Please check all items for damages
before leaving the Library.
Thereafter you will be held
responsible for all injuries
to items beyond reasonable wear.

3   3/13
4   8/14
5   8/15

OCT   2004

Highway 61 Revisited

Also by Gene Santoro

Dancing in Your Head (1994)

Stir It Up (1997)

Myself When I Am Real (2000)

Highway 61 Revisited

The Tangled Roots of American
Jazz, Blues, Rock, & Country Music

Gene Santoro

OXFORD
UNIVERSITY PRESS

2004

OXFORD
UNIVERSITY PRESS

Oxford   New York
Auckland   Bangkok   Buenos Aires   Cape Town   Chennai
Dar es Salaam   Delhi   Hong Kong   Istanbul   Karachi   Kolkata
Kuala Lumpur   Madrid   Melbourne   Mexico City   Mumbai   Nairobi
São Paulo   Shanghai   Taipei   Tokyo   Toronto

Copyright © 2004 by Gene Santoro

Published by Oxford University Press, Inc.
198 Madison Avenue, New York, New York 10016
www.oup.com

Oxford is a registered trademark of Oxford University Press

Library of Congress Cataloging-in-Publication Data
Santoro, Gene.
Highway 61 revisited : the tangled roots of American jazz, blues,
rock, and country music / by Gene Santoro.
312   p.   cm.
ISBN 0–19–515481–9
1. Popular music—United States—History and criticism.
2. Jazz—History and criticism. I. Title.
ML3477 .S21 2004
781.64'0973—dc22
2003024872

Book design and typesetting: Jack Donner, BookType

1 3 5 7 9 8 6 4 2
Printed in the United States of America
on acid-free paper

Contents

IV. In the Garage

V. Possible Futures

Highway 61 Revisited

A chronicler who recites events without distinguishing between major and minor ones acts in accordance with the following truth: nothing that has ever happened should be regarded as lost for history.

—Walter Benjamin

Music reveals a personal past which, until then, each of us was unaware of, moving us to lament misfortunes we never suffered and wrongs we did not commit.

—Jorge Luis Borges

Introduction

HIGHWAY 61 REVISITED OFFERS, I hope, alternate ways of seeing the evolution of American pop culture, especially music, over the last century.

It opens with twin chapters on Louis Armstrong and Woody Guthrie. In the book's unfolding narrative, this complex pair of geniuses represent the headwaters of significant and twisty currents flowing through the last hundred years of American pop-music history, here separating into isolated backwaters or bypassed channels, there merging into an unavoidable river with many deltas, but always, whether incrementally or with white-water force, shaping key portions of the cultural landscape. Both Armstrong and Guthrie began as folk musicians performing for small marginal groups. Armstrong became the dapper virtuoso who survived endless varieties of racism while inventing the musical language that transformed jazz from folk music to art, though he never stopped insisting (unlike many of his more recent progeny) that entertainment was an indispensable aspect of his art; he enthralled a mass multiracial audience, which made him forever synonymous with jazz as well as rich, though he insisted on living relatively simply. Guthrie kept his talents deliberately rude, at least on the surface, because he wanted to dissolve the stage's fourth wall by not seeming any more professional than his listeners; he smelled bad and dressed like the hobo he'd been, dynamited mass success whenever it got too near him, and became famous anyway, the catalytic icon energizing the wavelike resurgences of American roots music that have punctuated every decade since. Armstrong, a black outsider by birth, wanted in, in his genial way—though thanks to America's color bar, he rarely forgot where he stood. Guthrie, a white insider by birth transformed by family tragedy and Okie alienation and leftist politics, in his brusque way wanted out. But both challenged many of American society's cherished imperatives and ideals, implicitly as well as explicitly, in their art, their opinions, their attitudes, and their lives.

Highway 61 Revisited traces how these dynamics and their corollaries spool through post–World War II American culture via selected figures and moments that illustrate the interplay at work in various contexts. In the process, it argues that these interactive tensions—between races, between musical art and pop entertainment, between high art and functional art, between art and commerce, between art and politics, and between America's mainstream and marginal subcultures—form the fertile tidepools incubating most interesting modern American popular music, up to contemporary hip-hop and neofolk.

Since this book isn't encyclopedic, it tries to demonstrate how this works by telling several overlapping stories in a variety of formats and styles. One portrays a colorful cast of characters from the American Parade whose art surfaced marginal subcultures into mainstream US cultural life, usually with political and social impacts. Another follows the mingling of jazz (and its attitudes, especially its improvising drive, the risky business of American existentialist art) with some of the nation's many pop culture streams: folk, rock, country, soul, hip-hop, poetry, comedy, TV, and movies. Yet another traces the development of genuine popular or "folk" cultures within (and often despite) the growth of corporate mass media, like the ubiquitous homemade garage bands that sprang up mushroomlike among boomers between the 1960s and 1980s, inadvertently creating a rock "canon" out of a patchwork of material while inculcating in millions the endangered pleasure of making their own music. And yet another suggests that if our politics over the last two decades has been recycling into a new McCarthy era, our culture is also doubling back to revive and reexplore modes of alienation and expression from those Cold War days. (This isn't to say history repeats itself, exactly. Today's hipsters aren't 1940s Beats, but they do share a certain inchoate alienation; poetry slams at little bars and bookstores today aren't just reissues of 1950s coffeehouses; the Web isn't merely a technological update of fan lists, postwar radio, and independent labels; *South Park* doesn't just reprise Lenny Bruce or the Firesign Theatre. But they form potentially suggestive parallels.) Connecting these are thematic leitmotifs like oral culture, racism, authenticity, drugs, outsider art, white versus black marginal subcultures, and so on.

There's an autobiographical thread as well, varying in thickness. Partly that's because the process of discovering the affirmation of human creativity and possibility that music and art, whether "folk" or "high," represent in the face of evil, greed, stupidity, and general human frailty changed my life, as it has so many, and shapes it still. And partly it's because I began this book after September 11, 2001, when the Twin Towers in my hometown came down and, like so many, I felt the need to retrace my footsteps, and America's, trying to understand how I wound up here—and where we might go next.

Most of these chapters began life in (often radically) different guises, in the following publications: *The Nation, New York Times Book Review, Chamber Music, Fi* magazine, *Jazzwise,* and *Pulse.* Others were specifically written for this project, to fill out its narrative and thematic arcs. I want to thank my longtime editor, Sheldon Meyer, whose patient intelligence is priceless, as well as his assistant, Peter Harper; my production editor, Joellyn Ausanka; and my agent, Denise Shannon. As for my family and friends, who offered sympathetic ears and shrewd feedback, no thanks are enough.

part I **Avatars**

Louis Armstrong

1

FROM 1925 TO 1928, Louis Armstrong made an astonishing series of recordings, the jazz-creating legacy of his Hot Fives and Hot Sevens, a succession of studio groups that virtually never performed live. In 1927, the young cornetist led his band into a meticulously hilarious version of a classic composition Jelly Roll Morton had made famous, "Twelfth Street Rag."

The track sounds like the opening shot of a revolution—except that the revolution in Armstrong's head and hands had already been in full swing for years. Unlike most revolutions, from the first it displayed an ingratiating, inviting sense of humor and charm. Dippermouth, as his early New Orleans pals dubbed him, used the rag as a trampoline. As his horn fractures the tune's familiar refrains, ragtime's precise, cakewalking rhythmic values suddenly coil and loop and stutter and dive, the aural equivalent of a bravura World War I flying ace dogfighting tradition. Every time Armstrong comes precariously near a tailspin, he pulls back the control stick and confidently, jauntily, heads off toward the horizon, if not straight at another virtuosic loop-de-loop.

The relentless joy brimming in the sound of young Satchemouth's horn, the glorious deep-blue and fiery-red tinged Whitmanesque yawp of it, has an undeniably self-conscious edge. Ralph Ellison and Albert Murray first pointed out a half-century ago that it is also the sound of self-assertion, a musical realization of the double consciousness W. E. B. Du Bois posited for African Americans. Within this almost Hegelian compound of power and pain, a racial revisiting of the Master–Slave encounter in Hegel's *Phenomenology of Spirit*, Du Bois explained that African Americans were inevitably alienated, stood both inside and outside mainstream American culture and its norms, prescriptions, hopes, dreams. Such alienation, Du Bois pointed out, could cripple black Americans by forcing them to internalize mainstream cultural values that held them to be less than human, but it could also liberate the brightest of them. The "Talented Tenth," as he called this group, could act on their perceptions of the contradictions between the high ideals grounding basic American cultural myths ("All men are created equal" in the Declaration of Independence, for example) and gritty daily reality, where blacks were not exactly welcomed into concert halls, schools, restaurants, or buses.

In the bell of Armstrong's barbaric (which means, in the sense Whitman inherited from Ralph Waldo Emerson, non-European) horn is the sound of a new, all-American culture being forged from the stuff of the social sidelines. In 1957, Ellison wrote to Murray, "I've discovered Louis singing 'Mack the Knife.' Shakespeare invented Caliban or changed himself into him. Who the hell dreamed up Louis? Some of the bop boys consider him Caliban, but if he is, he is a mask for a lyric poet who is much greater than most now writing. Man and mask, sophistication and taste hiding behind clowning and crude manners—the American joke, man."

Armstrong himself was no naive artist; he certainly wasn't a fool. From his earliest days he saw race as a key issue in his life, his art, and his country, with the wit and understanding evident in his music. As he wrote of the composer of "Twelfth Street Rag," jazz's self-proclaimed inventor,

> Jelly Roll [Morton] with lighter skin than the average piano players, got the job [at Lulu White, New Orleans' leading whorehouse] because they did not want a Black piano player for the job. He claimed he was from an Indian or Spanish race. No Cullud at all. . . . They had lots of players in the District that could play lots better than Jelly, but their dark Color kept them from getting the job. Jelly Roll made so much money in tips that he had a diamond inserted in one of his teeth. No matter how much his Diamond Sparkled he still had to eat in the Kitchen, the same as we Blacks.

IN *THE OMNI-AMERICANS*, Albert Murray explains how Armstrong's music limned human talents needed in the frenetic, fast-changing 20th century. Drawn from the pioneer, Indian, and slave, the key American survival skill was improvisation, the soloist's ability to mesh with his surroundings. (Historical accident though it may have been, in that context the meeting of Armstrong and Jimmie Rodgers, Father of Country Music, on tracks like "Blue Yodel No. 9," seems almost a foregone conclusion; it also forecast and encouraged later developments like Bob Wills and his Texas swing, Bill Monroe's bluegrass, Willie Nelson's jazz singing and partnerings with Ray Charles, and Merle Haggard's looselimbed improvising Strangers.) Ralph Ellison's *Invisible Man* uses Armstrong's version of "Black and Blue," a tune from the Broadway play *Chocolate Dandies* of 1929, to demonstrate the DuBoisian nature of improvising as epistemological tool.

This was the lesson Armstrong started teaching in the Jazz Age, when flappers reigned and sexual emancipation knocked at the doors of mainstream culture, when the Harlem Renaissance redefined African American, when Prohibition created a nation of outlaws who, thanks to associating with booze and gangsters and the demimonde's soundtrack of jazz, saw that Negroes, as they were called, were subject to legal and extralegal restrictions and prejudices just as arbitrary and stupid as the constitutional amendment forbidding Americans to buy and sell booze.

The elastic rhythms and fiery solos on the sides by the Hot Fives and Hot Sevens spoke to them, and illustrated the joys of the jazz-inflected life. On tune after tune, Armstrong cavorts and leaps and capers over and around his musical cohorts with the playful self-possession of a young and cocky top cat. Nothing can hold him down. He traverses keys and bar lines and rhythms with impunity, remolding them without missing a step.

"Black and Blue" made him a star. Originally written as a lament by a dark-skinned gal for her man, who's attracted to high-yellow types, Armstrong's brilliant, forceful reading renders it as mini-tragedy, the musical equivalent of Shylock's speech in Shakespeare's *Merchant of Venice*. "My only sin," he sings in that growl that compounds the earthy humanity of the blues with an unflinching dignity—this is no grovel—"is in my skin/What did I do to be so black and blue?" The short answer: in America, nothing. The color line did it all.

Subversive and powerful, Armstrong's music was the fountainhead of the Jazz Age and the Swing Era, when jazz was America's popular music, and the sounds of syncopated surprise filled the nation's dancehalls, while young folks skittered and twirled and flounced and leaped and broke out of Victorian constraints to looselimbed beats and blaring horns that emerged from America's Darktowns in New Orleans and New York and Chicago.

One of Armstrong's 1936 recordings is called "Rhythm Saved the World." Like many he cut, this banal tune is made something else by his subversive transformations. Its idea still echoes across America's teeming subcultures. Decades later, Parliament Funkadelic insisted, "Free your mind and your ass will follow."

ARMSTRONG ALWAYS CLAIMED HE WAS BORN on July 4, 1900, and who could blame him? As one of America's primary declarers of cultural independence (and interdependence), he should have been. But in his rich biography *Satchmo*, Gary Giddins both insists that all American music emanates from Armstrong and proves he was born on August 4, 1901.

Armstrong and his sister were born in The Battlefield, a hard district of New Orleans; their father left before either could remember him. In his early years Armstrong was raised by his grandmother, whom he credited with the Emersonian values—hard work, self-reliance, artistic daring coupled with personal amiability—that guided him. His mother may or may not have been a prostitute for a while; Louis returned to live with her when he was five.

At seven, he quit school and went to work for a Jewish family, the Karmofskys, and picked up his first instrument—a tin horn. He'd been dancing and singing on the street for pennies with other kids, but, working coal wagons with the Karmofsky sons, he learned to blow the cheap horn by putting his fingers together in front of the tube (he'd pulled off the mouthpiece). The boys encouraged him, their clients loved his melodies, and Little Louis, as he was called, had found his calling.

On January 1, 1913, he was busted for firing his stepfather's pistol and sentenced to the Colored Waifs Home. Here he joined the band and got his first musical training, which he characteristically never forgot. According to clarinet great Sidney Bechet, who in the 1920s was Armstrong's only peer as a virtuosic improviser, the cornet-playing 10-year-old Louis mastered the chops-busting clarinet solo for "High Society"—an astounding feat that only hinted at what was to come.

Little Louis danced in second-line parades, following cornetist Joe "King" Oliver in the Onward Band as they wound through the Crescent City streets. Oliver was a catalytic force for Armstrong, who always insisted he learned his stuff from Papa Joe. Certainly Oliver mentored him: when he left for Chicago, following the first post–World War I black migration waves from the South to northern and western cities, he left Little Louis his slot in the Kid Ory band, which led the young cornetist to the riverboats plying the Mississippi and to Fate Marable in 1920–21.

Marable, impressed by the young hornman's dazzling facility and ears, hired him for his riverboat band, and one of his sidemen trained the youngster to read and write music. What they played was a mix that, had they thought much about it, would have confounded the Dixieland revivalists who decades later took Armstrong as their figurehead: adapted arias and classical overtures, quadrilles and other dance music, and the like. (Historian Dan Morgenstern has pointed out the suggestive influence of classical music on Armstrong's music.) At Davenport, Iowa, when the riverboat docked, a young white kid named Bix Beiderbecke first heard Armstrong with Marable, and decided to make the jazz cornet his life. The first of jazz's white existential heroes, he would perfect his craft by jamming with Armstrong regularly, an exchange that led to mutual respect and friendship of the type still rare across America's color line.

Armstrong's multifaceted legacy, his music, would create a new subculture—the jazz milieu—where whites and blacks in America could meet on something like equal grounds, thanks to artistic respect. The institutionalized color line would hardly disappear; for generations, white stars would routinely get credit for musical advances developed by black musicians. In a historical irony enhanced by American racism, the jazz world became a site into which disaffected white Americans could exit, in implicit or explicit rejection of their society's mores and aims; for black Americans like Armstrong himself, it became one of the few precious potential entrances into the larger public visibility and acceptance.

In 1923, Oliver sent for his protégé, who kissed his mother goodbye, packed the fish sandwich she had made for him, and headed north to Chicago. When he got to the Lincoln Gardens Cafe, where Oliver's band was wailing, he looked like a rube, and was so shy he stayed by the door to watch and hear. He couldn't believe he'd be playing with these masters of jazz. In a very short time, first in his recordings with them, then with his own Hot Fives and Sevens, he would make them all sound like musical relics.

Rube or not—and his mode of dress quickly became Chicago-style sharp—Armstrong got the girl. His second wife, piano-playing Lil Hardin, married him while they were both playing with Oliver. Hardin was conservatory-trained and middle class, and for the next few years her ambition would drive the modest genius she married to make his mark in the rapidly exploding Jazz Age. Oliver kept Louis in his band partly to keep him from fronting his own, while Lil convinced her husband to grab Fletcher Henderson's offer to join his New York-based big band. When Armstrong arrived in 1924, Henderson's band was, as Morgenstern notes, "designed for Roseland's white dancing public . . . rhythmically stiff"; when he left 14 months later, both arrangements and soloists were extending his sound, and white America was learning to dance to them.

It was just the start. When Armstrong replaced New Orleans standards and blues with Tin Pan Alley tunes in the 1930s, he forged the model followed by the Swing Era, jazz's most successful invasion of American pop music—and thus of American society. His model was followed literally: key arrangers like Don Redman, who worked for many bandleaders, including Benny Goodman, adapted Armstrong's runs and rhythmic moves to section-by-section big band arrangements.

After Armstrong spent time in the Big Apple, working with Henderson and recording with blues singers, Lil persuaded him to come back to Chicago, where he joined her band, then Carroll Dickerson's, and rocked the town. The night he returned, he was greeted by a banner she'd had unfurled over the bandstand: "World's Greatest Trumpet Player."

Armstrong later told Morgenstern the reason he left Henderson's band was that the "dicty bandleader," college-educated and light-skinned and prone to look down on dark blacks, wouldn't let him sing, except occasionally for black audiences or for novelty and comic effect. Armstrong sang before he picked up a horn. It was a fundamental part of who he was and what he had to say. Ultimately, his vocals would make him a world-famous star. More immediately, they were another virtuosic tool he used to change jazz and, in the process, American culture.

ARMSTRONG PIONEERED SO MANY FIRSTS IN JAZZ (and America) that a list can seem unbelievable. Here's a sample. He invented the full-fledged jazz soloist and scatsinging. He introduced Tin Pan Alley and Broadway tunes as jazz's raw material. And he performed in interracial settings, sometimes for multiracial audiences. Once, in New Orleans, when a bigoted announcer refused to introduce his band, he did it himself—so well that the radio station asked him to do it for the rest of the band's stint.

He was transforming folk music into an art form without losing his willingness or ability to communicate his art to a broad audience—the vehicle for his penetration of mainstream American culture. And with him as point man, the submerged African American culture—largely known beforehand to most whites via caricature or appropriation—was transformed into something undeniable, tangible, concrete. His voice engulfed America. As Rudy Vallee put it, "No one in America sang the same after him." Among his major disciples was Bing Crosby, but his influence rippled across American popular and jazz singing like a submerged tidal wave. The apparently natural force of his voice's cagey dynamics and loose rhythms as he reconfigured pop tunes seized talents like Ella Fitzgerald and Billie Holiday, Bing Crosby and Frank Sinatra.

With his last Hot Sevens recordings for Okeh in 1928, where tunes like "I Can't Give You Anything But Love" were issued as b-sides, Armstrong moved closer to the new American cultural mainstream he was inspiring. When he started recording for Decca in 1935, the impetus accelerated.

In between, Armstrong had been pursued out of Chicago, then New York, by gangsters. The manager who helped him escape brought him to Europe, then made off with his passport. (The first time Armstrong played London, a deputation of British hornmen trooped backstage to examine his trumpet for gimmickry. As Morgenstern writes drily, "His virtuosity was still something not quite credible.") A couple of interim managers gave way, in 1935, to Joe Glaser, a thuggish, mob-connected scion of a well-off Chicago family. He and Armstrong shook hands on a deal that lasted till they both died. As Armstrong put it, "A black man needs a white man working for him." Jazz had originated as an ignored marginal subculture, played in whorehouses and bars by men who were often regarded as renegade heroes, tricksters, folks whose talents could help them get over on The Man. It was almost inevitable that the white American demimonde of gangsters and hookers and the like would be among the earliest exposed to jazz, and among the key white Americans in positions to employ black jazz musicians. It was no accident that so many of the clubs in jazz centers like Harlem and Chicago were mob-owned or affiliated, that hot jazz became the soundtrack of speakeasies from coast to coast during the Roaring Twenties that somehow, in quintessentially American ways, coexisted with Prohibition. Though it was often a marriage of convenience, it endured because it coupled the marginal and outcast. Among white folk, who else would choose to hang out with and deal with blacks?

His deal with Glaser marked the beginning of his crossover into mainstream American culture—another Armstrong first in undermining de facto segregation in America. And his years at Decca were his workshop in change.

He fronted a big band, which critics hated and fans enjoyed. The outfit was run by Glaser, since Armstrong, who occasionally hired and fired personnel, didn't want to shoulder a bandleader's nonmusical burdens. And he agreed with Glaser on a new musical direction: setting his solos off in sometimes inventive, sometimes indifferent bigband charts; smoothing his blues-frog vocals into a more sophisticated sound without losing their rhythmic slyness—something he was also doing with his trumpet solos, reshaping his early frenetic chases after strings of high-altitude notes into smoother, more lyrical solos.

Physical damage to Armstrong's lip and mouth from high and hard blowing forced the issue. Joe Muranyi, who played with him years later, says: "Part of the change in Louis' style could be attributed to the lip trouble he had in the early '30s. There are tales of blood on his shirt, of blowing off a piece of his lip while playing. This certainly influenced the way he approached the horn; yet what we hear on these tracks has at least as much to do with musical development as with physical matters." Limitation was, for Satchmo's genius, a pathway to a matured artistic conception. As Giddins argues forcefully in *Satchmo*, he'd never separated art and entertainment; jazz to him was a popular music that should be able to bridge that potential gap and allow him to open a beachhead where black figures could garner popular acceptance and respect. Jazz was his way into American society. And if his bands irritated critics, there were plenty of recorded gems amid the dross, and besides, he'd broadened his popularity by appearing in movies, with some inevitably racist parts and some brighter moments with Crosby, and people loved him.

By World War II, his audiences were more white than black.

THE WAR YEARS BROKE THE BIG BANDS. The culture had changed: singers and small groups were hip. It was the era of a new sound, what Dizzy Gillespie called modern jazz and journalists dubbed bebop.

Bop's frenetic, fragmented rhythms restated the postwar world's, and it deliberately presented itself not as entertainment but as art. The musicians creating it, like Gillespie and Charlie Parker, were fully aware of the stirring civil rights movement. World War II had fostered widespread entry of blacks into the American military and industry. Not surprisingly, after the war, they weren't willing to return to the old values of accommodation and deference. Instead, they demanded equality and freedom.

In this context, boppers and their followers saw Armstrong's lifelong mugging and entertaining as Uncle Tom-style pleasing of white folks rather than artistic integrity or entertainment. Dizzy Gillespie was rare among postwar jazz musicians in clowning onstage, his outgoing sense of humor a continuing counterpoint to the bop conviction that their art was being shortchanged by the music business, run by white Americans. Most record company executives didn't like or understand bebop and were sure it could never be broadly popular; they preferred older, familiar, and commercially tested forms. (It was another historical irony that Armstrong and Gillespie clashed about what the older man saw as bebop's pretensions, while Gillespie was, in many ways, Armstrong's truest heir in jazz at that time, with his beret and glasses and puff-adder cheeks and uptilted horn, his devotion to and adaptation of Afro-Cuban dance rhythms as well as his implicit claim to artistic status.)

Thus was set the stage for the Dixieland revival. Based in Chicago, the (mostly white) revivalists needed an artistic figurehead. With a healthy historical irony they ignored, they chose Armstrong—the very soloist who blew apart old-style New Orleans polyphony, their idea of "pure" or "real" jazz.

By 1947, Satchmo reluctantly abandoned his 18-piece outfit for the All Stars, a New Orleans-style sextet that included Jack Teagarden and Earl Hines. Though they often made fine music, the group was seen as a step backward by boppers. They jabbed at Satchmo, he jabbed back, and the split between revivalists and modernists escalated to a civil war that, in different stylistic and racial modes, still divides the jazz world.

Sadly, it was another Armstrong first. And his audiences began to turn lily white.

IN SATCHMO, Giddins deftly explains how Armstrong's world-famous onstage persona—the big grin, the bulging eyes, the shaking head, the brandished trumpet, the ever-present handkerchief, the endless vaudevillian mugging—was an organic conception of the artist as entertainer. Still, from the 1950s until just before his death in 1971, Armstrong had to deal with the accusations and slurs.

But if he never forgot who he was, while retaining his characteristically modest manner and only privately protesting how much he'd done to advance black civil rights, he could still be provoked, as President Eisenhower and the public discovered in 1957. Armstrong was poised to go on the first State Department–sponsored tour of the Soviet Union, a Cold War beachhead by jazz. He abruptly cancelled it because the southern states refused to integrate schools, and he publicly excoriated Ike and America. Surprisingly, even this didn't put a dent in his Uncle Tom image among the black audiences deserting him.

By all accounts, Armstrong was aware of his gifts and yet somehow was unassuming. His wealth meant little to him: he traveled on the same unheated buses as his bands 300 days a year. When his wife and manager wanted him to buy a Long Island mansion, he insisted on staying in his working-class bungalow in Corona, Queens, where the kids waited on his stoop for him when he came back from tours. When his wife persuaded him to put a brick façade up, he went up and down the block asking if other homeowners would also like their houses bricked, at his expense.

A prolific writer, Armstrong made his typewriter part of his road equipment. He wrote of everything—scattered impressions, concentrated history and biography, his love of marijuana and Swiss Kriss, a natural laxative. In his later writings, he contrasts New Orleans blacks and Jews like the Karmofskys, claiming, with uncharacteristic bitterness, that blacks didn't help each other to "get ahead" the way Jews did.

Antonio Gramsci wrote of proletarian intellectuals who could understand class struggle from an integrated perspective lacking to others, however sympathetic. Though he was writing about himself, he could have been describing Armstrong. Which is part of why African American intellectuals like Ellison and Murray saw Satchmo as an emblem of America's racial politics.

EARLY JAZZ MUSICIANS OFTEN REFUSED TO RECORD because they felt competitors could steal their best licks from their records. This was why the all-white Original Dixieland Jazz Band made jazz's first records; black New Orleans trumpeter Freddie Keppard refused, fearing for his originality.

No one knows for sure how many recordings Louis Armstrong made during the course of his half-century recording career. All agree, however, that he helped create both the art and the industry. After all, it was one of the numberless ironies of American racism that "race" records, a category of recordings aimed explicitly at nonwhite and other marginal subcultures that included Armstrong's hits, were as important as Bing Crosby's in saving the fledging record companies from collapse in the Depression.

But there was more to it than that. Through the phonograph Armstrong made infinite numbers of disciples, dispensing his vision and shaping what jazz would become. The phonograph transformed evanescent musical moments of improvisation into captured pieces of time, endlessly duplicable and repeatable, able to be studied and savored as well as experienced immediately. Also through the phonograph, as Morgenstern points out, we get a larger sense of what Armstrong himself listened to because of the records (of arias and the like) that he collected. And nearly three decades after he's dead, nearly all of us inevitably get our sense of how he played through the phonograph—though Morgenstern has noted that onstage Armstrong would often solo for half an hour at a time, an experiential perspective that the records, with their three-minutes-and-under limit, unfortunately can't and don't give us. What they provide us instead is a series of windows—imagine peering out an express train passing through a station—into Armstrong's world and art.

During the 1950s and 1960s, when he was largely considered a period piece, Armstrong recorded important documents, like his meetings with Duke Ellington and Ella Fitzgerald. The best thing about them is their apparent artlessness, the easy offhanded creativity that was as much Armstrong's trademark as his trumpet's clarion calls. The pleasure is doubled by the response of his disciples.

Ella fits that description easily, since her trademark scatsinging owes so much to Armstrong's. Yet she made it her own, purging scat of its overt blues roots. Producer Norman Granz supported them with his favorite Jazz at the Philharmonic stars—Oscar Peterson, Herb Ellis, and Ray Brown. The results: both *Ella and Louis* and *Ella and Louis Again* are incandescent yet low-key, full of generous pearls (from "Can't We Be Friends" to "Cheek to Cheek") that can almost slip by because of their understated yet consummate ease.

The 1961 session with Duke, *Louis Armstrong & Duke Ellington*, was hasty and almost haphazard, a simple melding of Ellington into Armstrong's All Stars, and yet it produced a wonderful, relaxed, insightful album. After all, Ellington had shaped his earliest bands around trumpeters and trombonists who could serve up Armstrong's New Orleans flair. And Morgenstern observed just how quickly and efficiently Armstrong soaked up Ellington's music at sight, shooting down any notion of Satchmo as a purely intuitive musician.

LIKE MOST POSTWAR BABIES, I grew up knowing Louis Armstrong as the guy who sang "Mack the Knife" and, most famously, "Hello Dolly." It was only later I'd discover the old blues stuff with singers like Bessie Smith, the Hot Fives, Ella and Louis, Fletcher Henderson, and—one of my faves—Armstrong's accompaniment on early hillbilly star Jimmie Rodgers's "Blue Yodel No. 9." But even as a kid I felt strangely drawn to the little black guy singing and grimacing on TV, wiping his perspiring brow with his trademark handkerchief. Although it all seemed corny, there was something, a hint of a subversion—though that wouldn't have been what his audiences, black or white, noticed unless they were oldtimers who knew the ironic physical language or Satchmo fans or, like me, just a kid.

Why would a white kid in America catch a glimpse of Armstrong's abundantly joyful and potentially dangerous ironies? I'd love to claim precocious brilliance, but it was a lot simpler. I could tell Armstrong was real because he filled the little blue TV screen so overwhelmingly that he made everything around him look, as it should have, fake.

2

Woody Guthrie

ON APRIL 16, 1944, a slight, wiry-haired man with a guitar and harmonica wandered into Moe Asch's little recording studio on West 46th Street off New York's Times Square. His sidekick, who played guitar and sang cowboy harmonies, joined him. They were between merchant marine voyages across the Atlantic, where they dodged U-boats and carried Allied supplies. With tall, lanky Cisco Houston, Woody Guthrie spent days in front of Asch's microphones, spilling out hundreds of the thousands of songs he'd collected or written during the preceding decade.

With Cisco's nasal high harmonies, simple almost haphazard lines running parallel to the melody, and energetic guitar, the duo sounded raw and homey, as if they spent their time playing saloons or roadhouses or dockside taverns. And that, along with a dizzying clutch of union and political rallies, is a lot of what Guthrie had been doing. Bumming around by himself, with Houston, with young Peter Seeger, he incarnated America's mythical wanderlust and noncomformity, lighting out for the territory in ways that inspired generations of road warriors, hitchhikers, trainspotters, pop stars, Beatniks, folk heroes, buddy-movie makers, and con artists.

On and off over the next three years, Guthrie returned to Asch's studio, performing alone and with various partners, as he unspooled the Memorex of material in his head. Asch, whose introduction to folk music was a copy of John A. Lomax's 1910 compendium *Cowboy Songs*, adored Guthrie. He first recorded Lead Belly in 1941, then watched his circle of artists expand: Pete Seeger, Josh White, Burl Ives. From this grew Folkways Records, whose treasures are regularly reissued on Smithsonian/Folkways.

By the time Guthrie surfaced at Asch's place, he'd long since been enshrined as the minstrel of the American left. He found his calling in Los Angeles, the highly polarized magnet for Okies during the Dust Bowl. Dust hadn't driven him to LA; family ties and ambition to be an entertainer did. But Woodrow Wilson Guthrie, born in Okemah, Oklahoma, in 1912 on Bastille Day (which he was as proud of as Louis Armstrong was of his claim to having been born on the Fourth of July), could reach these folks, speak to them and for them. When he sang in an offhand homespun manner flecked with sly timing out of Will Rogers, they responded to him: he reminded them of home, which looked so much better from here in the California heaven-and-hell of Steinbeck's *Grapes of Wrath* than when last they saw it, buried by dust. Suddenly this shiftless jack-of-a-lot-of-trades, this son of a middle-class land speculator and politician who went bust, this once small quiet boy whose mother was packed off to an asylum and whose older sister was rumored to have set herself on fire, this part Native American former teen vagabond who after hoboing each summer came prodigally home each fall to attend high school (where he was the paper's Joke Editor) and devour Kahlil Gibran and Omar Khayyam and Ralph Waldo Emerson and Walt Whitman in the local public library while he drew portraits of whores and copies of religious scenes and Whistler paintings (he loved Impressionism) to earn cash, this physically grown-up itinerant Huck Finn who shucked wives and lovers to go on benders and hit the road and whom his closest friends described as having barnyard manners, had discovered himself at age 25. He would be an American troubadour.

Guthrie didn't have a fabulous liquidy voice like his yodeling idol, the godfather of country music, Jimmie Rodgers. His was thin, often quavering around a pitch, a rough-hewn semi-amateur instrument. And he kept it that way. Lack of polish brought him closer to real people; for Guthrie as for Will Rogers, seeming unexceptional was central to his artistic presentation, compressed the gap between audience and performer—crucial for functional music sung at union rallies, labor camps, gatherings of left-wing urban folk enthusiasts. So, although he adored the Carter Family and spent hours learning Maybelle's influential guitar technique of picking out riffs on the bass strings while strumming, he generally kept his guitar serviceable and his mandolin the same. Despite a family fiddling tradition, his violin leaned toward sawing. The harmonica on his sessions he usually left to Sonny Terry, one of the folk revival's African American authenticators who blew the blues-and-train-whistle riffs of a Piedmont street performer, which he'd been with his partner, guitarist Brownie McGhee, who sometimes joined Guthrie too—a defiant color blindness in a nation scarred by institutional racism. (One of Guthrie's characteristically oddball "commercial" ventures fizzled when he tried to form an interracial country music group with Terry.) Like the old bluesmen he ran with, Guthrie regularly dropped and added beats, stretched verses, ignored bar lines, and seemed, to more "sophisticated" listeners like his second wife Marjorie, unable to count time properly.

He always performed better in informal situations. For Guthrie, folk art's apparent naivete made an artistic statement: it echoed and amplified its culture and inspired audience reaction—a folk version of Brecht. No wonder Steinbeck loved him: Guthrie stepped out of the American tradition of utopian muckraking antiheroes. His world looked Manichean, and prewar reality confirmed his instincts: the Great Depression ravaged the land while the rich squeezed the poor, Hitler challenged the rationale of Western industrial civilization, and there were bad guys aplenty of every size and shape—local cops and railroad bulls hassling hobos and turning starving Okies back at the California border or busting union heads, banks that slapped liens on everything down to a farmer's catch from his creek. Some heroes turn out bad: Mr. Charlie Lindbergh and his America First crowd are selling the country down the river to the Nazis. Some bad guys morph into folk heroes: Pretty Boy Floyd is a Western Robin Hood handing out Christmas dinners to families on relief. Jesus Christ is a hard-working hard-traveling sort. Communists and union men can do no wrong, unless they betray the cause. Hobos are going down the road feeling bad with no home in this world anymore and only the steel rails humming to go to sleep by, swapping tales from the cauldron that brewed Paul Bunyan and Babe and the Jumping Frog of Calaveras County laced with Will Rogers's dry timing. Mothers and home make us misty. Children get indulged, and the grown-ups (like they do now with *Sesame Street*) listen in and chuckle to the nonsense and game songs and riddles, everyone hanging on to find out where the shaggy dog finally winds up.

If his language wasn't so vital, you could say Guthrie merges Warner Bros. and MGM movies of the period for a picture of America in flux, from rural to urban, from agricultural to industrial. The country's sense of Manifest Destiny was punctured by the Depression and Pearl Harbor, but the war quickened its pace of change. By the time Guthrie was recording for Asch, a lot of what he sung about was history.

Woody Guthrie: The Asch Recordings Vol. 1–4 gathers 105 tracks in well-wrought fashion to outline the breadth, heights, depth, and limits of Guthrie's genius. Each CD has a loose theme. *This Land Is Your Land* includes Woody's greatest hits: most he wrote the lyrics for, setting them to existing tunes in the way oral minstrels do. The delightfully vitriolic "Lindbergh" ("They say America's First/But they mean America's next") adapts the melody from a song about the McKinley assassination. "Reuben James," a brilliantly compressed tale of a US destroyer sunk by a Nazi U-boat, is the Carter Family's "Wildwood Flower." And of course there's the famous title track, a Whitmanesque cascade of vivid lyric snapshots from Everyman's America to repudiate Kate Smith's saccharine "God Bless America." Its notorious deleted verse was a blunt attack on private property.

Guthrie was a too-willing follower of the Stalinist Communist line even after its widespread sympathizers of the hard-luck 1930s were disillusioned by the cynical Hitler-Stalin Pact of 1940, and he liked to see social issues in black-and-white terms, but he wasn't Joe Hill. He was larger and smaller, more artist and more human. "Car Song" is hillbilly Spike Jones rehearsing a parent–child dialogue with Ogden Nash–overlong lines and mimicked car horns; the final verse is "Why O Why O Why? Because,

because, because, because, goodbye, goodbye, goodbye." "Philadelphia Lawyer" sleeps with a cowboy's girl and gets his rightful comeuppance. And when you get to California with hungry kids instead of a banjo on your knee, the gallows humor of "if you ain't got the do-re-mi, boys" helps ease your gritted teeth and troubled mind when the cops turn you back.

In the 1930s, the Communist Party was one of the few organized voices consistently raised against racism in America—one reason Paul Robeson, for example, signed on. The Party showed Guthrie that poor whites and blacks were both marginalized in their own country. And so he wrote: a stirring ballad about Harriet Tubman and the Underground Railroad, his own "Strange Fruit," called "Slipknot," a potent series of questions about lynching set to relatively flashy guitar work.

Inevitably many of his political screeds have dated badly: "Sacco and Vanzetti" is insipid, and "Ladies' Auxiliary" is camp ("O the ladies' auxiliary is the best auxiliary"). But what endures about Guthrie's best work is its ambition and scope. He reminds us how music existed before Walkmen or MP3 players or Internet radio, how people made music for themselves to accompany daily life, remember events and deeds and characters, speak back to power and carry the news.

A man with a guitar has been an American symbol for a century. The guitar was made for folk music: it was easy to learn to play a little, was portable, and could be polyphonic or monophonic. On his Guthrie had a sign: "This Machine Kills Fascists."

But as this box set shows, he was many-sided: the Victorian sentiment of parlor songs like "Life's Other Side" and "Put My Little Shoes Away"; the drug songs like "Cocaine Blues" and "Take a Whiff on Me"; the hobo tunes like "Ramblin' Round" and "Hobo's Lullaby"; occasional pieces that celebrate the Bonneville Dam and rural electrification; "Farmer-Labor Train" ("Wabash Cannonball") and "When the Yanks Go Marchin' In" ("When the Saints Go Marchin' In"); square-dance calls on "Ida Red"; historical ballads like "1913 Massacre" about IWW miners. His textured naturalistic imagery and conversational delivery relay stories of good people misled, abused, looking for love and hope and a meal, in a magnificent land of abundance that manifests nature's inherent goodness—or would, if it and its people weren't raped and ruined, bullied and misled by evil men. This is Americana submerged or omitted from our history textbooks.

Listening now to Woody Guthrie's foxy, plainspoken wordplay lets us glimpse the patchwork of oral traditions, of local cultures that were fading at the moment Guthrie emerged at the vanguard of the gathering folk revival.

IN 1935, FRANK BURKE, the liberal owner of Los Angeles radio station KFVD, offered Guthrie's cousin Jack a 15-minute slot for a singing-cowboy show. But once Woody hooked up with Maxine Crissman, aka Lefty Lou, and formed a duo, mountain ballads and hymns took over. The audience surged, Burke expanded the show to half an hour, with a section devoted to "Cornpone Philosophy," and the letters from transplanted Okies poured it at a thousand a month and more. When Guthrie put together a mimeographed collection of old-time tunes he and Lefty Lou sang over the air, it sold briskly—50 to 70 copies per day; they plugged it over the clear-channel airwaves that wafted as far east as Texas, where his first wife and kids lived up with family until he sent for them, able to support them for the first time.

More offers rolled in, one from across the border. Mexican clear-channel radio was allowed more powerful transmitters than American stations. Their signals aimed north, covering the American Southwest and bouncing around the ionosphere on clear nights to as far north as Chicago. The allure of a huge audience brought the Carter Family to one station. Another, XELO, wanted Woody and Lefty Lou, and offered them $75 a week to assemble a hillbilly troupe for a nightly three-hour show. It ended after a few weeks, when no one got paid. And so back they went to tolerant Burke, who cut Guthrie's pay to a dollar a day—fine with Woody, since he could then skip out and sing at skid-row bars and labor rallies and mingle easily with workers while left-leaning Hollywood types marveled uncomfortably.

Guthrie was congenitally restless. Neither his wife nor partner could figure out why he didn't care about opportunities, career possibilities, stability and money. He could spend a day carelessly rolling down hills with kids in LA parks, squatting with bums in tenderloin districts, scribbling in his notebooks, sketching on his pad, watching clouds form. But he wasn't motivated to succeed. When Burke urged him to report on conditions at Okie camps for his new liberal newspaper, Guthrie started writing the sort of tunes collected in 1940 on his first commercial album, *Dust Bowl Ballads*. He inverted a traditional Baptist hymn popularized by the Carter Family, "The World Is Not My Home," into tight-lipped anger about the rich forcing the poor onto the road, ending with "I ain't got no home in this world any more." The Communist newspaper *People's World* noted his "native class consciousness" and signed him to draw cartoons and author a daily column, replete with misspellings and grammatical errors he adopted in the comic Western dialect fashion of Twain and Harte.

When the Popular Front collapsed after the Hitler–Stalin Pact, Guthrie persisted in defending the Soviet Union as he toured camps and sites of labor struggles and strikes with actor Will Geer and a makeshift troupe. (One early *People's World* booster dubbed him Prince Myshkin.) Others saw in him an effortless folk purity. The far-from-naïve Guthrie hit back at their condescension with burgeoning arrogance, armed by his authenticity. Of Burl Ives, he said tartly, "Burl sings like he was born in lace drawers." But when he made fun of Burke's anti-Soviet radio editorials, the station owner finally dropped him. Guthrie stashed his family back in

Texas and headed to New York, where Geer was starring in *Tobacco Road*. He sold his old Plymouth, put $35 in his pocket, and hitched and rode across the land, his dirty ears burning with "God Bless America," a huge hit, all the way.

IN A WAY, WHAT MOSES ASCH recorded with Woody Guthrie was a change in attitude toward American popular culture. Under the New Deal, the government sent out squadrons of researchers, writers, artists, and collators to document and disseminate local American folkways and history. This was part of the broader push to put to work the armies of unemployed, but it also reflected a country awakening from the social elite's Eurocentric cultural dominance, partly thanks to emerging mass media, and recognizing its *e pluribus unum* selves in the mirror of its artifacts. Jazz, the music of the urban sophisticate, was a prime example: a stew of African rhythms and chants, American marching band instruments, field hollers, and the blues that melded into something no one had heard before, the modern sound of the industrialized present, the big bands were the sonic equivalent of a 12-cylinder Jaguar. Bebop distilled the frenetic rhythms and jangled complexity of postwar American urban life. In contrast, the field trips of the Lomaxes and others like them were journeys into the past to gather scattered memories rendered into folk art. At Carnegie Hall in 1938, John Hammond aligned the elements of the musical continuum at "From Spirituals to Swing," an all-star concert. They would meet again in the civil rights and antiwar movements.

Dizzy Gillespie has said that he and the other young cats from Harlem clubs like Minton's had bebop's building blocks, but that Charlie Parker brought charisma and virtuosity that catalyzed their musical and extramusical visions. In 1940, when Guthrie hit New York for the first time and met Alan Lomax and young Peter Seeger, he completed a circuit that switched on the urban folk revival. He found disciples who could take care of his needs, deal with his outsized weirdness. They found someone who'd lived the life they'd been savoring via cultural artifacts. The tall tales Guthrie wove about his genuinely hardscrabble life added what leftists called authenticity to his critiques of The System. He was the People's Singer, their barbaric poet.

Alan Lomax was 23 when he first heard Guthrie in March 1940 at a "Grapes of Wrath" benefit for farm workers that Will Geer had organized. His world shook. Alan worked with his ex-banker father, John A. Lomax, from age 17, crisscrossing the South making irreplaceable field recordings of black inmates, adding oral histories and interviews that nest among the jewels of the Library of Congress. What he heard politically radicalized him; all he and his father agreed on was that the music was a singular American art form. For Alan, as Joe Klein observes in his thorough and well-written *Woody Guthrie: A Life*, "It was, potentially, a weapon in the class struggle. Throughout his career, he'd see himself as a promoter as well as a collector, someone who found ways to bring the music and the message to the widest possible audience."

The biggest prize the Lomaxes snared on their 1933 Library of Congress trip to Louisiana's Angola State Penitentiary was Huddie "Lead Belly" Ledbetter. Lead Belly spent most of his life in prison for crimes like shootings and attempted murder. He learned to work The System: he entertained guards for special perks, even won a pardon in 1925 from a 30-year sentence by singing for Texas governor Pat Neff. Though he dubbed himself "King of the 12-Stringed Guitar," Ledbetter's fretwork was solid but hardly flashy; you might not guess he'd rambled with Blind Lemon Jefferson, the great Texas bluesman and early "race" records star, as a youth. But his high keening voice, a powerful cri de coeur with a hard-to-decipher drawl, evoked Jefferson's, and he carried in his head a fathomless bag of Americana. The Lomaxes were enthralled. With their help and his own (this time he wrote a song for Governor O.K. Allen of Louisiana) he was released and retained as John Lomax's chauffeur and traveling companion; he joined the Lomaxes on their southern travels. For brief bursts his music supported him, but mostly he scuffled. Although he built an audience via weekly New York radio shots, his commercial recordings sold poorly, mostly because the big labels couldn't resolve how he fit their "race" catalogs. He did prison songs, ballads, cowboy songs, children's songs, lullabies, contemporary pop, accordion two-steps, and even the blues. They gave up, and left him to Moe Asch.

Asch is one of those independent label heads who played vital roles in postwar American music. At Folkways, Asch recorded culture that was vanishing beneath urbanization and the growing mass media. He ran his several labels on love and a shoestring. That means he doled out $20 here, $40 dollars there, to any artist who asked for it; he didn't keep books, and they didn't get royalties. It also means that many of his master discs no longer exist, and so the younger folk revivalists Asch's artists inspired later hunted his recordings with almost the same avidity they brought to their search for living songsters.

Lead Belly was the first folk artist Asch recorded, and his songs fed a powerful underground stream into folk and rock music of the 1950s and 1960s: songs he claimed to write (in an oral tradition, authorship is hazy, since change and adaptation are constant) include "Goodnight Irene" and "Cottonfields," which were covered by everyone from Seeger to Creedence Clearwater Revival, and defined others like "House of the Rising Sun." "Bourgeois Blues" is his scathing portrayal of racism in the nation's capital ("They call a colored man a nigger just to see him bow").

Asch saw Lead Belly as a victim of the expectations of even well-intentioned white leftists like the Lomaxes—a victim of authenticity. The two became friends. In his letters, Ledbetter complained that the elder Lomax was paternalistic—which included putting him in convict stripes for concerts. He didn't like being reduced to a symbol of oppression.

According to Asch: "He was one of the most formal human beings that ever existed. His clothing was always the best pressed, the best. His shoes were $60 shoes—in 1947! Where he might not have had much money to come home with, he had to have a cane. Lead Belly treated himself as a noble person."

Nevertheless, he always addressed the white folks as Mister in a low deferential voice. (Guthrie was "Mr. Woody.") He had recesses they could only guess at, depths they ascribed to him unclearly but in some awe. From 1940 on, he would be a sort of black doppelganger to Guthrie, who borrowed the older black man's adaptations of songs like "Jesse James," and used the melody of "Goodnight Irene" numerous times. On the other hand, when Nicholas Ray, then a radio director, wanted to replace Ledbetter with Josh White, whose diction was clearer to whites, Guthrie threatened to walk off the show; Lead Belly went on.

To most academics specializing in folk music—which to them meant the tracing transmission of Elizabethan ballads in America—Alan Lomax seemed like a Communist. He wasn't, but one of his chief allies was. Charles Seeger was a classically trained musicologist who championed American folk music as the authentic voice of the people, and thus inherently socially progressive. For Seeger, the fine arts belonged to the ruling elite, and commercial popular music was a pablumized travesty of the fine arts intended to lull the masses. With George Gershwin and Aaron Copland, who mined elements of jazz and country music, Seeger played a part in the broad intellectual trend fueled by the New Deal and the Popular Front into an outpouring of articles and books, documentaries and recordings: the desire to wrestle with the Emersonian question of American culture. As it went on, culture was redefined: rather than the fine arts, it embraced what people did and made, how they talked and loved and hated, what they ate and rode—the circumstances of human social life. For the elder Seeger, commerce and folk art were antithetical.

At the same time, Seeger and his wife Ruth, in partnership with the Lomaxes, struggled to find ways to transcribe the elusive musical qualities of rhythm and phrasing that, in all forms of American folk music from blues to jazz and beyond, evade European notation. The Seegers had a shy son named Peter who had gone to Harvard, tried his hand at political puppet theater, was an unpaid assistant to Alan Lomax at the Library of Congress, and studied the lute. Encouraged by his father and Lomax, he switched to five-string banjo. Like Lomax, he first saw Guthrie perform at the "Grapes of Wrath" benefit concert, and from that point was Guthrie's chief acolyte, student, and explicator. They hoboed and sailed in the merchant marine together, and at different points pooled their creative talents.

The Almanac Singers marked an apex of their rather asymmetrical relationship. In early 1941, Seeger and Lee Hayes, the Almanacs' core, and a few others lived communally in a seedy loft off New York City's Union

Square. They started holding Sunday afternoon rent-party concerts, and Lead Belly, Sonny Terry, Josh White, and Burl Ives showed up; nonmusicians paid 35¢ a head and a dime a beer. In the maelstrom of activity the Almanacs improvised lyrics of protest to old tunes and were shocked and thrilled when their audience of leftist urban sophisticates seeking America's folk-culture roots exploded like they were in a Baptist church. (The name "hootenanny" came a bit later.) They had watched Guthrie improvise lyrics, tinkering and rewriting constantly, the flux and flow of his heady language charged with risk and playfulness. They did it collectively to affirm solidarity; all their compositions were credited to the group. They called the creative improvising process "passing the song around."

In one of American history's odd symmetries, at around the same time, in Harlem, beboppers were taking old standards and drastically revamping the melodies and harmonies and rhythms in jam sessions.

A recording for a small leftist label got the Almanacs wide notice, including an ambivalent review in *Time*. They were now big fish in folk music's small pond. And if they tall-taled their lives to the media to authenticate their popular roots, it was to dramatize and credential their bona fides as outsiders. Isn't that what Woody did?

Guthrie had fled New York full-tilt in 1940 after deliberately detonating success. Following the "Grapes of Wrath" benefit, Alan Lomax and director Nicholas Ray arranged a deal with the CBS radio network. *Back Where I Come From* was a half-hour folk-music show Guthrie had a big hand in scripting and shaping; one episode featured the Golden Gate Gospel Quartet. Big-money offers followed when it was a smash: sing on Sanka's *We the People*, toss off a song about Wild Bill Hickok for *Cavalcade of America*, host *Pipe Smoking Time* for a tobacco company on network radio, with "So Long, It's Been Good To Know You" in a big-band version as the theme. The tightly controlled show reduced Guthrie to a prop—no spontaneity, no commentary, no politics, just shopworn hick-in-the-big-city stuff. "I can't take being told what to say, what to play, and what to wear," he said later. He hit a parade of bars, then he hit the studios of both programs in rapid succession and quit, and then he hit the road to California, where he languished, broke, saddled again with the family he'd dragged to New York and now dragged back out. Finally he caught a break: a month in Oregon, working for the Bonneville Power Authority on a movie that never materialized but inspired a couple of dozen of his finest lyrics, like "Grand Coulee Dam" (set to "Wabash Cannonball") and "Roll On, Columbia" (set to "Irene"). Then he got the transcontinental call: the Almanac Singers planned a summer tour and wanted him on it. So he dumped his wife and kids and hopped a cattle car for New York.

Soon after he arrived in 1941 the Almanacs cut two discreetly nonpolitical records for a small jazz label, and the headed out in an old Buick on a national tour to support striking CIO unionists. The group was giddy: they were riding with an original Road Warrior, and a frenzy of collaborative composition ensued that entered the legends and DNA of the folk revival. Guthrie insisted that protest songs should show rather than tell, but, beyond craft, there was only so much he could teach; they had to find it for themselves, like the jazz soloists who would soon follow Charlie Parker around. As he said, "Music is some kind of electricity that makes a man a radio." Only some people dial in to more static than others.

After a couple of months, Guthrie split and left Seeger holding the bag. Irresponsible? Or childish enough, free enough, to shrug off career, getting ahead, even changing the world, so he could ramble and create? He whined and complained when hard times cramped him, and he treated his women with both love and scorn, and he never really knew his kids, but he couldn't sit still, couldn't take the harness. His evasions of The System were so casual and complete neither Lomax nor Seeger could match them. Was this what the Communists meant by his "native class consciousness?" Seeger paid his bills promptly. Guthrie never paid attention. It was remarkably like the complicated relationship between Dizzy Gillespie and Charlie Parker.

When he met Woody Guthrie, Pete Seeger saw his father's vision of an American Brechtian troubadour incarnate. And he translated his father's ideas into action. The folk movement bloomed from roots Seeger tended devotedly for decades, and then, during the 1960s, the vision infused rock.

BEFORE THE NEW DEAL, record companies dug into rural American roots music for their own reasons: survival. During the Roaring Twenties, radio nearly killed off recording sales: why buy music when it wafted over the airwaves for free, interrupted only by commercials? (Does this sound a little like the 21st century battle between entertainment conglomerates and digital piracy? Why did Americans accept ads so quickly on mass media, as if commercial interruptions were acts of nature?) The desperate labels turned to the marginal poor white and black sounds that urban markets didn't initially want.

Ralph Peer was the initially unwitting instigator of new rural and regional markets. He worked the South selling records and sheet music to appliance stores and similar outlets when one customer suggested he could use a few country discs to spruce up sales. Peer didn't know much about it, but he signed up a few Atlanta artists. The discs sold decently, so he scanned for more talent. In 1927 he hit the jackpot with Jimmie Rodgers and the Carter Family, whose hits not only spread hillbilly music far and wide but, Midaslike, recast them into commercial gold.

Enter the major labels and the development of "race" and "hillbilly" records. The strategy was lovingly parodied in the film *O Brother Where Art Thou*: find local musicians, pay them a small flat fee if anything, record them cheaply, usually at a local radio station, press a limited quantity of discs, and advertise locally. In this way dozens of regional American subcultures, from the black and white Appalachian communities to hot-jazz urbanites to Hawaiian cowboys, were captured on shellac for Victor and Okeh and others who turned a handsome profit from the spare change that the marginalized subcultures provided within the industrializing society.

When the Depression ballooned, radio rapidly replaced expensive live broadcasts with DJs, many airing regional and "race" records. Two of the country's most popular programs were the *Grand Ole Opry* on Nashville's WSM and the *Barn Dance* on Chicago's WSM. Soon Hollywood signed "singing cowboys" like Gene Autry, whose yodel and style were a relaxed impression of Jimmie Rodgers's.

American folk music and commerce had galloped out of the gate together and left a cloud of questions and nostalgic notions of authenticity in their wake. Was Jimmie Rodgers, the tubercular Singing Brakeman whose hard-lived music embraced country, blues (he learned to play guitar from black railroad hands, though his rhythms mostly stayed whitebread stiff), Hawaiian, and even jazz (with Louis Armstrong), inauthentic because he recorded for a big label and sold stacks of commercial records and built a mansion in Texas? Was he authentic because he played benefits for local flood victims with Will Rogers?

The young Woody Guthrie studied and mimicked the records of Rodgers and the Carter Family with an energy he devoted to nothing else. He imagined himself as a performer early, and the performer in him saved him time and again: when he bought off boyhood gangs by entertaining them, when he rode the rails with hard cases who relaxed after a tall story or tune, when he flopped in fleabags where everyone was prey, when he played for Okie camps and labor rallies armed only with his guitar and its motto. Like Louis Armstrong, he learned very young that dancing in the street paid better than working or begging. He devoted his free time, when he wasn't bitching or bragging about his Okieness or chasing women or drinking, to pursuing his creative desires in a dozen directions, usually at once. He never quite told anyone what he really thought. He slept in his boots on other people's clean sheets and always smelled bad and snuck off before anyone else got up and Tom Sawyered his way out of any kind of work. But he sketched and painted reams, read Rabelais and Darwin and Lao-Tzu, wrote brilliant letters of staggering wordplay and emotional directness as well as novels and stories and hundreds of songs that are now part of the foundations of modern American popular culture.

What, in this context, does authenticity mean?

EVER WONDER HOW BRUCE SPRINGSTEEN got an Okie drawl? The next Woody Guthrie is always in the wings. Ask John Mellencamp or Steve Earle.

Lee Hayes remembers when Guthrie adulators first lined up to head for Coney Island, where Woody was living at the time with then-wife Marjorie and their kids Arlo and Nora. Guthrie had early symptoms of Huntington's chorea—though no one, except him, knew it. He'd been creatively dry for months, years. The sketch pads were blank, the novels abandoned, the songs reduced to squibs and notes, the whole huge clattering Rube Goldberg creative apparatus spinning its wheels ever more crazily as he tried to dodge or ignore the fate that had haunted him since childhood.

A waiter at an Adirondack resort where Hayes was talent coordinator told him: "Most kids reach a point where they really want their freedom. You hate school, your parents—anything that stands in the way. All you can think about is getting OUT. You want to hitch a ride, hop a freight, go wherever you want. Woody, I guess, represents that kind of freedom for me."

By then Washington Square Park and Cambridge were magnets for scruffy-looking kids with acoustic guitars and a college education and a need to get OUT.

Ramblin' Jack Elliot showed up at Coney Island Hospital, where Guthrie was recovering from a nearly fatal ruptured appendix, in 1951, carrying a guitar and decked out like a cowpoke and calling himself Buck Elliot. His name was Elliot Adnopaz, and he was the son of a Brooklyn doctor who heard Guthrie on a radio show and saw him at a regular downtown hootenanny. He could mimic Woody's every inflection, physical movement, attitude. For years I've had a postcard of them on flophouse cots, their thick mops of tangled hair and long thin features not so vaguely twinlike. But as Guthrie fell under the disease's power, he resented Elliot's uncanny accuracy at aping his slurs and stumbles and bouts of aphasia.

When Bob Dylan showed up, serious folkies said he was stealing Jack's scene. But Dylan's relationship with Woody was different: Guthrie was deathly ill by then. Dylan was less ever-present doppelganger than entertainment and relief—as Guthrie wound in and out of hospitals over the years, even his old friends, many worn out by years of demands and erratic behavior and self-righteous arrogance, stopped coming. Dylan played and wrote songs for Woody, as if he were seeking a kind of benediction from the songster, the poetic gift, the human touch. After his 1966 motorcycle accident, Dylan's first public appearance was at the benefit-tribute for Guthrie.

Springsteen, inspired by "Bound for Glory" and the movie *Grapes of Wrath*, became the blue-collar voice of the Rust Belt Age. But those jobs and plants and folkways are eroded and lost now, two decades later, and his audience's links to him are loaded with loyalty and nostalgia as much as solidarity. Can The Boss be as free as Guthrie, tethered as he is by commercial demands and a mass audience's expectations?

What, in these contexts, does authenticity mean?

O Brother Where Art Thou sent acoustic music wide once more, but the format never left, just ebbed and crested. White singer–songwriters have abounded since Guthrie, but young black musicians with acoustic guitars playing backporch music dropped off drastically after Muddy

Waters's generation until Keb' Mo' and Chris Thomas King, who not only win Grammys but take contemporary risks—like mixing in hip-hop. What does this mean? Where will it lead?

As for hip-hop—well, Guthrie didn't invent the talking blues, the white man's rap, though the form is so identified with him he should have. Think about freestylin', where rappers improvise and "pass the song around." Isn't hip-hop folk music a recycling of old cultural parts into something dramatically new that finally surfaced into commercial media? And what do hip-hoppers in full blingbling driving Humvees to swank club parties mean when they insist, "I'm keepin' it real?"

I FIRST HEARD A WHOLE ALBUM by Woody Guthrie because of the 1966 New York City subway strike. I couldn't get to school from where I lived, so I stayed over at a schoolmate's house. He was a serious guy, deep, smoked a lot of Camels, and had a sly and wicked dry sense of humor. We sat up for a couple of nights going through his stacks of folk records. I heard Lead Belly for the first time; I couldn't understand half of what he sang, but I liked its rough immediacy. Folkies like Joan Baez, Simon and Garfunkel, the Kingston Trio, the Weavers all bored me—they sounded so bleached and passionless and sincere and safe, even when I liked the lyrics. I had heard lots of people sing Guthrie tunes, but until that night I hadn't heard the man himself sing more than a couple. It didn't fit my half-baked notion of blues. "It's the white man's blues," my friend said. Within a year, the antiwar movement ratcheted up, and "This Land Is Your Land" was one of its anthems.

part II The Postwar Jazz Era

3

Mary Lou Williams

MARY LOU WILLIAMS was the first girl who really made it into the boys' club that was (and mostly still is) jazz. Sure, girl singers by the dozen fronted the big bands. And there were always women who played jazz, though most of them worked in all-female outfits, like novelty acts. Think of *Some Like It Hot*, with Marilyn Monroe as the ukulele-strumming vocalist.

Like Monroe, Williams was drop-dead gorgeous, though she was tiny and in her prime weighed barely 100 pounds. Also like Monroe, she had a creative personality crosshatched with neurotic paradoxes, which she managed to transmute into art that was distinctive, eccentric—all hers. She had a rollicking boogie-and-stride piano touch that would have done her early idol, Fats Waller, proud; she liked to brag that she "played heavy like a man."

Born in 1910, when Louis Armstrong was a preteen and jazz was unrecorded, Williams, at the age of four, could hear a piece of music and play it back. At seven, she began her long working life in Pittsburgh and earned a chunk of her near-destitute family's keep. At 12, she had mastered parlor-piano favorites, light opera, ragtime, stride, boogie-woogie, waltzes, marches, and Irish-tenor hits. She played at private parties and silent-movie houses and whorehouses—financial mainstays for jazz musicians like Waller and Count Basie. At 13, she hit the road with Boise De Legg and His Hottentots. But she did not learn to read or write music until she was 20, when she became arranger for the Swing Era band, the Clouds of Joy, led by Andy Kirk. A "territory" band, focused on the area around Kansas City, it rode Williams's distinctive arrangements to fame.

Williams's arranging style was witty and deft. She wafted "floating" chord voicings via unusual instrumentation, and stacked punchy riffs and flowing melodies over a light, looselimbed beat. Later she did charts for bandleaders like Duke Ellington and Benny Goodman—and was often underpaid or not paid at all. This was typical of the way she was under-appreciated and overlooked even by men who perceived her talent. Still, she managed to keep growing and writing, despite a husband who lived off her and beat her. In the 1930s, she wrote self-assured tunes like

"Froggy Bottom," "Cloudy," and "Roll 'Em," which became a hit for Goodman. In 1939, she mentioned to John Hammond that she'd heard a young guitar player from Oklahoma City who was translating Lester Young's quick-witted rhythms and melodic sense onto his instrument. Hammond, the Vanderbilt-descended leftist who was Goodman's brother-in-law, arranged for Charlie Christian to take a train for Los Angeles, where the clarinetist's quintet was performing at a restaurant. One night, Goodman showed up to find a guitar amplifier onstage; Christian, wearing a purple shirt and yellow shoes, waited backstage. When Goodman called "Rose Room" to stump the newcomer, Christian instead played so brilliantly he inspired the group in a round-robin of solos that lasted nearly an hour, and was hired by Goodman on the spot.

Two years after Williams finally divorced her husband in 1940, she started a sextet with the young Art Blakey and trumpeter Shorty Baker, who became her next husband—a marriage that lasted only two years. Leaving Ellington's employ, Williams decided to settle in New York, where Barney Josephson hired her to hold piano-queen court at his club, Café Society, the famed Greenwich Village nightspot that catered to the rich and intellectual left and was one of the first to break the color bar. It featured jazz, blues, folk music, and comedy, usually with a liberal/leftist slant to match its integrationist policy. Here in 1938, Billie Holiday would sing "Strange Fruit," encouraged by Josephson and the omnipresent and extraordinarily influential (if often disliked and feared) Hammond.

In 1945, Williams unveiled the ambitious, stylistically wide-ranging *Zodiac Suite*. She had read a book about astrology, she told historian Dan Morgenstern, and "decided to do the suite as based on musicians I knew born under the various signs." She had been at a creative impasse compositionally; the thematic approach freed her muse. "Aries" was for tenor saxophonist Ben Webster, whom she'd known since her Kansas City days in the 1930s; its stride feel owed its logic to his love of the form and its practitioners; and also for Holiday. "Taurus" was dedicated to Ellington and herself, and has willful whole-tone scales and tempo changes to match the sign's character. "Gemini" was meant for Goodman, Baker, and Miles Davis, with its contrasting themes and piano-bass divergences. "Virgo" is a boppish blues dedicated to critic/historian Leonard Feather, a great friend of and advocate for beboppers. "Libra," with its gorgeous Impressionistic ambience, she wrote for Dizzy Gillespie, Bud Powell, Thelonious Monk, and Art Tatum. "Aquarius" she wrote for FDR and Josh White, the black folk-blues singer who was also a regular performer at Café Society. "Pisces," a Chopinesque waltz, was for Josephson. She recorded the entire suite as piano solos, duos, and trios for Moses Asch, the key figure in the folk revival. who also recorded the likes of White, Woody Guthrie, and Pete Seeger. In an early example of jazz being adapted to the concert hall, the New York Philharmonic performed three of the movements from *Zodiac Suite* at Carnegie Hall in 1946.

Meanwhile, like the young guitar player she'd recommended to Hammond, Williams had become a central character behind the scenes in bebop. She mentored bop outlaws like Thelonious Monk (who wrote "Rhythm-a-ning" from one of her riffs), Bud Powell (who fell in love with her), and Dizzy Gillespie, whose big band she wrote scores for. She worked briefly in Benny Goodman's Sextet, taking Teddy Wilson's chair, and in the early 1950s led a trio with bassist Oscar Pettiford and drummer Kenny Clarke, the nonpareil bebop rhythm section; besides their own performances, they played with a range of bop instrumentalists and vocalist Billy Ekstine. It's evident that Williams's capacity to absorb new sounds and idioms into her own voice and her restless quest to forge new forms of jazz composition had few equals.

As a Taurus—the sign she shared with Ellington and Charles Mingus—Williams offstage was, perhaps not surprisingly, a complex, fascinating maze of crossed motives and ideals: selfless and haughty, paranoid and primly determined, fiercely stubborn in artistic matters and always craving a business handler, self-abasing and overbearing, articulate and mystical, tempestuous and controlling, the highly private possessor of a steel will and cavernous insecurities who also just happened to be a superior all-around creative musician.

Mary Lou Williams was by turns a wild woman living the freewheeling jazz life and a passive, self-flagellating soul scarred by an insidious array of guilts. In 1954, she suddenly left her gig at a Paris nightclub, stopped performing, and opened the Bel Canto Foundation, which she funded by means of a thrift shop, for which she badgered musicians from Armstrong to Ellington to donate clothes and whatnots. She lived a hand-to-mouth existence once again. In 1957, at the age of 47, following at least one probable abortion and several tormented years of visions of saints and demons, she converted to Roman Catholicism. Even then she had her own angle: she went to St. Ignatius Loyola, the Jesuits' magnificent Park Avenue Baroque church. Her favorite Jesuit told her she could be more effective if she dropped her Christlike good deeds (she gave away most of her possessions and money and refused to play in nightclubs) and returned to her art to revamp it as a vehicle for her new beliefs. From then on, priests guided her career and spiritual life, and she tried heroically to become a saint. She prayed several hours a day, wrote a series of jazz masses (one a masterwork for the black South American saint Martin de Porres), tried in vain to solicit a papal commission, and acted as spiritual counselor for just about everyone she knew or met.

An intuitive personality riddled with nooks and crannies can make a stunning character in search of an author, but Williams has found her writing soulmate in Linda Dahl, and the engrossing result is *Morning Glory*, the detailed and revealing biography titled after one of Williams's hits. A tireless researcher, Dahl sounds Williams's resonant depths, tapping her diaries, unpublished autobiography, and previously unseen papers as well as interviewing dozens of her colleagues and friends. The book has some flaws: pedestrian prose, overlong quotes, and occasionally zigzagging chronology. But the final product overcomes its relatively minor drawbacks to present a serious and engaging historical portrait of one of jazz's greatest underappreciated figures. In the process, it throws down the challenge of reevaluating and reviving her work.

As Dahl sees it, Williams learned early to live in her head. The dark-skinned five-year-old discovered both intra-black and black-white racism when her family moved from Atlanta to Pittsburgh. Her mother was a party-girl drunk, with a slew of children who raised themselves; the family would often teeter on the brink of starvation. When a friend of her step-father was teaching the 12-year-old Mary Lou to drive, he tried to rape her. She fought him off, warning that her stepfather would come after him. But she needed to learn to drive: "Being stubborn, I kept going with him . . . yelling 'stepfather!' as a threat until I learned to shift gears and start in first." It is a parable of her dealings in the world of men.

At its best, *Morning Glory* pulses with that sort of vignette. Dahl, who previously wrote *Stormy Weather: The Music and Lives of a Century of Jazzwomen*, does not put Williams in a straitjacket of psychopathology or feminism. Instead, she keeps her sense of historical context sharp, and probes rather than labels her subject's teeming contradictions.

Dahl explores Williams's endless jousts with business moguls and family, her financial and musical and emotional ups and downs, the relentless commercial pressures and repeated episodes of racism. She keeps her judgments oblique but usually telling; after she documents how Williams had to overcome sexual discrimination time after time, she drily observes that Williams may not have been as accepted in the boys' club as she thought. And always there is her well-laid foundation of research: watch how she locates Williams's compositional stream of masses and never-ending push for a papal commission within Vatican II–era American Catholic political agitation, reminding us that Williams worked with Dorothy Day, cofounder of the Catholic Worker movement. Obviously, though her eyes were directed toward heaven, she still felt the need to alleviate earthly suffering.

Williams died of bladder cancer in 1981, following four years as artist-in-residence at Duke University. The one-time boogie-woogie queen, who hated rock and roll as commercial evil but saw jazz as spiritual because of its roots in the redemptive suffering of the blues, was eulogized by jazz critics but otherwise soon forgotten. This clear-eyed biography, along with the reissue of Williams's long-out-of-print recordings and recent versions of her work from artists as diverse as pianist Geri Allen and trumpeter Dave Douglas, should help fix that.

4

Max Roach

FOR DRUM LEGEND MAX ROACH AT AGE 72, which he was when this interview took place, life was good. He could look back with satisfaction on a lifetime of innovation—and controversy, something Roach, an outspoken, even combative fellow who has never lost the "street" elements of his complex character, is as adept as ever at stirring up. That same restlessness marked his persistent musical explorations of the last 50 years, which have helped map the postwar era in jazz. From the work he did as a teen with bebop innovators Charlie Parker, Dizzy Gillespie, and Bud Powell to his offbeat classical-meets-jazz forays, from his definitive hard bop quintet, featuring Sonny Rollins and Clifford Brown, to his championing of hip-hop artists as the newest wave of African American cultural renewal and change, Roach has been on the cutting edge—and unafraid to speak his mind.

Twenty years ago, when I first interviewed him, he straddled the fence on Wynton Marsalis, then a hot, divisive topic of discussion: he thought the trumpeter's classical chops outpaced his jazz abilities (which I agreed with) but added that it was about time jazz musicians themselves and American institutions like Lincoln Center recognized the value of what Roach, like many in the jazz world, sees as America's greatest contribution to the arts. Then, when Marsalis unveiled his rather Mingusy but jumbled extended work, "All Rise," in the late 1990s, Roach was furious: "Those churchy sections," he sputtered at me during the intermission, "are shit! He's never even been in a Baptist or Holy Roller church, and it shows." In my review, I attributed the cleaned-up quote to "a jazz legend in the audience"; Roach told me the day the piece ran that he got a sharp phone call from Lincoln Center officials—they'd guessed it was him and wanted to know why he'd talked such trash to me. "Because it's what I think," he shot back.

As countless people, including his old cohort and erstwhile business and musical partner Charles Mingus, have discovered over the years, it's not really worth arguing with Roach. Especially now that he's garnering the sorts of accolades that his achievements should bring—and, all too rarely in the arts, while he's still alive to enjoy them.

In spring 1996, Roach made one of his periodic leaps into new turf: an album featuring him in an extended composition with the New Orchestra of Boston as well as a shorter piece with the So What Brass Quintet. That is why I'm up on Central Park West to see him. While he and his office assistant are dealing with phone calls and inventory—one of the assistant's tasks is to go over the unorganized but extensive tape and wire-recording library of live shows Roach has stashed over the decades, some of them riveting performances with the Brown–Roach Quintet featuring Rollins—Roach hands me a video, which I pop into the machine. The tape, a live performance of *Festival Journey*, as the orchestral piece is called, starts, and I daydream in front of the TV, waiting for Max to finish with the phone. There in his spacious 14th-floor apartment overlooking the park, I'm surrounded by the memorabilia of a lifetime—African and Asian percussion instruments, an upright bass, a guitar, books that cover African American history, world mythology, all manner of art and musical catalogs and essays. It is only a sampling of the breadth of mind the most interesting jazz musicians display, an aspect of the music that informs it deeply but that too few listeners know or appreciate, and as my eyes wander the rooms I let myself play back some peaks of Max Roach's illustrious career.

Born in 1924 in the South, he moved to Brooklyn with his family when he was four—part of the migration of southern blacks leaving sharecropping for work in northern factories. Daycare for him and his older brother, as for many black kids of the time, came from the church, with its rich musical traditions that have left their indelible fingerprints on Roach's music. FDR's New Deal had its impact as well, an impact Roach has never forgotten as he's complained bitterly about the disappearance of arts, and in particular music, education from elementary and high schools across America. "It was free, Gene, that's how poor kids could learn to play an instrument," he says to me whenever the topic comes up. As a boy, he took maximum advantage, studying trumpet, piano, and then drums under the WPA program, which, seeking to make the arts an integral part of American daily life, sponsored artists teaching in the schools. His early experiences, and the lifelong benefits he's reaped from them, instilled in Roach a lifelong commitment to arts education (he was on the faculty at the University of Massachusetts at Amherst for more than 20 years) as well as strong social views.

But Roach's formal schooling combined with what he calls "the university of the streets." Growing up black in prewar Depression-era Brooklyn was in some—maybe too many—ways something like life as depicted in a Spike Lee movie. (Roach admires Lee's work and attitudes.) Besides his studies and rehearsals with the jazz band and symphony at Brooklyn's Boys High (now Boys and Girls High), Roach scuffled for paying gigs—at after-hours joints, backing chorus girls and fire-eaters and the carnival like, honing his chops, pocketing the cash, biding his time. So when he was 16, he was ready to replace Duke Ellington's stalwart drummer Sonny Greer for a couple of days—which he did so well it opened new doors for him, as the right gig in those days could for a young musician. Soon jazz stars like tenor sax pioneer Coleman Hawkins were hiring him, and the teen became a fixture at Harlem clubs like Minton's and Monroe's, where Dizzy Gillespie, Thelonious Monk, Kenny Clarke, and Charlie Christian were putting aside the big band charts that earned them their daily bread in order to toss their evolving ideas about harmonic extensions and rhythmic twists into the communal pot. Christian's upbeat, Lester Young–flavored guitar solos fired the imagination; Gillespie and Monk were, in their different ways, expanding jazz's language beyond the blues and pop, internalizing, as it were, the language of Gershwin and Debussy and rewriting it to new beats, which were Clarke's insights, developed out of the need to redefine the drummer's role in small groups. Once a Kansas City alto saxist named Charlie Parker landed in the Apple in 1943, he brought the apparently volcanic flow of ideas, motifs, and convoluted melodies into the mix, and the chemistry that would yield bebop was catalyzed.

What Roach, following Clarke's lead, did with the drums changed the shape of postwar jazz. His attack is compositional, melodic, in a way few drummers before him, aside from Count Basie's Papa Jo Jones, had mastered. (Roach has for years done a solo drum tribute to Papa Jo, a stunning example of how the drums can indeed speak the language of tonality and inference—a 20-minute lesson in why Roach's attack has deeply influenced latter-day drummers from Tony Williams to Joey Baron.) Brandishing offbeats to match the hornmen's slippery lines, flourishing a quick press roll or a rimshot or cymbal smash to reply, Roach abandoned simple timekeeping to enter into complex conversations with the "front line," sculpting the improvised arrangements as he proceeded. This sort of playing required a compleat musician. So Roach hit the books at the Manhattan School of Music; his classmates included the Modern Jazz Quartet's John Lewis and historian Gunther Schuller. Following with the drum solo compositions he began showcasing in the late 1940s, and the adventurous drum-and-bass outings he mustered with Mingus in the early 1950s, he formed M'Boom in the mid-1970s, an all-percussion ensemble intended to highlight the rounded possibilities he's nurtured for the drums.

Bop was cool, the ultimate cool to younger musicians like Roach and Sonny Rollins and Jackie McLean. But it didn't pay anyone's rent; the industry, reeling from the postwar collapse of the big bands, the midwar musicians' strike led by mob-connected union czar James Petrillo, and a variety of luxury taxes, had moved to highlighting singers backed by small, often anonymous combos, and was hardly interested in a clearly esoteric, even exotic new musical idiom. And so, like virtually every avant-garde music in America before or since, bop found other outlets—small entrepreneurial record labels often loosely (or tightly) allied with gangsters, mob-owned or mob-connected booking agents and venues. Prestige and respect the movement's leaders gathered aplenty from their acolytes, but in the mainstream press they were jeered at and pilloried, depicted as goofy European aesthete wannabes wearing funny clothes and talking crazy lingo—the same kind of treatment the Beats faced shortly afterward. Even the name bebop was a condescending media creation.

And so Roach like his vanguard confreres, hustled for paying gigs. He found himself on club-lined West 52nd Street, now renamed Swing Street, going from venue to venue, backing Charlie Parker, New Orleans revivalists, vocalists like Louis Jordan, who walked the line (which had not yet been drawn) between rhythm and blues and jazz. He learned from it all. That same versatility and curiosity made him essential to Miles Davis's *Birth of the Cool*, the groundbreaking sessions that united Lewis, Schuller, Gerry Mulligan, and a few others under the direction of Gil Evans, a former arranger for the Claude Thornhill band whose apartment became this ersatz group's crash pad, headquarters, and unofficial nerve center. Riding the swing of history's pendulum, this nonet eschewed bop's small-group freneticism, its dependence on the head-string-of-solos-head format, and instead ventured into a more understated, orchestrally arranged palette—a harbinger of what Evans and Davis would later bring to classic recordings like *Sketches of Spain*.

Roach had been studying Baby Dodds, an early New Orleans drummer with, among others, Louis Armstrong, who maximized the use of his entire drum set in ways that had never been significantly picked up on. On *Birth of the Cool*, you hear Roach expanding Dodds' approach, the subtleties of his colorations, the nuanced responses to the other instrumentalists and their interactions—quite a different road from Swing Era pathfinders like Buddy Rich and Gene Krupa, whose showboating, indebted to black drummers like the diminutive Chick Webb, could all too easily overshadow their artistic gifts.

By the mid-1950s, the jazz pendulum had swung yet again, back toward bebop without simply reiterating it. As the jazz spectrum devolved into Third Stream chamber jazz, junked-up bop, and West Coast cool, groups like Art Blakey's Jazz Messengers with Horace Silver began to delve into what became known as hard bop, a harmonically stripped-back, gospel-flavored stepchild of bebop. Charles Mingus adapted this style to his own Jazz Workshop idea, mingling the notion of improvisation as spontaneous composition with the idea of working compositions out on stage in performance, often confounding his musicians (and audiences) in the process. Roach was one of the powers of this movement, with a fearsome lineup that included saxist Sonny Rollins and trumpeter Clifford Brown. This group was one of postwar jazz's finest and most kinetic; their deft tempo shifts and odd-sectioned tunes, framing fiery solos, upped the performance ante and lifted audiences out of their seats. People could dance to jazz once again.

Like and often with Mingus, Roach participated in political demonstrations and movements from the McCarthy era onward—marching in Alabama with Dr. Martin Luther King, Harry Belafonte, and Pete Seeger. And he used his music as a platform for his views. *We Insist—The Freedom Now Suite* was commissioned in 1960 by the NAACP to celebrate the 100th anniversary of the 1863 Emancipation Proclamation; the piece is an outpouring of rage and frustration at American racism that, not surprisingly, makes for hair-raising, provocative music. I once asked Abbey Lincoln, Roach's wife of the period who sings on that album, how she felt doing all the painful, at times blood-curdling, screams and vocalizing. Lincoln is a regal woman with a soft storyteller's voice often rightly likened to Billie Holiday's, and in the last decade she's finally come in for much of her due, as both composer and interpreter. At the time, she gazed back at me in her resolutely queenly way and said, "It was what the music and its mood required, but I'm not sure I think of it as singing." Maybe for the sake of comparison I should ask Cathy Berberian how she thinks of her role in Luciano Berio's music.

Roach refuses to let age make stale his apparently endless variety. He has continued to multiply his musical languages and their creative outlets: M'Boom, his Double Octet (with strings), his symphonic material, his series of one-on-one jousts with musicians as resolutely unalike as Cecil Taylor, Dizzy Gillespie, Anthony Braxton, and so on. It should have been no surprise in 1988 that he became the first jazz musician to win a MacArthur "genius" award.

I have no idea how many times I've seen Max Roach play, and how many times I've listened to his recordings: *The Quintet at Massey Hall*; *Birth of the Cool*; *A Study in Brown*, with Clifford Brown and Rollins; *We Insist: Freedom Now! Suite*; *Survivors*, with his long-running quartet of trumpeter Cecil Bridgewater, saxist Odean Pope, and bassist Tyrone Davis; *Historic Concerts*, with Cecil Taylor; *Max and Dizzy*; *Easy Winners*, with his Double Quartet, his own plus daughter Maxine's Uptown String Quartet; *M'Boom Live at S.O.B.'s*. Among the last few times I've seen Roach onstage, two stand out in my memory. The first was in Harlem, where he played solo for a benefit audience of glitterati that included ex-mayor David Dinkins and congressman Charlie Rangel. Roach's legs were clearly showing their age: he needed some help climbing the drum riser, and there was a scary moment when he slipped and the crowd audibly drew its breath. The second was at Tompkins Square Park in the East Village, where Roach headlined the annual Charlie Parker Jazz Festival. He played his tribute to Papa Jo Jones, and the crowd of 10,000 went wild, bursting into a prolonged standing ovation at the finale.

Here, then, is Max Roach.

GENE SANTORO: You've always been adventurous. It's something you
    shared with Dizzy and Miles—the people who changed music in the
    1940s, say. They didn't stop; they kept changing, evolving, developing.
MAX ROACH: Right, right. I think that's the essence of what we do. It really
    comes out of writing. You have to keep renewing yourself. It's like the
    university: publish or perish. With us, it's the record companies. No
    matter what you do, year after year record company presidents, A&R
    executives say, "Man, you've made all these records. But what have you
    got that's new?" So you're constantly searching so you can record.
        The people you just mentioned, and people like Abbey, that's what
    they've done. It's one of the earmarks of what American music is about.
    The kinds of things that are coming together now, for instance, are
    amazing, unpredictable. Take Willie Nelson: jazz singing, country
    music, nylon-stringed classical guitar. He's like Ray Charles; he wants
    to do it all.
GS: The impetus, the urge to change, seems tied to something very
    American—the need to disregard categories, whether social categories
    or other sorts.
MR: Absolutely. That's not what this country was supposed to be about.
    This country was supposed to eliminate that, and it's gone a long way,
    though it's obviously far from done. And the same thing should happen
    artistically. It's like you said: there's no hierarchy of the arts here—or
    at least there shouldn't be. It's supposed to be a fluid situation, not like
    in more traditional societies, where art tends to stay more fixed and
    immutable, or even in Europe, where there are different kinds of stan-
    dards. Here it's like there's this town square in the middle of everything
    where anybody should be able to work, where everybody should be
    able to meet with other artists and have a conversation.
        In a couple of weeks, we're going into the studio to record with
    M'Boom, along with Tony Williams and Ginger Baker. [Williams, who
    had broken into the big time with Miles Davis's so-called second great
    quintet with Herbie Hancock, Wayne Shorter, and Ron Carter and
    reshaped the use of cymbals and polyrhythms in jazz, subsequently
    died; Baker, one of the founders of Cream, the blues-rock improvising
    trio that helped launch jazz-rock fusion, soon after this formed an
    offbeat power trio with guitarist Bill Frisell.] What we're doing is some-
    thing we've already had a trial run on; we did it in Verona last year. We
    had 15,000 people in the arena. I must tell you, I'm looking forward to
    it, but I'm also thinking Tony can really dance.
GS: I've seen the old man dance pretty well.
MR: Yeah, well, Tony and Ginger will keep me at it, I tell you. And
    M'Boom, of course, has been together over 20 years now and made the
    point that the drums can do a lot more than just keep time. But when
    Tony and Ginger and I get together, it's three different styles, a few years
    apart, anyway, but the way they mix becomes something completely

different. That's why over the years I've played in duos with so many different kinds of people—to check that chemistry out.

GS: Cecil Taylor is somebody you've played with in a duo, somebody whose approach is totally distinctive, who some people consider to be on the extreme edge even after 40 years of being on the scene and recording and getting artistic, if not commercial, accolades. But you take your thing and you get with it, wherever you want, and make it work.

MR: That's exactly what this music we call jazz is about, Gene—exploration. Cecil is something; he's always pushing when you're playing with him, he's always got another flood of ideas ready to go. He's a very strong musical personality; it's like getting into the ring with Mike Tyson. So usually you have to struggle to get a foothold in there. But once you do you set up a give-and-take. With Cecil, you have to keep doing that during a concert. But that's the fun—and the artistic challenge, the meeting of the minds. And that makes him a joy to work with, especially for a percussionist. The interaction is so fluid, and he's so aware of rhythm, what he does with it is so subtle. And at the same time he's so . . . insistent.

I remember one time I did a duo with Dizzy. He was touring around Europe with his band. Now, Dizzy worked every day if possible; he always did that, claimed it kept his chops up. He could never understand how Mingus, for instance, could go for days without touching the bass. Anyway, I met Dizzy in Paris, but I got there ahead of him. When he came in, it was late, so we didn't have a chance to talk about what we were gonna do. In fact, we didn't get a chance until the next morning—in the car, on the way to the sound check. Dizzy turns to me and says, "Who's the bass player?" "No bass player," I say. "Who's the pianist?" "No pianist." He turned and looked out the window for a second, then turned back with a little smile on his face, and said softly, "So I'm free, huh?" Harmonically and rhythmically, he could stretch the bar lines any way he wanted to, stretch the progressions any way he wanted to. He wasn't restricted to hearing any particular way somebody else on stage wanted him to. So he just kinda smiled and shook his head from side to side. Of course, when we got onstage he proved one more time that he still had more tricks than anybody else up his sleeve.

GS: The way you roam around stylistically reminds me how jazz musicians have traditionally resisted definition, having themselves or the music pigeonholed. Definitions could hem in what they were trying to do.

MR: Well, I think some things have changed. I think younger musicians like Wynton Marsalis and those guys began to realize that they could study Roy Eldridge and Dizzy Gillespie, and Louis Armstrong for that matter, and learn big lessons from them. That's good. But the important thing in jazz is still that you develop who you are. You have to have a personal signature. Miles went to the conservatory, but before he went there he'd developed his personal signature. So had Monk. The way he dealt with space and so forth, for instance, was like nobody else—he was Monk, he was saying something about himself, the way he related to the world. The way he sounds is the way he was, and he was like nobody else.

GS: There's a story you once told me about playing with Lester Young. You stopped by his room, figuring it had been a good night on the bandstand. And he said, "You can't join the throng till you write your own song."

MR: Oh, yeah, he had that way of talking. See, playing with him, I thought I'd be doing the right thing by playing like Papa Jo Jones. That night, we finished, and I thought, "Boy, Papa Jo would be proud of me." But Prez was saying, "Look, kid, get your own signature. You've got to find your version." It's like Bird said: "If you don't live it, it can't come out of your horn." You've got to live it, then believe it. Doing what somebody else did isn't the point. In this music, you have to find out who you are, what you feel, what you want to say. That's one of the ways that it's so American. You have to be yourself.

That's also one way jazz is different from classical music. In classical music, you learn to study and come up with the finest interpretation of a work that you can. That's a different way of expressing your personality. You have to learn to use what's written already to express yourself. In jazz, you have to learn to be who you are, and create the music from that.

GS: One analogy I've used is a library. In classical music, people are trained to read fluently, and naturally each person reads differently, adding shades and nuances to the work. In jazz, it's like the books are missing pages that the musicians have to fill in, connecting the dots in their own ways without destroying continuity.

MR: That's exactly it. You've got to come up with something that's individual to you and true to the music. That's why you're playing, that's why you're on the gig.

GS: That's kinda what you and Kenny Clarke did for bebop, no? Rearranged the rhythms?

MR: Right, right. Well, you've gotta remember what was happening at the time. The demise of the big bands had put all the weight on small groups and small clubs. First, there was the war, drafting most of the musicians, then there were special taxes—on dancing, for instance. And there was the rationing—tires, gasoline—that made it hard if not impossible to tour like in the Swing Era. All that made it pretty close to impossible to keep a big band going. Duke Ellington was one of the only bandleaders who could, and that's because he had the royalties coming in from his music, which he used to support the band. So the big bands basically died out and gave way to the small groups. That meant that the role of the drums had to change too. The small groups needed something different, not somebody keeping time. It had to be more active.

For me, Dizzy was actually the catalyst of that whole bebop period. He was on top of everything about it before everybody else, all the guys of our generation. He was working for and writing for Cab Calloway, writing for Claude Thornhill—he started very young. So he'd make the round of nightspots and sit in with you, with anybody. When I first heard talk of Charlie Parker and Oscar Pettiford it was because Dizzy had heard them in Kansas City and would come back to New York and talk to us about them. So by the time Bird got to New York I was already playing at the places he started to hit.

I first heard about Charlie Parker in 1943, at a joint called Georgie J's 78th Street Tavern, on East 78th Street. We played down there from say nine until three, then we'd pack our gear and go uptown and play from four until about eight A.M. That's a lot of playing time, but we were all young, and so there was a lot of energy. Charlie Parker heard us playing around the clock and looking for jam sessions after we got off high school, and he was amazed. If the music happened, if bebop took off artistically, it was because of that: the enthusiasm, the commitment, people wanting to do something new. It was fresh.

What Kenny Clarke brought to it, especially from my perspective, was his overall musicianship. He was a good pianist, a good composer, played mallets. I saw that and said, "Ah, so you've got to do all that to think like he thinks." That whetted my appetite to get more involved with theory and harmony and all those other things necessary to full musical training, 'cause up until then usually drummers just played the drums—they didn't know or need to know anything about the musical architecture, say. But when I saw how Kenny dealt with everything, it was an education. For me, it was like Dizzy bringing Miles over to the piano and saying, "You've gotta know how this works if you wanna be a real musician."

I remember recording "Un Poco Loco" with Bud Powell. I was doing the standard Latin rhythm thing I'd learned on it, and he just stops the tune and looks at me funny and says, "You're Max Roach. Can't you do better than that?" So I fooled around and came up with something different. A few weeks later, when the record comes out, I see him on the street. "Hey, Bud." He just glares at me: "You fucked up my record!" You know, we never did play that piece live after that, whenever I worked with him. But on the other hand, we were playing in so many odd meters that jazz hadn't much used before—5 or 7 or 9—and feels, that it all became almost intuitive. We internalized them. They became second nature.

Of course, at the same time I was doing that stuff I was going out on the road with rhythm and blues folks like Louis Jordan and Red Allen.

See, a drummer's like a chameleon—you deal with all kinds of musical situations or else you don't work. That may be one reason there aren't that many drummers who find their own voice to the extent that they have something so different they become bandleaders: Chick Webb, Buddy Rich, Gene Krupa, Cozy Cole, Art Blakey, Elvin Jones. It's not as easy to find something that makes you stick out on a tympani instrument as it is on a melodic instrument.

GS: Bebop bred its reaction, the cool.

MR: The *Birth of the Cool* sessions were amazing. Miles and I had been working with Bird for years already, so we knew each other well. And Gil Evans had been there during that whole period on 52nd Street. In fact, during intermissions and after we got our dough, as often as not we'd go to Gil's place. Gil was arranging for Claude Thornhill, as was Dizzy, and that's how the whole thing hooked up. We'd been going to Gil's tinkering with ideas for that music for weeks, an incredible mix of people: Miles, John Lewis, Lee Konitz, Gerry Mulligan. There was really some kind of chemistry.

Speaking of small groups, I remember when Mr. Ellington played with me and Charles Mingus. Listen to that record. He really kicks our butts, he's all over the place. And we were supposed to be the hot young guys, but we were scrambling. He had that left-hand stride thing going, his real sharp sense of time. Mingus got so unsettled he just decided to pick up the bass and leave. So we all went into the lobby, and Mingus was just beside himself. Everybody from all over the jazz world had come to see this particular session, to see Duke on his trio date with the younger guys, so the pressure was on—really on, if you were as sensitive as Mingus. So we had to calm him back down to finish off the rest of the session. Duke had to coax him back into the studio, telling him how beautifully he was playing, and then he calmed down and we could get back to work.

GS: In 1952, you and Mingus started your own label, Debut, and recorded the fabulous *Quintet at Massey Hall* with Dizzy, Bird, Bud, and yourselves in 1953.

MR: Yeah, we started Debut because nobody was banging down our doors to record us. He was a bass player, I'm a drummer, and record companies look for lead players. So we had to start our own record company to record our music. But we also recorded Charlie Parker, Miles Davis, and everybody else we could, because we were all struggling during that period. There was no work. The clubs were closing down. The record companies were cutting back. It was hard to make a living.

So I remember when we did *Massey Hall*. It was Mingus's idea to record that, the so-called dream band. At that time the only one of us who was signed to any label was Charlie Parker. Since he was signed with Norman Granz for Verve records, we said, "Bird, you negotiate for all of us." So he went to see Norman and asked him for $100,000.

Norman said, "Well, uh, I'll call you back." Of course, we never heard from him. So we put it out on our own label, but we couldn't use Bird's name—Norman threatened us about that—so he became Charlie Chan.

GS: M'Boom and your solo pieces, like "Drum Conversation," have long been vehicles for you to foreground what the drums can do besides just accompany.

MR: You know, Gene, you just hear so much in New York. When I heard Segovia do a concert and saw him deal with that instrument alone onstage, I felt that this could be done with a drum set. When Ravi Shankar first came to the United States he had a wonderful tabla player who had spread in a semicircle maybe eight tablas that he did some wonderful solos on. And I was always fascinated by Art Tatum, what people like that could do with solo instruments. So in the back of my mind I felt that the technique and knowledge of how to create form— in other words, how to take music and look at it architecturally—is the key to the drums. You build. Of course, you're not dealing with melody and harmony, but certainly you can relate to poetry and sentences, you can ask yourself questions and answer them, and you can do the same kind of things writers do to make what they're doing make sense.

M'Boom came about because I needed some people who felt about percussion the way I did. The front line has always been the horns, the second line was the rhythm section. So I got some people who felt like, "Okay, we're gonna be the front line, the second line and every other thing too." The percussion family, after all, runs the complete spectrum of sound, of determined pitches, from bass marimbas and tympani all the way up to bells and chimes at the top. Harmonically, we can cover everything with mallet instruments. As far as instruments of undetermined pitch, it's limitless: tire irons, shakers, everything. This was the basic idea: we wanted percussion to do the whole damn thing. That isn't original, of course, because you have people like Stockhausen in Europe, you've got the Japanese kodo drummers, and of course the Africans. But I think the unique thing I was after was that this percussion ensemble would reflect that music that's created in the United States—jazz or whatever you want to call it.

See, the drum set is an innovation that comes out of the United States. Nowhere else that I know of do percussionists play with all four limbs. So a new language is being developed here. As each generation starts dealing with the music, the drums take on a more prominent role, as in bebop, as in rhythm and blues, and in rock, as in rap now.

GS: A few years ago, you created some controversy by championing hip-hop and working with Fab Five Freddy.

MR: One of the things that fascinated me when I first heard rap was that there were no melodies or harmonies, just rhythm and poetry, rhyming. It was exciting to me. I think it was the most revolutionary sound out here as far as people of the inner cities are concerned, the ones left out of society. Okay. So first what the rappers have done is rejected what everybody else says is the proper way to deal with sound—that you must have a perfect balance between melody, harmony, and rhythm. They took rhythm and made it into something else; they obliterated melody and destroyed harmony. They spoke to their neighborhoods, to the life led there. And they came up with something that people are relating to all over the world.

5

Sonny Rollins

THEODORE WALTER "SONNY" ROLLINS has been called jazz's greatest living improviser so many times it's become his virtual Homeric epithet. In 1959, musicologist Gunther Schuller wrote an essay using "Blue 7" from Rollins's *Saxophone Colossus* to explicate the saxophonist's thematic way of worrying at melodies to unfold variations, often so subtly that they recall the attack shared by his idols Lester Young and Billie Holiday. Ask any significant contemporary saxist, from Joshua Redman to Joe Lovano to Branford Marsalis, about influences; expect Rollins's name to be at or near the top of the list.

In concert—the only way to experience Rollins at his best—he stalks the stage wielding his tenor like it's a toy, twisting and turning down the corridors of his restless imagination with such fluency that he seems less a purely musical, and more a natural, phenomenon. His burred, fluid tone shifts as he ransacks his bottomless memory banks for quotes, fragments of tunes he can warp into the crucibles that are his solos. His love of pop culture, from cowboy movies to dancing, led him to annex to jazz styles like calypso, in his "St. Thomas," and rework Tin Pan Alley schmaltz like "Toot Toot Tootsie." At the time, few jazz artists aside from Miles Davis—Rollins's most frequent bandmate in the early 1950s—could touch that sort of vehicle without going soft. But that's Sonny Rollins—and so that's what you get. The integration of his personality, the focus on the flow of his jazz voice as it articulates the pools of his psyche, is what makes him so formidable, as a player and as a person. He is a nonpareil jazz existentialist.

The quick précis of his life and career runs like this: his mother was born in the Virgin Islands, but Sonny Rollins grew up in Harlem, alongside other jazz-musicians-to-be like Jackie McLean. His older brother and sister studied music and became classical professionals, but Sonny was drawn to jazz and the jazzy pop of the Swing Era. He met his bebop idols hanging out on the Harlem scene: Charlie Parker, Max Roach, Thelonious Monk, Bud Powell. And like the teenage McLean he worked with them, rehearsing with Monk: "He used to sneak me into bars after school." In

1955, he was recruited for one of hard bop's powerhouses, the Max Roach–Clifford Brown Quintet. Two years later, he went out on his own.

Rollins has gone his own way ever since. His two "retirements"—one in 1959 to study himself and his music, when his practicing on the Williamsburg Bridge prompted a now-famed short story; the other in the late 1960s to travel to the Orient and delve into Eastern philosophies—are the best-known manifestations of his singularity. He doesn't quite fit the standard categories of jazz history or life. He's played almost everything there is to play, and it has all, for better or worse, come out him.

When you interview him, it's like playing in his band. He expects room to rove and develop his ideas—and they are ideas, not prefab riffs that fall easily under the fingers—but he also gets bored or impatient if you don't have the chops to feed him variations on the changes.

And so I lead off by asking why he hates recording.

He dives in: "I'm reading a book called *War of the Worlds*—not the H. G. Wells book. It's about the world of cyberspace, a sort of doomsday prophesy of what's happening in that world, how people are getting so far away from contact with each other—what the author calls "f-to-f," which means to face-to-face contact. This is getting to be a thing of the past, just like playing a musical instrument is getting to be old-fashioned. Some people can sit down in front of a screen and punch in an atmosphere of some kind and then experience those things via the Internet. I think that's a dangerous trend, but I don't like technology anyway, so I was converted before I read the book.

"I think that, whereas recordings are good, and I'm very happy to have made successful ones that helped people find out about me, the actual playing experience is nothing like being with real people, and creating music for real people, and getting the feedback from real people. That hasn't been replaced. In cyberspace, it's gotten to the point of cybersex. To me, that's a type of insanity. Now, playing music and recording isn't as extreme an example, of course, but playing live is like having sex live, as opposed to recording, which is like having cybersex. So I always like to have that contact with the audience. For quite a while, a lot of my records that I like were live. When I started out, everything was done in the studio, but that basically meant recording live anyway—no overdubbing, no going back and forth. In effect, it was live, but no audience except for the engineer and producer. Now, of course, I employ overdubbing and other modern techniques myself for my recordings, but I prefer f-to-f. I think there's something that happens in actual live performance. It can't really be captured; even a live recording is not like being there live. Does that sound crazy?"

I shake my head no. I've been at lots of shows that have been recorded, and the record, no matter how good, never feels the same. The vibe is gone, or at least diminished; you have audience noises, not the electricity, the looks on bandmembers' faces, the movements and colors of the crowd.

He nods. "All right. So there's no way to capture what's happening right at the moment, which is what jazz is all about anyway—that creative spontaneous thing. That's why I hate recording. I believe in this spontaneity, so I like to play in front of people."

Spontaneous communication, I suggest.

"Music is just a language," he observes, "and you speak to people in ways they and you can understand. You want to communicate without condescending. Every great musician I've ever known, all very serious guys, wanted to reach people; not all of them succeed in the same ways. Music has a spiritual aspect that needs to be communicated to people. Spiritual, mystical, whatever you want to call it, there's something mysterious that you can't get by punching a button. That's what makes life not humdrum."

"THIS AIR CONDITIONING—I HATE IT, but it's necessary," Rollins apologizes as he stops answering a question to clear his throat. He uses the time to step back from what I've asked him, scrutinizes it like it's a tune to blow on, and says, "Aren't these questions kinda technical for a general audience?" Our conversation—for this interview has turned into a conversation over the course of its three-plus hours—unfolds in Rollins's small 39th-floor Manhattan pied-à-terre (his real home is a 120-acre farm in upstate New York), a few blocks north of the World Trade Center, which hasn't yet fallen; its windows glare with the rising heat of this early summer day, and the Hudson River below glints its way to the sea. Rollins is sitting up in bed, his head swaddled in a blue turban, his eyes hooded by dark glasses, his muscular torso draped with sweatclothes and a sheet. I shrug, and explain the technical stuff sets up and fills in around more general stuff.

He answers, "Well, as I've said a lot of times I consider the saxophone to be a very unique, mystical instrument. The conical shape goes all the way back into antiquity. I remember when I first saw a saxophone I got hooked because it was so pretty—the keys and the gold, you know. I was just always attracted to it, and I still think it's the greatest instrument—you can do so many things with it, it's open-ended. The instrument is there to bring out the sounds of the individual artists, their personal sounds. The first sax players I learned to appreciate, like Coleman Hawkins and Benny Carter and Lester Young and Louis Jordan, represented an incredible range of possibilities on the instrument."

That is a fascinating list.

Ever since the mid-1920s, when Coleman Hawkins, after sitting near Louis Armstrong in the Fletcher Henderson orchestra, began to consciously replace his old-style vaudevillian slap-tonguing antics with the looselimbed emotional and creative rapture he absorbed from Armstrong's surging triplets, dotted and tied notes, and melodic leaps, the saxophone, especially the tenor sax, has been considered jazz's primary instrumental voice, elbowing aside the cornet and trumpet—an ironic inversion of how

Armstrong himself had elevated his cornet above all the other instruments in the old New Orleans jazz bands. Hawkins, trained on classical piano as a child, had little of Armstrong's instinctive and intensified blues feel, nor had he yet made the underlying connection Armstrong did between arias, say, and instrumental solos. But as Armstrong's power swept over Hawkins, as it did all of "hot" jazz, it liberated his thinking: his lines grew more legato, his rhythms percolated, and he drew on the harmonic understanding his childhood lessons had instilled. The tenor saxophone had left vaudeville's barnyard mimickry to become a jazz voice.

By the late 1920s, Hawkins's solos connected arpeggios across chord changes, replacing the largely "horizontal" (melody-derived theme and variations) soloing that Armstrong and early jazz featured with "vertical" (harmony-derived lines linking notes from chords) soloing—and thereby opened the conceptual door for most jazz improvisers since. In his early days, Hawkins at times sacrificed Armstrong's dancing subtlety and exuberance; like John Coltrane during his later free-jazz period, Hawkins tended to alternate heavy and light beats, in ways that rhythm and blues and rock and roll musicians could adapt. On his famed 1939 version of "Body and Soul," Hawkins filled a 78 rpm disc with an improvised saxophone solo of gorgeous construction and rich masculine tone that suggested dim lights, dreamy eyes, and a discreet fade-out.

Benny Carter's alto sax also mined legato smoothness, an economy of effort that climbed and descended across the song's harmonic motion via seamless arpeggios, though his silken tone, like that of Duke Ellington's Johnny Hodges, unwound with yearning, in contrast to the sexy insistence growling in Hawkins's (and in disciples like Ben Webster's) tenors. And of course, with his charts for big bands like Henderson's and his own, Carter joined innovating arrangers like Don Redman (the longtime sonic sorcerer behind Henderson's band) in formally restructuring big bands along the rhythmic and melodic lines suggested by Armstrong's trumpet solos.

Lester Young, a professional carnival and show musician from childhood, ended up in Kansas City in the early 1930s, where he met and left Count Basie for an abortive stint with Henderson's band. He was hired to replace Hawkins, but Henderson's personnel derided his playing; he had a light, airy, almost alto tone, and his long-lined solos, departing from the arpeggiated guidelines Hawkins had staked, seemed to float almost arbitrarily from one chord to the next on passing tones and flexible rhythms that helped inspire bebop. One reason Prez, as he was called, was often accused of homosexuality, a nasty putdown in the macho jazz world, was his distinctly un-Hawkinsy, unassertive yet brainy solos. And Young always insisted that his major models were Jimmy Dorsey and Frankie Trumbauer, two white saxophonists with classical training who played in "sweet" bands with dry, almost withdrawn tones; Charlie Parker, who always cited Young as the central influence on him, called the same pair. This was not politically correct.

Finally, there is Louis Jordan, a shaper of postwar rhythm and blues, once it had hived off from jazz evolution into bebop, cool, and the like. Jordan's father led the Rabbit Foots Minstrels around the TOBA vaudeville circuit, and as a high school kid he played sax and sang with the troupe on tour. When bebop demanded attention as high art, Jordan's jumping jive, like Illinois Jacquet's honking and screaming solo on the 1939 smash hit "Flyin' Home," was art as entertainment.

Rollins's list restores integrity to the fallen Humpty Dumpty of post-Armstrong jazz. Art and entertainment are assimilated. Rollins can touch the thrilling intellectual heights of modernist jazz while reviving its audience-grabbing panache. Even in 2002, he was one of the few jazz instrumentalists who could sell out Carnegie Hall, where thousands of fans endure the horrible PA, which reduces Rollins's edgy, often trebly tenor to an electronic kazoo, to catch a glimpse of the process of his jazz thinking.

His improvising approach reminds me of holding a melody up to light and rotating it. How does he know when it's done?

"Like a jeweler, almost," he says. "That's what I try to do. I never really think that it's done, and it's difficult to get the people I'm playing with to realize that it's not done. It's never done. The problem for me is that musicians will often feel it's done. For instance, I've got a new rhythm section. I always tell guys when they start with me: say you're playing a song, 'Somewhere Over the Rainbow.' Now, this is jazz, I know, so we're not just gonna play the melody. But after we state the melody, I don't want you to stop and go into that jazz 4/4, extemporize on the chord changes. Don't make that clear demarcation from one into the other. Go slowly into it. We may play the melody ten times. Each time it's gonna be a little different. So keep going on; as we keep playing, we'll get into the place where it's more jazzlike. But it has to come in a more natural, flowing way.

"Looking at it that way, things can go on forever. There's no limit to what you can do, as long as everybody's thinking that way. It should go on and on and on, until it gets to the point where it's not happening. I'll leave that up to me, though, and then I'll make the ending—much later than most guys would think it should be."

"NEWK" IS WHAT THEY CALLED HIM in the early days, because he resembled Brooklyn Dodgers hurler Don Newcombe, one of baseball's early black color-bar breakers. His saxophone contemporaries—John Coltrane, Ornette Coleman, Albert Ayler, Eric Dolphy—fomented angry, shearing revolutions that blew off what they heard as a calcifying Tradition. Rollins in many ways stood aside from the postwar rush of developments around him, anchored only in the moment, his voice and material an existential response to change. Think of the Buddhist concept of immanent reality, potential elicited into motion by human activity, or of Heisenberg and particle physics.

He says: "A lot of musicians approach their instruments through sound, by trying to develop a particular sound that will be theirs. As far as a sound goes, I have an individual sound, because each individual plays in a particular sort of way. But if I listen to my sound over the years there have been some changes over time. Therefore I don't identify myself with a sound, don't think of a Sonny Rollins sound. Miles has a sound; Coltrane at a certain time at least had a definite sound. I don't think I have that kind of a sound. I'm sure to people listening that's there's something they hear that tells them it's me, but I think of things in terms of ideas. My tone changes more than a lot of other people's; I use it to make statements with, to color different phrases different ways when I'm repeating them or working them. So I don't think of a Sonny Rollins sound because I'm always changing my sound to get out something I want at a certain time. It's completely ad hoc, and has to do with a lot of things like different instruments and the different environments as well as how I'm feeling. I'm trying to portray an idea."

Portraying ideas is an abstract pursuit that, in music if not always philosophy, demands a firm grasp of the concrete, if you are to communicate effectively. For Rollins, as for Armstrong and Davis, jazz is a mode of being as well as a musical genre, a method for querying and revising popular culture and ideally society. Foraging across the rolling plains of American pop music, Rollins, like Armstrong and Davis, has subjected the sounds of American daily life to jazz's Socratic interrogation, wringing dry Tin Pan Alley of sentimentality via the ironies of the marginalized.

This is not abstract. The calypso for "St. Thomas" is rooted in Rollins's family background, utterly transformed. "There's No Business Like Show Business" and "Toot Toot Tootsie" were radio hits during his young manhood. "Way Out West" nods to the cowboy movies he loved as a black kid. (Aaron Neville's lilting falsetto blends Sam Cooke with Gene Autry, his Saturday afternoon hero. Charlie Parker loved the stories of country music.) You could say Rollins's polyglot music represents America reimagined.

"There was a period," he says, "when I think that by playing a so-called popular tune it enabled a lot of people to relate to jazz. So a lot of musicians played these tunes partly as a way of communication, from jazz's very early days. I like a lot of pop songs, and of course I heard a lot of them when I was growing up: 'I'm Gonna Sit Right Down and Write Myself a Letter,' 'I'll Get By,' Fats Waller playing popular tunes, things like that. So I like to play them a lot, and intersperse them into things that I'm doing, because they're in my mind already and they come out when I'm playing.

"Fitting melodies from other songs onto other changes is a whole other area. You can't take an old song like 'Sunbonnet Sue' that you'd hear in an old cowboy movie and put it into any thing anywhere. The chords have to match, and not only the chords but the feeling has to match. I like the way Ella Fitzgerald does that; she's got it down. But it's one of the tools of jazz improvisation, and it has to be done the right way to work. The beautiful thing about jazz is that it can absorb everything else and still be jazz. So it's not incongruous for me to use these materials I heard in the movies or on the radio when I was a kid growing up." His 1951 recording with Miles Davis, *Dig*, is instructive: the swinging, somewhat sardonic reading of "It's Only a Paper Moon" takes an astringent tack, stripping sentimentality out for more complex emotions than even Nat King Cole's version, a proto-rhythm-and-blues hit in the late 1930s. You can hear the love Davis and Rollins share for melody, the hook the audience can follow through the gyres and tumbles of improvisation.

What, I ask Sonny, was it like playing with Miles Davis?

He smiles. "Playing with Miles was great because I love Miles's playing in the same way I love Lester Young's playing. I put them together because of that whole lyrical approach, the focus on melody and feeling. Miles and I both liked to take pop tunes that no jazz musician at the time would have thought of as the basis for improvisation and use them; Miles did it with 'Bye Bye Blackbird' and 'Surrey with the Fringe on Top.' And in fact—a lot of people forget this—Coltrane did the same thing. What was that song that people first began picking up on him with? 'My Favorite Things.' People had been hearing Coltrane for a long time, but when they heard that song they said, 'Wow.' So using pop tunes like that serves a purpose: communicating with the audience. People would say, Oh yeah, that's a song I know. I don't think anybody wants to be so abstract that they're beyond comprehension—especially in those days, when most jazz musicians were starving. There wasn't that much work around. And besides communicating, using these songs shows off the depths of the possibilities of jazz.

"In retrospect I'm sure that's had an effect on what's been called my thematic improvising—though I wouldn't have realized that at the time I was starting out. Part of the way I play is that I'm creating melodies. That's different from what most beboppers were trying to do—to run the chords as fast as they could. I'm not putting that down at all; it takes a great deal of skill to play that way. There's just different ways to do it. And I had to do some of that kind of playing too, on the way to getting closer to my own musical soul. The jam sessions alone would have pushed you into that; you had to compete, you had to learn certain kinds of lessons. But my natural inclination is more of the melodic style."

THE SHADOWS ARE LENGTHENING as the sun flows into the west-facing windows of Rollins's apartment. I ask him what it was like when he came of age and into jazz.

He shrugs. "Black people had fought and died in the war, and were tired of waiting to get on the front of the bus. Same old crap. We know the history from the time of the slaves; no different. And there was bebop, a new music that kinda linked up with that. This was one reason a lot of people liked Charlie Parker, because he had a certain dignity about the way he played: he'd always be very erect, talk in a very erudite manner. So as young people coming up, we saw this as the next wave, you know. We weren't going to be buffoons or clowns anymore. This is great music, and you must accept it like this, and we are people, and you must accept us as people. It all ran together. That was one of the great things about Charlie Parker that people haven't talked too much about. That attitude was one big reason we looked up to him."

On the recordings Rollins made with Bird in 1953 under Davis's leadership, Parker, redubbed Charlie Chan with characteristic whimsy because of contractual snarls, plays tenor sax—only the second time he'd recorded on it. His bluesy cries, unflagging lyricism, pungent rhythms that glide over bar lines and time signatures sound far closer to Lester Young and Sonny Rollins than they do to the frenetic imitations of bebop's myriad Little Birds who thought the secret to Bird's brilliance was his needle, not his soul. As for heroin—there was the complex sociology of the postwar era, when black soldiers and workers were expected to return quietly to the status quo ante, which charged a powerful current of rebellion—and repression. Was it coincidence that the McCarthy era and the early civil rights movement coincided with the flooding of heroin through Darktowns from New York to Los Angeles? Not according to musicians like Rollins, canaries in America's cultural coalmines.

So I ask him about the politics and drugs of bebop.

He explains, "A lot of it was imitation of Bird, a lot of guys like myself who played saxophone and looked up to Charlie Parker just wanted to imitate whatever he did to be able to play more like him—and that included shooting up. That was the bane of Bird's existence. He tried to stop the guys, but he couldn't stop himself; that was his downfall. But see, it wasn't so much the drugs themselves as much as the fact that black musicians couldn't use drugs and get away with it. I mean, Billie Holiday was a big drug addict, but even though other white artists like Judy Garland were big drug addicts, they as a rule could get away with it. So black musicians felt that this was a way to penalize them more.

"So in the larger sense, for a lot of people it was a sort of social protest to use drugs. This was the first generation that wouldn't go quietly to the separate hotel, the back of the bus, the separate food counter; they got into fights and lots of hassles about it. That's what I mean by the social aspect about the drug abuse.

"Billie Holiday was one of my all-time favorite people; she may have been on drugs, but she also sang that powerful protest song 'Strange Fruit.' I remember Eddie Davis telling me that when he and Bud Powell were in Cootie Williams's band, Bud got beat up really badly, which turned him to drink and drugs. The same thing happened to Miles at Birdland, when a cop beat him up for standing outside the club between sets. That was a bad night, because everybody came downtown when they heard about it on the radio, and it nearly became a riot. Then there used to be a place called Cafe Society in the Village, which was one of the first places to have integrated audiences and integrated bands. But there were a lot of incidents in the Village about it: I remember hearing that Sarah Vaughan got beat up there. So it was a very volatile era. In a way, all that rage about racism ended up making people hurt themselves with drugs—that's the saddest part about it. They were so alienated, they had so much difficulty dealing with the double standards, they felt they had to turn to drugs.

"Now, drugs were a form of rebellion, that's true, but they were something more. I know when I was using drugs, back in those days we felt that gave us a sense of community, among ourselves, against a hostile world, okay? Nobody really liked the music, it was always played in small, smoke-filled nightclubs—you know. So it gave us a sense of having something against the larger society. So there was that element in there. So we got into it, and then later you realize you shouldn't; you have to find other ways to exist. But it's a very complicated subject, because a lot of artists use some kind of legal or illegal drugs. Drinking we considered old-fashioned, for instance. But it was something artists have often used to put their minds in a different place. It's so old, and so valid in many ways, that the two, drugs and art, have gotten mixed up. You know how many great writers have been juiceheads. We knew that then."

EVEN BY THE ELASTIC STANDARDS of the jazz demimonde, Thelonious Monk was a highly eccentric man who carried a satchel full of random loose pills and bottles that he would periodically dip a hand into, and come out with a mouthful of whatever. He was also a founder of modern jazz, the anchorman at the sessions at Minton's and Monroe's.

Monk's piano attack was as laced with idiosyncrasies as his famously unpredictable personality, captured painfully and painstakingly by the movie *Straight No Chaser*. He was radical in his jagged melodies and rhythms and percussive piano attack with its unbelievable bent notes and crushed chord intervals, conservative with his solid foundations in church music, pop, blues, and stride.

Most young beboppers and critics considered Monk a clumsy primitive, interesting but a byway, a footnote, an inconvenience in the rush of modern jazz; for Rollins, he was an existential artistic guide. In 1953, Rollins joined Monk, Max Roach, and Oscar Pettiford to record *Brilliant Corners*, a collection of Monk's original, gnarled tunes. "On the title cut," wrote David Rosenthal in *Hard Bop*, "both saxophonists and Roach, challenged by the tune's eccentricity (they never did get the head right, and the take finally released was spliced together from various attempts) and by Monk's suggestive comping, turned in inspired performances." Certainly Rollins's solo, elbowing its phrasing into odd shapes and looming, leaping intervals, and Roach's, all percussive melody, are exceptional.

Rollins says: "Monk had a very different style from anybody; something like Duke Ellington but more extreme. I heard Monk play a lot of regular standard songs, not just his own stuff. His rhythmic and harmonic conceptions were so unique. He was a catalyst, a definite hero. He energized both Coltrane and myself to go out and do our own things after we played with him. Part of it was that he was so dedicated to the music, it's all he cared about. I picked up on that right away."

Rollins's next stop on his quest for self-development came in late 1955, the Clifford Brown–Max Roach Quintet. He had recovered from his heroin addiction; now came a period of peak creativity. Roach's kinetic drums underlined and partnered Brown's slashing trumpet solos, those rich, fat sound and ultralong lines and doubletime tempos that seemed the polar opposite of Miles Davis's cool, clipped, introspective horn, until you listened to his ballad work. Tracks like "Parisian Thoroughfare" suggest a Mingusy marriage of *musique concrete* and jazz. On *Brownie Lives*, a live recording shortly before Brown's tragic death in an auto accident, Roach reroutes the band by recalibrating rhythms or suggesting—on the drums!—changes in melodic direction. Rollins isn't as polished as Brown, but he bubbles with ideas: his opening on "Gertrude's Bounce" is startling, fiery, a clarion call. Here we hear Rollins coming into his promise; the man and the instrument, like the archer and the arrow, meld into one.

And so I ask him about his beating heroin and joining Roach. He doesn't flinch: "Gene, that group came at a very interesting time in my life. I had just made the break away from narcotics myself. You know the story: I wanted to show Charlie Parker that I was straight, so I went away to Chicago and got straight, and then he died before I could show him. Anyway, I came back on the scene determined to be straight, because I realized this was a negative way, that you can't really destroy yourself and play music. Sure it might give you a certain sense of being together against the world, but that wasn't enough. If we're all gonna die, what's the point? I realized that, and determined to stay away.

"Anyway, I joined that band when Harold Land left, and the music was very successful. It was a beautiful experience. I knew Max from New York: he was an idol to me, like Bird. And I'd met Brownie: he'd recorded a couple of tunes I'd written with Elmo Hope, and I went to the sessions. So I was out in Chicago, getting clean, working a lot of menial jobs and getting ready to come back to New York. I'd been around nightclubs, stood the test of guys coming up to me and offering me drugs. So I was ready. Then, when I joined the band in Chicago, I found that Brownie was the type of personality who exemplified everything that I felt jazz musicians should be, who wasn't destroying himself. He was playing great, he looked great, he was a plain-living guy, very humble, beautiful individual. That was a revelation to me. I was on the right track, but that band helped me stay there. Brownie was an anomaly: to be hip then, you had to shoot up. For a guy to be playing a horn that great and be clean was really something. He was an angel."

Rollins and Coltrane, who struggled with his own drug problem, met in the studio for "Tenor Madness," where the contrasts are suggestive. Rollins digs deep and patient into his bluesy roots, while Trane arcs aching note fusillades, sheets of sound; but when they trade fours at the tune's close there's been a meeting of the minds.

In 1957, Rollins made his debut as a leader with *Saxophone Colossus*. Here he is becoming himself. He synthesizes what he'd learned from Monk on "You Don't Know What Love Is," scrambling time, warping tonality, leaping odd intervals. And there's "St. Thomas," of course, with its undulating rhythms and complex personal penumbra: Rollins's friend Harry Belafonte, who popularized Caribbean folk music in America, marched in Alabama with Roach, Pete Seeger, and Dr. Martin Luther King.

A year later Rollins cut "Freedom Suite," nearly twenty minutes with a pianoless trio—the format Ornette Coleman had just begun to explore. And Rollins's reliance on melody as his improvising road map grew stronger with *A Night at the Village Vanguard*, the remarkable *Way Out West*, and *Sonny Rollins in Stockholm 1959*.

Martin Williams wrote of *Way Out West*, "Some reviewers heard 'anger' or 'aggression' in his saxophone sound. There is much humor to be sure; there is parody and even sardonic comedy. . . . There is more than a hint that he was taking a cue from the airy, open phrasing of Lester Young's later work. . . . Rollins shows he had absorbed ideas from Monk about how to get inside a theme, abstract it, distill its essence, perceive its implications, and use it as a basis for variations—without merely embellishing it or abandoning it for improvisation based only on its chords. . . . By 1957 Rollins had moved so far along as a kind of one-man orchestra that on the title piece of *Way Out West* he returns for his second solo with a spontaneous imitation of Shelly Manne's drum patterns."

BY THE SUMMER OF 1959, Sonny Rollins was widely regarded as the hottest saxist in jazz. But as anyone who's witnessed a Rollins cadenza can testify, the man runs by his own clock. So at his acme, he created a legend by taking himself out of the musical rat race: no nightclubs, concerts, recording dates. Until November 1961, he kept pretty much to himself—except, of course, for those marathons on the Williamsburg Bridge. When he came back on the scene, Martin Williams shrewdly noted, "The Rollins who returned to public performance in the fall of 1961 was the same Rollins, only more so. One's memory of that Rollins is a memory of performances which nostalgia might exaggerate but which exact memory could obscure."

It's impossible to imagine a contemporary jazz musician of Rollins's stature doing anything like this. Back then, young audiences, lured by the tang of rebellion and cheap tickets, came back and back again to watch the improvised music unfold, the process at jazz's heart, its existentialist soul, over extended gigs that could run weeks, even months. Now, club rents are sky-high, and so are ticket prices. A week-long run is a gift; one-nighters are the norm. The more leisurely and personalized oral tradition Rollins trained in has given way to academic classes and relentless industry pressures. As a label executive put it: "Jazz and sports these days have a lot in common. Art used to be the thing you strove for, your goal. Sonny Rollins wanted to be the best he could on his horn. Now the goal is career management. That doesn't preclude art completely; it just makes it part of the equation, instead of the whole. And there are so many ancillary possibilities now: videos, movies, multimedia. These guys have a much broader horizon to scope out and choose from. For them, music may only be the means to a number of ends."

I probe Rollins about the idea of career. He eyes me a minute, and responds: "I wanted to do some more studying, right. And woodshed for a while. But I think it's difficult to get away from music. Even now, I have made a point of managing my career so I don't work as much as I can, so I can keep myself energized and have some kind of stable life away from the business, and I'm able to work in better venues when I do work— raising the level of jazz, in a small way. I usually take off the end of the year, a couple of months. But sometimes it's harder to come back; what you missed. Duke Ellington used to work every day, and every moment there is to create something you're doing it. Even practicing at home, writing, it's not the same as being on the stage. That's where it really comes; that's where you have the intuition; that's where you have the ideas; that's where you learn what you should be doing. So the stage is still it.

"When I went away in '59, I really had a focus: I knew what I wanted to do, and I knew I had to do it. It had to do with my music. I felt I wasn't playing as much as I should be playing. I had a lot of people—the press, fans—who built me up to the point where I couldn't deal with that without really feeling that I could deliver. So I knew that I was gonna go back and get myself together; I had a strong motivation. I wanted to break some bad habits I had, like smoking. I'm a person who appreciates solitude anyway, so it's easy for me to be alone.

"Gene, the music we're involved in is very serious. And the people I've been fortunate enough to be around . . . well, it's something you don't want to defile. I never set out to have a career—no, no. We wanted to communicate, sure. And when I started playing I wanted to be like my idol, Louis Jordan, have those 8 x 10s and one of those nice tuxedoes and that kind of stuff. But what it meant, I had no idea. The thing was the music. There are fine lines. You want to get across, but you don't want to condescend. In the late '40s, early '50s, there was so much happening in the music we were too busy to think about it. I'll tell you this: I don't think jazz is or will ever be something one can have a career in. Maybe it's changing; if it is, I hope it's a good thing.

"But I always considered jazz to be outside the mainstream, because that's the way it's been in my experience. The guys that played, the great artists that created this music, always scuffled. It got a little better as the years went on—Coltrane began getting a little success right before he blew himself out and died. Miles—you could say he had a successful career. But for Miles to get to that point—if you accept that he viewed it as a career, which is not completely true—the music was the key part of his life, of all our lives. That was it. Anything that interfered, we tried to get to the concert each night, and get the music right. This is what it was. I still think that jazz is like that.

"Career is a funny word, Gene. I don't have a career. People know me because I've been around a long time, okay? And fortunately, I'm a survivor. But I'm not rich, and I'm not trying to get rich. Trying to get rich playing music is an oxymoron; there's something wrong with that. The society's different now, though, so maybe that will change too."

When Rollins ended his exile, his first LP added guitarist Jim Hall to his trio for a mix of standards like Billie Holiday's "God Bless the Child" and "Without a Song" and sawtoothed originals. *The Bridge* was an instant classic. The empathetic interaction between the guitarist, whose chords shimmer with the Impressionistic beauties pianists like Ellington and Bill Evans brought to jazz, and the saxophonist, whose lyricism winds through the densest harmonic thickets without losing ebullience, produces some of jazz's most luminous moments.

THERE HAVE BEEN PINNACLES in Rollins's work since, especially on stage, and stretches of lackluster recordings. *On the Outside* documents his interest in the 1960s avant-garde with mixed if provocative results. Equally uneven is *All the Things You Are*, where Rollins faces off with Coleman Hawkins, using free-jazz overblowing and chordless soloing, while Hawk remains magisterially aloof. In 1966, he scored *Alfie*, orchestrated by Oliver Nelson for a 10-piece band. In the 1970s and 1980s his albums suffered from a kind of multiple-personality disorder. Trying on funky fusion, Rollins lost his mercurial edge within formulaic jazz-rock backing. (The exception is Stevie Wonder's "Isn't She Lovely," an extended romp equal to anything he's ever cut.) He soloed on "Waiting on a Friend" for the Rolling Stones' *Tattoo You* because Mick Jagger heard him at the Bottom Line and called him up. Rollins first heard the finished track at a market near his upstate home: "I thought, Gee, there's something strange about that guy playing saxophone, and finally I realized, Wait, that's me! I wasn't credited on the record, and didn't want to be: I was doing it as a lark, as a challenge to see if I could relate to it."

Live, Rollins remains a cauldron of creativity, a saxophone Bach able to overcome mediocre concepts and flagging bands with his fugues. But he has his off-nights, when entropy closes in. In 1985, his concert in the outdoor garden of New York's Museum of Modern Art was recorded as *The Solo Album*, a major disappointment. It sounded as if jazz's greatest improviser had forgotten to prepare and relied too much on intuition; he stumbled uncharacteristically into solipsism—fragmentary quotes, scales and finger exercises untouched by his usual alchemy.

So in the 1990s he performed a series of concerts with younger musicians like Branford Marsalis and Terence Blanchard that the press billed as duels. He doesn't like the word, laughs and shakes his head: "Duels?! Aieee! Do they ever refer to Pavorotti and Placido Domingo singing together as a duel? I wonder. . . . No. They give those people more respect. 'Duel' is sort of derogative. The whole attitude is demeaning to jazz, because jazz shouldn't be looked at like a boxing match. That puts it into a different area. Jazz is entertaining music, it's serious music, but it's both at the same time. So you don't have to say that jazz should be a museum piece—no. But it shouldn't be looked at as a duel; with Branford especially there was a lot of that type of thing. No, jazz is more like a conversation between people who maybe haven't had a chance to discuss certain ideas before. We push each other in different directions, but the music is what benefits. And it should be entertaining at the same time, because people are seeing something real happening.

"You know, Gene, that's how the music was always transmitted. 52nd Street wasn't just Bird and Dizzy. All kinds of people were playing the Street then—Billie Holiday, Coleman Hawkins, Ben Webster, Don Byas. It was like a Golden Age. That kind of scene doesn't exist anymore. And of course there were jam sessions on the Street, but there were jam sessions all over; they were just the way things were done in those days. I played in the jam sessions on the Street—I was just coming of age, you know. But there was also a place called the Paradise in Harlem on 110th Street where everybody would come and play: Hot Lips Page, Charlie Parker, everybody. It was a different time: in those days, you had to compete with another guy on trumpet, another guy on sax. Nowadays, it's a different thing. Young musicians can listen to records—they've got all these records, they've got all this audio equipment, they've got video equipment where they can see guys playing. But that's not the same thing as getting up on the bandstand with Monk or Clifford Brown and playing with them.

"On the session dates, for instance, if you made a lot of mistakes you'd have to go, because there were always a lot of other guys waiting to get up on stage and blow. So you didn't have too many chances. If you sounded fairly good you could come back and maybe they'd let you play, but you had to show what you could do pretty quick and hope that you could make it, hope that it sounded okay. I guess guys still get together, but it's not like before where there were definite places to do it and everybody would come in after working, especially in big bands, where they had to read a lot of music, and just jam.

"Jazz at its best is the perfect picture of democracy. We're all playing on this different level; we're not down here on this material plane, physicality. So of course you transcend race and all that stuff. It really is American music, it really is—it fits so much of what the country is all about. And this is the place it's most ignored. Here it's treated like a second-class citizen—like blacks. The official culture can't recognize it for what it is. That makes life hard for a lot of great musicians. Now everybody talks about jazz being America's classical music, but it's mostly an empty phrase. Even the way the big jazz festivals are put on here shows that: they're usually sponsored by big corporations who want to use the music as an ad for themselves. In a way, that diminishes the music. It's a tricky subject.

"I'm very proud of the fact that jazz musicians can survive without having to be funded by the state; I think in a way that's good. Look at the way symphony orchestras are always looking for money from benefactors; a lot of jazz musicians are able to make it without having to ask anyone for money, which in a way shows the power of jazz, and I'm proud of that. I'm proud of the fact that jazz teaching is burgeoning in the schools. The only thing I would want is the official recognition from people in high places that jazz is America's music—there should be more of it on TV, more on the radio, just more generally, so that it permeates everything. But it can't be divorced from the whole racial hangup in this country. In a way, jazz is still going in and out the back door."

Chet Baker

6

IT'S EASY TO REPHRASE TOLSTOY'S OPENING to *Anna Karenina* so it describes junkies, who all share an essential plotline: who and how to hustle in order to score. But in the world of postwar jazz, Charlie Parker gave junk an unprecedented clout and artistic aura. Bebop, the convoluted frenetic modern jazz he and Dizzy Gillespie, among others, formulated, demanded intense powers of concentration. Bird played so far out of nearly everyone else's league that his heroin habit seemed to explain his godlike prowess. So heroin became an existentialist response to racism, to artistic rejection, a self-destructive way of saying Fuck You to mainstream America's 1950s mythologies. Parker warned everyone from young Miles Davis to young Chet Baker away from smack, but few heeded him. In 1954, Davis weaned himself from a four-year addiction; in 1988, Baker died after decades of living in Europe as a junkie, found in the street (Did he jump? Was he pushed?) below his Amsterdam hotel window.

Oklahoma-born and California-bred, Baker had one amazing artistic gift: he could apparently hear nearly any piece of music once and then play it. He intuitively spun melodies on his trumpet with a tone critics compared to Bix Beiderbecke's, and spent his long and uneven career relying on that gift and coasting on his remarkable early breaks. In 1952, Charlie Parker played with him in Los Angeles, giving him instant cachet. When Gerry Mulligan hired him for the famed pianoless quartet that is the quintessential white West Coast Cool band, it made him a jazz star. After a drug bust broke the group up, Baker began singing; his wispy balladeering and Middle America good looks gave him entrée to a broader public. During his early 1950s stint with Mulligan, he unbelievably beat Louis Armstrong and Dizzy Gillespie to win critics and fans polls; his first album as a vocalist, which featured "My Funny Valentine," got him lionized on the *Today* and *Tonight* shows and in *Time*. From there on, his life took on a downward bias within a junkie's relentless cycles.

Deep in a Dream: The Long Night of Chet Baker aims to synthesize all the information about the trumpeter and tries to interpret him within the broader contexts of popular culture. Author James Gavin had access to unpublished autobiographical notes and interviews with Baker's erstwhile memoir collaborator Lisa Galt Bond, and also draws extensively on books like Jeroen de Valk's *Chet Baker: His Life and Music* and *Chet Baker in Italy*; he apparently scoured archives for interviews, profiles, pictures and video and audio materials as well, stirring in dollops from Bruce Weber's 1988 overripe movie about Baker, *Let's Get Lost*. Gavin has tracked Baker across Europe and America, has distilled the divergent attitudes toward him and his work, and attempts to make a case for what endures while not flinching from calling clunkers. He confronts black jazzers' resentment of Baker's playing: most heard him, with excellent reason, as a paler, milder Miles Davis, yet he won polls and looked like he was making big money. As Gavin points out, Baker's lilting lyricism and even his demeanor owed almost everything to Davis's, but Baker wasn't raking in sales like college favorite Dave Brubeck, though he was churning out streams of highly variable product. In fact, Gavin explains the popularity of the sappy *Chet Baker with Strings* album, the trumpeter's best-selling 1954 disc (which sold an uncharacteristic 35,000–40,000 copies the first year), by comparing it to popular contemporary mood music—an apt and telling linkage.

Gavin's discussion of that record strikes one of his leitmotifs, Baker's charismatic visual appeal: "William Claxton's cover photo was so dreamy that record shops all over the country put the LP on display. Claxton showed Baker at his peak of beauty, staring out wistfully at the session, cheek resting against his horn's mouthpiece. Many of the buyers were young women with little interest in jazz, who bought the LP for its cover. They were surprised to hear music as pretty as Baker was. It was his looks, more than his music, that the Hollywood crowd cared about."

He's shrewd about Baker's singing: "Record producer Dick Bock listened in alarm as [Baker] struggled to sing on key, pushing the session into overtime. Baker's dogged persistence didn't impress the musicians, who were reduced to near-invisible accompanists, tiptoeing behind his fragile efforts. But as people stared at the cover and listened to Baker's blank slate of a voice, they projected all kinds of fantasies onto him. He became the first jazz musician to attract a strong homosexual following."

Gavin is quite good at debunking longstanding myths about Baker, many of which Baker started himself. He didn't beat out loads of trumpeters to play with Bird in LA; a studio pianist, not Parker, hired him. It's highly unlikely Bird told East Coasters like Davis and Dizzy Gillespie that "there's a little white cat on the coast who's gonna eat you up." For Gavin, this self-mythologizing is a key to Baker's recessive, almost invisible character: "Just as he discovered how to seduce the camera lens into depicting him in make-believe terms, he learned to glamorize the truth into a fairy tale of romantic intrigue."

Naturally, the biographer seeks the man behind the layered tales. Here Gavin circles a black hole, because Baker was, as one witness after another testifies, nearly completely unrevealing. He didn't read, or speak, or other-

wise express: he was "cool." Longtime junkiedom only hardened this character trait into manipulative blankness. So Gavin looks at Baker's doting,
pushy mother and his violent failure of a father, checks out Baker's high-
school beatings for being a pretty boy, intimates that Baker's brief and
harsh version of heterosexual sex may have covered for repressed homosexuality, and links him to the waves of rejection, from the Beats as well
as Hollywood types like Marlon Brando and James Dean, rippling the
1950s. It's suggestive, though not necessarily convincing, since, unlike
other jazzers—Davis and Charles Mingus, for instance—Baker had no real
contact with or interest in other artistic subcultures.

Baker's critical reputation kept crashing after the Mulligan quartet
disbanded in 1954, and his drug use continued to escalate from around
that time, when his heroin addiction began. By 1966, he hit bottom: he
was badly beaten, probably because he ripped off a San Francisco drug
dealer, and his upper teeth had to be pulled. His embouchure wrecked, his
career, already smoldering, looked like it was finally in ruins. He worked
in a Redondo Beach gas station and applied for welfare. Against the odds,
record-label head Dick Bock bought him dentures, and for more than a
year he worked—probably harder than he ever did before or after—to
rebuild something of the limpid trumpet sound that once made girls
shudder.

In 1959, he had relocated to Europe, where he stayed for the rest of his
life (except for a couple of brief homecomings) to avoid prosecution for
drug busts. (Inevitably, he got busted in Europe instead.) Gavin rightly
notes that the Europeans, especially the Italians, adopted Baker as a
familiar bohemian archetype: the damaged genius, an artist in need of
understanding and patronage. It didn't help. His trajectory careened
mostly down; upward bursts of musical lucidity flashed against a churn of
mediocrities and an ever-more snarled life. His talent languished: he never
expanded his musical knowledge, nor did he really learn to arrange
or compose or even lead a band. He relied on producers and agents to
direct his musical life; he didn't bother conceptualizing his own creative
frameworks. He always demanded cash payments—no contracts, no
royalties—on his endless scramble to score. And as women revolved
through his life or fought over him and were beaten by him, he tried a
few bouts at detox but compressed even further into a junkie's two-
dimensionality. By the time he died, most American jazz fans thought he
was already dead.

For this last half of his book, Gavin, even buoyed by research, swims
upstream against the cascading flow of a junkie's essential plotline. For
decades, Baker is mostly chasing drugs, screwing anyone within reach,
tumbling downward creatively and personally, and alternating manipula-
tively between victim and abuser. Except as a voyeur, it's hard to care,
especially since, with exceptions I think even rarer than Gavin does,
Baker's music was generally worthless. Junk didn't make him a musical

superman; it simply drove him to make fast, sloppy recordings with under-rehearsed bands, playing horn that was so unpredictable in quality it could sound like an abysmal self-parody. Sympathetically balanced as he desperately tries to be, even Gavin can only cite a handful of ex-sidemen as Baker's musical legacy of influence. Instead, he depicts Baker as a kind of cultural icon rather than a cultural force.

It was one of history's ironies that Baker was resurrected after his death by a film made shortly before it. Bruce Weber, a fashion photographer famed for his homoerotic Calvin Klein and Ralph Lauren ads, has a sharp eye for the scandalous, and decided to make *Let's Get Lost* when he saw Baker at the trumpeter's brief fling at an American comeback in 1986. He fell for what an associate described as "beauty that looked kind of destroyed." Weber bought him a French beatnik wardrobe from a Paris designer, and paid him $12,500 for a performance that Gavin describes: "eyelids sagging, slurring his words, all but drooling. Unless he got what he needed, [Weber's assistant] said, 'he wouldn't have sat still for us a minute.'" The documentary refired interest in Baker among boomers and Gen Xers, who responded to the bathetic junkie glamor of his apparent frailty, personal and artistic, just as their 1950s avatars had. Reissues of Baker's albums on CD have gathered mass and sales since.

That leaves us with Baker's mysterious death, long haloed by a host of theories. Gavin rejects accident, reporting, "the window [of the hotel room] slid up only about fifteen inches, making it difficult, if not impossible, for a grown man to fall through accidentally." Dismissing speculation that Baker might have lost his room key and tried to climb the hotel's façade, Gavin feels it's unlikely he could have gone unnoticed on such a busy thoroughfare. He dismisses homicide, as did Baker's remaining friends and the Dutch police, and concludes that Baker was shooting his favorite speedballs and committed a sort of passive-aggressive suicide by "opening a window and letting death come to him. . . . [He] had died willfully of a broken heart."

That's a pretty sentimental final fade for a hardcore character like Baker, who for all Gavin's determined nuance ultimately seems far less rebel than junkie. Maybe Gavin should have pondered *Naked Lunch*. Then he might have ended his book with, say, Steve Allen's take, since Allen was one of the many Baker burned: "When Chet started out, he had everything. He was handsome, had a likable personality, a tremendous musical gift. He threw it all away for drugs. To me, the man started out as James Dean and ended up as Charles Manson."

7

Miles Davis

IT'S DRIZZLING ON AN UNSEASONABLY WARM spring day in New York in 1988; even the huge bay windows in this suite in the upper reaches of the swank Essex House, which sits on Central Park's southern edge, reveal only the muted greens of the reviving foliage below and the dull gray sky above. The plush suite's hallway is crammed with huge cardboard boxes; the living room has a Yamaha DX7 keyboard and a four-track recording machine set up within reach of an armchair where, across a coffee table littered with magazines (*Details*, *Interview*, *Vogue*) topped by a score pad and a couple of trumpets, sits Miles Dewey Davis III.

The disarray is partly because Miles's apartment is being renovated and partly because he just signed himself out of the hospital the day before. Once again, his body, which over the last 40 years has been ravaged by heroin, alcohol, cocaine, Benzedrine, barbiturates, sickle cell anemia, and car accidents and their after effects, is fighting off another onslaught, this time by the diabetes that has plagued him for years. "I got these sores all over my right leg from taking the insulin," he rasps in the world-famous cough of a voice that somehow, like his muted trumpet, projects crystal-clear. He pulls up his pants leg to reveal a swaddle of bandages and tape beneath a metal brace; his shirt hangs open to show a cotton pad taped to his chest. From time to time he shifts uncomfortably in his seat, his leg semi-stretched out beneath the table. When he gets up to open a window, he's stooped and achingly slow: the pain he's repressing becomes unavoid-ably, horrifyingly manifest. "I was in the hospital for three weeks," he says offhandedly, playing off his reading of the reactions on my face. "I've got an infection right here from taking insulin. They say it was a floor germ that comes from the rug, y'know."

I don't say anything. I don't know what to say. Rumors are milling around the entertainment world about what is ailing Davis, and the spec-ulation runs right up to AIDS, hemophilia, cancer—you name it; if it's deadly enough, Miles Davis is supposed to be stricken with it. This is a typically double-edged mark of his stature: those who admire him and those who disparage him are abuzz with the same stories. He wants to dismiss the talk, but he clearly also doesn't want to dwell on it, give it credence or heft by answering it. And so, held in proud check by the same remorseless combination of focus and discipline and self-awareness that has driven his art and persona for half a century, he gets up and shuffles haltingly but with apparent purpose around his suite briefly, as if to prove by willed movement that he will endure, come back, live to upset his detractors and cheer his fans, and cheat his own demons one more time.

And so once he settles back down, for 90 minutes he talks into my tape recorder, taking questions and working them the same way he'll take a melody into his trumpet and, in giving it back, tease the unexpected angles out of it, stamp it his. Most of the time his sketch pad sits on the table before him, and while he talks he chooses a pen to color and fill in his current work-in-progress; he's sketching and painting a lot these days. When he grabs my arm to underline this or that point, his grip is strong— surprisingly so, for such a frail-looking little guy, as if all those years of boxing have left their sturdy residue despite years of ailing—but friendly. He pulls his sunglasses on and off, peers over them at me and then around the room, finally casts them aside; when he does his eyes burn, the gleaming windows of an inner intensity multitudes have witnessed and been drawn into by his art, but few have fathomed.

I'm nervous but trying to stay focused. Ill as he looks, Miles Davis in person is quick and sharp. I'd interviewed him before briefly over the phone a couple of times, but this is different. There are umpteen stories about Davis flash-frying interviewers in person when they stumble or screw up or just trigger some invisible tripwire inside his psyche. Add that he's been one of the sounds in my head since I first saw him at the Fillmore East in its heyday, one of those mix-and-match three- or four-act shows that Bill Graham mounted so memorably, shaping the tastes of a generation. So I'm not real interested in getting crisped without getting at least some of the goods I've come for.

I lead by asking a couple of musical questions, general ones, feeling my way. He watches me, characteristic hooded eyes, not quite indifferent, not quite engaged, a predator, it seems to me as I try to concentrate on my notes and his answers and the window in my tape recorder, where I can see the cassette hubs turning reasssuringly around like they're supposed to. He's waiting. I ask a third musical question. He ignores it, leans forward, grunts assertively in that trademark slurred rasp, "You a musician?" Pause. I feel like maybe I've done it, whatever it is. Too late. So I say, "Yeah, I play." "Whatchu play?" "Guitar, mostly." "Not trumpet?" "Nope." "Never?" "Nope." "You sure?" "Uh, yeah." Pause for two very long beats. "Too bad. You got great lips for a white guy." One beat. I bust out laughing, his eyes lose their cowling, open briefly into a dancing light. From then on, he talks. When he's done improvising on a particular topic, he pauses for a moment and then asks, "What else you wanna know?"

Opinionated, outspoken, and usually outrageous, Miles Davis has been at the center of some of the most important musical and cultural upheavals of the last half-century. Even a casual flip through his catalog of albums uncovers more precious touchstones than most artists dream of mining in a lifetime. From the glory days of bebop to the birth of its cool reaction, from the hard bop swing of the pendulum to the introduction of modal structures, from jazz-rock fusion to getting back to the funk, Davis has stood in the eye of the hurricane, riding its twists and turns through the tumultuous postwar renaissance of American popular culture with a remarkable agility. The success Davis's art has brought, however, is hardly mirrored by his disastrous personal life, where he repeatedly paid the price of moving on via multiple wrecked marriages and relationships, alienated families and friends, and the extensive physical damage he is, here at Essex House, trying to overcome one more time so he can play, perform, become himself in the one place where he incontestably is: making the music that has consumed his being.

LISTING THE CAST OF CHARACTERS Davis has played with can be like taking a name-dropper's tour through the history of jazz since World War II. How he entered the scene, however, is more revealingly characteristic. Son of a dentist, a well-off African American who owned a horse farm outside East St. Louis, Davis told his dad, who was paying his way and sending him an allowance, that he was headed to New York to study at Juilliard. Instead, once he got there he, like dozens if not hundreds of younger jazz musicians, went on a pilgrimage to find and play with Charlie Parker. He succeeded big-time; he barely brushed through Juilliard before he was playing, haltingly, semicompetently, with the crew that created bebop at after-hours jams in Harlem clubs like Minton's and Monroe's, including Bird himself. Encouraged by Bird, who plugged Davis into Gillespie's slot when the older trumpeter left his quintet, and Dizzy, who famously taught Davis to look to the piano keyboard as the method for understanding the complex developments in modern jazz, he soon emerged as a remarkably young leader of the modern jazz movement.

In 1949, Tadd Dameron, the theorist and composer, asked Davis to join his band for a European tour; there Davis was introduced to intellectuals, love (in the enticing person of Juliette Greco), and acceptance as an artist rather than a black jazz musician—a trade that in America was still barely considered an art even as its mass popularity withered with the death of the Swing Era. Like so many African Americans before and since—Sidney Bechet, Josephine Baker, Bud Powell, James Baldwin, Jimi Hendrix—Davis found the disparity between Europe and his homeland jarring. When he came back to the US, he got hooked on heroin. (In 1956, he returned to France to improvise the soundtrack for Louis Malle's *Ascenseur pour L'Echafaud*, which was screened a scene at a time for the musicians, who then outlined a few chords and a mood and recorded.)

Despite his increasing drug dependence, he starred on the recording called *Birth of the Cool*, with the Modern Jazz Quartet's John Lewis on piano, Gerry Mulligan on baritone sax, Lee Konitz on alto sax—an all-star nonet of rising younger musicians. The album made his name. Here his haunting lyricism and natural melodic flow were freed from bop's frantic virtuosity. Bebop's complex harmonic sense was reabsorbed into a small big-band format, whose éminence grise was the then 30-odd-year-old Gil Evans. Evans's softly burnished harmonies, his jazzy reformatting of the classical concerto form of tutti response to Davis's solo calls, glowed with an introspective light somewhere between the apparently unlikely Claude Thornhill big band, where Evans had worked, and Duke Ellington's "concertos." Davis himself thought no other arranger came closer to Ellington's uncanny skill at creating new sounds.

His life, however, slid downhill. There was his accelerating descent into pimping and heroin addiction, which led him to steal from friends and marks alike. Then there was the operation to remove polyps from his larynx, which could have ended his career but instead left his voice a famously, permanently husky ruin. Finally, there was his cold-turkey recovery at his family home, powered by his father's iron faith in him and his own iron will. In his unquenchable search, determined autonomy, and fierce rejection of expected norms, Davis, so black in skin and so bourgeois in background, seemed as if he had to overcome his own history in ways roughly parallel to those of the overwhelmingly white Beats and bohemians of the 1950s, for whom the jazz milieu was their exit from a society of Organization Men and Gray Flannel Suits, Nuclear Apocalypse and Cold War, and electroshock and lobotomy-prone Snake Pits. As Bird had been, so Davis became for those outcats whom Norman Mailer, with his typical combination of excesses and misunderstandings and unerring deftness, characterized as White Negroes, the ultimate hipster—a jazz existentialist.

And yet because Davis was black, even those apparent parallels fell short. Unlike his bohemian fans, he was a recurrent target for cops even in supposedly liberal New York simply because of his race. Even after he kicked the habit and had become a jazz star in 1959, he walked a white woman to her car outside Birdland, where he was headlining, and then smoked a cigarette, and a cop started hassling him. Davis was a bit nonplussed; the cop, who musicians later rumored was drunk, kept trying to get him to move along, then started swinging. When Davis blocked the shots, he was felled from behind; a detective billyclubbed him. This hit all the New York City papers, accompanied by pictures of Davis's head swathed in bloody bandages; he became something of a *cause célèbre* in the media and liberal circles. When he tried suing the NYPD for $500,000, the lawsuit disappeared, via legal machinations and threats of revoking Davis's cabaret license—the time-honored method the largely Irish police force and its WASP bosses had used to shut off work and money for black musicians.

Also unlike his bohemian fans, Davis was far from antimaterialist. He drove a Ferrari to his gigs—the same yellow Ferrari he was regularly stopped by the cops while driving because they couldn't believe he could own it, because he must have stolen it. Onstage he was so cool that he could turn his Italian mohair–suited back on his audiences and listen to them murmur in approval. And since those audiences were largely white, he (and they) could revel in the reversal of power those moments in the spotlight conferred.

IN THE MID-1950s, George Avakian, the patrician producer for the jazz and pop divisions at Columbia Records, began luring Miles Davis away from the indie labels he'd been recording for. Avakian, a fine connoisseur of jazz, was an apt representative of the label chief executive William Paley thought of as the Cadillac of the record industry. The company's classical catalog was all high sheen and big names and prestige, and Avakian, who thought of Davis in similar terms, had to overcome the corporate scruples and fiscal worries of his bosses, who feared they were taking on a junkie who might well be dead within the year. Eventually Avakian signed Davis, and his first move was to reunite the trumpeter with Gil Evans, whose arrangements, he said, were the sonic equivalent of Davis's horn. Classic discs like *Sketches of Spain*, which was prompted by Davis and his then-wife seeing a Spanish dance company, followed. Avakian also helped enhance Davis's romantic image—the sharp pricey Italian suits, the sports cars, the artsy covers of his albums, the hipster reticence surrounding him.

First with Avakian, then with producer Teo Macero—who produced Davis as he did Charles Mingus, in very hands-on fashion, often composing bits and pieces of necessary music, then spending hours editing the tapes that continuously rolled in the studio for both their sessions into albums—Davis crafted brilliantly enduring music that also doubled as makeout platters for the postwar generations.

Other jazz artists, like Dave Brubeck, sold more records. But with Davis, Columbia felt certain it was buying a future and would recoup its payments and whatever troubles it suffered with the star it was helping create from the mid-1950s on, via big publicity splashes and tours. The strategy worked: to this day *Kind of Blue* remains jazz's best-selling recording. So maybe then it shouldn't have surprised anyone when in the 1980s Columbia decided once again to create a star from a trumpeter identified as the next Miles or the anti-Miles, depending on your perspective, one Wynton Marsalis.

Davis may well have been the monumental egotist his detractors charged, but his willingness to risk his creativity and reputation was, in his eyes, the inevitable accompaniment to his quest for challenge and change. "I finally figured out," remarked bassist Dave Holland of the 1960s sessions he did with Davis, "that when we were in the studio and the tape was rolling all the time that Miles was into recording the process of discovery, as we came to terms with new and unfamiliar ideas." By contrast, Marsalis has been much slower to grow as a musician at least partly because of the rigid boundaries he himself imposed on the idea of jazz when he was younger. Unlike Davis, he seems uncomfortable outside scripted opportunities, musical and otherwise; he likes to be assured of approval and/or control. Davis, on the other hand, may at times have dared foolishly or without what others considered significant musical payoffs, but his catalog of work is defined by risk, which is part of why it is studded with classics. And he was willing to work with so many diverse people on his way to the top and afterward: Sonny Rollins, John Coltrane, Cannonball Adderley, Bill Evans the pianist, Red Garland, Philly Joe Jones, Ron Carter, Tony Williams, Herbie Hancock, Wayne Shorter, Chick Corea, Keith Jarrett, Jack DeJohnette, Airto Moreira, John McLaughlin, Pete Cosey, John Scofield, Mike Stern, Marcus Miller, Al Foster, Bill Evans the saxophonist, Mino Cinelu, and so on. This too stands in stark contrast to Marsalis.

"I don't lead musicians, man. They lead me," Davis explains casually in his hotel suite, as he has before, without a trace of condescension or contempt, with the sort of easy understanding that has led a few perceptive writers to compare him to jazz's other long-lived band leader nonpareil, Duke Ellington. Ellington famously listened to his musicians and wrote for them, often using their improvised phrases as the basis for composition, always trying to suit the composition to the improviser's strengths. Davis has done the same for generations, urging his musicians to stay totally in the moment, to call on that strangely bifurcated consciousness any artist, but especially jazz musicians whose art revolves around improvisation, must have of their work as it unfolds: the intensity to pursue (or recognize) lines of investigation and the self-awareness to shape and edit those lines as they appear. Davis again: "I listen to them to learn what they can do best. Like Darryl (Jones) play a bass line, and he forget it. I won't. I'll say, 'Darryl, you did this last night, do it again.' He'll go, 'What?' I'll say, 'It's right here on the tape [of the show].' That's what gives playing that feeling, like when you see a pretty woman and say, 'Shit, wait a minute.' Listening to what they do and feeding it back to them is how any good bandleader should lead his musicians.

"Can I categorize the different generations of musicians I've played with? Well, you know how that goes: the sounds change. You have to match this now," he says wryly, patting his Yamaha DX7 keyboard, the mainstay of studio work in the increasingly electronic end of the 20th century, which is seeing studio musicians turned out in ever-growing numbers, ironically recalling the end of the big band era, when so many first found refuge in studio and TV work. "It's not the same thing. You've gotta kick musicians to do that, any kind of musician. I mean, jazz: I never did hear the word jazz in St. Louis or anyplace else when I was a kid. Anyway, young musicians now are hearing this constant subconscious

things about critics. 'If I play this real fast and run all over my horn . . .'"
he mimicks, a startlingly squeaky, insecure voice, a flash of Davis parodic
wit. "But they're so lazy they don't even want to change the clichés. The
clichés are boring for me. And the approach of playing into a microphone,
bowing, and stepping back—like the *audience* did something. Hell, you
listening to the audience or are they listening to you? You giving *them*
something. But the younger guys been so brainwashed by critics and stuff,
they think it's cool. Everybody wants to play their own style, but how can
you play your own style when every person who can ride a scale and back
has a record out?"

He pauses, eyes me. "My idea is you surround yourself with talented
people and make them uncomfortable. Then they gotta come up with
some shit." And then, as generations of his bandmates testify, he coun-
terthrusts, putting his own creativity on the line and pulling together the
improvised threads of their solos in his own, summarizing, recapping,
underlining, making sure the process was foregrounded, embracing their
ideas while bringing them to fruition. This is the capacious generosity
listeners instinctively respond to in Miles Davis's music.

FOR YEARS ONE OF THE CENTRAL CONTRIBUTORS to Davis's music was the
late great Gil Evans, who worked on or behind the scenes for many of his
most historic projects. Evans's friendship and collaboration became one
of Davis's pillars; he saw Evans as his artistic soulmate who could, without
cheerleading or malice, help him see and understand and realize his
musical needs and directions. "Gil Evans is the only serious musician I
ever met in my life," he says. "Like myself, he'd listen to anything and
wouldn't have to comment on it, just sitting there enjoying it, everything's
okay." He snorts derisively. "But you get those guys who want to play one
phrase 'cause there's a girl out there—I can feel it and see it and hear it."

The tall white soft-spoken Canadian and the short, combative African
American shared a lifetime of musical passions. They met on Swing
Street at the beginnings of both modern jazz and the postwar civil rights
movement, which was embodied in how boppers, mostly black, and
hipsters, black and white, made that scene. The Irish cops kept their
wary eyes on mixed-race couples on the Street—and this one of the
hippest streets in New York, the cosmopolitan center where a generation earlier Harlem had spawned a cultural revolution via theater and
literature and fine art and jazz. Because of the way it attracted young
white America from the Flapper era on, jazz created a kind of idealized
space in which some of America's myths—like the myth of equality
regardless of race—almost became reality, where the usual hierarchy of
blacks dominated by or invisible to whites was inverted, at least on stage,
where it became clear that the prime inventors and movers of jazz were
African American. And so within the privileged, marginal site called jazz,
racism could, at least temporarily, be suspended or overcome by mutual

respect for cultural achievement, which ultimately had significant social and political ramifications.

The passions Davis and Evans shared spanned a wide imaginative range. Several years before our 1988 meeting, I had interviewed Davis about his projected sessions with Jimi Hendrix, whom he'd first seen in *Monterey Pop*, when he went to the movies with John McLaughlin. Producer Alan Douglas oversaw a number of posthumous Hendrix records that had to be assembled from bits of tape, noodlings, partial tracks, and raw takes; he told me that he had been working to set up the Davis–Hendrix date when the guitarist died in England, after a lackluster set at the Isle of Wight festival, choking in his sleep on his own vomit. Davis hadn't wanted to say much to me about it: "What's the point? I wanted it to happen but it didn't. I loved the way his guitar sounded, and wanted to play with that." Soon after Hendrix's death, Davis started feeding his trumpet through a wah-wah pedal, cloaking his trademark breathy rasp with its electronic wash, reaching for his version of Hendrix's engulfing sound. It was a drastic change from his introspective lyricism, however acid that could be at times, to this new aggressive attack, and critics hated it, though he gained young fans like me at places like the Fillmores. It was no accident that Evans, too, was drawn to Hendrix; he reharmonized and orchestrated a batch of Hendrix songs for his big band, and in the process demonstrated how rock music could be adapted to acoustic and jazz sensibilities in ways different from those of the first wave of jazz-rock fusion.

Evans died only days before my 1988 interview with Davis, and so, as we sit in Essex House, he is very much on the trumpeter's mind—not least, I suspect, because Davis is himself staring death in the eyes once again. After a pause, he says slowly, "Like I just wrote a little something 'cause Gil was dying—I knew it, it just came to me. I'd been trying to get him for three months; by the time Anita [Evans's wife] called me, I'd written this piece. The next day, he died. She called me to tell me he knew I was trying to get him, and to tell me where he was. But the next day he died, so she called me to say he was dead. And she said, 'I think he orchestrated the whole thing by going away, you know, like Indians do.' 'Cause nobody wants you to say, 'Hey man, what the fuck is wrong with you, why do you look so bad,' that kind of shit? He'd lost all his fluids, he had dysentery for a month. So it was just a matter of waiting. I knew it was coming, 'cause I done died ten times thinking that he was gonna die. Which he did. So anyway, I wrote this thing for him that just sounds like him. I might play it at the end of every night on this next tour.

"Gil," he drawls, shifting positions uncomfortably, "gave me an album by Harry Partch in 1948, where there were drums and keyboards that really sounded like what John Cage was doing. This piece I did for Gil has all of that in it, but it has a key, a tonality. Sounds good to me, it's refreshing. It's always nice when you have a bouquet of herbs all mixed together, and you drop 'em into a gumbo or a bouillabaisse. So when you have all these drums you can listen to and something else, that's nice. But not if you can say, 'Oh yeah, that's a bass drum and a snare and a cymbal.' You like to be *teased* a little bit, you know? And I've used a lot of just *sounds* on here; that shit sounds good after you've heard so much of something else—kinda clears it off."

Partch was America's own classical-music renegade, an outsider visionary whose Emersonian ideas and influence and Bukowskian prototype—after wandering as a hobo during the Great Depression, riding the blinds like Woody Guthrie, he got a Guggenheim Fellowship in 1943 and then became a research associate at the University of Wisconsin—eventually reached from 1950s bohemia to more recent artists like Tom Waits, who has refashioned himself into Partch's descendant via both his eccentric sonic ideas and outsider-hobo image.

Partch has been described as a totally unrepressed individual and a nasty bastard. Of John Cage, Partch, the man who invented some 30 instruments and a notation system and then, unhobolike, lugged increasing loads of stuff around, once snarled, with at least a touch of envy alongside the righteousness, "All Cage needs is a gong, a carrot juicer, and a toothbrush." He also said, "The extent to which an individual can resist being blindly led by tradition is a good measure of his vitality." Certainly he and Miles agreed on that.

In the late 1980s, producer Hal Willner put together an album featuring younger musicians like John Zorn, Geri Allen, Vernon Reid, and Robert Quine enacting another of his characteristic ideas: a tribute to Charles Mingus that radically redesigned his music to include the use of Partch instruments. The final results were uneven, but the best of it was highly suggestive. And its irreverence and willingness to go for new sonic and conceptual territory over literal-minded interpretations would have made both musical renegades smile beneath their snarls.

THE EMPHASIS ON THE HERE AND NOW in its endless passing and flux, the affirmation of life in the face of death, beats at the heart of Miles Davis and his music; fundamentally, if reductively, it's one reason he has repeatedly sought out new avenues of artistic expression. A true disciple of Charlie Parker and Louis Armstrong, he starred from the 1950s as the jazz equivalent of a matinee idol, an outsider who was also tres chic. While other no less talented players were polishing their bebop chops, their modal spiralings, their fusion war cries, they'd turn around and find Miles had already moved on. The restlessness that fuels him never seems to quit. He needs to constantly reimagine the sounds in his head, where most musicians inevitably slip, however imperceptibly, into a set working method, a hardening musical vocabulary, a recycling of the glory moments of youth to please a crowd. Miles, by contrast, is driven.

Still, as Ian Carr, among the most detailed and perceptive of Davis's biographers, has said, "People say Miles Davis never looks back, but of course he does. Only an idiot doesn't look back. But Miles just keeps moving forward anyway."

When Davis felt he had nothing to offer in the 1970s, exhausted by deaths and his own deepening dependence on cocaine and other drugs, his increasing involvement in sexual orgies and bacchanals at his West 77th Street brownstone in New York, he withdrew for several years into silence—but a silence very unlike Sonny Rollins's. And yet his jazz existentialism, like Rollins's, like that of the postwar American generations who have followed his trumpet's wordless siren song so beloved by singers, its patented parched and introspective yearning from the romantic behind the cynical shades, the upper-crust boy who became a junkie and a pimp and a jazz icon, has become so deeply entwined in American countercultures it's hard to extract his influence even in the abstract play of imagination. Jerry Garcia wanted his band to play like Davis's great quintets of the modal era, and hence were born peaks of the Grateful Dead experience like "Dark Star." (When Davis shared bills with the Dead at the Fillmores, the band was thrilled, though they never played together.) Such examples are manifold. In effect, Davis's life and art mark one central place where acidhead/counterculture synchronicity and bop/Beat life-in-the-moment met. I don't know that Davis and Bob Dylan ever met, but Dylan is one of Davis's few equals in the art of being an artistic chameleon, a disciple of Heraclitus, and projecting an image that stirs the mass imagination by leaving so many areas blank, to be filled in by the fan.

"If I want to go back, I just think back," is how Davis responds to my question, which he's been asked one way or another about a million times: why doesn't he go back and recycle his classic material? He looks at me openly and directly for a moment, stops fiddling with his drawing materials. "It makes me feel sad when I hear the old stuff, you know? Because you can't get the same feeling; I can't get the same feeling. And I don't want to try. When we made certain things, it was like, 'Hey Miles, listen to this,' or, 'Look at how this'll work.' Like Gil Evans playing Ravel for me. But that's over. When I listen to *Kind of Blue* now, it's too slow; it's like somebody walking underwater. Now things are more upbeat—even the commercials are motherfuckers, they sound better than bands I've had. So I don't go back because I feel too sad, man. I think, 'How would it sound if we had this part on drums, this pattern going.' The only things that sound good from then are the singers (he hums a verse from James Brown's "I Got You") 'cause that ain't too long and drawn-out like we used to play. Some things we did, like 'Little Church,' I'm trying to find, 'cause I'd like to do that again."

You could say Davis's music in the 1960s and 1970s became so aggressive and turbulent partly because it mirrored the world around him. His notes to his soundtrack to a movie documentary that was also a homage to a great black athlete, Jack Johnson, make clear his identification with Johnson's struggles—bedeviled by gangsters and the IRS, one of the long line of visible African Americans to be targeted by the powers that be, an especially resonant notion in the wake of the wave of 1960s assassinations of black leaders like Martin Luther King and Malcolm X. He wrote, "The rise of Jack Johnson to world heavyweight supremacy in 1908 was a signal for white envy to erupt. Can you get to that? And of course being born Black in America . . . we all know how that goes. . . . Johnson portrayed Freedom. . . . He was a fast-living man, he liked women—lots of them and most of them white. . . . He had flashy cars. . . . He smoked cigars, drank only the best champagne, and prized a 7-foot bass fiddle on which he'd proudly thump jazz. His flamboyance was more than obvious." Flamboyance could be seen as one of the black man's cardinal sins in America. Johnson was convicted of violating the ironically named White Slavery Act, and went into exile in Paris.

The album bearing Johnson's name is the most overtly blues–rock-oriented of anything Davis ever did, opening like a postwar South Side Chicago electric blues, Muddy Waters with escalating twists realized by guitarists John McLaughlin and Sonny Sharrock. "Yesternow" spends its first devastating 12 minutes reworking a James Brown riff. Its recording and editing were informal and elastic even by Davis's deliberately loose standards: Herbie Hancock happened to be walking through the building where the band was recording when he was recruited to sit behind the organ. Producer Macero drastically edited the four sessions' worth of material into the finished album; some outtakes were included on later discs like *Big Fun*.

Two years before we meet at Essex House, Davis recorded *Tutu*, in honor of the South African archbishop who was among the most visible and effective antiapartheid leaders. Produced by Marcus Miller, one of his bassists from the 1980s fusion era, this tribute to Tutu, second only to Nelson Mandela in his power to command world reaction and esteem in the fight to rid South Africa of apartheid, marks Davis's meshing once again of politics and music. For this album, Miller self-consciously modeled himself after Evans. "I set up all the backgrounds, played and recorded all the instruments pretty much myself, and then Miles came in," he told me while they were editing the disc. "I wanted this record to be like something Gil Evans would have done in our time, with contemporary instruments and sounds. Miles sat in the studio and listened to what came over the headphones. BAM! He'd suddenly bend over and look like he'd been hit. Then he'd start to play. It was amazing to watch."

"Recording studios have changed a bunch of times since I started recording," Davis continues, back here at the Essex House, "so naturally I've changed what I do while I'm in them. Musicians are so nervous about playing perfect to a critic that it has its own effect. Critics are always criticizing the way we make records now. That's because they don't have nobody to write about: They can't say, 'Oh, that was Herbie [Hancock] playing the drums'—hear what I'm sayin'? He knows what he wants to hear, and he can get the same sound without the drummer and program it, even that drummer's same sound.

He's talking about his next album, a project that will become *Amandla*: "There's a number I wrote that never repeats, the phrases are completely different from beginning to end. And I *had* to get my drummer to leave that space open, because that's what had to go there. But wouldn't you know, Darryl [Jones] *must* play in that space. I said, 'Darryl, we don't do that anymore. I don't want you in the space.' He said, 'I know, but I bet you like that way I play it.' I said, 'Yeah, but you know when people write a melody, it's because they've exhausted all other melodies.' He'll learn that difference when he plays his own music. I've seen Stravinsky do that. And Mingus. In 1946, I rehearsed with Mingus every day. I'd rehearse with him just to hear what he wrote. You through with me?"

Almost. There's the inevitable final question, the one where Miles is asked to sum up a lifetime of artistic endeavor. He tolerates the clichéd question, looking around me almost evasively at first, then suddenly locking into full focus on my eyes. "Well," he begins, "I really didn't realize what I did until I came back to play and there were all these books: 'He did this and this and that and that.' Sounds like Columbus. Then I finally said, 'Damn, that wasn't that much'; what I did somebody was gonna do that anyway. Know what I mean? After we did it, somebody named it and said it was this or that, but we didn't do that. It's like jazz; I don't know what that means. Besides, *we* did it; I didn't do it by myself. It's just like you hear so many hints all in a row. Somebody say, 'Why don't you go outside and see if the paper's there?' Or, 'Why don't you do this outside?' Or, 'Why don't you do that outside?' Finally you say, 'Damn, they want me outside.'" He pauses, laughs. "So I might go see the African Ballet with Gil Evans and hear this thing, this thumb piano, where the guy starts on one chord and one side and when he gets to the other side he's finished with it. And I'll say, 'Damn, why can't I do that? I can't play that piano, what sound can I get?' The sound that I could get with the band—you gotta realize this was *then*—was that I figured, 'Maybe I'll have the piano player trill.' So that's how it came out on "Flamenco Sketches"; all I could do as say, 'Hey Bill, trill.' But the *bottom* had the thing in it. That's the difference between now and then. Nowadays a bass player would make that downbeat so you could hear it more; then it was in the middle part, around the third beat. Prince is always talking about get up on the one, and come down on the three. It'd be nice to play it that way, wouldn't it?"

Under his thinning hair and frailty, Miles Davis shakes his head and hums a few bars of what it would sound like. "Yeah," he says, pleased. "I might just do that."

Herbie Hancock

TECHNO IS FAR FROM NEW. After forebears like Stockhausen and Kraftwerk (who synthesized, in several senses, the psychedelic era's sonic radicalism), Herbie Hancock and Bill Laswell were among the earliest big names to start messing with it almost two decades ago. On February 8, 1998, Hancock's 1980s techno landmarks, *Future Shock*, *Sound System*, and *Perfect Machine*, were reissued—just in time—or so the corporate thinkers at this major label, facing the precipitous sales drop decimating their industry at the onset of the 21st century, must have hoped—to catch the lastest heaving waves of house, techno, and electronica. Hence the following meditation on Hancock's long and prolific career as an eclectic and catalytic sonic explorer.

IT WAS 1951, AND THE 11-YEAR-OLD piano prodigy was onstage with the Chicago Symphony, performing a Mozart concerto for his debut.

That would have been unusual enough. But in addition, to make things more intriguing, the youngster was black, in an era when virtually all American symphony orchestras were lily-white and, unthinkingly or not, were determined to stay that way.

Welcome to the life of Herbie Hancock. Musically speaking, it seems to have started far far away from the sound we call funk—especially since funk, when Hancock was a boy, was a backyard word polite folks listening to Mozart certainly didn't utter: it meant the pungent smell of sex.

Hancock's talent hasn't been limited to his gifted fingers, though there have been few greater or more versatile keyboard players, whether on grand piano or Macintosh computer, in the annals of American music. No, he is also a cultural synthesizer, a reimaginer, a visionary artist whose ears have been able to pluck fascinating sounds, the sounds needed or useful as grist to his creative mill, regardless of their pedigree. He is one of those artists who is continually reintegrating the changing culture around him, and in the process helping to change it. Funky, after all, was not a word young Herbie Hancock would have used to describe nice people or places. It was suggestive, lewd, laidback, downhome. It was for roadhouses and the back seats of cars, not symphony halls. It was usually pronounced *Fonky*, with a blue-collar, ex-slave southern drawl that Hancock's family would, like most upwardly mobile African Americans then and now, have found déclassé.

Beginning in the late 1980s, postmodernism seemed to proliferate, become everybody's style de jour, and critics routinely tacked phrases like "genre-busting" on to every artistic nitwit who managed to staple bits of one musical genre to another, as if that in itself were revolutionary or meaningful. From one perspective, this hyperbole was merely an outgrowth of the brand of rarified academic Marxism, dominant over the last two decades, that finds potential revolution in every act of reinterpretation or cultural "transgression." Meanwhile, Herbie Hancock keeps doing what the best musicians have always done—pursuing his art, using whatever works to get where he wants to go creatively. "Genre-busting" and other critical ideas are largely irrelevant to that process, where the focus is on realizing the artist's vision through any means necessary. The point of creativity for Hancock isn't to violate rules for the momentary cheap thrills of imagined or real cultural transgressions, but to forge a new sensibility, a different understanding, another perspective—in short, the complex set of social and personal communications we call art.

No good artist, not even the "primitive" cave painter of Lescaux, is a simple mirror of his times. But if he's any good at all, his heightened sensibility acts for his audience like a lamp shining into previously darkened corners, allowing us to see what's been hidden in the shadows from a new and revealing perspective. Thus have the artistic products of Hancock's synthesizing mind over nearly four decades given us glimpse after glimpse into some of the undertows and paradoxes, bafflements and triumphs of American culture.

FROM ITS EARLIEST DAYS IN NEW ORLEANS, where it was born of European, African, and Caribbean stock, jazz has always been about synthesis, about fusion. And yet this mongrel cultural art form has been periodically swept by the angry reactions of purists, who demand that its artists stop the clock, so to speak, freezing jazz (or, more accurately, their prescriptions for jazz) in some alleged moment of purity. That happened in the 1940s, when Dixieland rose like a phoenix from the "rediscovery" of pre-Swing Era figures like trumpeter Bunk Johnson to oppose bebop, which no less a colossus than Louis Armstrong infamously dismissed as "Chinese music." It happened again in the 1960s, when Miles Davis was on point for the rapidly arriving waves of new mixes of popular music, like rock and funk, with jazz, and won new younger audiences, to the derision of the jazz crowd, who in insular postbop fashion derided anyone who managed to touch large audiences with anything less pure than derivatives from Charlie Parker and Dizzy Gillespie. (Gillespie himself, of course, was joyfully pirouetting and winking through jazz explorations of Afro-Cuban and other "foreign" material, demonstrating once again that epigones, as Harold Bloom has noted, are far more fearful of change, which risks their status, than genuine avatars.) It happened again in the 1980s, when Wynton Marsalis attacked anyone who dared to dabble in jazz that wasn't based on his notions (originally distilled and dispensed by his father Ellis and his mentors like Albert Murray) of blues and swing. "Anyone" included his brother Branford and Herbie Hancock, who'd given the young trumpeter early exposure.

From either a historical or creative viewpoint, that sort of demand—enforced neoclassicism—is both foolish and impossible, and whatever its useful and beneficial side effects (in this case, a salutary restoration of a public sense of jazz history and its role in American life and culture), it often heralds a sterile age of cultural decline. Time, after all, doesn't stop, partly because people don't. Culture shrivels if it stalls. (Witness the diminished role of classical music as a cultural force and the concomitant shrinking of its audiences—a continuing downward trend over the last generation, which led directly to the installation of Wynton Marsalis at Lincoln Center within the framework called "Classical Jazz"; the hope, then and now, was that younger jazz enthusiasts would replace the dying classical subscription ticket holders in those plush seats.) No surprise, then, that the most durably significant jazz artists have rarely succumbed to the temptation to cry, "Halt."

What Herbie Hancock sought to do from early in his career was to reconcile and revivify the many musical styles he knew, the different faces of culture that spoke to him as an artist. In the process of doing that creatively, he helped open jazz up to new, pop–music inspired ideas and structures. And vice versa: he interpolated jazz improvisation and sophistication into earthy, seemingly basic and even oversimple (to the sophisticated jazz mind) pop formats. As a by-product of cultural miscegenation, his internal creative dialogues yielded music that could, as a by-product, provoke a frank discussion of the racial and class-based interrelationships underlying American society.

This achievement wasn't a foregone conclusion in the late 1950s, when Hancock was a young self-described "jazz snob" who listened devotedly to Gil Evans and Bill Evans and classical music and ignored most contemporary pop. There was nothing inevitable about his transformation and development, although his personal background—middle class and educated, yet marginalized in key ways because of his color—put him in a special, even privileged position to decipher the enigmas of American culture, are outlined by W. E. B. Du Bois in his discussions of the "Talented Tenth."

So time and experience, the interactions of American history with his own history, and artistic curiosity led Hancock away from notions of aesthetic purity, beginning, however obliquely, with that day he joined the

Chicago Symphony on stage. He worked closely with Miles Davis, Wayne Shorter, Ron Carter, and Tony Williams in a legendary 1960s quintet that unraveled and rewove the threads of jazz. "We liked finding our way into the unknown," Hancock has said. "We liked getting lost." Hence the title of his most famous tribute to Davis, "The Sorcerer." He told Nat Hentoff, "I know him well but there is still a kind of musical mystique about him. . . . There are times I don't know where his music comes from. It doesn't sound like he's doing it. It sounds like it's coming from somewhere else."

Hancock alternated his own acoustic recordings with the Davis outfit's increasingly electric dates. It was while playing with Miles that he discovered the Beatles, Cream, Sly and the Family Stone, Jimi Hendrix, African music. His own music began to host a no-holds-barred examination of how the manifold branches of African American-originated sounds—indeed, *any* sounds—could creatively interact. That lively and inexhaustible topic, at the heart of much American postwar culture, is still Hancock's creative focus to this very day. Witness his late 1990s recording, *Gershwin's World*. There he deftly puts the composer, whose debt to black American music was at least as enormous as black American music's debt to him, in the context of Scott Joplin and Duke Ellington and the rest of the web of influences that made Gershwin possible, and quite possibly necessary.

Let's put it this way: imagine a world without Herbie Hancock, especially without his most pivotal albums, like *Takin' Off*, *Headhunter*, and *Future Shock*, and you've got to reimagine how funky jazz and early fusion and an awful lot of contemporary funk and electronica, acid jazz and hip-hop jazz would have turned out.

Or to put it another way: despite fashionable intellectual trends, individuals can and do change the course of history. They work within contexts, naturally. No man is an island, even if he is a cultural catalyst. And ideas, even musical ones, have potential political effects: witness Wagner's cult within Nazism or the American folk revival's effects on the civil-rights and antiwar movements. Evolution teaches us the theory of parallel development, which says that key adaptations arise in several places at roughly the same time to allow for a better chance of survival. As anthropologists keep discovering, this is as true in cultural history as in biology. The rise of funk with James Brown, Sly and the Family Stone, Fela Kuti, and Miles Davis created a context for Hancock, a set of languages he could learn, intermingle, retranslate, reformulate within his art, finding a voice of his own in how he did that. That is his genius.

And it's why, for nearly 40 years, Herbie Hancock has been making things that didn't quite exist before.

HANCOCK WAS BORN INTO A MUSICAL FAMILY. He describes his father as "a bathtub singer" and his mother as a gifted amateur piano player. The Hancocks recognized their son's musical potential early, starting him on classical piano training when he was seven. He got a degree in musical composition from the respected Grinnell College in Iowa. And even after he'd become a star, he continued his studies at the Manhattan School of Music.

Hancock has never stopped being a student. His wide-ranging musical skills, intuitive empathy, and shrewd intelligence propel him to roam across the musical spectrum, from African folk music to European concert music. He is perpetually looking for yet another learning experience in a lifetime already crammed to bursting with them.

Here's a revealing example. In the early 1990s, I was at the Montreal Jazz Festival when Hancock was a headliner there. He delivered a terrific jazz set, and then bypassed the mainstream-jazz jam session the promoters had set up in the lobby of the hotel where musicians and press types were quartered. Instead, Hancock hit the town, and found a couple of tiny acid jazz and hip-hop clubs. He listened, then sat in. I dare you to name any other jazz musician of his stature and age who'd be doing *that*. Then I dare you to name any other jazz musician of his stature and age who'd have good enough chops with funk rhythms, with pop-music concepts, to be *able* to do it. And to do it without condescending, as if peering down from high art to low.

Sonny Rollins once said to me, "Jazz isn't a thing. It's what you do. The material is what you make of it. It can come from anywhere." That openness is why Rollins and his peers in the 1950s and 1960s could explore so many interconnections between jazz and other styles with such richly enduring results. It was an analog of the social movement toward integration, and proffered an artistic complex of interrelations that shadowed contentions by Malcolm X and Franz Fanon that racism in America was directly related to international policy. Similarly, part of why more recent Hancock albums, like *Headhunters*, *Future Shock*, and *The New Standard*, are so impressive artistically, and so important historically, is that they offer the listener a chance to overhear ongoing dialogues between cultural formats from funk to classical to jazz, to witness their histories entwine. It's a vision of hope, of inclusiveness.

When *The New Standard* came out in 1996, Hancock asked me pointedly, "What was the pop music of the '20s and '30s? It was called jazz. Frank Sinatra was a jazz singer, according to the ads. The schism between pop and jazz came in the 1940s, with bebop. So the material of those older songs by Irving Berlin and Cole Porter and George Gershwin was easier to bring into jazz, and still is.

"Rock and roll started as a branch off jazz roots, but it moved pretty far away. The harmonic content, generally speaking, wasn't as rich as the older pop tunes, which were closer to the same roots as jazz. Groups like the Beatles started the self-contained model of songwriting and performing. Nowadays, it's not the song itself as much as the singer, the sound. That's why there aren't that many cover tunes any more in pop.

Exactly the same thing happened in jazz. We used to have a lot of jam sessions, and play pop tunes. We used to cover each other's songs more than we do now.

"So for this record, I said, 'Okay, let me see if I can take contemporary pop tunes and reconstruct them so that they sound like they were originally written to be jazz tunes, something more provocative for improvisation.' And then I decided I wanted to take tunes that would make people say, 'Nope, there's no way to do a jazz version of this.'"

Each song's arrangement is strikingly different. Dave Holland's bass limns the melody for "Norwegian Wood" against an initially stark backdrop; Kurt Cobain's grunge translates into a modest piano-sitar duo (with John Scofield), impromptu, relaxed, sonic and musical warts and all. The band came up with usually fascinating strategies for taking these songs—some of which, in their original forms, are to older jazz ears pretty stiff harmonically, melodically, and rhythmically—into the more elastic zones jazz improvisers prefer. Hancock and arranger Bob Belden reformatted them, jazz-style, with generally striking results. Take "Mercy St." While Michael Brecker's tenor sax states the melody over the signature chattering percussion that reminds us this is a Peter Gabriel song, Hancock's piano begins to prowl in the background, introducing the jagged rhythmic variants and expanded harmonic palette that soon kick in. I can't stand most Simon and Garfunkel, but "Scarborough Fair" swirls through eddies of white-water interaction, furious multipart conversations that transfigure it from a delicate folkie lament into a gutsy, bluesy celebration. "Thieves in the Temple" finds the rhythm section chugging the Crescent City-inflected funk steadily, while the soloists embroider and explode the winding melody, each in his own way: where Hancock eases into glinting dissonance, Scofield digs into biting, hot-blooded B. B. King guitar, snapping off lines like the heads of crayfish.

Not every tune is successful. The least satisfying is Baby Face's, with its string wash, its tinkling piano, its generally simplistic commercial feel. Ditto Sade's, which veers near easy listening, saved by a ferocious brawny tenor solo. Still, just when things threaten to go limp, in comes Stevie Wonder's piece, all lunging ferocity with breakneck sax wailing and a triumphantly joyful spirit of play.

That appealing mix of artistic daring and populism underlies the best of Hancock's syncretic music, from "Watermelon Man" to today. It's not mere historical coincidence that younger jazz artists, from Cassandra Wilson to Charlie Hunter, from Greg Osby to Matt Shipp, from Jason Moran to Bill Frisell, from Liquid Soul to Soulive now tread similar paths as they reforge connections between jazz and contemporary pop.

In fact, you could easily argue that the dialogues Herbie Hancock has created between pop music, especially funk, and jazz on albums like *Headhunters* and *Future Shock* have shaped the younger musicians who've emerged over the last few years as they look to stir jazzy solos with rock and hip-hop atmospherics and contemporary dance rhythms. Hancock, after all, has been doing that—and often doing it with unique brilliance—for decades. And his singles and albums sell in far bigger numbers than is usual for jazz, partly because audiences sense Hancock's lack of condescension. They may not grasp all his artistic subtleties, but they're moved by what they hear.

Hancock started learning about ways to reach audiences right after he arrived in New York. The story goes that Mongo Santamaria's regular pianist, a youngster named Armando Corea, couldn't perform one weekend in 1962, and so trumpeter Donald Byrd, who had Hancock in his band at the time, suggested Hancock as a substitute. The audience was tiny, and so the band decided to amuse itself, jamming and talking. Byrd was discussing the complex historical and musical relationships between black American and Afro-Cuban music when he turned to Hancock and said, "Play that blues that you wrote." One by one the band found the groove and jumped in; the finished tune became a permanent staple in their repertoire, and when Santamaria saw how it wowed full houses, he decided to record it. (It was, he later said, the only time he knew he was cutting a hit single.) "Watermelon Man" zoomed onto *Billboard*'s Top Ten pop singles in early 1963. Hundreds of musicians have covered it since.

At the time, Hancock said, "I remember the cry of the watermelon man making the rounds through the back streets and alleys of Chicago. The wheels of his wagon beat out the rhythm on the cobblestones." That quote is telling. Music, for Hancock, is fundamentally about experience. He's always looking to push the artistic envelope, but he wants his audience involved. He doesn't want them to just appreciate his music abstractly, as art.

In the liner notes for his classic 1969 album *The Prisoner*, he said, "I am trying to write hummable tunes with a kind of rhythmic element people can be infected with. It's an extension of the concept of simple melody and rhythm related to a more advanced harmony. It's like a huge door with a lot of little doors to the outside public, and I'm trying different doors."

In 1969, Hancock's former boss Miles Davis was already coming under fierce attack for helping to launch jazz fusion. Jazz purists were disgusted that anyone would leave bebop behind for concepts coming from pop music. They overlooked the fact that Charlie Parker loved the schmaltzy Guy Lombardo Orchestra, that his favorite alto player was Jimmy Dorsey. They apparently forgot that Duke Ellington wrote hit dance tunes as well as "serious" works. They saw jazz as having evolved into a high art to be observed and enjoyed by learned insiders, in the European courtly tradition. Though there was truth to this, they simultaneously chose to ignore the implications of jazz's African and American folk roots, where the distance between artist and audience was smaller and more interactive than in Europe. (In Harlem and Washington and Newark clubs, for instance, jazz and R & B still inhabit the same sliding musical scale. Is this because the clientele is largely African American?) On the other hand, jazz fans and critics regularly make implausible claims, like how, if only serious jazz were played on the radio as often as Madonna or Britney Spears, its often minuscule cult followings would balloon. Of course, radio play didn't help classical music, which until the end of the 20th century had a well-established broadcast support system, subsidized by the usual elites.

Hence Hancock's slightly defensive tone about reaching "to the outside public."

CONTEXT MATTERS. The tumultuous 1960s, when he was working with Miles Davis's great quintet, turned Hancock around from jazz snob and back toward an eclectic curiosity driven by his panoramic musical interests. "The times," Bob Dylan wrote, "they are a-changing." In many ways, the decade culminated the rich postwar outpouring, a cultural renaissance of painting and writing and music that gradually swamped the American cultural landscape and changed a repressed society into one ripe for mass creative experimentation.

The Beats like Jack Kerouac and Allen Ginsberg and William Burroughs, and the New York School of painters like Jackson Pollock and Willem de Kooning and Franz Kline, and jazz musicians like Charles Mingus and Miles Davis, Sonny Rollins and John Coltrane tapped into the same molten core of postwar energy that drove America's expanding economy and military might and space explorations. And they rewrote the established rules as they did it. Mingus reimported slave spirituals and worksongs into jazz, as well as drawing on Stravinsky and Debussy and Ravel and Strauss. Rollins introduced West Indian rhythms, like calypsos. Coltrane stacked implied harmonies on top of simpler tunes with the audacity of a brilliant air traffic controller overseeing rush hour at La Guardia Airport.

Miles Davis, part of it all, registered it all like a cultural seismograph, and shared it with his sidemen. A painter as well as classical music fan, he was floored by the sounds emerging from black America during the 1960s. He adored the airborne, doppler-shifted sounds of Jimi Hendrix's guitar, and plotted to record with him—an encounter that sadly never came to be. "Why," Davis once asked me, "would anybody expect me to play bebop *now*? That was then. Charlie Parker was about what was happening then. My music has to be about what's happening *now*. Why go back and repeat yourself?"

Sly Stone catalyzed Davis. Funk's modal structure gave him a way to redeploy the methodology he'd developed since 1959's *Kind of Blue*: find the right creative mix of musicians, give them musical sketches, and work as an enabler, challenging them to fill in his outlines with their art. Hancock watched his boss, and learned. "Miles used to change my tunes, Ron Carter's tunes, Tony Williams's tunes," he explained to me. "He would take what we had, boil it down to the bare bones, and put it back together—still just bare bones, because the band put the meat on it every night."

Funk brought back into jazz an element that had been downgraded by bebop purists—popular reaction, audience participation. Funk's rhythmic insistence was irresistible. You had to move to it. That made it approachable, accessible to anyone. Perhaps predictably, that made it distasteful to those who wanted to model jazz after European high art, with its emphasis on more distanced, "intellectual," or "reflective" appreciation.

"Inside jazz," Hancock once observed to me, "there's been a backlash against fusion, against a lot of pop music. A lot of the young lions like Wynton Marsalis steer away from the pop side of things. But to restrict yourself to studying the past, even if it's Ellington, isn't the spirit of jazz. It's my understanding that jazz has always been very open, that it's always borrowed from different musical genres and contributed to the shaping of other genres too. Take that away, and you won't have anything I want to hear. It may be jazz, but it ain't gonna feel good. It's gonna to be cold, and it ain't gonna have no soul.

"So a lot of jazz people still hate fusion, but they forget that there were several kinds of fusion back then. One was jazz-rock fusion—very notey. Lots of notes being played. Modal solos. A lot of grandstanding. Me, I took the funk side. I wasn't trying to play modally the way a lot of guys were."

Perhaps the most significant trend for contemporary jazz is the rediscovery of Hancock's funky kind of fusion, the kind that didn't lionize noodling soloists, that kept the structures tight and focused on the funky polyrhythms, the dialogic interactions, drawing audiences in and letting them find their own levels within it.

When Miles Davis was teaching Hancock to boil down his jazz tunes, James Brown and Sly Stone were boiling soul music down to its bones, its more African foundations, the insistently roiling polyrhythms and feverish call-and-response formats that mesmerized listeners and hauled people up onto dance floors. By 1972, when Davis released *On the Corner*, a powerfully compressed album of tonal colors and funky rhythmic displacements, jazz aficionados and musicians everywhere detested it—and detested Davis for making it. Uncharacteristically, he retreated into guitar-driven fusion until the 1990s.

But *Headhunters*, Hancock's matchless 1973 record, extends that funky facet of Davis's influence into a more pop-based sensibility. The hit single "Chameleon" is clearly partly homage to Sly Stone, but reimagined, updated, jazzed. It became a hit, and made *Headhunters* one of the biggest-selling jazz records of all time.

A decade later, "Rockit" laced hip-hop turntable scratches with computer-generated industrial sounds over funk beats, and rode to the top of the MTV charts with an audacious and hilarious cartoon video that poked implicit fun at racism. With his deft artist's touch, Hancock was breathing human life into the first wave of techno via his sinewy and sinuous funk. The album *Future Shock* was a smash—even with the jazzy acoustic piano in the middle of the industrial-strength "Auto Drive."

THE WAY HANCOCK TELLS IT, in the early 1970s he discovered that even his friends, after buying his records, didn't play them. "I realized," he said, "that I could never be a genius in the class of Miles, Charlie Parker, or Coltrane, so I might just as well forget about becoming a legend and just be satisfied to create some music to make people happy."

In fact, his genius resides precisely in his willingness and ability to make people enjoy the challenges of his art. And it's made him a star, and a legend, and a cultural innovator of the first magnitude.

part III Rebirth of the Blues

9

The Gospel Highway

THE GOSPEL HIGHWAY, the church-based circuit toured by African American preachers and religious entertainers, was paved largely by segregation, but it also meant to bypass the world's sinful mores. To trace its twists and turns is to follow strands of America's cultural DNA, peer into its cognitive dissonance and paradoxes. Observers, for instance, may discuss the genetic relationships and stylistic affinities of gospel and blues, but for true believers, one is holy and the other satanic—period. That explains why Ray Charles was so viciously reviled by the faithful in 1955, when he rocked an old spiritual in the then-new soul gospel style, added leering lyrics, called it "I Got a Woman," and scored a hit that helped launch soul music: He had blasphemed, as surely as if he'd had sex in Sunday school.

Charles's new sound transposed the Pentecostal moans of soul gospel's male quartets into popular culture, with indelible results. Among the outstanding quartets developing that style were the Dixie Hummingbirds, and in his thoughtful, well-organized *Great God A'Mighty! The Dixie Hummingbirds: Celebrating the Rise of Soul Gospel Music*, Jerry Zolten both recounts their career and uses them as a lens to view larger contexts. He sees the Hummingbirds consistently reinventing themselves within the evolution of African American religious culture, and positions them as key movers in the between-the-wars shift from old-time "Sister Flute" spirituals to the denser, more driving hard soul gospel of the male quartets. These four-part-harmony groups (actual numbers could vary; the 'Birds were usually a quintet or sextet with multiple tenors) shouted with a raucous call-and-response fervor that fused Holiness Church grace with devil blues, attracting women, young folk, and integrated audiences. In the process, they helped link the Gospel Highway to the vast interconnected web that the postwar American entertainment business was becoming.

Drawing on seminal books like Anthony Heilbut's *The Gospel Sound* as well as his own research and interviews, Zolten skillfully navigates these sometimes explosive changes. He conveys the complex moral codes of the churches in which the Dixie Hummingbirds sang while illustrating how crucial developing business acumen, building a fan base and booking skills, and projecting a unique sense of style were to the group's success in the sharp-toothed business of gospel entertainment. And he regularly pans and dollies back to set this subculture within larger American themes: the day-to-day effects of segregation; the Depression-era growth of radio and recordings; the emergence of the church-based civil rights movement; the upsurge of independent labels and booking agencies thriving on nonmainstream sounds in postwar America; the relations between Jewish showbiz entrepreneurs and black entertainers; and the ineluctable appeal of African American culture to white America.

As they labored for six decades within and sometimes outside gospel's walled vineyards, the Hummingbirds certainly helped blaze interesting trails. In 1942, they became the second gospel group to play Café Society, the landmark political-musical cabaret; their band boasted tenor sax great Lester Young, and they were hailed and befriended by glitterati from John Hammond to Paul Robeson. In 1956, they participated in the second all-gospel show at the Apollo Theater. (Characteristically, Zolten observes that the Apollo's change of music policy was prompted by its slumping box office.) At the 1966 Newport Folk Festival, a year after Bob Dylan was booed off the stage for "going electric," the 'Birds were among the front-rank gospel singers who joined bluesmen Son House, Skip James, and Howlin' Wolf as well as rock and roll godfather Chuck Berry. In 1973, they laid their distinctively kinetic blend of voices and rhythms on Paul Simon's "Love Me Like a Rock."

Along the way, the Hummingbirds' lead tenor, Ira Tucker, one of gospel music's most charismatic growler-and-shouters, and bass Willie Bobo, who originated trademark "walking" vocal lines, first inspired doo-wop idols like Little Anthony and the Imperials and then soul groups like the Temptations to adapt the quartet's approach to less exalted material.

From their 1928 North Carolina genesis as a staid, sweet-singing old-style quartet until their retirement in the late 1990s, the Dixie Hummingbirds remained, as early member Barney Parks put it, "a clean religious group." Tenor James Davis was the leader, and at age 12, he already enforced "our first rule. No drinking." Other strictures banned women and demanded professional reliability; the rare rulebreakers paid fines.

To travel to their first big performance, the youngsters borrowed a car and coasted downhill to save gas. But as Zolten points out, "They were entering a long-standing performing arts tradition, one that unlike other entertainments afforded African Americans the opportunity to present themselves with dignity. . . . Strict adherents to the quartet tradition, the group performed in their Sunday best, dark suits and ties. They stood in a straight line and simply sang without moving, instead allowing the emotion to come through in the expression of their voices and the words of the song. They performed a cappella, no instrumental accompaniment at all."

Their approach got jolted at a late 1930s quartet competition. Gospel's equivalent of jazz's cutting contests, these often attracted integrated audiences. Faced with the more assertive and incendiary delivery of the northern-based Heavenly Gospel Singers, the shrewd Davis developed the two-step contrarian approach that netted the 'Birds decades of competitive victories: "If a group in front of you goes over well enough, the last thing you want to do is the same type of stuff they're singing. A group get up and raise a lot of sand, you get up and be as sweet as you can get! Get sweet as a honeycomb before you get up there hollering." And then, to ice the victory, he stole their handsome, dynamic lead singer who drove kids wild.

By the late 1930s, the group was changing rapidly, thanks partly to the spread of radio and recordings, which aired formerly regional styles to national markets and reshaped audiences and performers alike. As Zolten explains, "The Hummingbirds were able to draw on a variety of traditional a cappella techniques—African American vocal conventions like stretching and playing on notes, switching leads, carrying the rhythm along in the bass voice, adding soaring falsetto ornamentation, shifting tempos, and introducing counterpoint harmony weaves. As always, the first and foremost goal of any Dixie Hummingbirds performance was to sing for the Lord and guide listeners to spiritual epiphany. But now as professionals, they also had to think about putting on a show. There was room for spontaneity and improvisation, but they had to be highly practiced."

Radio became one of their marketing stalwarts; at the local level, as anyone who has seen O Brother Where Art Thou may recall, the medium was frequently color-blind and easy to break into. Zolten avers, "Station owners cared only that listeners stayed tuned, heard the advertisements, and bought the products. Radio also regularly put black performance style in close proximity to white Americans." In fact, these qualities were exactly what later allowed Alan Freed and Wolfman Jack and a handful of white and black DJs across postwar America to break the overwhelmingly black world of rhythm and blues into the white teen universe.

With handshakes and verbal agreements as their contracts, gospel singers were prey to ripoffs; with little cash but an aura of glamor, they were also ripe for seduction. Unlike many of their peers, the Hummingbirds learned the business, eventually promoting and producing themselves, and evaded temptation. "'You had to walk the line' [Tucker] says. 'If you didn't, the church people would take you down.'" Adhering to Davis's strict moral code, they eschewed the sinful carousing that permeated gospel's sacred precincts and produced titillating gossip and accusations about luminaries from Clara Ward to Sam Cooke.

Sexual and musical dalliances could cause equal scandal. Even established stars like Sister Rosetta Tharpe were subject to censure if they crossed too far over the stylistic line. Tharpe found success singing the Lord's praises over blues-guitar runs out of Charley Patton—a dicey enough proposition in itself for many within the fold, but one that brought her growing renown among white as well as black audiences. Then in 1938 she joined John Hammond's groundbreaking "From Spirituals to Swing" concert at Carnegie Hall. "Appealing to record buyers both black and white," Zolten writes, "Sister Rosetta Tharpe would not only fuel the taste for rocking hard gospel within the black community but would propel a growing interest in black religious music among whites, especially in the urban East." But she narrowly skirted danger: "Tharpe . . . had succeeded in broadening her appeal by performing not only in churches, but also on records and in nightclubs, cabarets, and concert stages backed by the jazz combos of bandleaders like Lucky Millinder and Sam Price. She was walking a fine line and in late 1946, the *New York Amsterdam News* reported that her indecision was costing Tharpe some credibility with her religious constituency." It was only when she returned to working churches steadily that the tongue-wagging of the faithful slowed.

For the churchgoing, Sam Cooke was a far more pointed exemplar of the unholy tensions that always exist in American culture between the sacred and the profane. As a beautiful boy with a heavenly voice traveling with one of gospel's premier quartets, the Soul Stirrers, young Sam seduced and was seduced with something like abandon. But then in 1956, in parallel with Brother Ray Charles, he turned to pop. He crafted hits—crooning ballads like "You Send Me" and "Cupid," party-time fun like the clave-inflected "Another Saturday Night," the gospel-flavored "Chain Gang" and "Bring It on Home to Me." He'd crossed over to mass white audiences—something that brought politically correct but misguided accusations from later white critics like biographer Daniel Wolff, who charged that Cooke's white handlers, the Italian producers Hugo and Luigi, had forcibly bleached the singer's music. This sort of thing had clearly happened before—think Jackie Wilson, for just one instance—but the unavoidable fact is that Cooke made those artistic and commercial decisions for himself; as he fought for (and gained) control over his music, he didn't have the white hipster's hangup about hard gospel being "blacker" (and therefore "truer to the black experience") than his hits. For Cooke, these were simply different aspects of his voracious musical personality, much as gospel and soul were. And if he wanted to be a major mainstream star, and garner the rewards and celebrity thereof, what of it? But the Christian gospel world never forgot or forgave his apparent treachery; when he was shot at a motel in 1964, apparently by a prostitute, they nodded righteously, serene in the knowledge that the Lord's will had finally been done.

By contrast, the Hummingbirds never ceased their rounds of churches as they rose toward gospel's version of commercial success. Early on, they'd established a comfortable touring schedule: Florida in winter, the Northeast in summer. Guided by Davis, they cemented fan loyalty by arriving well ahead of concerts to mingle with their fans, and they steadfastly honored commitments to church and religious promoters despite more lucrative enticements. This devotion to their core audience and repeated refusal to stray into overly secular material helped propel them up gospel's ladder.

In 1942, they joined the millions of black Americans who had migrated north since World War I, leaving Carolina for Philadelphia. There they soon appeared regularly on WCAU, a 50,000-watt clear-channel station that was white-owned and catered to white listeners; they were rechristened the Swanee Quintet. Ironically, the radio spot led directly to their following the Golden Gate Quartet into Café Society, whose progressives dubbed them the Jericho Quintet. Apparently Hammond et al. weren't quite progressive enough to forgo the need to control every nuance of black artists' career choices.

From 1952 on, following a series of small-label record deals, the Hummingbirds landed with Duke/Peacock, a black-owned independent whose secular stars included Little Richard, Big Mama Thornton, Johnny Ace, and Bobby "Blue" Bland. The relationship embraced their 1950s commercial and musical peak, when they added more instrumental backing to their patented vocalizing. Their biggest hit, "Let's Go Out to the Programs," had them imitating in turn all their contemporary gospel competitors—a tour de force that made them national headliners. In 1959, they posed for the photo for their first LP: "The cover . . . against the backdrop of a star-studded sky, showed the white-tuxedoed Birds from the waist up, handsome faces with pencil-thin moustaches smiling up." Later that year, they headlined at the Apollo and joined a salute to Mahalia Jackson at Madison Square Garden. Gospel was at its commercial apogee, but, as Zolten notes, "The Dixie Hummingbirds . . . would follow their usual course—top of the world one night, a small country church the next."

That pattern held even through their flirtation with Simon, secular material, and broader fame: And yet they complained to *Sepia* magazine in 1973, "We have already lost some of our audience. . . . It would be a blessing if *Sepia* could help make it clear to our people that the Dixie Hummingbirds are religious men, living God-fearing lives, who function as ambassadors for Jesus."

Zolten unfolds this story, with its sundry subplots and themes, fluently. His musical descriptions are evocative, and he neither minimizes nor exaggerates the gospel world's fierce moral and showbiz competitiveness. He shows how, like all the top-flight gospel quartets, the 'Birds drilled on staging and presentation as well as music. And while he periodically overstates their broad innovating impact and their direct influence on doo-wop and soul, overall he makes a case that they were exemplars and conveyors of cultural and musical changes then at hand in America.

For aficionados, this book inevitably covers familiar historical ground. But Zolten has an eye for telling details and counterpoints. Take his periodic snapshots of the gospel business: "That year [1953], according to figures compiled by *Billboard*, the Soul Stirrers had earned $78,000, the Pilgrim Travelers $100,000 on 173 dates, and Clarence Fountain's Mississippi Blind Boys, $130,000 in 40 weeks. . . . [Duke/Peacock owner] Don Robey reported a million and a half records sold in 1953, most of them Willie Mae Thornton's 'Hound Dog' but 500,000, 'Let's Go Out to the Programs'" by the Dixie Hummingbirds, an exceptional tally for a record in any genre."

He also has a nice feel for history's ironies. When the Hummingbirds auditioned for Hammond to play Café Society, they were sure they knew from experience what white folk wanted, and polished up their sweet singing. The patrician radical was completely put off: "He said, 'You all from the South I know. Gimme some corn bread, baby.'"

And he offers some tasty vignettes: "Tucker still remembers the night in Norfolk, Virginia, when the Dixie Hummingbirds stayed in the same 'colored' hotel with Big Joe Turner, Ray Charles, Teddy Wilson, Duke Ellington, and Louis Armstrong. . . . Tucker admired Armstrong for his 'rags to riches' climb to success. . . . 'I talked with Louis seven hours that night. We talked all night and he missed the bus. So he said, "What the heck." Got him a cab from Norfolk to Reading, Pennsylvania.'"

10

Chess Records

THE EVOLUTIONARY HISTORY of American vernacular music over the last half-century-plus has often hinged on entrepreneurs who hung out in the shadows between mainstream culture and its marginal cousins. In ways they didn't intend, these businessmen became mediators, even advocates, for cultural outsiders.

Take black musicians. They had limited opportunities at major labels (where they, like other ethnic and regional groups, were usually cordoned into "race" and specialty record lines), major booking agencies, and major venues. And so again and again, small labels offering blues or rhythm and blues or gospel, black-driven musical formats not plugged into mass-market distribution pipelines, popped up across postwar America. The label heads, almost all of them white, had individual motives, of course, but most shared a vision of potentially profitable niche markets going untapped.

Such were the Chess brothers, Leonard and Phil, who after World War II started what became Chess Records. Born in Poland, the boys emigrated to America with their family in 1922, and grew up in Chicago. Though they kept links to their Jewish heritage, their businesses—a junk store, a couple of liquor stores—moved them steadily into the tangle of racial and ethnic relations that crisscrosses American culture like fault lines.

In 1946, Leonard, the elder dominant Chess brother, took over a bar in one of the black Chicago neighborhoods filling with southern migrants. The liquor license was in Phil's name. Like other tavern owners, the brothers saw that live bands drew customers, that there was money to be made in black music and its audience—and that idea shaped the rest of their lives. They improvised shrewd, streetwise business tactics, and they learned fast. By the time Leonard died of a heart attack in 1969, at age 52, he and Phil owned several record labels, a recording studio, a record distributor, a couple of music publishers, two radio stations, and a batch of real estate. More important, they had recorded more than their fair share of the best and most influential sounds of the postwar era.

As Nadine Cohodas recounts in *Spinning Blues into Gold: The Chess Brothers and the Legendary Chess Records*, Leonard Chess formed a bond with his customers and artists that went beyond money. Phil and Leonard apparently didn't feel African Americans were Other—or, if they did, as immigrant Jews they understood what that could mean. They were assimilated and secular: the word most frequently on Leonard's lips referred to, uh, Oedipal sexual contact. And they had drive and determination, so in black neighborhoods in Chicago, then all over the country, they absorbed local culture and sounds, made connections and friends, signed up musicians. They hustled records to DJs, record-store owners, and distributors on a road that stretched for years from dusty shacks to cities. By the late 1950s, Chess had grown from an ad-hoc two-man operation into a hitmaking group of record labels, a kind of mini-major label wrapped in myth. On an early US tour, the Rolling Stones came to Chicago so they could record in the same Chess studios their blues and R&B idols, whose songs they covered and "crossed over" to a white audience of millions, had used.

For in the minds of fans like the Stones, Chess was more than a record company; it was a matrix where key elements of postwar American popular culture were catalyzed. The births of gritty electric urban blues, rhythm and blues, then rock and roll are among the moments Chess Records helped create and chronicle. Framed by a world where the white-bread mainstream and racism and payola and cutthroat competition were daily facts of life, the Chess brothers produced pivotal innovators like Muddy Waters, Chuck Berry, and Etta James, and nearly signed James Brown and Elvis Presley. They not only made money from selling black music to black Americans; like their friend, legendary DJ Alan Freed, they also introduced countless white American kids to those sounds.

This is the by turns fascinating, complex, and dry-as-top-40-charts story Cohodas wants to flesh out. Overall, she succeeds pretty solidly. A former reporter for *Congressional Quarterly* and author of *The Band Played Dixie: Race and Liberal Conscience at Ole Miss* and *Strom Thurmond and the Politics of Southern Change*, Cohodas connects a lot of dots and corrects earlier versions of Chess history by music writers who relied too heavily on unchecked hand-me-down anecdotes. (Just one example: a story Keith Richards has loved to tell journalists, including this one, over the years relates how when the Stones made their first pilgrimage to Chess Records on their first US tour, he met Muddy Waters—who was painting the ceiling. Though he hardly got a fair financial piece of the profits he generated for Chess, Waters never did menial work for the brothers, who treated him well, in their ersatz plantation-mentality fashion.) Still, Cohodas has done her homework: first-hand interviews with a variety of witnesses enliven her wide-ranging research materials, which include artists' biographies, local newspapers, city directories, and trade magazines like *Billboard* and *Cashbox*, useful for tracking any record label's history.

Spinning Blues into Gold has a larger-than-life cast of characters. Berry, Waters, James, Howlin' Wolf, Little Walter, Bo Diddley, Ahmad Jamal, Ramsey Lewis, James Moody—some of the brightest stars from blues, jazz, R&B, and soul waxed their music for Chess, and their records were instrumental in changing the shape of postwar popular music. What combo of magic and "ears" and instinct led the Chess brothers to hear a dim wire recording of a tune called "Ida Red," played for them by a disciple of Muddy Waters, and realize that young Chuck Berry probably had a hit—which he did, once the tune's name was changed to "Maybellene." With that, truly distinctive rock and roll guitar, Berry's onstage duck-walk, and an entire genre of car–kids–love songs, were launched.

So very much of what the Chess brothers recorded became part of the fundamental soundtrack for the 1960s garage-band efflorescence across America, at first entering the standard repertory by way of white blues-rock covers (the Stones, Eric Clapton, the Blues Project, Paul Butterfield) and then, as larger rock venues like the Fillmores began to book artists like them as part of their deliberate mix-and-match musical presentations, directly. And then there are key DJs like Freed, who from the 1950s on helped cross black music over to white radio listeners and drew (make that demanded) steady and steadily increasing payola from the brothers, as he did from nearly everyone, until the payola scandals broke and his prominence and attitude combined to cast him as the industry's available fall guy. (In this Congress and Freed were ushered toward each other by Dick Clark, himself a walking conflict of interests—he owned record labels, ran overpoweringly important teen TV and radio shows like American Bandstand—who came off, by deliberate contrast, as the battered industry's Mr. Clean.) Finally, there are other independent label heads, an always colorful cast, which here includes the Bihari brothers and Evelyn Aron, as well as a small host of behind-the-scenes Chess players.

It's almost inevitable that an institutional history like this will at times lapse into somewhat potted thumbnail sketches of individuals, but Cohodas usually keeps them evocative and on point as they intersect in the buzz of life around Chess Records. Her delving into the business ledgers and background, too often glossed over or reduced to easy and comforting art versus commerce clichés by music writers, is particularly strong. However, she does sometimes undercut the depth and strength of her reporting by overinterpreting scenes and characters. She seems defensive, for instance, about calling Leonard and Phil anything tougher than "frugal," though she quotes plenty of witnesses testifying to their notorious unwillingness to part with money. When production head Dave Usher asked for a raise after a string of late 1950s hits, Leonard's typically tart reply was, "What do you think, you're one of my family?" Usher left Chess soon afterwards. His successor, Jack Tracy, negotiated a better deal, including producer royalties. At the end of his first year, the royalties totaled $750, and Leonard barked in his unilateral way, "We're going to change things. . . . You won't be getting a royalty again." Tracy didn't even bother to protest.

Perspective can change a lot, and Cohodas rightly, if a bit defensively, tries to contextualize the Chesses' financial practices. They bought new Cadillacs and rented apartments and paid lawyer's fees for their artists, but almost never handed out royalty statements. Atlantic Records' honcho Jerry Wexler, a friendly rival of the Chess brothers, saw their approach as updated paternalism. Cohodas points out that many if not most labels at the time did similar things, and eventually wound up in disputes with their musicians over money, copyrights, and the like—and that very much includes Wexler's pioneering Atlantic label. She also points out that most of the business (as was often the case with small indie labels) was in the brothers' heads, so there's frequently no way to verify Chess Records' numbers and transactions. But once again, she's done her homework: the book's epilogue, "Lawsuits and Legacies," narrates the staggeringly numerous financial and copyright clashes Chess had with its musicians following Leonard's death.

There are disconcerting moments when Cohodas's sympathies overreach her facts. She describes the role played by the brothers' wives, who were kept completely in the dark about Chess business, as "important" because they kept their houses neat and raised the children, and Leonard's wife Revetta packed the suitcases for his trips and got up early to make breakfast. In fact, as her book inadvertently makes clear, the Chess brothers were mainstream-traditional in terms of home life; what set them apart, as it did their indie-label peers, was the raw, unanswerable desire to document this music and culture they'd been drawn into, find a hit, then another, and avoid the postwar straight world's straitjacketed visions of life's possibilities, personally and professionally. After all, how many straight business execs hung out with motorcycle gangs and con men and thieves, the way Leonard Chess liked to?

Overall, though, Cohodas's dogged reportage powers her book past its relatively minor flaws and serviceable prose. Dotted by irreconcilable memories and unresolvable disputes that she lets stand, *Spinning Blues into Gold* adeptly mimics the often Rashomonlike residues of historical memory from its various protagonists. One example: when Chuck Berry was busted, tried, and ultimately imprisoned on Mann Act charges in 1959–61, the Chess brothers paid for his lawyers—according to them. Berry's autobiography, as Cohodas duly notes, denies it. Then again,

Berry, who always demanded to be paid in cash for his shows often before he even went onstage, then carted the proceeds around in paper bags, was probably the only Chess artist as cheap as the Chess brothers.

In the end, Cohodas has crafted an in-depth, fact-and-story-rich tour through an important site in American popular culture. If ultimately it leaves Leonard and Phil Chess themselves as informed sketches rather than full-lit characters, that's probably how they would have liked it.

11

The Folk Revival

I WAS IN HIGH SCHOOL in the 1960s, when I first saw Dave Van Ronk at the Gaslight, one of those little cellar clubs that used to line a Greenwich Village that now lives in myth and legend. I didn't understand what he was doing. It didn't fit anywhere neatly, musically speaking. It seemed like a jumble whose elements I recognized—folk tunes, ragtime, early jazz, Delta blues—but couldn't line up into what my 15-year-old mind thought was coherence but was really my expectations, which were being uncannily exposed and exploded. I felt like Dr. P in Oliver Sacks's *The Man Who Mistook His Wife for a Hat*, scanning deconstructed faces for that single telltale feature that would reveal to me who I was looking at. It took me several days to recover from that set, to piece together what had hit me. Aside from nagging annoyance, I didn't know how to think about it. I couldn't have been more confused if Louis Armstrong suddenly ambled onto the *Ed Sullivan Show* and followed "Hello Dolly" with "The Times They Are A-Changin'."

Two things, however, I knew even as I was alternately squirming and transfixed through Van Ronk's show: he was a hellacious guitar picker, a real—and therefore, in pop and folk circles, rare musician (I later studied with two of his students), and he was the only white guy I'd ever heard whose singing showed that he truly understood Armstrong and Muddy Waters. When he roared and bellowed, it felt like a hurricane blast shaking that little club.

Oh yeah: Van Ronk was funny. Really funny. He did bits from W. C. Fields, whose irreverently transgressive movies were being revived, part of the 1960s rediscovery of great American anarcho-comics like the Marx Brothers. He did "Mack the Knife" in mid-show with a suddenly acquired tremolo I later found out was Marlene Dietrich's; it threw my teen spirit and forced me to rethink what I thought I knew about folk music. When he did "Cocaine," the perennial crowd-pleaser and set-closer he'd adapted from the Reverend Gary Davis, his friend and teacher, his asides ("Woke up this morning and my nose was gone") seemed made to order for the drug counterculture. (Of course, some of us had already discovered how deeply braided into American history and society drug use was—word was out on how Coca-Cola got its name.) Decades later, Jackson Browne revived this tune on his tours, his band parsing out the implications of Van Ronk's guitar.

There are many Van Ronk undercurrents flowing through American pop culture. The acclamation and small forest of obituaries that followed his death of colon cancer in early 2002 ironically mirrored his ghostly omnipresence during life. He was a missing link, an authentic songster who voiced folk-made music. He directly connected the vision of the folk artist, which Woody Guthrie and Pete Seeger shared with Alan Lomax, with both its black cousins in Piedmont and Delta blues and the white, largely middle-class collegiate audience drawn into the postwar folk-revival waves. In fact, from the early 1960s until his death, Van Ronk became the éminence grise behind those revivals. (Christine Lavin presented him his 1997 ASCAP Lifetime Achievement Award.) And he was more: the man who reconnected jazz to the other forms of folk music that he, like his avatar Woody Guthrie, pursued, learned, reclaimed, and kept alive—and, with the wit and humor that prevented homage from freezing into reverence, even dared to reimagine without prejudice or hierarchy.

A big burly guy whose personality was as oversized as his voice, Van Ronk never "crossed over" to commerciality, never got famous, never signed a major-label deal, never played arenas. In those ways, he was a true descendant and avatar of the folk-music aesthetic: becoming too visible or successful equaled selling out. He followed the time-honored American path into this culture's musical heart: he studied African American sources and learned directly from their living purveyors. These included Piedmont ragtime pickers like Blind Blake and Blind Boy Fuller and Delta deep-bluesmen like Son House. Then there was the Reverend Gary Davis. He'd dazzled 1940s Harlem streetcorners with his stylistically wide-ranging guitar and whooping singing, careening from biblical shouts to leering lipsmackers, and by the 1960s had become a teacher who drew Village hipsters to his small brick house in Queens. This was the era when Moondog, the eccentric jazz poet, took up his daily post near the Museum of Modern Art and did, well, whatever he felt like that day.

Maybe it's not so surprising that I was so fascinated and confused by these figures that I didn't guess until later that I'd stumbled into the last stages of America's older oral culture.

HUMAN SOCIETY, being a conservative creature, tends to close its books slowly, and revisit them often along the way, with however many misunderstandings and blindnesses of reinterpretation as it stumbles toward its futures. But the acceleration of technological change, and the increasing absorption of even apparently marginal subcultures into industrial models, has inevitably altered the oral process of folk art transmission. In the 21st century, it's pretty clear that, for better and worse, technology has probably rendered the Van Ronks oddly superfluous, apparently redundant. In evolution, if not always in architecture, form follows function. The concept of folk music hatched by Charles Seeger and the Lomaxes and embodied by Woody Guthrie, Lead Belly, and Pete Seeger has, in the age of mass recording and mass media, lost its daily functionalities. Where once songsters were the repositories and transmitters of our polyglot national folk heritage, where Van Ronk's generation of amateur and professional musicologist-sleuths sought out records tossed into attics and garages to find artists obscured by the mists of time, now, thanks to the omnipresent, profitable avalanche of record-company CD reissues, almost anything they had to dig for is readily available. Of course, the artists and their cultures are not.

So our easy connection with the cultural past is shaped by the recording studio, with its time constraints and pressures and implicit notion of a fixed performance guarded by copyright and potentially paying off in the publishing royalties that are the core of the music industry's economy. That inevitably alters performances from folk art, where borrowing and repetition are demanded. Thus we've lost the idiosyncratic twists to the oral/aural tradition that an artist of Van Ronk's caliber introduces, almost casually and yet integrally, however much they appear like asides.

"This song has changed since Gary used to do it," he growls in introduction to one recorded version of the Reverend Davis's "Cocaine Blues," as he used to do onstage. Which was, of course, part of the point, as well as the method of transmission, of real folk music: culture is a conservative mechanism, a cumulative record of human activity, and change results from disconnections and accretions precisely like Van Ronk's sharp-witted alterations of Davis's barbed blues, originally improvised add-ons drawn from his memory of lyrics the way a jazz musician pulls riffs from history and reworks them into his own voice. Millman Parry's deductions about the Homeridae, the ancient bards wandering Hellas singing Homer's epics, from his study of Yugoslav oral poets who used metrical patterns and preset textual chunks to recall and recompose their "source" texts, apply to America's bluesmen and songsters and jazz artists, describe some of the armature of what we call improvisation, which is based in memory and practice. As jazz historian Dan Morgenstern has pointed out repeatedly, even figures like Louis Armstrong who are usually thought of as improvising titans rarely just blow off the tops of their heads; they rely on preset phrases and ideas as raw vocabulary on which to draw, to recombine, to anchor them, at least, in the process of creation.

What Bruce Springsteen, another of Van Ronk's collateral relations, called "the human touch" describes the process underlying Van Ronk's creativity. Naturally, Van Ronk was a die-hard collector of sources, living and recorded. As the liner notes to the 1962 album *In the Tradition* put it, "Dave Van Ronk has established himself as one of the foremost compilers of Jury Texts regarding traditional tunes. (Jury texts are when many verses are sung to one tune, usually with some new words appearing with each subsequent recording.) Here, in 'Death Letter Blues,' Van Ronk has arranged some of the most moving verses of this song into a dramatic slow blues." Behold the songster at work—a process found in early Armstrong, Guthrie, and Robert Johnson.

Although the building blocks of oral culture are plastic, preservationists in a non-oral culture tend toward reverence, simpler imitation, and homage. A lot of that happened in the post-McCarthy era folk revival. (As Van Ronk observed in a late 1970s *Sing Out!* interview, "It was all part and parcel of the big left turn middle class college students were making. . . . So we owe it all to Rosa Parks.") While black rhythm and blues was revving white teenagers into rock and roll, black folk artists were becoming heroes to young white collegians. The left cast a romantic, even sacramental aura over black (and white) folk art and its traditions, which implicitly stigmatized creative change. The central notion of folk-revival culture, authenticity, meant avoiding commercial trappings and artificial personas and trying to replicate an idealized past from recordings, to see oneself as the latest worker in a continuum devoted to reviving music that served as the repository of oral traditions while maintaining for it some sort of contemporary functionality—a social dimension. Seeger, Guthrie's friend and follower, insisted that was essential.

And so college men and coeds, enticed by his concerts and proselytizing during his blackballed McCarthy exile, studied recordings of antique ballads, which they sang along with songs of popular protest to audiences largely made up of people like themselves. Nevertheless, their cultural effects—or, perhaps better put, the effects of their having created a culture—somehow eventually spilled into larger political and social arenas, became a fundamental set of motifs in the soundtrack for the protest movements of the 1950s and 1960s. Thus despite the inevitable tensions between authentic preservationism and contemporary relevance, between folk culture and industrial commerce, the notion that Guthrie and Seeger shared with Bertolt Brecht and Kurt Weill, say, that art could create a climate that would galvanize ideas into action, has been a bedrock belief of leftist cultural politics from the postwar era until today.

Perhaps it was Van Ronk's deep study of and familiarity with the past that helped him avoid fixing it. Part of what made him different from, say, Mike Seeger and his New Lost City Ramblers was that he so internalized what he'd learned that he couldn't help altering it, in the deceptively creative manner of human memory. He could (and did) annotate what he played and discuss it in musicological terms. In a late 1990s interview dealing with Harry Smith's *Anthology of American Folk Music*, which he rightly called "the bible" of his generation, he noted dryly, "I sat up and took notice at how many tunes that, say, Doc Watson does that are on the *Anthology*. . . . Some he would have known [via oral tradition]. But you can tell. There are hundreds of possible verses. When someone does [lists three verses in order], you know they've been listening to Bascom Lamar Lunsford."

For Van Ronk, folk music was a living tradition—meaning he allowed himself the authority, within somewhat squishy limits, to tinker with, if not radically alter, what he knew to fit his own needs as an artist—a modern Homeric singer. Would I rather hear Son House's recording of "Death Letter" than Van Ronk's live take? Was Van Ronk, as he once acidly rephrased the record business's conception of him, "an albino Muddy Waters"? What, in the context of these questions, do the notions folk music and authenticity mean?

THE REVEREND GARY DAVIS was one of the prize discoveries of the postwar folk revival. He was as authentic a folk artist as they come, and his blindness and blackness only added to the aura of inevitability his outsized personality and music projected. It was one of the many ironies of the folk movement that some questioned Davis's authenticity and depth of real feeling because of his undeniably gripping and looselimbed virtuosity—a foreshadowing of garage-band and punker credos about technique numbing raw feeling. In this and other ways, they'd certainly out-Guthried Woody, who, though he kept his own skills carefully homespun, would never have denied the emotional depths of his pals Sonny Terry and Brownie McGhee just because of their superior technical prowess.

Terry, McGhee, and Davis went way back, to the heyday of streetcorner performers in their shared home base of Durham, North Carolina, in tobacco country, not far from Thelonious Monk's birthplace of Rocky Mount. Davis had moved to Durham in the 1920s, after coming of age in Greenville, a seedbed of songsters: Josh White also hailed from there. Guitarist Willie Walker, a local hero who played a now-shadowy but legendary role for Piedmont pickers akin to the one Buddy Bolden played in New Orleans jazz, was then in his prime. White, who was almost twenty years younger than Davis, said of his skills, "Walker was like Art Tatum. They don't teach that kind of guitar."

Now, of course, there are piles of transcriptions and tapes and a fair number of albums aimed at teaching Davis's music, although few among even ace pickers, whether the well-known Van Ronk or disciples like Jefferson Airplane's Jorma Kaukonen and blues guitarist Woody Mann, can go past a certain point to duplicate the edge or depth or looseness, the humor or raw sexuality or godfearing truth Davis had. "There is an authority about his playing," wrote Duck Baker, "that always makes me listen. His sound is hard, almost brittle, uncompromising—and perfect for what he is doing. It is true that you will not hear the kind of dynamics used by classical players any more than you will get them [sic] from a sanctified choir." You could say the same of Louis Armstrong—and his

Dixieland-revival followers. And you could note the same rhetoric—authority and authenticity being the two key terms—used to describe them. And you could further note how these two illusory terms are still in heavy rotation around the land of hip-hop, with its rote insistence, however misdirected and (self-) deceptive, on "keeping it real" in the glossy, advertising-heavy, contemporary pages of *Vibe*.

Davis was real enough. Born in 1896, he lost his sight as a child. In small southern towns at the time, songsters found well-traveled corners to park at and serenade folks, and bands often walked or rode a wagon through town to gather a public. "The first time I ever heard a guitar," Davis told historian Sam Charters in the mid-1950s, "I thought it was a brass band." It was a telling analogy with apt historical overtones. In post–Civil War New Orleans, the brass bands that incubated proto jazz came into being partly because of the availability of army instruments abandoned in warehouses; the black bands adapted the instruments to new sounds, new uses Sousa never imagined. In much the same way, hip-hop "found" music and art in old turntables and records just as technological advances were scrapping the formats, once more high-lighting one recurrent role for black American culture within the larger society: a piecemeal underclass cultural enactment of Nietzsche's re-evaluation of all values. Junk, in this sphere, can be—indeed, should be, must be, will be—transmuted, Midaslike, into art.

Told what the sound he heard was, Davis demanded a guitar, and to learn to play made one, as so many did—his was a pie pan and a stick. He soon got a banjo and learned the technique called frailing, heard his first blues at a carnival in his teens, and began playing in earnest. His wrist had broken and been set very badly, so his hand was at an angle that should have made playing the guitar difficult if not impossible. Like Django Reinhardt with his fire-welded fingers, Davis turned liability into a conceptual leap—he fingered chords no one had seen before. He performed in church as well as on the streets, where he sometimes joined string bands, so his repertoire, which he'd play for knots of passersby and at factory gates at shift-change time, rapidly grew to encompass gospel, ragtime, reels, marches, blues, jazz, even minstrel-show tunes.

Davis left Greenville when his first wife moved in with another guitarist, and hit Durham around the late 1920s, where he was apparently recognized almost immediately as a master street musician. By the 1930s he'd hooked up with Blind Boy Fuller, another ragtime guitarist, and Sonny Terry, and the trio played Durham's sidewalks for years. Charters thought that Davis's style was "too flashy" to go over well with street audiences, and he only recorded two blues sides with Fuller—one of them called "Rag Mama Rag," a title and spirit The Band would later adopt. (J. D. Long, the producer for the American Record Company, inserted his name as coauthor, in the time-honored fashion that ran from W. C. Handy to Leonard Chess, Dick Clark, Alan Freed.) And guitarists, though they couldn't mimic Davis's off-the-cuff yet coiled brilliance, tried mightily, as Piedmont blues recordings from the 1930s attest—Fuller's own and Blind Blake's and Josh White's among them.

In the way of some bluesman, like the Georgia Tom who wrote "Tight Like That" and then transformed into Thomas A. Dorsey, foremost composer of gospel, Davis gave up the blues for the Lord in the 1930s. He was ordained and got $23 a month in welfare, while he sang praises on the Durham streets for the rest. A welfare worker wrote, "He has a very aggressive manner . . . a religious obsession which influences his activities in an almost impractical manner." By the late 1930s he disappeared, in 1944, he married his second wife Annie and was living in Raleigh and visiting her children in New York, where later they settled in Harlem. Davis soon became a familiar figure on uptown streets, an ironic down-home counterpart to the suave, urbane demeanor and concert-hall appearances of Duke Ellington. Davis yelled, stomped, banged on his guitar, slid up and down the strings for onomatopoeic effects, and otherwise hollered for the Lord. He also returned to the studio in 1949; those startling, unconventional efforts, along with his equally unique earlier sides, are collected on *Reverend Gary Davis 1935–1949*.

Davis's holler, his fluid voice with its baritone gravel, matched the jaunty looseness of Armstrong's best vocals; his stuttering guitar, pausing to run oblique twinkling riffs in the midst of contrapuntal fingerpicking, is a one-man band. Only Joseph Spence, the Bahamas picker who became a folk-revival stalwart thanks to his own jagged, irregular guitar stylings and croaking vocals, approached Davis's self-confident musical exuberance. In a world where Robert Johnson had barely been rediscovered by enthusiasts, Gary Davis was a living revelation of the power of the blues.

So, by the mid-1950s searchers and folkies began finding their way to Davis's Bronx apartment, Charters being among the earliest. Soon he brought his friend Van Ronk along; they played and studied and researched together. Davis was recorded by students like John Cohen (whose 1953 home tapes have been reissued by Smithsonian Folkways; others have been reissued on Smithsonian Folkways as *Pure Religion and Bad Company*). By the early 1960s, Davis was performing again, a star on the folk-revival circuit, and he even mixed into sets of his fervent religious hymns like "Samson and Delilah" and "Twelve Gates to the City" some of the lewd blues and wild instrumentals, like the digit-twisting "Buck Dance," he'd eschewed for decades. He said he did them for his growing number of students, so they could learn. "I ain't no miller, ain't no miller's son, but I can grind you a little corn till your good miller come," he sang in his long salacious version of "Hesitation Blues," far longer than the three-minute limits of recording before the postwar LP.

His sentiments weren't quite disinterested, though: he was notorious for groping female folkies, planting himself in tight spots backstage, in corridors, at parties, so they had to manuever past him while getting felt up. Such are the confusing ways of the Lord, as gospel artists like Sam Cooke and Al Green (we'll only touch on preachers like Jim and Tammy Bakker, Jerry Falwell, and their eternally recurring Elmer Gantry like) have borne witness.

"ONE THING I WAS BLESSED WITH is that I was a very, very bad mimic," Van Ronk said in a 1997 interview. Which is another, better way of stating how oral tradition straddles conservation and creativity. Van Ronk's background allowed him to understand this uniquely.

He was born in Brooklyn on July 30, 1936, a Depression baby to a mostly Irish working-class family. His father and mother split, and he grew up in blue-collar Richmond Hill, where he went to Catholic school— which is to say, he played truant until the system gave up on him, at 16. In 1998, he told David Walsh, "I remember reading Grant's memoirs, the autobiography of Buffalo Bill. Lots of Mark Twain. . . . My brain was like the attic of the Smithsonian. . . . The principal . . . called me 'a filthy ineducable little beast.' That's a direct quote." For the rest of his life, he remained, like Guthrie, a formidably wide-ranging autodidact, another Gramscian prole-intellectual.

While Van Ronk hung out in pool halls he was listening to jazz, his first love—bebop, cool, and increasingly traditional, aka New Orleans or Dixieland jazz. (He always cited Armstrong and Bessie Smith, with Lead Belly and Bing Crosby, as his major vocal influences.) For a while he was a self-described "moldy fig," a true believer that the only pure jazz was from New Orleans and the era of King Oliver. (The concept of authenticity in jazz and folk is almost identical, as are the cultlike implications of the term and its exclusionary uses. This shouldn't be surprising: jazz, after all, was a folk music until its gradual transformation to commercial and art music starting with Armstrong himself, and the almost millenarian revivalism that attended the "rediscovery" of Bunk Johnson was like nothing more than the similar contemporary "rediscoveries" of ancient blues and folk masters from Skip James and Son House to Mississippi John Hurt and Lightnin' Hopkins.) One of young Van Ronk's first gigs was playing tenor banjo with the Brute Force Jazz Band, one of thousands of Dixieland revival bands serenading postwar America.

On Saturday afternoons, Van Ronk recalled, he headed to the Briarwood (Queens) apartment of guitarist Jack Norton, who'd hung with Bix Beiderbecke and Eddie Lang. Norton taught him "old orchestral jazz school" fingerings à la Count Basie's Freddie Green, and did near-continuous blindfold tests with jazz records. "The Old Man," recalled Van Ronk, "used to put on recordings and we would play 'name that sideman' . . . but it was listening training. You had to listen with a focus and an intensity that normal people never use. But listening that normal people do will not serve for a musician." He began toting his guitar around to clubs to sit in, and played with the stellar likes of Coleman

Hawkins, Johnny Hodges, and Jimmy Rushing. He'd later remark in his acid way, "They were always very polite."

Like Odysseus, Guthrie and Houston, Kerouac and Ginsberg, and Pynchon, without a clear calling for his energies Van Ronk decided to take to the sea. He ended up in the merchant marine, a way to see the other sides of the world without going military, a tramp tradition for American artists. In 1957, the young seaman got a shore gig at the Café Bizarre, one of the Village's now-legendary spots. Odetta, the gospel-voiced black singer who gave the 1950s folk scene there a sense of authenticity and interracial connection as Lead Belly, Sonny Terry and Brownie McGhee, and Josh White had to the first Depression wave, heard him, liked what she heard, and convinced him to make a demo tape that she'd pass on to Albert Grossman, folk-music maven, Chicago clubowner, wily semi-thug, and future manager of Bob Dylan, Peter Paul and Mary, and a host of 1960s folk-music stars. Popping Benzedrine in the best Beat fashion, Van Ronk hitchhiked to Chicago in 24 hours, got to Grossman's club, found out the tape hadn't, auditioned, got turned down (Grossman was booking black songsters like Bill Broonzy, and Van Ronk accused him of Crowjimming), hitchhiked back to New York City, had his seaman's papers stolen, and thus decided that he would, after all, become a folksinger.

It's the sort of story that threads the Beat Generation, but also marked Van Ronk as different from those who would come in his wake, the white middle-class kids answering Guthrie and Seeger's pied-piper call for cultural reconsideration and escape from 1950s conformity, the Baezes and the Zimmermans, the Rambling Jack Elliots and Richard Farinas, the Tom Paxtons and Maria D'Amatos and John Sebastians, and the rest. Van Ronk wasn't playing at being an outsider; he was one—a blue-collar kid with little formal education, a self-proclaimed leftist, a member of the Workers League who could utter decidedly un-Romantic lines like, "I have more in common with a carpenter than you might think." (Think of Springsteen in concert, unveiling a new song by announcing to the crowd, "This is my job, right?") Or "Technology always determines the forms of music. The bow and arrow *had* to precede the first stringed instruments. The bellow principles *had* to precede the organ. You can't have an organ without smelting, right? You couldn't have a fugue without math. Or math without a concern for who owns how much of what."

Given his sardonic realism, it was fittingly ironic that he and his wife Terri became quasi-parents for that younger generation of dewy-eyed collegiate folkies inspired by Guthrie's songs and Seeger's indefatigable college-campus concert proselytizing. Seeger's concerts had planted folk music on campuses across the country, but Harry Smith's *Anthology* provided the rich soil and nurture for the next generation of folk musicians, whose connection with the oral tradition was far from Van Ronk's and even farther from Guthrie's and Seeger's. "Cast your mind back to 1952," he told one interviewer. "The only way you could hear the old timers was hitting up the thrift shops. When the *Anthology* came out, there were 82 cuts, all the old time stuff. I wore out a copy in a year. People my age were doing the same." And the people who became his musical stepkids, especially the young Bob Dylan, inhaled the set like a drug.

Van Ronk once said of Seeger, "What am I supposed to say about the guy who invented my profession?" But by the late 1950s that profession was already migrating far from Lead Belly and Guthrie, actual songsters who lived the lives they chronicled, and far from Seeger's fiercely idealistic anticommercialism, that descendant of German Romanticism's emphasis on the purity and truth of folk culture. Once McCarthyism ran its course, Seeger, though he had refused to testify before the House Un-American Activities Committee, had managed to resurface in the post–McCarthy era. Still, less threatening figures like Burl Ives became the public commercial faces of folk music. As Joe Klein noted in *Woody Guthrie: A Life*, the folk revival offered record companies an exit from the latest witchhunting: they were swamped with payola scandals stemming from rock and roll (a new congressional fixation that paralleled "investigations" into TV's quiz-show riggings), and inundated with public outcries based on racial and sexual fears that had generated mainstream disapproval of rock and roll. The patina of integrity and authenticity covering white collegiate folk music helped the labels repolish their corporate images.

Starting in 1958, the Kingston Trio cleaned up old tunes like "Tom Dooley" and "Tijuana Jail" and scored 10 top 25 hits. Neat folk groups proliferated, feeding into the Village and Cambridge, where earnest young men and women in recently acquired rural accents and denims recycled the *Anthology*'s songbook and hoped to catch a record label's ear. It was no accident that Albert Grossman followed the money and sold his Chicago club, then moved to New York.

In 1959, when Bobby Zimmerman was leaving behind his pounding piano à la Jerry Lee Lewis in front of a rock band for college and the *Anthology*'s lures, Van Ronk made his first records for Moses Asch's Folkways, now compiled on *The Folkways Years*. They reveal a singer misclassified. As Van Ronk once put it, "I never really thought of myself as a folk singer at all. Still don't. What I did was combine traditional fingerpicking guitar with a repertoire of old jazz tunes." Here he does a Gary Davis-derived staple of his repertoire, "Hesitation Blues," and more blues and gospel. His big, rough voice and guitar dexterity are self-evident, as is his improvisational feel. Both, however, seem contained; he hasn't yet found himself fully.

In 1964, he yanged with Dave Van Ronk's Ragtime Jug Stompers, recording high-energy versions of old tunes with a wild and ragged Dixieland outfit. "Everybody Loves My Baby" has the sheer delight and seat-of-the-pants playing that marked the best garage bands of the decade's second half. This was his recurrent folk-jazz dialectic. On his solo album

Sings the Blues, Van Ronk's coarse voice and nimble fingers got looser—like the irrepressible Davis's—and thus he found himself.

"It was more academic than it is now," is how Van Ronk in the 1970s remembered this era. "It was 'de rigeur,' practically, to introduce your next song with a musicological essay—we all did it. There was a great deal of activity around New York—not so much you could make money at. But there were folksong societies in most of the colleges and the left was dying, but not quietly. So there was a great deal of activity around *Sing Out!* and the Labor Youth League, which wasn't affiliated with the old CP youth group. There was a lot of grassroots interest among the petit-bourgeois left."

Spoken like the slyly sardonic observer who once told an interviewer from the International Committee of the Fourth International, "I've always like Trotsky's writings as an art critic."

BY 1961, BOBBY ZIMMERMAN was Bobby Dylan and arrived in New York, Van Ronk had become the ultimate insider in the self-constituted Village folk scene of social misfits and deviants and critics and would-be revolutionists, and the two, probably inevitably, gravitated toward and around each other. Ramped up by commercial success, the folk revival's second major peak was about to be reached even as debates about authenticity and commercialism crescendoed. "All of a sudden," Van Ronk recalled a few years back, "there was money all over the place. If there was ever any evidence to the trickle-down theory, the only evidence of it I've seen was in that period of 1960 to 1965."

At the height of the folk boom, pop was largely barren and formatted. Elvis came out of the army domesticated, the first generation of blue-collar rockabilly rebels were either dead or incapacitated, and the Mickey Mouse Club–bred predecessors of N'Sync and Britney Spears and Christina Aguilera grabbed the top of the charts with echo-chambered confections. College campuses turned to more overtly intellectual pursuits, which meant what is now called roots music and jazz. Kids were necking to *Kind of Blue*, Mississippi John Hurt, and Odetta. Buttoned-down acts like the Kingston Trio were all over radio and TV. Some of the lids were popping off the repressed cauldrons of cultural energy seething just below the postwar gray flannel era.

Van Ronk settled into the Gaslight Café on Macdougal Street, a hub for noncommercial folkies. Small sleazy pass-the-hat Beat-folk clubs proliferated. Café Bizarre, where Odetta had heard him onstage in 1957, was the first, but within a couple of years several other coffeehouses, like the Café Wha?, opened. By 1962, Dylan settled in down the block, at the grander Gerde's, where Izzy Young of the Folklore Center, part of the older folk-revival wave, had set up a folk-music showcase, and WBAI broadcast the shows, and clubowner Mike Porco soon realized he'd stumbled into a salable product and ousted both, lining his bar with record company covers of folk albums and his seats with earnest young beatniks. Porco's Monday night Hoots were the dollar-admission descendants of Young's and Seeger's more informal loft gatherings, and he showcased "rediscovered" legends like John Lee Hooker with Dylan as the opener. Tom and Jerry, later known as Simon and Garfunkel, and Judy Collins cut their teeth there. Kids flocked to see, hear, and participate in this word-of-mouth semi-underground. Jug bands emerged as the intellectual's equivalent of the 1950s blue-collar rockabilly outbreak in the South and doo-wop in the North, prefiguring the nationwide garage-band explosion of the 1960s after the Beatles and Dylan. The link: everyone felt empowered to pick up an instrument. These were all modern folk musics.

Still, Van Ronk was both figurehead and outsider. His versatility and wide-ranging interests, his methodology and study aligned him more with the radical Bob Dylan who would soon emerge than it did with the folkies who hung around his Village haunts. "Musically," he later recalled, "it was very interesting. [The folk revival] attracted a large number of talented people, who probably wouldn't have been interested in folk music had it not been so popular. Someone like Jose Feliciano. He played the guitar, he sang, ergo, he was a folk singer."

Van Ronk always questioned the musical credentials of his ersatz flock. "I was one of the worst musical snobs that ever came down the pike," he once said by way of explaining why he ignored the era's mushrooming singer-strummers in Washington Square Park. Few of them had his training, his credentials as a collector and interpreter who went back to sources, his expansive notion of folk music, which he periodically redefined as "saloon music" or "a grabbag." Few individual younger performers imitated his complex grasp of arranging, which he repeatedly traced to apparently abstruse influences like Ellington's horn section voicings or Jelly Roll Morton's piano or even Scarlatti harpsichord pieces. Most of them lacked his sarcastic sense of humor, his cynical sense of the world as fundamentally resistant to change. Children of the idealistic strain coursing through Lomax and Seeger and Guthrie himself, they believed they were creating an alternative world, that revitalizing cultural roots could create an awareness that would somehow remake society. The irascible Van Ronk saw through the glass walls.

The Newport Folk Festival, the crowning triumph of the postwar folk revival, was first organized in 1959 by jazz impresario George Wein and Albert Grossman. It graduated even the purer wings of the folk movement to big-time concerts; Seeger himself was deeply involved. "I never liked those things," Van Ronk recalled. "It was a three-ring circus. . . . You couldn't even really hear what you came to hear. Put yourself in my position, or any singer's position: how would you like to sing for 15,000 people with frisbees?" Most, of course, would have answered, "I love it."

For Van Ronk, though, if there was a point to the tradition, it was person-to-person communication, focus, the kind of outreach he saw as implicit in Guthrie.

Along with his own musical catholicity, that may be why, even after the Dylan-goes-electric blowup at the 1965 festival, he remained a defender of Dylan, both personally and professionally, against more sectarian folkies—which included nearly everyone from Seeger on down.

"Nervous. Nervous energy, he couldn't sit still," is how he spoke of young Bob to David Walsh in 1998. "And very, very evasive. . . . What impressed me the most about him was his geniune love for Woody Guthrie. In retrospect, even he says now that he came to New York to 'make it.' That's BS. When he came to New York there was no folk music, no career possible. . . . What he said at the time is the story I believe. He came because he had to meet Woody Guthrie. . . . Bobby used to go out there two or three times a week and sit there, and play songs for him. In that regard he was as standup a cat as anyone I've ever met. That's also what got him into writing songs. He wrote songs for Woody, to amuse him, to entertain him. He also wanted Woody's approval. . . . [Dylan's music] had what I call a gung-ho, unrelenting quality. . . . He acquired very, very devoted fans among the other musicians before he had written his first song."

Van Ronk was among the first to record a tune Dylan claimed to write, "He Was a Friend of Mine," on *Dave Van Ronk, Folksinger* in 1962. (It was actually on old folk tune somewhat revamped.) Three years later, the Byrds redid it on *Turn Turn Turn*, whose title cut remade Seeger's setting of Ecclesiastes into folk rock, the new sound Dylan had kicked into high gear during his 1965 tour.

VAN RONK ONCE OBSERVED, "The area that I have staked out . . . has been the kind of music that flourished in this country between the 1880s and say the end of the 1920s. You can call it saloon music if you want to. It was the kind of music you'd hear in music halls, saloons, whorehouses, barbershops, anywhere the *Police Gazette* could be found." That's not exactly a full description of what he did over 30 albums and countless performances from clubs to festivals to benefits for CORE.

"They'll call me a blues artist even if I sing Pagliacci," he said once, with some bitterness, though his first albums were steeped in the early blues. But it's better to think of him as a songster, that older, more encompassing sort of folk artist. Lead Belly and the Reverend Gary Davis are outstanding examples of this type, which goes back to the earliest recorded bluesmen. They drew from multiple local and regional traditions that, in the early days of radio and phonograph, still defined American musical styles. Dance tunes, blues, ragtime, ballads, gospel—anything to keep the audiences on street corners or in juke joints interested and willing to part with some cash. This was, after all, performance. Entertainment was its primary goal; improvisation, found in the vocal-guitar interplay and instrumental backing as well as verse substitutions and extrapolations or shortenings, played to audience reaction. This performance modality reaches from Eastern Europe and ancient Greece to the Mississippi Delta and Cuba's son vocalists, and ad-libbing has always been at its core.

Like Lead Belly, Woody Guthrie's black analog and one of his foremost models, Van Ronk covered a wide stylistic geography, embracing the blues' regional dialects: the Delta skills and sounds of Son House, the dark stylings of Blind Willie McTell, the laconic attack of Mississippi John Hurt, the ragtime-based fretwork of Blind Blake and Blind Boy Fuller and Davis, the Texas laidback sound of Mance Lipscomb. But almost always, as Van Ronk sought to remind newer waves of guitar-based kids who would be faster and harder and cleaner and outer, the music was about the dance between voice and instrument, the antiphonal approach under-lying most black American music—and therefore much, if not most, of American popular culture.

In 1962, with the Red Onion Jazz Band, he cut *In the Tradition*, which, along with the solo *Your Basic Dave Van Ronk* album, has been reissued as *Two Sides of Dave Van Ronk*. This somewhat odd couple makes a wonderful introduction to the breadth, depth, and soul of his songster's legacy. The smoothly idiomatic Red Onions pump joyful New Orleans adrenaline and Armstrong trumpet into a raucous "Cake Walking Babies from Home"; a sinuous "Sister Kate," that early dance hit built from an Armstrong melody; and Dylan's characteristically caustic "Over You." Amid the Dixieland offerings are solo spots: a stunning version of Son House's "Death Letter Blues" (later recorded by Cassandra Wilson), Lead Belly's "Whoa Back Buck," the virtuosic ragtime of "St. Louis Tickle," signature pieces like "Green, Green Rocky Road" and "Hesitation Blues." There is no diminishing of talent or narrowing of perspective evident on the tunes selected from *Basic*: Billie Holiday's "God Bless the Child" (sung with a tenderness that scorches periodically into Howlin' Wolf) and "St. James Infirmary" share space with songs by Davis and Mississippi John Hurt.

In 1967, he cut *Dave Van Ronk and the Hudson Dusters*, a deliberately amateur cross of jug band and electric folk that foreshadows the Blues Project, the improvising garage band that the guitarist on this date, Danny Kalb, later formed with fellow Van Ronk disciple Steve Katz. There was doo-wop, Joni Mitchell—whose "Clouds" develops anguished depth thanks to Van Ronk's deft use of his torturous voice's breaks as interpre-tative device—a move he learned from Armstrong and Bessie Smith—and the balls-to-the-wall garage rock "Romping Through the Swamp," which sounds more akin to Captain Beefheart than anything else.

Recorded in 1967, *Live at Sir George University* is time-capsule Van Ronk on guitar unspooling favorite parts of his vast repertoire: "Frankie and Albert," "Down and Out," "Mack the Knife," "Statesboro Blues," and "Cocaine," of course—all masterful, each distinct, a polished yet raw-edged gem.

By then the folk boom, whose audience was bleeding into folk rock, electric blues, and psychedelia, stalled and ended. Van Ronk continued (except for a hiatus in the 1970s) to perform and record and gather new-old material. And he had time, before his death, to deliver some acid reflections.

On 1960s folkies: "The whole raison d'etre of the New Left had been exposed as a lot of hot air; that was demoralizing. I mean, these kids thought they were going to change the world, they really did. They were profoundly deluded. . . . Phil Ochs wrote the song 'I declare the war is over,' that was despair, sheer despair."

On 1980s folkies: "You're talking about some pretty damn good song-writers. But I'd like to hear more traditional music. . . . With the last wave of songwriters you get the sense that tradition begins with Bob Dylan and nobody is more annoyed with that than Bob Dylan. We were sitting around a few years ago, and he was bitching and moaning: 'These kids don't have any classical education.' He was talking about the stuff you find on the *Anthology [of American Folk Music]*. I kidded him: 'You've got a lot to answer for, Bro.'"

12

Willie Nelson

On April 30, 2003, Willie Nelson turned 70, and celebrated with the release of his latest greatest hits collection. *The Essential Willie Nelson* (Columbia/Legacy), a two-CD set, has an intriguing 1970s-vintage cover shot that sets exactly the right tone for 40 years of selective tracks. Nelson's unkempt long red hair and scraggly beard frame his thin, almost Bob Hope nose. His mouth twists slightly, a smile just short of a sneer, in sardonic, knowing reaction to the world behind the camera. His eyes, couched in wrinkles and bags, stare straight and deep into the lens, and suggest hard-to-fathom distances and recessions at the same time they focus you into connecting. This interaction, evasive, seemingly casual, direct and subtle, represents the essence of Nelson's sly, almost unobtrusive art.

The Essential Willie Nelson demonstrates once again that the Red Headed Stranger's nonchalant gospel-flavored, jazz-inflected voice and guitar have remained essentially themselves for decades despite an ever-expanding variety of musical backdrops: barebones string bands, sleekly glossy Nashville productions, twangy 1970s Outlaw country rock, jazzy standards with strings, gospel-laced soul.

Maybe that breadth is a major reason Nelson's recurrent duets with Ray Charles are almost always so charged—and so much fun. After all, only Charles and Bob Dylan have traveled as sure-footedly across as far-flung a constellation of genres and expectations as Nelson has and still remained themselves; Charles and Nelson have long shared material and appearances. (A 1984 show at the Austin Opera House, captured on *The Willie Nelson Special*, features excellent versions of "Georgia," "I Can't Stop Loving You," and the old hillbilly fave "Mountain Dew.") Part of this odd couple's magnetism stems from their representing opposite poles of the American spectrum. Charles, the consummate be-suited black professional trained in the tough world of low-rent postwar rhythm and blues whose nonpareil voice influenced countless singers, is a hard-bitten recluse who heads a thriving business dynamo and a drilled band. Nelson, the white country-music renegade, tried pig farming for a while when his career soured, comes onstage in hippie-cowboy-Indian costume, calls his band Family, and is the epicenter of the self-consciously laidback Austin music scene (his disciples include Van Zandt, Lyle Lovett, Joe Ely, Jimmie Dale Gilmore, and alt-country outfits like Uncle Tupelo) he helped seed and feed for the 30 years since he first strode onstage at armadillo world headquarters. Even on an off night, Charles can suddenly burst whatever frames the ragged churchy elasticity of his scuffed and soaring trademark voice. Nelson stays introspective: lacking Charles's explosive interpolations, he subsumes his surroundings, enticing the audience into his voice's unexpected contours.

Think of Charles as Louis Armstrong's direct descendant, and Nelson as a cross between Bing Crosby, Jimmie Rodgers, and Woody Guthrie. Their duets are like oil and vinegar, always about to separate if not stirred up, delicious because they don't. Thanks to the gospel-jazz core of their artistic personalities, their encompassing self-assurance in their craft's portability of application, they make singing symbolic of existential struggle. It helps that they both love what Charlie Parker loved most about country music—storytelling.

Like Charles, Nelson absorbed the breadth of American music by living it. Born in poor Texas cotton country, Nelson and his sister Bobbi, who still plays piano for him, were raised by their grandparents, devout people and gospel-music fans who encouraged their grandchildren to pick up instruments. By the time the boy was seven he was writing songs. "I worked in the cotton fields around Abbott," he has said, "with a lot of African Americans and a lot of Mexican Americans, and we listened to their music all the time." So blues and Mexican ballads underpin Nelson's phrasing and narratives, along with the hillbilly and Western Swing (13-year-old Willie once duetted with Western Swing founder Bob Wills) his radio picked up from Nashville and the border. Following a quick hitch in the air force and a tempestuous marriage to a Native American, Nelson moved to Fort Worth in 1954, became a country DJ, and played bars, mixing honky-tonk and preaching. (Nelson's longtime drummer Paul English originally played with the Salvation Army.) In 1956, he made his first record in Vancouver; it sold 3,000 copies. Then he wrote (and sold for $50 apiece) a couple of hits, which got him a publishing contract and brought him to Nashville.

There producers had little interest in demos of his nasal voice with its eccentric phrasing and capitalized on his songwriting. And yet now that those demos have resurfaced on various reissues, they actually outline a central portion of Nelson's work, since most made the top 20 country charts, though almost always as performed by others. The low-key style of his barebones demos, however, grants Nelson's lithe voice more space for embellishment, pauses, and inflection than his released 1960s Nashville recordings while showcasing his off-kilter lyrics, which refashion clichés from unexpected angles, like "Hello Walls" or "Crazy." One outstanding example is "I Never Cared for You," whose opening lines cleverly subvert Tin Pan Alley macrocosm/microcosm imagery: the sun never shines, the rain doesn't fall, and I never cared for you. In the liner notes to *The Essential Willie Nelson*, Emmylou Harris's longtime collaborator Rodney Crowell recalls the song's effect when he heard it over the radio in the mid-1960s: "A voice rivaling Bob Dylan's in authenticity delivered the fantastically ironic lyric to a weird-sounding gut-string accompaniment."

Ray Price was the first star to cover Nelson's tunes; for a while Nelson played bass in Price's band and wrote hits for Faron Young ("Hello Walls"), Billy Walker ("How Time Slips Away"), and Patsy Cline ("Crazy"). But Nelson the singer suffered: his first label closed, and he kept being wedged into the curtain of syrupy strings that defined Nashville countrypolitan—a very 1950s sonic confection spun by producer Owen Bradley, modeled after the bland but influential approach to contemporary pop that A&R head Mitch Miller had fashioned at Columbia. Countrypolitan gave the likes of Cline crossover appeal while trying to erase the singing rube/cowboy image that, via earlier movie and radio stars like Jimmie Rodgers and Gene Autry, first brought hillbilly music into mainstream markets. Nelson, who stubbornly resisted conforming, was a problem child.

He scored a couple of middling hits, but even though he joined the Grand Ole Opry and signed with RCA in 1965, as a performer he spent the next several years in limbo. The then-pudgy Nelson's idiosyncratic, limber vocalizing and noncomformity, insistence that his songs could sell themselves, and unwillingness to glitz up his act caused a constant debilitating battle. Still, in the midst of a few blandly uneven countrypolitan discs, he managed to cut one of country music's first concept albums, *Yesterday's Wine*, a dazzling song-cycle about a life from cradle to grave that demonstrated what he could do given his head.

By 1972, he quit Nashville and moved to Austin, where he noticed that young rock fans were turned on by honky-tonk and folk. (His way had been prepared, in part, by friend and colleague Johnny Cash's 1970s eclectic TV show, which showcased the Man in Black, who had been performing at folk-music festivals for years, with folk-revival stars from Dylan to the Carter Family.) Shrewdly, Nelson resurrected the country-folk-rock style Nashville had rejected, enhanced by his lengthening hair and cowboy-Indian duds and hippie-crossover ideas. His old Music Row pals thought he'd killed what was left of his career. In fact he had finally found his audience, post-1960s types who thought rock was too corporate and responded to Guthriesque storytelling minus the whiny self-indulgence of James Taylor, Carly Simon, and Carole King—the same crowd Emmylou Harris would wow and Bruce Springsteen would tap with *Nebraska* and *Tom Joad*.

After an abortive stab at his own indie label, Nelson recorded with Atlantic, by then a major label that had mostly jettisoned rhythm and blues and jazz for The Rolling Stones and Led Zeppelin. With soul-music producer Arif Mardin and his own band (including pianist Leon Russell), Nelson cut killers like "Shotgun Willie," which crossed funky soul back into country and rock, laced with the introspective touches and wry phrase-turnings Nashville had scorned. In 1974, "Bloody Mary Morning," a Texas-swing smoothie with characteristic witty lines ("It's a bloody Mary morning 'cause she left me without warning sometime in the night"), hit number 14 on the country charts. At 42, Willie Nelson was hitting his stride.

One of my Austin-based colleagues comments with bemused affection, "Willie is the Buddha. He's also a duet whore." In terms of consistent quality, he's right, but Nelson's duets, which have included outings with Charles, Cash, and Dylan as well as U2 and Julio Iglesias, if nothing else do reveal Nelson's prismatic musical curiosity. Two classics ("Good Hearted Woman" and "Mammas Don't Let Your Babies Grow Up To Be Cowboys") boast Waylon Jennings, that other Outlaw who, with Nelson, launched the 1970s back-to-the-roots country movement, its revisionist rock and rockabilly and folk ingredients contrasting sharply with contemporary countrypolitan productions. Merle Haggard, another perpetual Nashville outsider, shows up for Townes Van Zandt's evocative border ballad "Pancho and Lefty," where Nelson's nuance nicely plays off Haggard's swagger while making clear that Haggard, whose band The Strangers routinely improvises, is among the few country singers whose jazzy phrasing—the dancing rhythms that infiltrated the best American singing after Louis Armstrong—compares to Nelson's.

Red Headed Stranger in 1975 marks a pinnacle, Nelson's *John Wesley Harding*, an artistic restatement of purpose in the guise of an Americana concept album about an Old West preacher who loved women; its brilliantly sparse, country-folk production features his voice and trademark nylon-stringed guitar, and "Blue Eyes Crying in the Rain" shot to the top of the charts to make him a star. RCA, tailgating his success, compiled an album of Nelson and Jennings and others called *Wanted! The Outlaws*, the first country album to go platinum thanks to "Good Hearted Woman." A movement begun as a rejection of the Nashville music business became the business's newest stack of chips in the hitmaking casino.

Nelson hit number one again with Lefty Frizzell's sardonic "If You've Got the Money I've Got the Time," then cut a fine album of Frizzell tunes. When Crosby died, to his label's dismay Nelson abandoned what corporate types saw as a winning formula and zagged into the unsure turf of jazz-pop standards; he scored again: 1978's *Stardust*, arranged and produced by the MGs' Booker T. Jones, triumphs with slow tempos and strings, as if Nelson internalized Nashville and subtly refocuses it. His jaunty phrasing genially enlivens classics like "Georgia," "Someone to Watch Over Me," and the title track. The album hung on the country charts for a year.

Nelson never played it safe, as in career-building, and so success, like failure, didn't stop his eclectic wanderings: a jam-based feel (*Willie and Family Live*); covers of another renegade songwriter (*Sings Kris Kristofferson*); pallid reprises of *Stardust* (*Somewhere Over the Rainbow* and *Always on My Mind*); reunions with Price (*San Antonio Rose*) and Russell (*One for the Road*). By 1985, however, old-timers like Nelson began to be swept away by New Country, the latest Nashville formula brewed from reheated George Jones and Buck Owens. That year, he founded Farm Aid, which lured performers like Dylan. He also joined forces with Cash, Jennings, and Kristofferson in The Highwaymen, a band of Nashville misfits who revivified the roots of country music and expanded the genre's possibilities—and in the process extended its reach to the post-Eagles rock audience, eventually helping to make country music pop's best-selling style with the widest radio play. In 1990, the IRS whacked him for nearly $17 million in back taxes and seized practically all he owned. *Who'll Buy My Memories*, a 25-cut compilation of Nelson-only demos, outtakes, and keepers, was issued in 1992 to help pay off the remaining debt; it remains one of Nelson's most effective and affecting albums. The following year, he was solvent.

A collapsed lung, a pot bust, induction into the Country Music Hall of Fame, an ersatz acting career (*The Electric Horseman, Thief, Wag the Dog, Austin Powers: The Spy Who Shagged Me*)—Nelson is now legend enough to have songs written about him. Like Charles and Dylan, he's grown so powerful and centered in his artistry that even his lesser efforts outgun the best of others.

13

Lenny Bruce

THE SCENE: MIAMI IN 1951. A 25-year-old strip show emcee initiates his first public demonstration of what would, decades later, be called performance art. It is built around a scam: the Brother Matthias Foundation for Lepers. Just out of the merchant marine, recently married to a stripper, nearly broke, and meditating on contemporary defrauding evangelists, Lenny Bruce decides he'll raise money for lepers. And he'll only keep 50 percent. That, he argues forcefully, is far less than other charities, even respectable ones like Community Chest, keep. So he lifts a priest's garb from a local rectory and starts soliciting on the street. Almost immediately, he's invited into people's homes, thanks to his Roman collar. He's making a good haul. His second day out, he gets busted.

Welcome to the world of Lenny Bruce, where "accepted" and "normal" values are regularly, ritualistically turned inside-out. A twisted yet compelling figure, part brilliantly flawed pharmakos and part implacable junkie, part perpetual adolescent and part First Amendment crusader, he was reborn as a hero to the 1960s youth rebellions, and with the rock revival of the 1980s again became an icon; he joins rock critic Lester Bangs, Leonid Brezhnev, and Leonard Bernstein for a stream-of-consciousness catalog of alternative-culture luminaries in REM's machine-gunned "It's the End of the World as We Know It." This is typical of the way Bruce's name tends to pop up in pop culture, a mismatched juxtaposition that unwittingly says as much about punker-slacker attitude as it does about Lenny Bruce, who, as the old bumper sticker goes, died for our sins of a morphine overdose in 1966 at age 40.

Bruce pioneered an outsider form of in-your-face standup comedy, a kind of jazzy verbal performance art (think of George Carlin and Richard Pryor, Bruce's self-professed and best disciples, or Firesign Theatre, who made Joycean improvisation into high-level pop art) that is now widely accepted and widely practiced. Or is it? Certainly the perpetual-teen side of Lenny Bruce is on display all over the media, on *Saturday Night Live* and *Comedy Central*, in the late Andrew Dice

Clay's small-minded filth and Howard Stern's flatulent shock-jock self-importance. Anyone can easily claim Lenny as avatar and saint—as long as they elide the motives generating the best of his satirical art, the stiff-armed jab he thought he was landing on America's square-chinned hypocrisy with each dirty word.

But thanks to them, almost half a century after he died we've discovered that Lenny Bruce was wrong: using words does not necessarily defang them. Is nigger less potent because gangstas throw the word down? Academics can pirouette in debate forever over that, so try something less theoretical. In the post-Reagan era, where taxes have been decoupled from social programs by slogans like "tax-and-spend politicians," where access to legal abortions is shut by bomb-wielding "right-to-life" supporters, buzz words are more loaded and less culturally transparent than any time since the 1950s; their invocation is enough to preclude discussion of the issues they cloak.

Miraculously enough, the coarsening of American popular culture has accelerated at the same time that the fundamentalist Christian right demands a society conforming to its clear moral sense. Is this the outcome of social repression or the wages of sin? "Reality" TV deepens the confusion between what's on and off the tube and deadens the need for the distance between the two. The motto of the Fox News Channel is "We Report. You Decide," but nobody except the most rancid couch potato could mistake its overbearing right-wing biases. The Patriot Act, passed in the wake of 9/11, strips off protections guaranteed Americans by the Bill of Rights, and the few who protest are mostly pooh-poohed or ignored in the media. Here is the work of language as obfuscation. The forces of social repression in America look stronger than at any time since the late 1950s, when the slow-breaking cultural thaw began to examine or reject America's dominant mores via art, pop culture, social movements, and eventually mainstream politics.

As a central character in the Great Postwar American Morality Play, Lenny Bruce is usually framed by stark dichotomies of good and evil. And so he has usually been painted as avatar or prophet, tragic hero or manipulative junkie. But Bruce still fascinates not because he was larger than life but because he so clearly wasn't: in many ways a failure of a man and a fluctuating undisciplined artist, he was both in and out of sync with his time and place; he could oscillate between Holden Caulfield and Sammy Glick. But in contrast to a fellow junkie like Chet Baker, he was at least aware of that; he articulated it in his routines, and shivered at it when he heated his needle and spoon. In the end, Bruce didn't transcend his time; he made periodically brilliant stabs at representing it.

As he crossed the tracks into the forbidden zones of America, unearthing race and sex and drugs and religion, Lenny Bruce was right and wrong about a lot of things at the same time, the way Elvis was; he shared a sort of druggy naivete with The King. Crossing the tracks was the direction that mattered for white rebels in the 1950s. African Americans didn't have to question The System; exclusion by color gifted them with the curse of Du Boisian double consciousness. But for white Americans, opting out of The System meant rejecting its ideology of goals and money and The Future that was dedicated, at least in theory, to them. Almost as a fulcrum to escape, lots of them tuned in to the marginal sites and people of America, turned on to drugs both to escape the world of gray flannel suits and to become more like the sainted outsiders and, in the process, touch what they saw as natural spontaneous creativity more deeply. They dropped out to become hustlers, collect the trust fund money, or wake up in rubber rooms after electro-shock.

Let's back up to that opening scene, performance art before there was a name for it. What makes it funny is the deliberate moral confusion it evokes, its unsettling of symbols and their corollary economics. What makes it disturbing and truly provocative is its blithe confusion of fantasy and reality: is it a scam masquerading as art or vice versa—or both? This question threads Bruce's legacy.

Maybe Lenny Bruce's was the necessary and even predictable symbiotic reaction to a culture so desperately repressed it practically screamed for outbreaks of adolescent revolt. Think of him as a talkative James Dean. Or think of him as a burlesque comic: in the late 1950s and early 1960s, he single-mindedly rebuilt Borscht Belt humor into social shtick with outrage as its engine and humor as its fuel. His mother, one of his legend's most zealous promulgators and guardians, proudly insisted she raised him free of contemporary mores and guilt, which gave him new eyes; his eternal adolescence, perpetuated by dope, fired up his frequently infantile demands on everyone around him. In the unfathomable ways of art, these qualities also made his best work endure.

The hypocrisy that he attacked in America was something he reviled in himself. A jazz musician who knew Bruce well told me a revealing story of the 1950s. Bruce, he said, had been screwing his girl; Bruce's wife Honey got mad and screwed the musician. Bruce walked in on them; his eyes filled with tears, and he backed out of the room. The musician explained, "He thought that kind of sexual freedom was natural, the right thing, but he just wasn't ready. He couldn't really do it, and it murdered him inside." A stupid scenario? Throughout the Ozzie and Harriet 1950s, wife-swapping and "swinging" caught the eyes of perceptive chroniclers of suburban America like John Updike and John Cheever.

Twenty years after Ronald Reagan, cultural hypocrisy and repression is in vogue again, its agents are legion, and, as Pogo said famously, They Is Us. A society transfixed by TV reality believes what it sees on The Tube: one survey reported that most Americans in early 2003 believed

Saddam Hussein toppled the World Trade Center, without proof, solely thanks to George W. Bush's repeated linking of the Iraqi with Al Qaeda. Clarence Thomas? Rush Limbaugh? Pedophile priests? The 2000 election? Camille Paglia? Monica Lewinsky? O. J. Simpson? Anthrax by mail? "Shock and Awe" War with Iraq? These sound like punchlines for routines Lenny Bruce, unfortunately, never got to try out.

I FIRST HEARD LENNY BRUCE not long before he died. A Creole drummer I knew lived with his stepmother, his father's third wife, and two stepsisters, product of his father's second wife, next to the house his father lived in. Driving his chrome-covered Riviera, dressed in sharp threads cut to transform his fat into beef, his hair conked and coiffed, his mustache seductive, Mr. X sporadically gave money to his not-quite-ex-wife the nurse to help support the kids, but reserved the right to his own life. That meant a New Orleans-style second line of women visiting his house.

The first time my father saw my friend the drummer in my room, he flipped but waited till the kid left, then cornered me and demanded, "What is that nigger doing here?"

It was the era of "white flight," and we lived in a neighborhood mostly of working-class Italians and Irish, city workers and truck drivers and small shopowners, surrounded and, as they saw it, increasingly penetrated by the growing black population of Jamaica, St. Albans, Hollis, and Laurelton. As a kid, I watched the local gangs lock and load zipguns, knives, and chains for forays across the Belt Parkway, where they'd fight black gangs. I wondered why the white guys dressed in the same loud clothes and listened to the same music and drove the same flashy cars as their enemies.

Mr. X overheard our band when we practiced in the basement of the house where his son lived. One warm day, we were messing with Young Rascals' tunes when he leaned out a side window and yelled, "You guys wanna hear real organ trios? Get your asses over here."

For us, the Rascals were a real organ trio. Felix Cavaliere, the Italian who sat behind the big Hammond B-3, and the others hailed from the New York metro area. Ahmet Ertegun of Atlantic Records had signed them after a set at a floating West Hampton bar called The Barge. It was a gas watching Cavaliere pump those footpedals to create soulful funky bass lines while he worked the Hammond's throaty tonal shades, via its whirling Leslie speaker, to modulate the sustained chords that revved the fans.

Nobody in garage bands had Hammonds. They were too heavy and ridiculously expensive. Farfisas, lighter and far cheaper and sounding it, were ubiquitous. Many a Farfisa organist punched tone keys trying vainly to dial in that unbelievable thick, sexy Hammond sound, with its microtones, its gritty smoothness, its siren's call. My colleague Bob Blumenthal once described the Hammond as the synthesizer of its time; it sure was like nothing we'd heard, until we heard Jimi Hendrix.

The Rascals seemed odd and cool at the same time—named after the movie shorts that had been TV staples during our childhood, wearing knickers and short jackets and schoolboy hats, visual clowns with an obviously deep love of black music. Cavaliere once told an interviewer that the Rascals' musical concept was "Marvin Gaye's voice, Ray Charles's piano, Jimmy Smith's organ, Phil Spector's production, and the Beatles' writing—put them all together and you've got what I wanted to do." They were inventing blue-eyed soul. In bands like ours, their hits—"I Ain't Gonna Eat Out My Heart Anymore," with its Stax–Volt-style combination of endlessly sustained organ chords and soulful vocals; "Good Lovin'," with its zooming guitar chords and hammer-down rhythms; "I've Been Lonely Too Long," with its choked pleas and octave-bumping bass—were part of the basic vocabulary, the shared language that opened doorways into music.

For whatever reason, the Rascals also opened to us Mr. X's record collection. When he wasn't there, we'd wipe our feet on the front door mat, take our shoes off before we crossed the white carpet in the living room past the overstuffed, plastic-covered sofas, and flip through his wall of LPs and 78s. Organ trios with Jimmy Smith and Jimmy McGriff and Lonnie Smith, bebop and hard bop, Billy Eckstine and Nat King Cole, big band stuff from Chick Webb and Duke Ellington, early R&B and soul—it was gold.

And comedy: everything from Moms Mabley to Redd Foxx, Dick Gregory to Lenny Bruce.

Bruce zinged us with one-liners: "Another martini for Mother Cabrini." He startled us with his by turns bored and vehement rejection of the attitudes and language he'd inherited and snidely, violently, crudely dismissed. We loved his adolescent moral inversions: the pope as an evil businessman partnering with Billy Graham and Oral Roberts to swallow the planet's wealth while denying its inhabitants of color any piece of the pie, or even human dignity, put us into stitches.

For the varicolored teen rebels I knew, Lenny Bruce spoke clearly, directly, hilariously, unmasking the phony heart of the American Dream. We felt like we'd joined a secret cult. It was how we felt reading *Mad* magazine or watching Rocky and Bullwinkle or, a bit later, listening to Frank Zappa's Mothers of Invention.

THINK OF BRUCE AS THE ELVIS PRESLEY of standup. Short but well-built with darkly striking good looks, a babe magnet, he was star material for the bohemian crowd: sexy and dangerous. Like Presley, he made visible to mainstream America a range of previously underground or segregated, black-derived cultural streams that broke through in his jazz-inspired satirical thrusts. The effects are legion and culture-wide. Or, to put it succinctly, no Lenny Bruce, no Dick Gregory, Richard Pryor, Flip Wilson, Chevy Chase, George Carlin, Eddie Murphy, Robin Williams, Chris Rock, *The Simpsons*, or *South Park*.

(Gregory, who knew and admired Bruce, once called him "the eighth wonder of the world." A remarkable riff Bruce improvised on the word "nigger" when Gregory first saw him perform in 1962 inspired the black satirist to call his own 1964 autobiography *Nigger*.)

Maybe the most singular thing about Bruce's turbulent, headline-grabbing, bust-and-court-filled career is how it helped open doors for black standup comics, who by the late 1950s had begun venturing into such street-grounded satire in front of black audiences, to play before integrated and white audiences. (Hugh Hefner, whose chic *Playboy* magazine published excerpts from Bruce's autobiography, also booked Gregory into his Chicago club—Gregory's first big-time shot at white folks.) Bruce's language flowed and bucked with a feel that paralleled Jack Kerouac's prose or Charlie Parker's bebop sax; it was a hipster's jargon compounded of black jazz slang, Yiddish expressions, four-letter words, and neologisms ("toilet" for crummy club, for example). And he aimed his motley, disreputable bullets, compounded of frustration, cynicism, and edgy, mordant humor, at America's collective nerves and social pretenses.

Take a sampling of a few titles of the classic 1950s monologues that brought him the fame, major bookings, and big bucks at the short-lived apex of his career. In "Father Flotsky's Triumph," he lampoons old prison movies by flagrantly using "Uncle Tom" blacks and gay whites, along the way firing off digs at such American movie icons of saintliness as Pat O'Brien. "Adolf Hitler and the MCA" imagines how the huge talent agency-turned-entertainment conglomerate would have discovered and shaped the career, even the name, of the Nazi leader—a prescient collusion of showbiz and politics that has even greater resonance in our time than it did in Bruce's, when Richard Nixon hadn't yet learned to wear TV makeup. Nixon himself is burlesqued in "Ike, Sherm, and Nick," which opens with Ike worrying about Sherman Adams's famed vicuna coat, but quickly turns to Nixon's ill-fated trips abroad, where he was routinely stoned and abused ("They spit on me," he tells Ike, who responds that the problem isn't Nixon, but his wife Pat—"she overdresses"—a reference to her famed cloth coat).

"Religions Inc." depicts the pope and American evangelical preachers like Oral Roberts cozying up to plot conspiratorial moves as the routine links church and business interests and sales tactics ("R.C. up 9 percent this year"). What would be better guaranteed to rattle America in 1958, when Bishop Fulton J. Sheen appeared on TV weekly to inveigh against Communists and for Christian morality, not long after the phrase "under God" had been added to the Pledge of Allegiance to reaffirm America's role as Chosen People and counter the godless Soviet threat? Especially since Bruce throws in jabs to that other American sore spot, race, when he, as Roberts, goes off about how civil rights activists are pushing church leaders: "They want us to *say* something." Meantime, the evangelical preacher assures the pope, "We put in two bathrooms on each school bus."

His unsettling, cynical humor put cops and district attorneys on the lookout for Bruce's appearances. They scanned his recordings and found bits called, "How To Relax Your Colored Friends at Parties," with its bumbling well-intentioned white racists; "Psychopathia Sexualis," with its playfully knowing allusions to Beats like Allen Ginsberg and jazz-poets like Lord Buckley; and "To Is a Preposition, Come Is a Verb," the most abstract, jazz-inspired composition of his oeuvre, an ingenious, almost Dadaist hymn to sex. (These routines, now collected on *Lenny Bruce Originals Volumes 1 and 2*, most directly inspired Richard Pryor, as is especially clear on the early tracks of *And It's Deep Too*, which collects Pryor's complete Warner Bros. recordings.) Then there's "The Kid in the Well": Bruce takes a basic clichéd "human interest" story then in the headlines, twists it so the doctors who treated the kid get sued, and finally asks, "How come this gets headlines and a black guy can't buy a house doesn't?" The juxtaposition blew minds in 1958, when this sort of information was usually left buried, unarticulated. How times have changed: now Bruce would probably be accused of advocating class and racial warfare while his charge would be denied, spun, evaporated.

Sometimes the laughter Bruce drew was full-throated, a release of tensions; sometimes it was strained, or seemed to be pulled out of an audience almost against its will, as his raw wit—"sick humor," as it was labeled—strained listeners' ability to step outside convention to the emotional breaking point. With Bruce, the theater's "fourth wall" disappeared. His audience was forced to confront whatever he did as he did. Standup, after all, was the art of process, enhanced by Bruce's improvisational impulses.

He honed his act in strip clubs, where jazz musicians like Philly Joe Jones, one of Miles Davis's drummers and a friend of Bruce's, made up the house band. Is it surprising, then, that Bruce understood jazz as a kind of existentialism, used jazz as material besides adapting its process, insisted on inserting improvisation into every show? In "The Interview," he parodies a nodding-off junkie bebopper called in for a job by a Lawrence Welk-style bandleader—the epitome of white-bread America. It's hipster versus square. The staid boss doesn't understand "in" locutions like "I have a monkey on my back"; "I don't want no animals on the bandstand," he barks in an accent hovering somewhere between Yiddish and German.

Charlie Parker had said, "If you don't live it, it won't come out of your horn." Bebop insisted that the art of black jazz musicians was not mere entertainment but worthy of respect because it demanded talent and risk. Like Kerouac and most of the myriad "Little Birds" who flocked to bebop, Bruce flew recklessly, without Parker's all-consuming genius: he could soar like Daedalus or fall like Icarus in performance during his few minutes of improvised shtick. On *The Carnegie Hall Concert* or *Live at Curran Hall*, his improvisations can tail off into dead ends; you can sense his language failing at the outer bounds of his frames of reference. Even before he capitulated completely to addiction in the mid-1960s and lapsed into self-absorption and despair and grandiosity, maybe his complicated sensibilities just couldn't always find fittingly complex expression. He was as adolescent as the society around him; sometimes he sounds like a kid making faces while spitting out dirty words.

On the other hand, maybe Bruce grasped the banality of so much of the evil in America, especially in black American life. Pharmakos or egomaniac? Before junk and The Law took him over, you can hear the humanity in his best bits.

BY THE MID-1950S, after he'd garnered his first burst of notoriety by traipsing onto a strip club stage naked, Lenny Bruce found his vocation: to go onstage and, improvising from sketched-out routines, strip what he, like other Outsiders in this era, saw as self-serving hypocrisy from the powers-that-be, from the day-to-day mores of society, and project an alternative picture of how America actually worked. And, in the process, prick nerve endings and be funny.

He could also seem as stiffly self-righteous as his hip audience. "Conditions of unspeakable poverty, filth and humiliation exist right here in 'the richest country in the world,'" he wrote in his autobiography *How To Talk Dirty*. (He had a heavy ghostly hand from Paul Krassner, a New Left activist-journalist who later co-founded the Yippies with Abbie Hoffman, one of Bruce's truest and tragic disciples.) "This country, which magnanimously balms its conscience by helping Greek orphans and buying bonds for Israel, but manages to pass up the appeal for bail-bond money needed desperately by sixth-generation Negro Americans fighting for their human rights."

Unlike Mort Sahl, whose more professorial political satire was detached enough to make him a hero in liberal quarters, Bruce traveled wide and deep in this demimonde of outsiders and weirdos, drug and sex fiends, whores and musicians and artists—which meant he wasn't quite trustworthy. Still, this was where cultural change produced Abstract Expressionism, the Beat Generation, postwar jazz, noir film, and the new form Bruce himself was instrumental in shaping—standup comedy.

A descendant of Mark Twain's comic 19th-century lectures and Will Rogers's between-the-rope-tricks observations, arising in the 1950s from the entr'acte bits by cabaret and burlesque emcees, popularized by late-night TV talk shows like Jack Paar's and Steve Allen's, standup comedy turned on addressing the audience directly. This was a new tack—despite common misconceptions, vaudeville comics didn't traditionally address the audience, except for occasional asides. Most standup comics smoothed their new format with familiar themes, the stuff of blackout sketches and sitcoms, to win over audiences. Some, like Milton Berle, thrived on one-liners, many of them lifted from black comics at Harlem's Apollo Theater. Some, like Redd Foxx, machine-gunned raucous crowds with "blue" jokes. At his best, Bruce used sex and situations to draw audiences into the contours of his off-angle worldview. And for a few years he attracted bigger and better-heeled crowds as he surfaced toward the mainstream despite the assumption-jangling nature of much of his material.

Onstage, Bruce's intensity—the hooded eyes, the ready sneer, the darting movements—made him look almost like a human seismograph registering the tremors and tensions building beneath the surfaces of American society. And as often as not during his peak, Bruce's humor—or, at least, the audience's laughter—was as much or more cathartic relief from the satirical and verbal onslaught as it was spontaneous belly laugh. Not that he couldn't be funny: one-liners like "My mother-in-law broke up my marriage: one day my wife came home early and found me in bed with her" stippled his routines like surreal signposts from the Borscht Belt, marking places listeners could ease up for at least a breath.

With Bruce, as with later counterculture heroes like Ken Kesey and Abbie Hoffman, part of the frisson for his hip followers was having to maintain their insider status by keeping pace with chameleonic shifts of attitude from the Leader—having to fight, without seeming to struggle, to stay On the Bus. It could be a rocky ride. Few non-cultists clambered aboard for long.

IN AN AMERICA WHERE CONFORMITY was the social norm, maybe it's no surprise that Bruce's life followed a course far beyond what most contemporary Americans considered the pale.

His mother was an erstwhile vaudevillian and performer-wannabe herself, he married a stripper, and he came to artistic maturity in the 1950s nightworld populated by America's disappeared characters—black jazz musicians, strippers and hookers, homosexuals, junkies and dopeheads, disaffected college students, straight men and women who wanted at least a glimpse of something else. He played to them, on them, with them, in his multifaceted psychological ways.

When his cult status grew big enough, the stories started about him and his "sick" humor. In May 1959, the *New York Times Magazine* brought his underground reputation to wide notice, as writer Gilbert Millstein primly warned, "The newest and in some ways the most scarifyingly funny proponent of significance is Lenny Bruce, a sort of abstract expressionist stand-up comedian paid $1750 a week to vent his outrage on the clientele."

By 1961, his troubles with the law started to overtake sick humor as the major theme in stories about him. In December 1962, he was busted by the Irish Chicago DA and largely Irish police, who were upset by his parodies of Catholicism; that followed back-to-back busts for obscenity in California. Soon his arrests escalated. It was easy pickings for The Man: Bruce was using methamphetamine, heroin, Benzedrine, you name it.

Like the subculture he spoke for and to, Bruce saw drug use as rejection of society's constraints and hypocrisy. After all, millions of Americans were using drugs—prescription and over-the-counter drugs for sleeping and waking and dieting and whatnot. So what was the big deal? In "Three Message Movies," Bruce muses about making a Hollywood film about a normal, law-abiding, suburban family that lays aside budget money for its drug needs. It wasn't the sort of advertising parody—the exchange "Isn't all marijuana the same?" "That's the mistake a lot of people make" is right out of a Madison Avenue spot about cigarettes—that a society believing marijuana use led to heroin addiction wanted to hear, however funny it might seem to hipsters.

By 1964, Bruce couldn't get work. His passport was voided, his New York cabaret license was revoked, and clubowners understood that if they hired him they risked being shut down or fined by the law. And so they didn't. His deepening involvement in court cases sapped his creativity: he made it his personal crusade to prove to the courts that his act, in its own words, was satire. He grew convinced he was being persecuted for poorly transcribed, randomly lifted, and out-of-context police versions of what he actually said. And so he marshaled strings of star witnesses, including Nat Hentoff, Ralph Gleason, and Kenneth Tynan, to testify that what he did was art. After all, he figured, Ginsberg and the Beats, even old James Joyce's *Ulysses* and D. H. Lawrence's *Lady Chatterley's Lover*, were either threatened with censorship or banned in the United States.

Bruce grew more and more obsessed with First Amendment law when work dwindled and disappeared and drugs became his life instead of his recreation. He argued with his lawyers about tactics and presentations, constantly hiring and firing them. He took over parts of trials himself; for one, as he tried to deliver what he really said before the jurors, the judge admonished them, and courtroom observers, not to laugh—an order the bailiff found hard to enforce. But that was earlier on. For a year and a half before he died, Bruce's increasingly ragged, rare performances outside courtrooms matched those within: he'd read from and rebut transcripts from his trials for obscenity. He was a trench-coated shadow lurking in the spotlight, an obsessive disjointed defender, a nonstop self-explainer; there were no laughs left. Junk had stripped him of his human power to connect; the law had used it to turn him inside out. How now to distinguish scam and reality, satire and transcript, performance and life?

Before he died, he had ballooned in weight and virtually sequestered himself in the Hollywood house that he kept redesigning while he was running out of money and working endlessly on unfinished and frequently incoherent legal briefs. The grimy black-and-white shots of his fat naked sprawling indignity, taken by a river of press photographers the LA cops happily let pass through the dead man's house, washed across front pages around America and the world.

14

Sweet Soul Music

> When Martin Luther King, standing on a platform, addressing
> an off-stage white society, says, "You don't have to love me to
> quit lynching me," he is disinfecting his doctrine of agape from
> sentimentality—from the notion of easy solutions by easy love.
>
> —Robert Penn Warren,
> "Who Speaks for the Negro?" (1965)

> To the white protagonists of this book ... Ray Charles was a
> god for almost the very reasons the White Citizens Councils had
> warned about: sex, barbarism, and jungle rhythms.
>
> —Peter Guralnick, *Sweet Soul Music* (1986)

As TRENT LOTT STRUGGLED to "repudiate" segregation 50 years after it
was outlawed, about the only point he left out of his incoherent counterattack is that he was a soul-music fan. Now, I don't know that he was,
but as a southern frat boy, he would have been ironically typical of the
initial audiences for Stax Records, the Memphis-based label whose music,
along with Motown's, helped transport cultural integration to a broader
plain. Good ol' boys who wouldn't eat with "the colored" steadfastly
booked fledgling southern soul acts year after year, providing steady
income and a tour circuit before singers like Carla Thomas and Otis
Redding found their ways into America's mainstream.

For so they did, in that era of hope and recovery, of reopening possibilities after the McCarthyite witchhunts and hysteria had narrowed America's
options. By 1965, the year after the first landmark Civil Rights Act, when
optimism seemed to permeate the economy, the culture, the scent of the
air—when the false dawns and cataclysms forming on the distant horizon,
presaging the long twilight of Thomas Pynchon's *Vineland*, were still fist-
sized bad dreams—Motown, a black-owned independent record label
rocketing from outsider to insider status, was already a top-of-the-pops
(read white crossover) hitmaking factory. In the mid-1960s, it suddenly

seemed that black Americans owned the top of the pop charts, breaking out of their longtime racial enclave of rhythm and blues. In July 1964, "Where Did Our Love Go," cooing, lightweight pop by the Supremes, elbowed Dean Martin out of the *Billboard* number one American slot. Just as suddenly, it seemed, black entertainers zoomed from occasional to continual sightings on TV, especially teen-oriented music programs like *Hullabaloo* and *Shindig* and those hosted by Dick Clark and Les Cole.

Over the next couple of years, in a trend started by the British Invasion bands, the idioms of black singers' hits, from "What'd I Say" and "Do You Love Me" to "Respect" and "Midnight Hour," became a core part of the shared language of largely white garage bands across the land. For a few years there, it seemed like Dr. King's dreams were being enacted in the arena of popular culture. As historian Peter Guralnick writes in *Sweet Soul Music*, "It was as if the rhythm and blues singer, like the jazz musician and professional athlete before him, were being sent out as an advance scout into hostile territory." It looked like the civil rights movement—which had always deployed the church music that gave birth to soul for its uplifting anthems and rallying cries; whose leaders, from King to Malcolm X, moved masses with the same churchy cadences that soul singers finessed—might infuse a new generation via the genetic structure of American popular culture, white and black, right down to the grassroots levels of homemade entertainment.

This had never happened before in quite the same way. In early jazz, the best white players like Bix Beiderbecke and guitarist Eddie Lang worked with black innovators; Beiderbecke jammed with Louis Armstrong, and in 1928–29 Lang (born Salvatore Massaro) recorded duets with Lonnie Johnson, his great black counterpart; to avoid appearing interracial, Lang was credited as "Blind Willie Dunn." Jimmie Rodgers, the Singing Brakeman and godfather of modern country music, learned to play guitar and sing the blues from a black railroad man. Before the war, the Swing Era produced countless young white wannabes who lifted black jazz innovations and styles and then proceeded to stardom. In the postwar era, doo-wop found blacks and Italians synthesizing similar elements in abutting neighborhoods on the streetcorner hangouts of the lower classes. Rock and roll was essentially rhythm and blues, as the black style (formerly lumped under "race" music) was dubbed by the white executives running *Billboard*'s charts, with a rockabilly twist. Soul music, however, was different: it had few white stars. And yet, as the film *The Big Chill*'s best-selling nostalgic soul soundtrack demonstrated in the 1980s, the spectrum of sounds soul offered in its heyday captured young white American ears on a scale that foreshadowed (and would only be rivaled by) hip-hop for later generations.

To me, the Supremes sounded like black cotton candy—exactly what Berry Gordy Jr., Motown's founder and maximum leader, wanted. (In

New York, even "white" AM radio stations spun slices of black music, and at the far right of the dial were "black" stations like WWRL and WLIB, and after midnight came the erratic clear-channel stations from around the country, crackling over the transistor radio hidden beneath the covers pressed to your ear.) But I was drawn ineluctably to the springy, powerful bass lines and drums driving the songs. The tensile rhythm sections produced a chug-a-lug of interlocking parts often buried beneath layers of vocal schmaltz and period-piece echo and overblown orchestration. (It was rumored that there were 2 by 4s stomping through "Baby Love" to make sure white Americans could learn to feel the backbeat—a cultural twist I remembered years later in Perugia, when I watched a churchful of enthusiastic Italians at a gospel music concert by African American groups clap resoundingly on the one and three.)

Hits—mainstream hits made for white teenyboppers—were Motown's raison d'être, and its stuff sounded transparently like what it was—assembly-line product. Now, the history of American pop is stuffed with songs written to imitate hits; that sums up the role of Tin Pan Alley. But Gordy made Motown self-generating, self-sufficient. He hired songwriters and producers, and at the weekly production meetings held votes to decide which songs sounded most like potential hits; they'd make it to the release schedule. In that context, it shouldn't be surprising how repetitive the Motown Sound could get. There were exceptions: Smokey Robinson and the Miracles, whose material and arrangements were usually hipper; Martha and the Vandellas, who unlike the Supremes slashed and burned on "Dancing in the Streets" and "Heat Wave"; The Four Tops, who essentially kept recording the same old song (an egregious example of Motown's prefab product) made irresistible by Levi Stubb's charismatic gospel shouting and some of the funkiest bass and drum parts on the label. Ironically, the sameness of the material crafted for each artist conveyed a lesson that soul, molded from blues and gospel and jazz, could teach, a lesson as applicable to bebop as hip-hop: what mattered more than stylistic range was emotional power and technical finesse in its variations.

Years before the Supremes' triumph, the press had been snuggling up to Motown and Berry Gordy Jr. The son of a southern immigrant-entrepreneur with a large close-knit family, Gordy started Motown, after failing at other ventures, with money borrowed from the family credit fund (all the Gordys used this for their business start-ups). Motown grew rapidly from its 1958 launch, and Gordy spread the company vertically across buildings on West Grand Boulevard. He encouraged a family-style feeling (with many of his actual relatives at top jobs) in the informal day-to-day operations; it yielded big benefits.

Set in Detroit, the city's only significant record label, Motown attracted a formidable but overlooked pool of local black talent of all musical stripes. There were jazz musicians and modified doo-woppers, songwriter and producer wannabes, kids who wanted to be stars—they all hung out in the connected stretch of little buildings that housed Motown's operations. There was the recording studio, a converted garage that usually ran 24/7 as producers lined up to record their demos for the Friday production meetings. There was the array of offices for ever-expanding departments: the charm school, which taught poise, right down to how to sit; the booking agency, which handled all Motown's acts; spaces for tutorials in dance steps and fashion and image-making; Quality Control, which judged the hit potential of each week's production output and culled likely winners for the big Friday meetings.

While they swept floors and answered phones and typed and oohed and ahhed huddling in the hallways, young Motown wannabes absorbed the surroundings like Hollywood contract players hoping to be stars: here they could learn, be remade, reborn into the record biz—which, after all, had supplemented boxing and other sports as possible paths into mainstream American life, culture, and economy, something the movies had yet to do for them. And if Gordy paid most of his salaried employees comparative peanuts, and some of them not at all, well, he also, like a benevolent paternalist, oversaw an open, competitive shop where anyone could in theory (and often enough in fact, just like the larger American mythology, to make the myth credible) rise to the highest levels. His employees believed. In book after book, interview after interview, the constant refrain from everyone involved, however disaffected, repeats how the family feeling shaped the corporate structure, reiterates the intimacies and give-and-take of the constant creative flow. Motown was the black corporate equivalent of garage-band heaven, a garage label, the cousin of hundreds of backyard operations that sprang up in the postwar era to chase that latest new American dream: the hit single.

In service of that dream, Gordy replicated the Hollywood studio system, itself an adaptation of the auto industry's assembly line, annexing functions to his label in ways no one else had, to attain total control, a total product. Is it any wonder so much of it seemed interchangeable?

Gordy's unbending will, his dream to take the white pop market, powered Motown. Other black-owned labels, from prewar Black Swan to postwar Duke-Peacock in Houston and Vee Jay in Chicago, had produced great music but rarely broke it beyond black audiences; even though Vee Jay was one of Gordy's early distributors, signed the Italian doo-wop group the Four Seasons, and had released the first Beatles album in the United States, one of its owners ended up working for Gordy. As Nelson George, author of several books on Motown, explains in his *Death of Rhythm and Blues*, "Motown promoted Gordy as an affirmative, unthreatening symbol of black capitalism, one as acceptable in the New York Times as on the cover of *Ebony*." He had the perfect double image for showbiz: he was street (he'd hustled at pool halls and seethed with attitude) and middle class (his family was a hive of upward mobility). And he was himself talented, not just a suit. He'd written hits like "Reet Petite" and "Higher and Higher" for Jackie Wilson, the brilliant singer mired in soppy material and gooey arrangements by white handlers like Mitch Miller, the long-tenured head of pop music at Columbia Records.

The first record Gordy cut at his Hitsville Studios in 1960, the breeding place for what he dubbed "The Sound of Young America," was titled "Money (That's What I Want)." Thanks to his shrewd grasp of the music business and the culture, along with his paternalistic sense of company finances, over the subsequent decades he'd get plenty.

The national marketplace he sized up was still generally balkanized, serviced by small mom-and-pop retailers and regional distributors. Only a couple of the major labels and larger indies like Atlantic had national distribution pipelines; the rest was patch-quilt. The sprawling country was only slowly losing its longtime, sharply defined regional identities to the emerging mass media; it teemed with hundreds if not thousands of local subcultures, each with its own musical spins. Thanks to technological advances like the relative cheapness and portability of tape recording equipment, a kind of speculative bubble inflated the number of independent labels. Would-be producers wrote songs, put together sessions, recorded them, and peddled the results to a label or distributor. If a hot DJ broke your record and rode it—a process lubricated by payola, which small and large labels and distributors alike employed according to their resources—other local and regional DJs might well pick it up, and it could turn into a hit. In a society touting Organization Men, this life was a leap of faith into a crapshooting world where fame and glory and money could roll in and roll out with the same blitheness, where sex and drugs and creativity weren't stuffed into gray flannel suits, where the factory whistle put out a backbeat that, if you were lucky, would be yours. Conmen and hipsters and geniuses rubbed mohair-suited shoulders in a demimonde that rejected the square world that rejected them.

A fledgling indie-label operator needed a few traits. First was the "ears," that combo of instincts, training, and luck to spot a potential hit. Then there was grit: you had to be willing to bet your financial life over and over on recording a hit, getting it pressed, finding listeners and buyers. Maybe most important of all was access to deeper pockets. Collecting from regional distributors, who could coax airplay out of DJs that would up demand and sales, even on a hit single, was a difficult if not impossible task, and busted many or most independents. As you might expect, a black independent label head needed more of all these qualities than his white counterparts. Gordy had them. He understood early, for instance, that his newborn operation would be choked by the failure of Chess and other regional distributors to pay, and negotiated a national distribution deal with a major label instead. Moves like that certified Gordy as The Great Black Hope, and he cast his company as a vehicle for others; talent, which basically meant hitmaking ability, was the only currency that mattered at Motown.

That currency Motown produced in abundance. Between 1960 and 1979, it racked up more than a hundred top ten hits—more than 30 at number one—on the pop charts, the white listening gauges of where the real money flowed in the music industry. But Gordy's ambitions soon outstripped merely an enviable stream of chart-toppers. How many black acts before the Supremes had raked in big bucks playing the mob-owned Copacabana in New York or the mob-related hotels in Vegas? Virtually none. But that direction meant the already lightweight trio learned old standards with typical old-fogey charts. To my friends, the "Sound of Young America," as Gordy had dubbed his company, had become the sound of our parents, slightly modified.

Gordy had tapped into big money, somewhat ironically following the paths to mainstream stardom staked out for the rock and roll era by Elvis Presley and Colonel Tom Parker, Presley's greedy manager. And he made sure his people made no public missteps. Chuck Berry could be busted under the Mann Act at the height of his popularity. Jack Johnson and Joe Louis and Berry could all be bedeviled by the IRS. None of that broke Motown, despite the inevitable proliferation of sex and drugs in the West Grand Boulevard buildings after the money started rolling in and the IRS investigations inevitably followed.

GORDY WAS INCISIVE: he understood the crossover potential of black music but buttressed it with artist development, keeping acts on contract even for years until they landed a hit. But he was simultaneously a throwback to bad old practices black (and many white) artists had faced with white label owners since the industry's inception. Motown stars had apparently unlimited expense accounts, but in fact they were charged by the label for everything from recording and tour costs to wardrobes. Their royalty rates were extremely low to nonexistent; Motown didn't bother to issue statements. And Gordy controlled the finances of many of his stars right down to their bank accounts, which needed his co-signatures on checks. Then there were his strict divisions of labor: few Motown artists, aside from Smokey Robinson, were allowed to be songwriters or producers, and vice versa. There were the low salaries. There was the way he schmoozed the black DJs in the early days, when he needed them to put his product across, then slid to the white side of the aisle. (No black-power spokesperson, Gordy did start a short-lived label—one of the 39 he'd own—to release speeches by the likes of Dr. King.) Overall, Gordy's tactics were no better and often worse than those of white label owners like the Chess Brothers, or Syd Nathan, whose King Records became the ambivalent home of James Brown's soul revolution.

This stuff started to come out in the late 1960s, when the lawsuits began. Following the Detroit riots of 1967, Motown's music diverged in several directions. The Supremes, especially Diana Ross, now Gordy's lover and primo star, kept heading further into traditional showbiz.

Meanwhile, Norman Whitfield, a new young producer who had risen through the Motown ranks, was influenced by the riots as well as the sounds of Jimi Hendrix and Sly and the Family Stone; he edged the Temptations into socially relevant, psychedelic funk like "Cloud 9" and "Ball of Confusion," with improbable success. Then the shouting started. Holland–Dozier–Holland, Motown's key early hitmakers by then promoted to central positions, sued Gordy and the label. Angered by the ever-increasing time, money, and perks Gordy lavished on Diana Ross at their expense, other artists sued, or left the label, or both. Gordy's shoddy contractual practices, which let Motown cream not only off the top but the middle and even bottom of everything that happened at the label, began to surface.

The Jackson Five saved Motown from this first wave of deterioration via back-to-back hits that made them huge stars. But in negotiating contracts with iron-willed Joe Jackson, the clan's monstrous patriarch, Gordy pulled the same sorts of lowball stunts he'd built into his label's practices. By the late 1970s, Joe wanted his boys out of Motown, and signed them to Epic, a wing of Columbia Records, for comparatively huge advances and guarantees. Gordy was left to haggle about Motown's ownership of the Jackson Five name; the group became the Jacksons. And Motown the recording company was a hollowed-out shell.

In fall 1968, Gordy moved to Hollywood, and with his move Motown in Detroit lapsed into a vestigial operation, though Hitsville was officially open until 1975. The shift inevitably changed Motown's nature; whatever was left of the camaraderie and improvising informality died with Hitsville. But now Gordy wanted to conquer Hollywood, to make movies and TV, where the real money lay. Ross, his manipulative paramour, the would-be diva who graduated from Supreme to soloist, was his focus: he wanted to transform America's black sweetheart into a movie star, transfer his Svengali touch to the silver screen. It didn't work in *Lady Sings the Blues*, which miscast Ross as Billie Holiday, or in *Mahogany*, a muddled, turgid mess directed de facto by Gordy himself, or in *The Wiz*, for which Ross insisted on playing a ludicrous Dorothy. (She had by then broken up with Gordy after having his child.) Still, the royalties from all those earlier hits kept rolling into Gordy's Jobete publishing company, to the tune of millions per year, as he licensed scads of songs in the pop marketing explosion of the early 1980s, when Michael Jackson bought the Beatles catalog and licensed "Revolution" to Nike for its ads. Gordy, after all, was Michael's mentor. Remember the California raisins singing "I Heard it Through the Grapevine"?

FOR ME, THE REAL LURE AT MOTOWN was the backing musicians, a long-faceless shambling outfit who, unbeknownst to most outside Hitsville, called themselves the Funk Brothers. Aside from a couple of names gleaned from music and fan magazines and DJs and such, all we knew was that this floating crew of musicians was responsible for the propulsive sounds that outshone the vocals on so many Motown releases. Bassist James Jamerson was a hero for musician wannabes like me long before we knew his name; we could hear his afterimages in white bassists from Paul McCartney to the Grateful Dead's Phil Lesh.

During 2002, *Standing in the Shadows of Motown*, a documentary offshoot of the book by Alan Slutsky about the Funk Brothers, came out at a few theaters. Combining old footage with "recreations" and interviews with survivors, it also serves up musical segments featuring the band, which sounds terrific, backing a motley array of vocalists that includes Joan Osborne, Bootsy Collins, Ben Harper, Meshell Ndegeocello, and Chaka Khan.

The movie codifies and augments the information that only slowly leaked out about these people who controlled Motown's pulse. Most of the couple of dozen musicians involved hailed from the South, had come north with families looking for work at the auto plants, as southern blacks had done since the days of Henry Ford. So Detroit simmered sounds from raw country to urban sophisticate, and jazz thrived, yielding a crop of top-tier as well as lesser musicians during the postwar era. The Funk Brothers were among them: their members had played with Charlie Parker, Dizzy Gillespie, Miles Davis, Sarah Vaughan, Dinah Washington, John Coltrane, and a few hundred other jazz stars. Drummer Benny Benjamin backed Bird and Ray Charles, Muddy Waters and Chuck Berry. Pianist Joe Hunter worked to make his left hand like Rachmaninoff's and Art Tatum's.

Once you stripped the voices off Motown songs, you heard a tightly tuned rhythm machine, its camshaft rotating pistons in a chug-a-lug pattern of syncopated parts that put out enormous horsepower. At the heart pulsed Jamerson, one of this documentary's dead, unheralded stars. Born on Edisto Island in the Carolinas, Jamerson made his first diddley bow—the long-standing homemade string instrument rural southern blacks trained on, which in this case was a string and a bowed stick that the boy stuck down an anthole "and made the ants dance." Using one picking finger—most bassists use two or three—Jamerson developed his innovative attack, complex lines that dance within their patterns, subdivide time, create anticipation, build tension, and release into the rhythmic moving bottom of pop music, an unpredictable camshaft that somehow delivered more thrust. Harnessing the temporal creativity fostered by bebop and developed on bass by Oscar Pettiford and Charles Mingus to pop music, Jamerson seemed utterly free. Where he placed notes mattered intensely; they surrounded the beat, stuttered across it, loped with an exhilaration that was undeniable, uplifting—soul, the sheer joy of a self-assertive imagination cavorting across a musical canvas that somehow magically freed the listener as well.

In 1965, when the Motown Tour went to Britain, the musicians, generally unknown, were to their astonishment greeted by a James Jamerson Fan Club.

The idea that jazz sophistication and blues fervor could meld into popular music was the legacy of Atlantic Records, that feisty indie that became a major label on the strength of R&B and soul, then eventually signed the Rolling Stones and Led Zeppelin. In its pioneering days of the 1940s and 1950s, when it was one of the premier labels putting out jazz and rhythm and blues, Atlantic developed a methodology for its recording sessions: take an R&B vocal star like Big Joe Turner; hire jazz musicians for their range, creative spark, and reading skills, drawing again and again from a familiar rotating cast to encourage interplay and improvisation; put together charts and rehearse; have the bluesy or gospelly singer weave through them. Voila! Jerry Wexler (who as a *Billboard* editor had coined the term rhythm and blues) and Ahmet Ertegun, Atlantic's chief honchos, had essentially copied this recipe from Ray Charles, who had stirred it even in his early days as a somewhat colorless Nat King Cole imitator, and heated it to fever pitch with churchy sounds gone sinful on 1950s classics like "I Got a Woman" and "What'd I Say." Compared with most jazz recording of the time, which was low-budget and haphazard and further attenuated by widespread use of drugs like heroin, the process was surprisingly precise, well-tooled, and organized, and yielded artistically fruitful as well as profitable results.

Gordy adapted the Atlantic model to his Motown style. He hired the core of his studio crew in 1958, and kept adding (and occasionally subtracting) as time went by. He put most of them on exclusive contract; they flouted him by playing at jazz dives and strip joints, the kind of places where everyone packed heat. (Strip joints were staples of 1950s jazz life, when other gigs dried up. It was in that milieu that Lenny Bruce met the jazz musicians who were his earliest fans.) In the movie a couple of the Brothers point out in the movie how rhythms they cut in the studio came from gigging with Lottie the Body, an exotic dancer who'd worked with Count Basie—especially Afro-Cuban rhythms, like the sinuous lick structuring "I Heard It Through the Grapevine." There's footage of Joe Hunter digging into bebop piano, and Joe Messina wailing bebop guitar on a 1955 Soupy Sales TV show; from their jazz gigs, the Funk Brothers transported voicings and melodies and lines into the Snake Pit, as they called the converted garage that was Hitsville's studio. "When the producers would hear those jazz changes, they'd say, 'That's hip,'" recalls one. And Motown may well have been the only label outside Atlantic to feature vibes, a jazz instrument, on pop hits.

The Funk Brothers were overwhelmingly African American, but there were longtime white participants, like guitarist Messina. "They used to call us the Oreo cookie guitar section," he reminisces during the film; for years, Motown's three session guitarists sat in black–white–black order. When Detroit erupted into its 1967 riots, another in the series that flashed across the country during those years, the Funk Brothers hung together: emerging from the studio, their workplace and prison, to a city in flames, the black musicians looked out for their white colleagues—their friends. Music, the intensity of prolonged side-by-side creative work under factory conditions, forged a bond that the movie periodically, to its credit, manages to capture without lapsing into sentimentality. It was the musicians' meshing at several levels, after all, that showed in Motown music's ease and power; their mutual respect was clear in the ways they wove around each other's parts. They created those parts, mostly, revamping sketchy arrangements into head Count Basie-style charts—arrangements improvised in the studio. Giggling among themselves as they worked out the next session's ideas, they locked their pieces into staggered place, thickened chords, enhanced the syncopations and slinky beats that Motown rode to hitdom.

In the late 1960s, Marvin Gaye began agitating to do a more involved brand of music that reflected the decaying reality of Detroit and America; when Gordy agreed, in 1970 Gaye cut "What's Going On," giving the Funk Brothers their first unrestricted shot at foregrounding their musicianship within Motown. Their jazz chords came up front, foreshadowing a new kind of soul that thrived in the early 1970s via producer–songwriters like Philadelphia's Gamble and Huff. For the first time, too, the musicians got credit on the album sleeve. At their peak, they might pull down between $25,000 and $60,000 a year, peanuts compared to what Ross or Gordy were raking in. So inevitably they cut tracks for other Detroit studios and risked getting canned to do it: Motown paid informers to shadow them, and fined or fired them when they got caught. The pressure on them was awesome: studio work rolled on continuously, and they were typically expected to complete four songs per three-hour session. By the late 1960s, they hid out in a nearby funeral parlor to escape the endless sessions.

WHEN THE BEATLES AND THE ROLLING STONES first hit the United States, their repertoire was mostly American roots music and Motown. They enthusiastically translated the complex Motown charts into arrangements for four or five musicians of middling ability–extracting the sound, as it were, to a rock quartet. This was like handing out keys to a musical kingdom, and numbers among the most lasting cultural effects of the British Invasion. Suddenly anyone in a garage or basement could take a crack at that irresistible Motown groove—and, in fact, the growing spectrum of soul music. From Chicago, Curtis Mayfield warbled his sweet calls to social awareness, like "People Get Ready" and "Keep on Pushin'"; his guitar style, with its hammer-ons and pull-offs running three-note moving chords behind his vocals, created the template Hendrix would psychedelicize. Otis Redding spearheaded Stax's penetration of white northern audiences; the second wave, led by Isaac Hayes, reaffirmed the music's blackness. On Atlantic, which pushed forward into soul with Solomon Burke and Wilson Pickett, Aretha Franklin, Ray Charles' truest heir, brought gospel jazz directly and fervently into soul, rocking her piano with a largely white southern rhythm section from Muscle Shoals, Alabama, reiterating and embodying the lessons Charles had laid out for white and black postwar American youth.

As Nelson George wrote,

> Motown and Stax were the twin towers of sixties soul, feeding ideas and energy into house parties and love scenes of all colors. Though connected by their simultaneous success, the two companies were total opposites. Motown in Detroit was black-owned, secretive, rigidly hierarchical, totally committed to reaching white audiences, with production styles that ultimately made its producers, writers, and musicians the real stars of the Motown sound. Stax in Memphis was initially white-owned, easily accessible to outsiders, filled with leaders of all kinds. Its records, the offspring of musical miscegenation, appealed primarily to black Americans.

Both relied heavily on black radio, at least at first, to build audiences.

Evolution, in culture as in biology, takes parallel paths to try to guarantee the survival of new attributes. At Stax in Memphis, a southern town more insidiously segregated even than Detroit and other northern cities, blue-collar white kids ran errands, tended the record store in the lobby of the old movie theater that doubled as the label's studio, boxed records, moved equipment, and learned—like their black counterparts at Motown, like kids at countless record stores across black and white and brown America—to analyze what made a hit. The foundations of the Stax sound were related to yet different from Motown's: a mingling of country and blues played with jazzy licks the young Stax players picked up from the local black musicians they idolized. It was a blend kicking around the South since World War II; its avatars included rockabilly and Chuck Berry.

By 1968, *Time* magazine ran a characteristically hyperventilating (and characteristically late) cover story opening, "Has it got soul? Man, that's the question of the hour. If it has soul, then it's tough, beautiful, out of sight. It passes the test of with-itness. It has the authenticity of collard greens boiling on the stove, the sassy style of the boogaloo in a hip discotheque, the solidarity signified by 'Soul Brother' scrawled on a ghetto storefront. . . . Soul is a way of life, but it is always the hard way. Its essence is ingrained in those who suffer and endure to laugh about it later." It was the sort of insufferable condescension *Time* had displayed, in turn, about jazz musicians, Beat writers, protest singers, hippie rock and rollers.

Contrast Guralnick, writing of a sound drenched in sex and love that

was generated as a cultural expression of the drive toward racial integration after a decade of demonstrations, attempted school desegregations,
backlashes, National Guard and federal marshal face-offs, battles over
housing, and job discrimination: "Musically . . . soul remains the story of
how a universal sound emerged from the black church. Historically it
represents another chapter in the development of black consciousness,
similar to the Harlem Renaissance, say, in its championing of negritude,
but more widespread in its impact. . . . It is the story of blacks and whites
together . . . of the complicated intertwinings of dirt-poor roots and
middle-class dreams, aesthetic ambitions and social strivings, the anarchic
impulse and the business ethic."

Soul music did give symbolic voice to the cultural changes in play. The
Atlantic and Stax-Volt varieties especially recombined black blues and
white blues, aka country music. The house bands at Stax-Volt and Atlantic
were integrated. Was soul music the cultural objective correlative of the
civil rights movement, a culmination finally come, thanks to the Kennedy
assassination and Lyndon Johnson's arm-twisting (which would lose the
South and many northern blue-collar areas for the Democrats for generations)? If Motown acts could play the Copacabana and Las Vegas, wasn't
that the American Dream?

It was, for Berry Gordy Jr., who by all accounts, including his own, was
utterly oblivious to the world around him. The civil rights movement
might have been peaking as Motown artists dominated the charts. Detroit
might have been going up in flames while Motown was beginning to
stagger and weave under Gordy's increasingly distanced paternalism. The
Vietnam War might have been radicalizing and killing thousands of
youngsters, but Gordy barely noticed what was going on beyond his own
adroitly jiggered bottom lines.

Stax, run paternalistically by white owners Jim Stewart and Estelle
Axton, was forced to stay in tune with changing times. In 1965, Al Bell
took over as the label's head of promotion. At first he seemed a token
black figure chosen partly as public relations, to balance Motown's black
ownership. But for artists like Isaac Hayes and David Porter, who would
create the second wave of Stax hits, Bell turned out to be secret hero, the
Jesse Jackson of in-house politics who changed the company's direction—
until it blew up.

IN THE LATE 1960s, the dream of integration was under attack. The 1965
Watts riots, which for many shocked Americans had buttressed the argu-
ment for integration, gave way to an apparently open-ended series of riots
and the rise of Black Power and figures like Malcolm X and H. Rap
Brown, who rejected the entire project of racial integration. On July 24,
1967, the riots in Detroit left 43 dead, 7,000 arrested, 1,200 homes and
businesses destroyed. Then as throughout the 1960s, it sometimes seemed
as if history was answering to earlier events: in 1943, as southern blacks

streamed into the converted auto factories for wartime labor, 25,000 whites rioted when 3 blacks at the Packard bomber engine plant got upgraded, leaving a wake of 35 dead, 29 of them black, almost all of them killed by a police force shot through with transplanted southern whites.

As African Americans disagreed ever more violently among themselves about what was to be done in America, a more complex cultural equation between visible black Americans and the mainstream came into view. Was it coincidence that James Brown, after hitting the charts and the radio (and having white teens sing along) with "Say It Loud (I'm Black and I'm Proud)," in the idiosyncratic, fiercely compelling syncopated funk he invented, announced that he supported Richard Nixon, the first benefi-ciary of the GOP's new southern strategy, aimed at hiving off white blue-collar, suburban, and southern voters via code words about simmer-ing racial issues? Is it odd or representative that Soul Brother Number One identified with the new ideology of black capitalism, its insistence on self-reliant separatism? How to reconcile this with the fact that at the same time Aretha Franklin, the daughter of Detroit's flamboyant and strong-voiced Reverend C. L. Franklin and, as George writes, "an heir to a legacy of redemption through music," was embodying how white America was open to the black cultural experience more directly than ever before? And what to make of how Jimi Hendrix and Sly and the Family Stone appealed to overwhelmingly white audiences but had little to no black following, with Hendrix especially being dismissed as a white wannabe, blackballed by black radio?

By 1969, as Hendrix was being played solely on FM rock radio, AM radio was changing. WLIB, one of New York's white-owned "black" stations, the "natural" homes of soul music, was sold to black owner Percy Sutton, who immediately moved the offices out of Harlem. "White" stations like WMCA and WABC had already stirred dollops of black music into their playlists. By 1971, the Harvard Report, commissioned by Columbia Records to study the rise of black markets again, observed that the CBS roster had two black artists, Sly and Santana, a Chicano-led outfit whose inclusion indicates both the scarcity of major-label black acts and the still-potent American color bar. It also observed that 30 percent of top 40 records crossed over from black radio. Surprise—by 1980, Columbia had signed 125 black acts.

In 1972, Al Bell signed Richard Pryor and Jesse Jackson to record for Stax and oversaw Wattstax, a black Woodstock at the site of 1960s riots. It was a bid for a black-power stance, an overt change apparently reflecting the power shift from Stax's white founders to its black managers and artists. But the venture was partly financed and distributed in movie and album form by Columbia. Schlitz poured in additional money to keep ticket prices to $1; naturally, the concert sold out. The vast Los Angeles Coliseum hosted all Stax's stars, after an opening invo-cation by Jackson. In the movie, intercut between scenes from the show, are interviews with Watts dwellers, overwhelmingly in the funky, offhandedly in-your-face style that was already as clichéd a hallmark of black-power rhetoric as *Time*'s stilted homages. Still, the concert raised close to $100,000 that was donated to causes from the Sickle Cell Anemia Foundation to Jackson's Operation PUSH. At the same time, Bell followed Gordy's drive to diversify—movies, a Broadway play, a basketball franchise, none of which paid off in anything but flash. Back in Memphis, as Guralnick reports, many white members of the Watts family saw this as "a direct affront: 'Whose cause was it—Wattsax or Al Bell's? Were they doing it for the people in LA, or were they doing it to promote Al Bell in LA? And what did they ever do for Memphis? Not a goddamn thing.'" Shades of Berry Gordy.

Two years after the Harvard Report, Columbia head Clive Davis was dismissed; the label said for expense account violations, but speculation claimed he'd been countenancing drug and other payola for radio DJs. As they had in the 1950s, the payola scandals would rapidly spread and help wipe Stax out by the late 1970s.

But even in the early 1970s, when Stax was vying with Motown for first place in album sales, cultural trends signaled changes on the horizon—like the surging, separatist movie genre dubbed blaxploitation, cartoony action flicks with black-power subtexts aimed at black audiences. In 1970, *Sweet Sweetback's Baadasssss Song* launched the wave, with a soundtrack by Earth Wind and Fire; the gentle if firm push toward integration represented by Sidney Poitier was being ousted by black versions of Charles Bronson and Clint Eastwood. *Shaft*'s soundtrack by Isaac Hayes made him a superstar; Curtis Mayfield wrote one for Gordon Parks's *Superfly*. The number of black entertainers topping the *Billboard* charts crested between 1967 and 1973—oddly but tellingly, the period when indie labels processed the bulk of the music into the market.

By 1976, as American society recoiled from terrorism and thuggery devolved from 1960s radicals like SDS and the Black Panthers, the blaxploitation wave ran out and soul music calcified into mechanized disco. The 1960s had that aura of optimism, that may seem foolish in the cynical 21st century; by the 1970s, after the Kennedy–King–X assassinations, Altamont, Nixon's election and reelection, Kent State, and so on, that optimism was dead or dying, and the reconsolidation of power taking place across the society found analogs in the record industry. Mergers among the majors, and the absorption of indies, accelerated. FM radio was formatted in ways more like the vilified AM playlist style—a straitjacket even more securely tied today by limited corporate ownership—than the looser album-oriented FM of the late 1960s; stations were increasingly chain-owned, presaging today's near-monopoly situation in the "market." Payola scandals and federal trials for the sorts of practices that also roiled late Motown—counterfeiting records, shipping new releases to industry accomplices as "cut-outs" and collecting kickbacks off the books while the company lost money, very like a classic mob scam out of *Goodfellas*—punctured the industry with the disco collapse of the late 1970s. Flexing their distribution capacity, major labels manufactured an artificial sales bubble of a musically sterile form that was among Motown's linear descendants by overshipping records and posting them as huge paper profits; the scam blew up in their fiscal faces when returns of unsold goods from record stores swamped their fictionalized bottom lines with red ink.

Enron, anyone?

Disco was the product of the new black-music departments at the major labels, first formed in the early 1970s in response to the challenge posed by indies like Gordy. One result: black music, with rare exceptions, was again ghettoized within new-minted formats like "urban contemporary," but, unlike in the old days of "black" radio, the urban contemporary playlists were perforated with white "crossover" artists. This was not, however, a two-way street: black musicians were once again, as they had been up through the 1950s, expected to play for "their" market. To take just one example: Chic, synonymous with disco hits, formed as a rock and soul band. When their demos circulated around record companies and got them appointments, the jaws of the executives across the table inevitably slackened or dropped when guitarist Nile Rodgers and bassist Bernard Edwards strode in. "You guys did this tape? But you're black," was one standard response. "You should be doing disco." Years later, both musicians told me, "We finally gave up."

"Giving up" meant a string of hits, and lucrative production work injecting new and fresh ideas and sounds into a few established black stars like Diana Ross as well as reshaping the flagging careers of white artists like David Bowie and Jeff Beck; without Rodgers formulating her debut, the fledgling called Madonna could never have flown. Is it worth considering Michael Jackson's ongoing self-mutilating reconstruction, along with his superstardom and degeneration into tabloid fodder, as the most apt physical symbol of the America's neurotic focus on and confusion about race?

In the 1980s, musicians like Vernon Reid, guitarist from the hard-rock quartet Living Colour, and vocalist Cassandra Wilson helped form the Black Rock Coalition to publicly counter renewed ghettoization. A small upsurge of black rock bands—Fishbone, go-go bands from D.C. like Chuck Brown and the Soul Searchers—got a few moment's notice. But only with hip-hop's cultural impact would the pendulum start to swing back. It was a nice historical irony that the Sugar Hill Gang's first 1980 rap hit and harbinger of the future, "Rapper's Delight," used Chic's "Good Times" as its backing track. Within a couple of years the success of Sugar Hill records, a black-owned indie with widely rumored financial twists, spawned small rap-oriented labels. The cycle was ready to repeat.

part IV In the Garage

15

Bob Dylan

Here I sit so patiently
Waiting to find out what price
You have to pay to get out of
Going through all these things twice.
                                        —Bob Dylan

Forward, into the past!
                                        —Firesign Theater

EVERYONE KNOWS WHAT HAPPENED when Bob Dylan fronted an electric band at the Newport Folk Festival in 1965. Which is why August 3, 2001, saw 100 scribes from all over the country merging into a crowd of 10,000, inching by vehicle and foot through the narrow tourist-choked streets of the former center of the triangle slave trade later known for its wealthy "cottages"; while others rode water ferries from the sailboats and power boats anchored like ducklings around a mammoth cruise ship, sandwiched by the graceful suspension bridge connecting Newport to the mainland and Fort Adams. The pentagonal sandstone bastion with the recessed barred windows, built to protect Narragansett Bay in the 19th century, backed the big stage. At 5:30 P.M., to a standing and expectant sea of sun-soaked bodies who'd been hearing Aaron Copland's "Fanfare for the Common Man" and "Rodeo" pumped over the PA, half an hour late but right on time, the short guy in the silver shirt and black suit with the fake beard and wig topped by a tall white Stetson bounded onstage with his four black-clad bandmates. A punchy acoustic string-band version of an old folk blues called "Roving Gambler" got started. At 61, Dylan had returned to the scene of the crime.

Or maybe he hadn't, and not just because of Heraclitus, with whom Dylan would surely agree about feet and the same river twice. For the assembled multitude who had come to the fabled rock where the prophet had stood and been dishonored, it was, as it should have been, an Event;

they made the biggest one-day crowd the festival's had in years. For the enigmatic bard himself, his Cassandra streak and razor wit evident again after years of trying to banish or submerge them, his restless decades-long quest for something to believe in an implacable universe transformed by his art into an uneven but awesome legacy crucial to American popular culture (40-plus albums, 500-plus songs, 200-days-a-year of roadburn), back in Newport and gunning his rapid-fire way through the 90-minute-plus set of revamped classics and breaking out periodically into a smile, like Mona Lisa with the highway blues, it's impossible to say. Is the shaman onstage for the umpteenth time more or less likely than we are to know or care what this specific moment is supposed to mean? Is it just another turn in the maze he runs outside the Gates of Eden, looking for love, jubilation, transcendence, apocalypse, hope, death—an answer, an exit? How can you tell the dancer from the dance?

"I'm mortified to be onstage," Dylan told the *New York Times* in 1997, "but then again, it's the only place I'm happy. . . . I don't want to put on the mask of celebrity. I'd rather just do my work and see it as a trade."

As listeners snaked through the dozens of vendors' stands and past the stages, they brushed against everything from traditional hill tunes to country and rock and the confessional singer–songwriter mode that is now, after Dylan, usually thought of as folk music. One early act on the main stage rammed home a Led Zeppelin cover. It was all far, far indeed from the hallowed tale of 1965, in which Dylan led musicians from the Paul Butterfield Blues Band and the Blues Project, two early improvising rock groups, into a blistering version of his anti-Village folk scene screed, "Like a Rolling Stone," that drew such furious booing they soon split the stage.

Myth can be more fun and sharper-sighted than history, and even, as Dylan the mythmaker knows, truer. Over the years, variant accounts of 1965 Newport have surfaced. The standard version ultimately comes from Pete Seeger—though Dylan himself helped. Seeger was then the keeper of the folk-revival flame. According to this dominant form of the story, often embroidered and heightened by succeeding writers for effect, the booing was loud, spontaneous, and universal, as folk fans rejected Dylan's contemptuous noise, demanded a return to the authentic socially aware sounds he'd made his folkie bones with, songs like "The Times They Are A-Changin'." But others have suggested that the booing came largely from backstage, from Seeger and his cohorts, shocked by what they saw as treason—or from fans complaining about the crummy sound system—or even that there was no booing at all. Still others noted that Dylan had used electric instruments on his records; that on 1964's *Another Side of Bob Dylan* he abandoned overt political protest for Brechtian parables about tortured love and striated life, thus bolting from the mission Seeger saw as central to contemporary folk music; that "Like a Rolling Stone" was hitting the charts across America (ultimately to reach number two on the *Billboard* rankings) and AM radio was bending its sacred three-minute limit to air it; that you would have to have been deaf indeed to have been shocked by what Dylan was up to at Newport.

Whatever. After three electric and three acoustic tunes, he quit.

As he moved over the last four decades from protest singer to surrealistic prophet, from born-again Christian to born-again Jew, Dylan's life and music registered, however unwillingly or elliptically, his times. This is one reason people have interpreted his Mona Lisa–highway blues smile and his amphetamine/Beat attitudes in their own images. They've translated him into hero, antihero, sellout, savior, asshole, religious zealot, burnout, political radical, and artist. Unless it was useful to him, Dylan usually resented being reduced in rank from prophet (he has always credited divine inspiration for his work, and his most apocalyptic imagery rages with echoes of Blake and the Bible) to mere mirror-holder, and he has usually managed to translate himself anew—the protean artist. That is part of his genius, the soul linking his tangled life to his web of art—and, for that matter, his art to his audience.

So like the decade he symbolizes, Dylan today is many things to many people. He's an aging rock star composer of some of the most powerful and enduring songs of the century who loves the gypsy life of the road; a multimillionaire with an Elvis-like entourage who has an un-American lack of interest in personal hygiene; a double-talking celebrity with a ferocious sense of privacy who has spent most of his life in studios and on the road with his ears full—to varying degrees, depending on exactly when we're talking about—of the transcendent sounds he hears in his head, as well as the roaring sound of the star machinery and its need for lubrication. Such is the dilemma of any commercial artist. Pop culture is full of the tales. But few if any other pop songwriters have been considered for the Nobel Prize in Literature.

THE SLIGHTLY PUDGY 19-YEAR-OLD came to the 1961 Greenwich Village folk scene with a Woody Guthrie playbook on his knee, but he loved Buddy Holly's *Stratocaster* and Elvis Presley's raw Sun recording sessions and knew he wanted to be a star. He told Joseph Haas in 1965, "I was playing rock and roll when I was 13 and 14 and 15, but I had to quit when I was 16 or 17 because I couldn't make it that way, the image of the day was Frankie Avalon or Fabian, or this whole athletic supercleanness bit. . . . I discovered Odetta, Harry Belafonte, that stuff, and I became a folk singer." It was easier, he added, because you only had to perform by yourself on acoustic guitar.

It was easier, too, because rock and roll had been supplanted as the music of rebellion—and wherever young Bobby Zimmerman was going, dissatisfied rebellion was the propulsion. For collegians, the folk revival doubled with jazz as rock and roll's more intellectual cousin, its stopgap replacement, a more exotic form of the postwar rebellion that everywhere just below the crusts of mainstream America threatened to undam its hot lava flows. While Park Avenue debutantes chased jazz musicians for sexual whiffs and actual liaisons to catch the frisson of rulebreaking, folk music lent buttoned-down collegians perspectives so alien to their obvious privilege, so hard to find alternatives to in this era. The sullen, inchoate existentialist forms of rejection that gripped white America worried about its kids—gangs? juvenile delinquency? *West Side Story*? heavy petting? refusal to slip into society's slots?—made *Life* magazine stories on the Beats and their passive willingness to scrape by, bypass careers and families, revel in drugs and sexuality, and follow black jazz more alarming and all too much of a piece.

Their fears were well-grounded. Jazz and folk shared obvious magnetic attractions for the disaffected—and for some of the same reasons: outsiderness, an exotic and yet authentically human, American nature that wasn't accounted for, owned, coopted, or polluted by the mainstream culture in its values or goals. That these simplistic oppositions became even more illusory as the period unwound does nothing to deny their mythic power.

Pete Seeger spent the postwar era as a college-traveling troubadour, spreading the gospel of True Folk Culture wherever he went. An engaging performer, all gangly and earnest with ingratiating and often self-deprecating humor, Seeger had been blacklisted at the height of his career, and relegated to American culture's back forty, which he turned into the pastures of plenty, the fecund seedgrounds for the urban folk revival that was part of the great postwar American Renaissance.

As Dylan recalled his early days in New York to interviewer Bill Flanagan: "All these black guys would come up from south of the border and recite poetry in the park. Now they'd call them rappers. The best was a guy named Big Brown who had long poems. Each one was about fifteen minutes long. They were long, drawn-out badmen stories. Romance, politics, just about everything you could imagine was thrown into his stuff. He came out of Texas, I think, and he was in jail a lot. I always thought that was the best poetry I ever heard. Streetwise poetry. There were quite a few of those guys around in the sixties. I heard them at Mardi Gras, too. They were just brilliant speakers."

In 1961 Greenwich Village, the scene's lodestars included Seeger, Reverend Gary Davis, Dave Van Ronk, and, of course, Joan Baez. Everyone knows how Dylan screwed—and then screwed—Baez after she'd helped launch his career by acting as his scene patron and covering his songs. Most recently, David Hajdu's *Positively 4th Street* puts early 1960s Dylan into a pas-de-deuxing foursome with the Baez sisters, Joan and Mimi, and Richard Fariña, whose role is inflated to make him almost Dylan's artistic equal, a major initiator of folk rock. It's the latest twist on the creative and sexual intellectually charged soap opera that insiders retold and reinterpreted over the years with *Rashomon*-style variations.

By most accounts (and over four decades there have been plenty) Dylan early on cast himself—first in his mind's eye, then, after he'd established the myths, in fact—as a shadow observer hoboing through life, with his BO and irresistible charm and coldhearted focus and spew of genius. According to a lot of the witnesses, Dylan lives in introverted, near-constant turbulence, buffeted by internal as well as external winds and by his own creativity, which produces constant alienation. The chorus for this troubadour's life has many members. There are women who sing his praises, care for him, want to protect him; they include sincere Minnesota folkie madonnas, Village political sophisticates like Suze Rotolo, celebrities like Baez, and his apparently endless lovers from white groupies to black backup singers. There are ex-acolytes and musicians and business associates wailing the I-been-abused blues. There are core loyalists and friends. There are fawners, often drawn from the same pool as the abused. They all generally agree, though, that the Bob Dylan they know is an unbelievably private, often surprisingly inarticulate man with nearly unshakable drive and talent. In book after book about Dylan, the star of the show flickers like a strobed and ultimately elusive image through the crosscut glimpses of his intimates. The facts and tales pile up; the figure behind the screen seems to come into clearer focus but never quite emerges. In one recent biography, *Down the Highway*, Howard Sounes gropes for the "inner" Dylan and often comes away silly. Trying to extrapolate insight from Dylan's visual artwork collected in *Drawn Blank*, for example, Sounes writes, "Mostly Bob seemed to be alone in empty rooms. He often drew the view from his balcony, a view of empty streets, parking lots, and bleak city skylines."

Perhaps, as Sounes and others have asserted, Dylan has "conservative" beliefs, in contrast to, say, the leftish countercultures of the folk and rock scenes he galvanized without fully inhabiting. Or perhaps he simply has always desperately wanted privacy for himself and his family and friends. After all, how many of us have an A. J. Weberman ready to lurk outside our houses and dig, on a daily basis, through our garbage, and then publish the lunatic *Dylanology*? It does seem that Dylan, like most people, has a floating mishmash of an ad hoc personal code of morality. I've never really cared, and so as I plow through version after version of his life, each with its ways to carp, I wonder why Dylan is supposed to be different from any other complicated human. Is it because his art delivers such emotional rawnesss, such a heightened sense of self and surroundings, that people are disappointed when the man dances interminably?

David Hajdu's variants of the Dylan-Baez saga start with the young Baez sisters seeing Seeger in concert and getting their own guitars, then follow Joan to the thriving Cambridge folk scene, where she became a star with a recording contract. We view her through a novelistic collage of perspectives: Baez herself, those she'd already left behind in California, those watching her rise in Boston. This technique shapes the book's storytelling. We see Fariña, for instance, through Mimi's eyes as a basically lovable, if hurtful, rogue genius; through Joan's by turns as accomplice, potential seducer, and parasite. We watch Joan's Cambridge friends fret and fume at young Bobby Dylan's riding her to the top while Joan loves him blindly, and meet other Dylan lovers like Suze Rotolo and Sara Lownds, whom Dylan later married. We wonder why Mimi can't see how Fariña is using her to get to Joan, since nearly everybody else, including Joan, does, and we wonder if he'll succeed. And we hear the chorus of disharmony around the charged moment when Dylan abandoned his image as folksinger; we note that Joan idealistically spurns manager Albert Grossman and a major record label and Bob signs with both.

Evoking the long-standing theme that early Dylan was the parasite creation of the people around him, Hajdu writes: "By the spring of 1962, Suze and Bob had known each other for about six months and had grown close, despite Dylan's reluctance to reveal much about himself. He tested his songs on her, played Elvis records for her to hear, and brought her to Gerde's; she loaned him books of poetry and took him to CORE meetings. 'A lot of what I gave him was a look at how the other half lived—left-wing things he didn't know,' said Rotolo. 'He knew about Woody and Pete Seeger, but I was working for CORE and went on youth marches for civil rights, and all that was new to him. It was in the air, but it was new to him. And poetry, we read a lot of poetry together'—Lord Byron and Rimbaud, as well as playwrights, especially Brecht, 'a lot of Brecht.' As Dylan prepared to begin recording again, the failure of his first album still fresh, he focused on writing his own songs. Perhaps Albert Grossman was right: he was a poet. And Suze might have a point: social protest was in the air."

Aside from the sleek innuendo there's no news here: Rotolo's role was established long ago, and Dylan has always maintained that he became a protest singer because it's what was happening around him. His commitment to it was as an artistic form, not as a life's work. It's easy to see why, once he'd mastered it, he would, as he would again and again with people as well as ideas, move on. It's less easy to see, after all these years, why so many around him register shock or surprise when he does.

THE VILLAGE FOLKIES, in full creative coffeehouse flight, were generally leftish, middle class, longing for cultural authenticity and artistic purity, and interested in making something apart from the loathed world of commercial showbiz—everything Albert Grossman, the ex-Chicago clubowner now turned folk-scene maven, who would manufacture and manage acts from Peter Paul and Mary to The Band and Janis Joplin while building a world-class recording studio outside Woodstock, soon came to represent.

After *New York Times* critic Robert Shelton raved about Dylan at Gerde's in print, Columbia Records brass inked him. They wagered little money on his success, though; one reason they could sign up folkies with such alacrity was the low budgets needed to record and promote them. Dylan's debut cost $403 to cut and sold 4,200 copies—not Elvis, but not the debacle some writers have made it out, given the small numbers most jazz and folk discs sold then and now. Goldman, however, decided shrewdly that, since the bulk of the money in the music business came from publishing rights, he would market Dylan the Songwriter. And so, in mid-1962, Dylan signed a three-year deal with Witmark Music, which would publish 237 of his songs. And Goldman formed Peter Paul and Mary, whose primary function was to record Dylan tunes.

One of those, "Man on the Street," ended in a Brechtian stab at translating words into deeds, art into social action, Woody Guthrie style. And there were caustic political tracts like "John Birch Talking Blues," which CBS's censor forbade Dylan to play on the Ed Sullivan Show. He'd drilled into America's nerves, and controversy and publicity dogged him: when "Blowin' in the Wind" rode high on the charts in 1963, first *Newsweek*, then *Time*, revealed his real name and background, sneering, trying to undercut his credibility as a protester, much as they had sneered at Beats and jazz musicians. But Dylan got it from all sides. In 1964, he courted a "storm of criticism," said critic Ralph Gleason, for the surreally tinged, fierce love songs on *Another Side of Bob Dylan*. The kicker was "My Back Pages," where he takes leave of the folk-revival movement with a typically acid-etched, paradoxical goodbye to the black-and-white ideologies of the folk world, as he heads toward making art of the tumultuous riot where his inner and outer lives meet.

Folkies, like jazzers and much of the left, distrusted and often despised American popular culture. And yet commercial pop culture is precisely where Dylan dove headlong as soon as he could. Even before his fabled fiasco at the 1965 Newport Folk Festival, Dylan drew electric guitars and drums—the evil talismans of showbiz and commercial sellout—from his toy chest, where they'd been waiting alongside Harry Smith's *Anthology of American Folk Music*, Hank Williams, Little Richard and Elvis Presley.

In 1964, Nat Hentoff wrote in *The New Yorker*, "'He's got a wider range of talents than he shows,' (producer Tom) Wilson told me." Later Dylan told Hentoff, "I don't want to write for people anymore. You know—be a spokesperson . . . from now on I want to write from inside me." "My Back Pages" heralded the next year at Newport.

FORT ADAMS PARK IS ACTUALLY SEVERAL MILES from Freebody Park, where the Newport Folk Festival was originally held when George Wein, who founded the Newport Jazz Festival in 1954, and his then-partner Albert Grossman, who later managed the biggest names of 1960s rock, including Dylan, started it in 1959. It died after two years. In 1962, Wein hooked up with Pete Seeger and Theo Bikel, and by 1965 the revamped fest drew 71,000 people and sported a 64-page program with 40 ads. Folk music, the major record companies had realized, was big business. Still, each artist was paid a democratic $50 per show; profits funded the Newport Folk Foundation's promulgating of folk music and musicians. This is the basic model Wein's Festival Productions still follows for the immensely popular New Orleans Jazz & Heritage Festival, as does Seeger, whose wonderful annual Clearwater Hudson River Festival at Croton State Park has floated the sloop and its miraculous river cleanup since 1964.

After 1965, Wein tried to realign the Newport Folk Festival with the erupting forces of the post-Dylan world via acts like Buffalo Springfield, but in 1971 it shut and wasn't revived for fifteen years. Even as Dylan walked off the Newport stage in 1965 he was reaching the first pinnacle of his 40-year career, and had already transformed American popular culture. So many roads led to him and so many emerged from him that his main rivals as transformative agents in popular American music may be Louis Armstrong, Miles Davis, and Elvis Presley—and, like all of them, he drew recurrent abuse from fans who saw him as betraying his talent, abandoning the purity of his early days. But for Dylan, purity is a pointless abstraction; like St. Paul, he believes virtue is manifest only in being tested. "To live outside the law," warns one of his most famous ruthless lines, "you must be honest."

Dylan incarnates the Great American Songbook, its worst as well as its best. Another Woody Guthrie manque when he hit New York, he grew up on Buddy Holly and Little Richard. During the early 1960s, he absorbed the totemic *Anthology of American Folk Music*, the last generations of true folk musicians, the folk revivalists who flocked to Greenwich Village and Cambridge to Travis-pick guitars behind traditional ballads and Guthrie tunes and whatever else they'd picked up. He was a deadly mimic, and learned to phrase inimitably from blues and soul, though his voice was often ridiculed; his guitar skills, like Guthrie's, varied from painfully rudimentary to quite accomplished. His creative outbursts, the nonstop writing, tumbled all he heard and read and did into his increasingly high-torqued personalized songs; tapped by the shades of Blake and Rimbaud, he'd become a seer or shaman, a seismic artist who quavered to the times' deep rhythmic structures whether he willed it or not.

The Beatles and Rolling Stones survived past the British Invasion largely because they jumped on Dylan's millennial bandwagon, adapting his Jeremiah's cry, his truthteller's story forms, his sly ironies and probing sarcasm and haunted paradoxical loves; his far-reaching grasp of forms, his impossible phrasing, his poet's fecund sense of language in play for its beauties and possibilities. They gave him back the gift of American rock and its pop and roots forebears; he gave them art. In the process, they morphed from talented cover bands of American roots music and R & B who wrote pop ditties and novelty tunes into singer–songwriters on Dylan's model, storytellers who strove to paint personal and social pictures that Tin Pan Alley couldn't. This self-contained model of artistry became the industry standard, aside from prefab acts. It happened almost immediately: no sooner was Dylan Dylan than the search was on for the Next Dylan, the New Dylan—a list that, over the decades, accumulated dozens like Donovan, Paul Simon, Arlo Guthrie, Springsteen, even Dylan's son Jakob. If the British Invasion upended the complacent American record industry by demonstrating that "the kids" wanted something else and would pay big bucks for it, Dylan altered the fundamental nature of what "the kids" wanted. He had realized Woody Guthrie's dream—a true popular art.

It's a big stone to carry, but it's Dylan's—and in the rollercoaster course of claiming it this guarded, caustic person has left a trail of human and other wreckage. Still, he earned it with the three classic albums of his amphetamine-surreal-Beat period, the multifaceted *Bringing It All Back Home, Highway 61 Revisited,* and *Blonde on Blonde.*

THERE ARE STILL ANTI-DYLAN FOLKIES as hardfaced about Dylan-goes-electric-at-Newport as jazz purists are about post-*Bitches Brew* Miles Davis. Like jazz, folk music enjoyed a wider commercial appeal while rock and roll regenerated through the early 1960s. They shared the cultural cachet of being the soundtracks for intellectuals and Beats, college students and hipsters. The versions of jazz and folk that dominated the radio—the Kingston Trio, Ramsey Lewis Trio—were dismissed as made-for-the-masses pablum. Insiders lamented them but shrugged; they, after all, had access to the real deal. When Dylan and Davis in the mid-1960s redefined for themselves what the "real deal" was, insiders faced a choice: take a similar shot at redefinition or excommunicate the heretic.

In his intuitive fashion, Dylan registered more jazz than most, just as he absorbed and extracted more country, blues, and other forms than most; his only real folk-scene rivals in musical catholicity were Pete Seeger and Dave Van Ronk. Dylan's tastes in jazz included Jelly Roll Morton and Billie Holiday. Nat Hentoff, writing about the new folk as well as jazz, interviewed Dylan in 1966 for *Playboy.* They'd done this before, and they had a score to even: *Playboy* had tried to edit an earlier interview, so they decided to do a put-on.

In it, Dylan whiplashed the jazz snob's intellectual pretensions with surreal humor, the common language of the counterculture, the Marx Brothers attitude Abbie Hoffman tried to make into Yippies. Hentoff asked him, "In recent years . . . jazz has lost much of its appeal to the younger generation. Do you agree?" Dylan answered: "I don't really know who this younger generation is. I don't think they could get into a jazz club anyway. But jazz is hard to follow; I mean you actually have to like jazz to follow it; and my motto is, never follow anything. . . . What would some parent say to his kid if the kid came home with a glass eye, a Charlie Mingus record, and a pocketful of feathers? He'd say, 'Who are you following?' And the poor kid would have to stand there with water in his shoes, a bow tie on his ear, and soot pouring out of his belly button and say, 'Jazz, father, I've been following jazz.' . . . Then the kid's mother would tell her friends, 'Oh yes, our little Donald, he's part of the younger generation, you know.'"

At the peak of his powers in the early 1960s, Charlie Mingus would bestow titles on his music like "Folk Forms 1." He was acknowledging the tradition of folk composition—adopt or adapt an existing melody or song form to your uses. Mingus's models were Bartók, Stravinsky, Copland, Ellington—people who made self-conscious art from the folk tradition's artifacts. By contrast, like Guthrie before him, Dylan's early compositions were new lyrics fitted to existing or modified tunes. These methods are genetically related. Jazz's common currency is standards, popular tunes literate jazz musicians are expected to know how to navigate. A favorite pastime at postwar hootenannies was to "pass the song around"—each person got a crack at improvising a verse or stanza. Think of these as the folk scene's jam sessions, a way of transmitting information as well as competitively rating players.

Improvisation is rooted in memory; its spontaneous creation is not totally ad-lib. Dylan practiced—spoke, ranted, typed, sang, performed—incessantly, honing his talent while he absorbed all around him like a psychic sponge. Revved to fever pitch by speed-freak restlessness and his shuttered but muscular sense of self and the power of his art, he had to keep moving on. What else could he do? Or, as my colleague Stuart Klawans put it, "Since he could write 'Subterranean Homesick Blues,' why would he not?"

MY FIRST DYLAN ALBUMS were *Bringin' It All Back Home*, *Highway 61 Revisited*, and *Blonde on Blonde*, so for me Dylan's real value has never been only as a political symbol anyway: he's got everything he needs, he's an artist, he don't look back. And his penetrating mysticism was blazingly clear then, way before he got involved with organized religions.

As Dylan told Flanagan: "Songs are supposed to be heroic enough to give the illusion of stopping time. With just that thought. To hear a song is to hear someone's thought, no matter what they're describing. If you see something and you think it's important enough to describe, then that's your thought. You only think one thought at a time, so what you come up with is really what you're given. When you sit around and 'imagine' things to do and to write and to think—that's fantasy. I've never been much into that. Anybody can fantasize. Little kids can, old people can, everybody's got the right to their own fantasies. But that's all they are. Fantasies. They're not 'dreams.' A dream has more substance to it than a fantasy. . . . So you can't say what it's about. But what you can do is try to give the illusion of the moment of it. And even that's not what it's about. That's just proof that you existed. What's anything about? It's not about anything. It is what it is."

As a friend of mine once put it, Dylan opened the toy chest of American popular music so that anyone could play with all of its contents. The remark underscores the breadth of Dylan's catalog. Only a few musical peers—Ray Charles comes to mind—have done anything as wide-ranging, have magnificently ignored the notion that genius lives, as the popular Malvina Reynolds song put it, in "little boxes." Or as Dylan snidely remarked to Hentoff in their 1966 *Playboy* put-on, "What does it mean, rock and roll? Does it mean Beatles, does it mean John Lee Hooker, Bobby Vinton, Jerry Lewis's kid? What about Lawrence Welk? . . . Are all these people the same? Is Ricky Nelson like Otis Redding? Is Mick Jagger really Ma Rainey?"

Maybe it's not surprising that, like Charles, Dylan seems to have two key qualities: genius and self-protective complexity. From the beginning, the Dance of the Seven Veils between the (initially few genuine) facts that surfaced about his private lives and the whirring rumors has been part of his celebrity allure; it amplified his gyrating lyrics, gave insiders plenty to guess and gossip about, and outsiders a contact high.

In 1965, when *Bringing It All Back Home* was released, D. A. Pennebaker tagged along for Dylan's last all-acoustic tour of Britain and filmed *Don't Look Back*. The tour, completely sold out in advance, repeated current songs like the epic "Gates of Eden" and the nearly epic "It's Alright Ma." The achingly bitter "It's All Over Now, Baby Blue" he pulls out one hotel-party night to gun down a very young Donovan Leitch, the Next New Dylan: Donovan leads off the battle with an insipid ditty, and Dylan retunes the guitar and mows him down, looking like a protopunk, black leather and closed tab collars and Cuban-heeled boots and that tangled mop of hair. "Subterranean Homesick Blues" is number six on the UK charts and everywhere on car radios while he tours. In sold-out Albert Hall, the crowd is hushed to reverence.

Released in 1967, the movie caused a stir mostly because it unveiled another few sides of Dylan. Now it's been reissued on DVD, with the usual enhanced menu of outtakes (here audio tracks) and commentary (some useful, some silly). The good news is that it looks just as murky as ever. With this backstage home movie, Pennebaker was inventing our notions of cinéma vérité: a wash of grimy, grainy images with weirdly impromptu light, in-the-moment vignettes and scenes.

Pennebaker wasn't interested in converting Dylan into a poster boy for activism or peace and love or the Francis Child ballad collection; he grasped the artistic multiplicity that often came out as duplicity. During the movie, Dylan reveals side after side: the manipulative creep; the defensive master of the counterlunge; the insular and sometimes inarticulate star; the smartass provocateur; the hyperintense performer; the chain-smoking, coffee-drinking, spasmic-twitching composer sitting endlessly at type-writers and pianos. And yeah, the nice guy pops up too. It's a portrait of the artist as Zelig.

In Pennebaker's film, this Zelig too has his handler: the owlish, pudgy Svengali that was Albert Grossman, who negotiates about money in a couple of thug-inspired, nasty scenes. Folk veterans tend to see him as a representative of Moloch, though he did encourage Dylan to write and experiment early on. He also produced the film.

According to Pennebaker, Dylan came up with the movie's famous opening: "Subterranean Homesick Blues" plays while Dylan, wearing a slight sneer, stands on one side of an alley. Allen Ginsberg and Peter Orlovsky stand off to the other. Dylan is holding placards with bits of lyrics from the tune, and drops each card to the ground when it goes by on the audio track. It's a neat piece of visual business that bridges Buster Keaton and MTV.

Hangers-on drift across the screen throughout the film: producer Tom Wilson, who carried over the acetates of *Bringing It All Back Home*; Alan Price, the organist who had been fired from the Animals, the blues group he founded, after they hit the charts with "House of the Rising Sun," which they covered because of Dylan; and, of course, Joan Baez. She had headlined a 10-day tour in the United States, which she thought was continuing in the United Kingdom; it wasn't. Dylan and his sidekick/roadie Bobby Neuwirth escalate from tolerating her to torturing her. They make fun of her small breasts. She sings one of Dylan's loveliest songs, "Turn Turn Turn Again," while he types, ignoring her. When he sings the Hank Williams classics "Lost Highway" and "I'm So Lonesome I Could Die," she tries to harmonize but doesn't know most of the words.

He shrugs off journalists, then as now, with "You're gonna write whatever you want anyway." But periodically he's exasperated into directness. "Do you think," he bursts out at one point, wriggling free of being pinned by a stream of questions about his roles as youth spokesperson, movement leader, artistic figurehead, "anybody that comes to see me is coming for any other reason than entertainment?"

The hero of Don DeLillo's brilliant satiric novel of rock and paranoia, *Great Jones Street*, is Bucky Wonderlick, modeled on Dylan with traces of John Lennon and Mick Jagger. He's in hiding when Running Dog News Service uncovers his rundown loft lair and presses deferentially, gently for information. "We know it's asking a lot expecting an interview. . . . What about the rumors?" Bucky's response: "They're all true."

WHEN "LIKE A ROLLING STONE" peaked at number two on the charts on August 14, 1965, in the number one slot was Barry McGuire's simplified Dylan protest soundalike, "Eve of Destruction." That didn't surpress the outrage from the folk world and older fans that trailed Dylan as he criss-crossed America, then Europe with members of the Hawks and keyboardist Al Kooper for much of the year. The fledgling new tour circuit for rock, cobbled together out of small clubs, old theaters, and ball parks, was barely aborning. As were all the engineering and logistics: only a couple of years earlier, 50,000 fans at Shea Stadium screamed while the Beatles played through tiny amplifiers. The technology of large-scale rock concerts hadn't gotten much better, until Dylan. Covering him for the *Saturday Evening Post* in 1966, Jules Siegal notes the custom sound system worth $30,000 being carted around in eight large crates. He also notes that to date *Highway 61* sold 360,000 copies in the US alone, that Dylan had sold 10 million albums worldwide, and that his tunes had been covered 150 times by artists ranging from Stan Getz to Lawrence Welk.

David Hajdu's neatly shaped narrative skids with deliberate abruptness to its finish in 1966. That April, after a publication party for his seminal counterculture book, *Been Down So Long It Looks Like Up to Me*, Richard Fariña died in a motorcycle crash. Three months later, Dylan had his own motorcycle crash, which pulled him out of the public eye for three years. Hajdu writes, "Precisely what happened to Bob Dylan on July 29 is impossible to reconstruct with authority." Except that, as with Greta Garbo, it multiplied his mythological status. In *Great Jones Street*, as DeLillo explores and exposes the mystique and business of American mores and the counterculture, Bucky Wunderlick withdraws, overwhelmed by fans' demands, the road's repetitions, the claustrophobic celebrity that closes him off from his creativity. His manager sees things differently: "The press is getting the dry heaves over your disappearance."

It might as well be Dylan who retorts, "There is no freedom without privacy." Sounes's biography retells familiar tales, as we watch obsessive fans stake out Dylan's houses, hassle his women and kids, ransack his garbage. We learn more of the grimy legal battles between Dylan and Grossman, who for several years, at least, earned much more from Dylan than Dylan did. According to Sounes's version, "In 1981—twelve years after they had stopped doing business together, Grossman sued Bob for back royalties. Bob filed eighteen counterclaims, complaining that Grossman had exploited and mismanaged him throughout their association. Bob refuted suggestions Grossman had 'discovered' him, pointing out he had already acquired an agent and a record deal before they met. Bob said he was completely unsophisticated in business at the time.... He felt Grossman had taken advantage of this naivete, and it was not just the money he had lost that rankled with him. He also felt hurt that someone he had trusted had betrayed him. This hurt was apparent when Bob gave a sworn deposition in 1981 in support of his counterclaims. By this time he had seen more than $7 million of his earnings siphoned off by Grossman. When asked how long he had known Mr. Grossman, Bob replied carefully, 'Well, I don't think I've ever known the man, Mr. Grossman.'"

He did know lots of women, though, and in book after book, article after article they parade dizzyingly by: Minnesota coffeehouse girls, Suze Rotolo, Baez, Suze again, his first wife Sara, Baez again, back to Sara, various sidetrips, a string of black backup singers like Clydie King and Carolyn Dennis, who, Sounes reveals, had Dylan's child and secretly married him.

Those he got closest to talk little: a Woodstock neighbor who remembers him as a family man waiting for his kids to come home from school, for instance. With such a rich, tumultuous interior life finding complex creative form with such immediate impact, Dylan constructed a persona of mumbled putdowns and monosyllables, a deliberate artifact of confusion, an existential challenge. His musical cohorts from over the decades retail variations of the same tale: little contact, minimal-to-no rehearsal, vague if any instruction. Even the Hawks, later known as The Band, arguably Dylan's closest creative associates in the late 1960s, shed little light on the man and his muse.

USING HIS 1966 MOTORCYCLE ACCIDENT as cover to withdraw from the circus, Dylan hung out at Big Pink with The Band, a garage-band funhouse where they played old songs and scrambled up some new ones. They all, but especially Robbie Robertson, learned the architecture of songs and the art of songwriting from The Master.

John Wesley Harding, released during this period, had been recorded earlier. After Dylan's first reappearance, at the Woody Guthrie memorial concert at Carnegie Hall on January 20, 1968, Lillian Roxon described it glowingly as "a completely folk record." Its plain gray cover had a Polaroid for its picture. What you saw was what you got: *John Wesley Harding* was back-to-the-roots; leave the overblown psychedelic heights to the Beatles and Stones. It also previewed the next stretch of Dylan's road: direct, unaffected songs, at their best dashed with his surreal humor and mystic moments. Within a month, *John Wesley Harding* sold 500,000 copies. His Big Three had each taken a year to sell that many.

Nashville Skyline, his 1969 silence-breaker, disappointed most fans— the newly lightened voice, the genially mild love songs, recalled why critics have always found Milton's Satan more fascinating than his God. Then came the bootleg *Great White Wonder*, the first version of the *Basement Tapes* of Dylan with The Band, again playing Janus, rooting around America's attic to find ways to speak to its present.

In 1970, Bob Dylan got an honorary degree from Princeton University. Academics armed with "relevance" taught his songs, his liner notes, his scattered poems, his life.

LIKE MOST, I WAS BORED, then lost touch with the 1970s and 1980s Dylan, who dulled his edge and his vehement sense of humor, it seemed; a dedicated family man engaged in legal battles with Grossman, whom embracing religions, evading stalkers, he slid further into irrelevance as his records grew thin, boring, annoying. There were musical spots of light: *New Morning* had some weird but wonderful spins like the tender waltz "Winterlude," the soul-recitative-with-backing-scatting "If Dogs Run Free." 1974's *Planet Waves* ranks with his greatest work. With "Tangled Up in Blue," 1975's *Blood on the Tracks* was hailed as a masterpiece, Dylan Redux. Once he was born again in 1979, his songs edged toward existential hymns, as on *Slow Train Coming.*

But most of the albums over 20 years lacked wit and durable material, as Dylan drifted through drug abuse, exploding relationships, financial crashes, religious fevers, public self-destruction at the Live Aid concert, and a host of problems that culminated in the late 1980s, when he floated a desperate offer to join the Grateful Dead. Dylan worshippers, the band gently sidestepped the issue, but one upshot was 1989's *Dylan & The Dead*, a reasonable album that marked the onset of his final turnaround. Always an improviser onstage and in the studio, he started to choose his bandmates and his sets more carefully, keeping the loose, sloppy jam feel (which grew whenever he played lead guitar); his bands got polished to a roadhouse sheen. He'd become the touring troubadour he'd imagined himself as a kid.

IN NOVEMBER 1994, dressed in iconic big-polka-dot shirt and black sunglasses, 53-year-old Bob Dylan appeared on MTV's *Unplugged.* He sang a handful of his greatest hits, mostly 1960s vintage, some of his most wondrous and paranoid and surreal creations: "Tombstone Blues," "All Along the Watchtower," "Rainy Day Women #12 & 35," "Desolation Row," "Like a Rolling Stone," "With God on Our Side" and "The Times They Are A-Changin'." Not long afterward, he licensed that last tune for use in ads by the Bank of Montreal and Coopers & Lybrand.

Yes, this is the enigmatic legacy of the 1960s, that tar baby of American cultural politics. But the selling of the counterculture was built into what was, after all, a pop phenomenon. The Grateful Dead started peddling T-shirts during the Winterland days with Bill Graham. By the time we got to Woodstock, "counterculture" was a squishy advertising concept. No one at the time saw this better than the artful enigma that is Dylan.

"I see pictures of the 50s, the 60s, the 70s, and I see there was a difference," Dylan told one interviewer in 1995. "But I don't think the human mind can comprehend the past and the future. They are both just illusions that can manipulate you into thinking there's some kind of change."

Thus spake Zarathustra.

By 1995's MTV *Unplugged,* Dylan was resurrected, though hardly the same. He stopped tossing his old tunes off almost contemptuously; they were persistently rearranged, reinterpreted, in jazz's (and 1960s rock's) restless fashion, far from the freeze-dried recording reproductions that now dominate pop concerts. At the time, his classic material was being reissued almost nonstop via the industry's rapid recycling of inventory onto the new CD format. This remains his concert mode.

His near-death experience in 1997 from a heart infection—an eerie bracket to 1966—grabbed him headlines, and refocused and energized him. *Time Out of Mind*, from that same year, was rightly hailed as his best effort since *Blood on the Tracks*. Produced by Daniel Lanois, its rootsy sounds drew from Delta and Chicago blues, rockabilly, and ballads; its lyrics had bite and power, reestablished his wit and humor about loss and hope and entropy and pain and faith and, of course, death in a hostile and indifferent world—topics for grown-up rockers. Songs with titles like "Not Dark Yet" and "Trying To Get to Heaven" were delivered in a weary, scuffed-leather croak whose phrasing danced with the rhythmic subtleties he'd learned from jazz and blues. One jazz musician told me, "I love to watch people try to sing along with him. He never does what they expect with the melody. The closest thing to what he does with his voice is Sonny Rollins's sax."

The album's epic tune, "Highlands," epitomizes the subtle smarts of Dylan Reborn. He never repeats his delivery; neither does the band, which mingles Pops Staples with Delta blues, mutating its licks almost subliminally for every single verse of the 15-minute track. Meantime, Lanois's patented mix, deep with tremolo, gently rotates the instruments through a roughly spherical soundstage, creating an unconscious complicity with the lyrics—which ultimately, after some very funny verses (including a vintage-Dylan shaggy dog story about a waitress who wants him to sketch her), are about going into that good night.

Then again, Dylan was always the grown-up at the party in the 1960s, disdaining airy talk of love and change. He was the closest thing to a real bluesman born of that time. I remember what Al Kooper, who played organ on *Highway 61 Revisited* and at Newport in 1966, once told me. Tom Wilson, the only black staff producer at Columbia, owned an indie jazz label before producing records by the Animals, Dylan, Simon & Garfunkel and the Velvet Underground. Wilson said of Dylan, "Put him with an electric band, and you'll have a white Ray Charles who's a poet."

That neatly describes both *Time Out of Mind* and 2001's *Love and Theft*. "His lyrics are so raw, so emotionally direct," said one friend who revisited these albums about the time I did, "that they're almost blank; you can project yourself onto them." At the same time, our own Heraclitus takes note of time's passage in oblique but telling ways. Where once he sang defiantly, "When you got nothing, you got nothing to lose," now older he grumbles realistically, "When you think that you've lost everything, you find out you can always lose a little more."

On *Love and Theft*, Dylan even more overtly embraces jazz, especially of the between-the-wars Swing Era when blues and jazz and early R & B all blended in the likes of Armstrong and Nat King Cole. "Bye and Bye" finds his croak skipping blithely, limberly, through sardonically high-stepping swing, recalling nothing more than Armstrong's vocals without the heft, somewhere near Billie Holiday's late singing. "Moonlight" is a suave torch song—Dylan as Astaire—tinged with threat. And there's heavy-duty Chicago blues, rockabilly, and rockers to fill out the album.

So maybe it shouldn't surprise anyone that in summer 2002 Dylan headlined the Aspen Jazz Festival with Willie Nelson.

Which brings us back to Newport 2002. "The Times They Are A-Changin'" followed "Roving Gambler" with Dylan's looselimbed phrasing framed by mandolin licks, his sliding slurs on the title line ironically accenting world-weariness rather than battle cries. "Desolation Row" too became less acerbic, less surreal, as if reality has caught up to Dylan's Boschian vision; he punctuated verses with a one-note lick à la Neil Young. "Mama You've Been on My Mind" had a bluegrass, Dead-inflected feel; the Dead echoed again through the first encore, Buddy Holly's "Not Fade Away." "Positively Fourth Street" shifted to a Percy Sledge–style plea—a delicious twist to this slashing counterattack on the late folksinger Phil Ochs, a Dylan acolyte who ran with Abbie Hoffman and ended his days dreaming of himself as Elvis. "Subterranean Homesick Blues" swelled with punk-tipped rage. The crowd, on its feet since Copland wafted from the PA, was moving to the music, its energies harnessed, the musicians onstage knowing they were doing their jobs.

And so it went: the tight, incredibly versatile and rapid-fire quintet—guitarist Charlie Sexton, multiinstrumentalist Larry Campbell, bassist Tony Garnier, drummer George Ricelli—worked with roadhouse precision and timing, switching between acoustic and electric instruments like race-car pit crews, dispensing (as usual with Dylan) with frills like talking to the audience, just finding the zone and feeding the beast. "Summer Days" revved up pedal-to-the-metal rockabilly. "North Country Fair" had a backporch feel that sat the crowd down, then "Tangled Up in Blue" snarled and brought them back up. "Mr. Tambourine Man," dazzling with phrases that skimmed like stones across a rippling lake, offered more modest, but maybe more real, affirmation than it might have in 1965. Here I am, the revitalized chameleon seemed to say, and we are now history—and thus open endlessly to reinterpretation. And then came "You Ain't Goin' Nowhere," ironically soothing, its lyrics a curse riding shining pedal steel licks like those of The Byrds' country-rock version.

They cranked into "Wicked Messenger," which waxed fierce, a Jeremiad blues; "Leopard Skin Pillbox Hat" flared with sarcasm. The encores included a powerful "Like a Rolling Stone." During "Blowin' in the Wind," a gull hung improbably motionless over the American flag atop the bastion while Dylan trilled, "How many seas must a white dove sail?" Then it dipped into the wind and wheeled off, and a few moments later the amazing band blasted out "All Along the Watchtower" in Jimi Hendrix mode, the jutting fortress walls their backdrop.

By the first encore the crowd had started to dribble out, but thousands remained: parents dancing with their smaller kids on their shoulders, next to their teens; Gen Xers wearing Born to Run and Woody Guthrie T-shirts, moving to the throbbing pulses and mouthing the words while Dylan's voice cut like a dolphin through the slippery beats and the sun sank through the glowering haze toward the lip of the mainland. And as I headed to the parking lot to inch oh-so-slowly out of Newport, I remembered how I used to carve Dylan lyrics onto desks in high school. Good thing I never got caught.

16

Electric Blues Revival

IN THE MID-1960s, a small West Village club called the Café Au Go Go became a key site for roots revival then thriving in New York's Greenwich Village. It hosted acts from folk to blues, old-timers and young wannabes all jostling for the small devout audiences that thronged alternative-culture centers like the Village, Cambridge, San Francisco, and Los Angeles. On the corner and upstairs from the Au Go Go was a small shabby theater: when the Mothers of Invention pulled into New York, they stayed in residence there, almost as if they were lost, for months, and drew almost as many fans each night as there were people onstage, while they performed their titillating onstage cabaret of satirical music and ersatz drama like "Ritual of the Young Pumpkin," involving a female doll and an array of vari-sized vegetables in ways guaranteed to make 15-year-old males crack up.

Down the block were scene stalwarts like the Village Gate, home to jazz, international music, folk music, revues, and shows; around the corner and up and was the Café Wha?, where the Fugs dug in with a hot black guitarist named Jimmy James, who soon went to England and became Jimi Hendrix. Also nearby were the Gaslight, where the folkie likes of Eric Anderson and Tom Paxton still performed, and the Night Owl, the plaster-dusted basement room where the Lovin' Spoonful were born and held court until they hit with "Do You Believe in Magic," now the score for a Mercedes-Benz commercial. Biker gangs like the Alien Nomads lined certain bars, their motorcycles neatly aligned at the curbs, and waited for prey. Dozens of acoustic guitars echoed and clashed in Washington Square Park, as kids and semi-pros drawled renditions of blues and Dylan and ancient folk tunes, while nickel bags of pot and small chunks of hash and occasional hits of blotter acid were peddled and imbibed. Times being what they were, the cops ignored as much of the activity around them as possible.

On weekends, the narrow crisscrossing cowpaths turned into streets crawling with kids from Long Island and Jersey and Connecticut and Brooklyn, most dressed in the military castoffs or pseudo–Carnaby Street toff fashions or frayed secondhand duds. They'd string out along the winding side streets, throng the park around the fountain plaza, knot into small huddles, and elbow out the street people in order to panhandle bemused tourists and increasingly bored and irate residents— the children of American privilege growing up absurd. Members of British Invasion groups like the Animals moved among them, hungrily roving the clubs, picking up on their heroes like Charles Mingus and John Coltrane, sussing out unknowns like Hendrix, setting the near-future in motion. The times they were a-changin' indeed.

Thanks to the explosion of media interest in the wake of Dylan Electric, the Village scene was changing fast. The no-man's land between the old Lower East Side, the Village, and Gramercy Park, a Ukrainian neighborhood where Beats like Allen Ginsburg and artists like Larry Rivers had moved during the 1950s to avoid the Village's overpriced rents and tourists, filled with teenyboppers and hippies and was renamed the East Village. FM rock radio didn't exist yet in New York, but within a year Scott Muni would get one afternoon hour of programming on all-classical WOR-FM, where he would air underground heroes like Hendrix and the Grateful Dead, people who until then depended on word of mouth. Alternative newspapers like the *East Village Other* sprouted, culturally outflanking the Beat-based *Village Voice*, which scrambled to catch the eye of the latest teenaged bohemian-wannabes. Bill Graham opened the Fillmore East with concerts that mixed the Grateful Dead and Miles Davis, Jimi Hendrix and folkies like Richie Havens and stone soul like the Ike Turner Revue. One unfortunate, inevitable side effect was the closing of the small clubs that incubated the scene Graham and the awakening record industry would cash in on.

It was a great time to be a kid with curiosity and ears in New York. New worlds seemed to be rising all around, and all you had to do was look. Nothing cost too much even for a poor student: the minimum wage was $1.35 an hour, but a ticket to the Fillmore was only cost $3, $4, or $5 for a three- or four-act show.

Before the Fillmore East opened, just before *Highway 61 Revisited* galvanized popular music, in 1965 the Café Au Go Go hosted a gaggle of high school and college kids for a week of afternoon live recording. A few of my teen friends enthusiastically showed up because the taping's subject was the Blues Project, who came out of the New York folk-blues scene captained by Dave Van Ronk; in fact, guitarist Danny Kalb was Van Ronk's former student and collaborator. The tapes became part of *Live at the Café Au Go Go*, the band's first album, which we naturally raced to buy once it came out.

We were probably weird even for the weird times. Other kids were into the Beatles and Motown; we were learning about folks like Muddy Waters and John Coltrane, Howlin' Wolf and Charles Mingus, Big Bill Broonzy and Robert Johnson by way of the Stones and the Yardbirds and the Project and the Paul Butterfield Blues Band and the like, digging for their records, checking out their performances. In much the same way we'd learned about Woody Guthrie from Dylan and Baez and Seeger. We made fun of top 40 radio and its bands, trawled around the dial in the wee hours when our parents thought we were asleep to find the clear-channel stations that bounced around the ionosphere from Texas and the South and even Chicago and Cleveland in the unpredictable post-midnight hour. We got earfuls of sounds we had no grids for and it was, as they said then, mind-expanding, a jolting rush of raw and unforeseen vitality, even if it meant you spent the school day skating through tests and classroom work while replaying the latest discovery in your head.

As we ventured into the clubs, nursing overpriced sodas to satisfy table minimums for the underaged, drunk on being 2 or 6 or 20 feet away from the musicians, we developed expectations. Songs were not to be performed, like they were on *Shindig* or *Hullaballoo* or the *Ed Sullivan Show*, as note-for-note renderings of a record. Live meant loose, spiking shows with the unexpected, and so we began to expect and chase the dynamics of live improvisation. Jazz, blues, R & B, rock, folk—we were surrounded by them, and they seemed to flow into each other, at least around the edges. The musical questioning we heard seemed part of the broader questioning that was rocking culture and society. We didn't have to understand the full possibilities we were getting a whiff of to be intoxicated, especially at 14 or 15.

And the Blues Project intoxicated us, partly because they could have been us, older and more experienced. Most of us didn't have too many preconceptions about things like authenticity or musicianship, though the dedicated young folk revivalists among us tended to be dismissive of anything that smacked of pop. But we all played in bands and were at least dimly aware of the folk revival and radical jazz and social upheavals all around us, and we knew what we liked. So we followed the Blues Project faithfully, from its 1965 beginnings through its recurrent splinterings to its final 1967 breakup. They opened unexpected doors into worlds where we'd meet other, older weirdos and intersect with the still-living past.

Late one school night in 1966, for instance, a couple of my pals and I showed up at Steve Paul's West Side club, The Scene, a downstairs hole-in-the-wall that rock history later deemed pivotal. We weren't late enough: the sets, we discovered, never started anywhere near the announced set time. While we hung out nursing glasses of whatever we were drinking, a tall, filthy, longhaired guy with a big nose appeared out of the back room. He did a double take when he saw us, then slid into a seat at our table. The interrogation began: How old were we? How did we get in? What were we doing here on a school night? What did our parents think? Didn't we know places like this could lead us astray to wickedness, drugs, booze, sex? He was, he said, brushing aside our questions, though not impolitely, the janitor, and Mr. Paul let him live in the club when he had nowhere else to go; he was also, as part of the arrangement, the club's usual opening act. Then he hurried to his back room and reemerged with a battered Bible, which he opened as he folded himself into his chair and began to read to us from Apocalypse. His name was Tiny Tim, and that night we saw the shtick, from "Hey Paula" to "Tiptoe Through the Tulips," that he would ride to fame via the *Tonight Show*.

Encounters like that began to teach us to read the scene's contours, and we tried to map them. We learned to hang out to spot where Jimi Hendrix headed after a Fillmore show, which was often The Scene, his Revox tape machine under some roadie's arm so no note would be lost as he roared through his space-blues. We saw him devour the fiercely competitive Buddy Guy, one of our new blues-guitar heroes, in an impromptu jam on that club's tiny excuse for a stage. We followed Jerry Garcia, an Eveready Bunny who wandered with a stoned smile and a guitar from spot to spot around New York looking to sit in with anyone still moving after he'd finished two long Grateful Dead sets at the Fillmore. We talked ourselves backstage wherever we could and hung out, awestruck and giggly as girls, listening to the musicians toss around names and ideas we tried to fill in later, like so many tantalizing ellipses.

So we weren't just thrilled; we were being educated, educating ourselves in the oral tradition of garage bands across America, spinning records and covering tunes and in the process creating a common folk-musical language. We were learning to make our own art, and that made us potential connoisseurs with a particular perspective. We respected and treasured old innovators like Gary Davis and Muddy Waters; we were attached to electric blues revivalists like the Blues Project and the Paul Butterfield Blues Band because we thought we could have been them.

And so we had debates about who was better, Danny Kalb or Butterfield's guitarist Mike Bloomfield, while we were copying their styles. We analyzed Kalb's nerve-jangling, hopscotching-round-the-fingerboard runs (which still sound to me like a talented dancing spider is being electrocuted on guitar strings, often in modal form) and his Danelectro's whining, nasal tone. We joked that, as he scrambled up and down the guitar neck in characteristically skittering haste, he could induce ear bleeds at 100 yards. We made fun of how he combed his hair up from above his left ear to cover his desperate balding on top. Still, when Kalb freaked out in 1967, one of my pals found his acoustic guitar, pictured on the back of the Project's second album, *Projections*, in a pawn shop and immediately bought it; another still has it.

As the guitarist/leader, Kalb bore the brunt of our attention, but there was plenty to go around. We mocked Al Kooper's raggedly asthmatic vocals and low-rent piano technique and learned all his Farfisa moves—especially since he'd played with Dylan on *Highway 61 Revisited* and at the infamous Newport Folk Festival of 1965, even if he'd written "This Diamond Ring," a mindless pop hit, for Gary Lewis (Jerry's son) and the Playboys. We goofed on guitarist Steve Katz's inflated psychedelic-folkie lyrics and Robert Goulet-ish baritone, and studied his gutsy harmonica solos. We memorized Andy Kulberg's propulsive bass patterns and winced at his inevitable 15-minute, jazz-simulated "Flute Thing." We laughed at Roy Blumenfeld's unsubtle drum flailings and felt our pulses race as the rhythms onstage pumped and oscillated, breathed in and out, as Kooper's organ and Kalb's guitar climbed and crescendoed in coiled, not quite coordinated sympathy, piling up tension that was aching for release, as the band's energies focused and spiraled into the kind of orchestrated group orgasm that we were beginning to intuit could be a key component of the best live pop music.

Confusion? Teenage ambivalence toward heroes? Sure, that too. But sitting here now, I think at least part of what we were learning was that pop music's spectrum is a wondrously expansive thing that thrives on both greatness and junk—in fact, depends on the interaction between the two for its raw materials and its evolutionary thrust. It's a cliché, for instance, that what has "survived the test of time" must be better than what didn't, but luck and quantity always have something to do with what lasts. Who knows what died with the burning of the library at Alexandria? And what if those Renaissance detectives who started scraping monastery palimpsests to discover ancient "lost" texts had decided they liked the top layers better? Then too, not even Umberto Eco knows what was lost with the scrapings.

This is one way I listen to *Anthology*, the two-CD compilation of Blues Project stuff that includes (usually rightly) healthy chunks of previously unreleased material, omits (sometimes, though not always, rightly) some previously released material, offers some titillating inside (if too credulous and overstated) views of the band in its time without always clarifying actual events and dates, and often sounds like it was recorded on a windy day by two mikes floating past on an East River garbage scow. And hearing this stuff now, a good quarter-century since I last listened to any of it, I have to admit I still love it and hate it, often at exactly the same time.

One reason is the music's sheer energy, its brash and raw vitality. Another is its audacity. They're not separable. After all, the Blues Project were nothing more than a garage band writ large—in other words, a potpourri of folk (an ethereal "Catch the Wind"), rock and roll (set highlights always included a Chuck Berry stomper like "I Want To Be Your

Driver"), blues (lots of Willie Dixon, like "Spoonful"), jazz ("Flute Thing"), taut pop ("Cheryl's Going Home"), schlocky pop (singles like "Love Will Endure"), classical touches ("Steve's Song"), and pretty much anything else they could think of, attacked in charmingly home-made ways.

Their grassroots naivete and openness were their greatest charm and virtue. This early, Butterfield was more the outsider purist, copping note-for-note charts from his black Chicago blues mentors. The Project, by contrast, took Muddy Waters's "Two Trains Running" and slowed it way, way down, filled it with space and spiky blowouts to run for 11-plus minutes. This was a recipe the Grateful Dead finessed. And Butterfield took up the implicit challenge: on *East West*, his band's second album fusing jazz, rock, blues, and raga, Bloomfield led a jam on Nat Adderley's "Work Song" that had a finesse the Blues Project couldn't have managed. But finesse wasn't why we liked them. Their raggedy edge was part of the fun: check out how they pump "Back Door Man" (included on this boxed set as a studio cut, not the live Au Go Go version) or "Who Do You Love" (an alternate Au Go Go take) into menacing, hurtling protopunk slashers.

With the passage of time, the band's technical limitations are even more painfully apparent, but ultimately they don't matter any more than the Ramones' or the Sex Pistols'—and for the same reasons. At its core their music was about heart and energy. They found enough of both to survive their constant schisms, reaching beyond their grasp, and a frustrating inability to make a splash outside New York. And yet without the Project's spacey extended arrangements, headlong organ-races-guitar climbs, unblended early Stones harmonies, all the inviting incompleteness of garage rock, the line that runs from San Francisco psychedelia to contemporary jam bands like Phish and Dave Matthews Band and String Cheese Incident might well have been different.

This somewhat garbled CD package captures some of this, with its sometimes whimsical track selections and stilted and too reverent, if useful, notes. Chronology dictates the track order. Some choices are downright weird: it doesn't make sense to replace fiery but muddy live versions of "Violets of Dawn" and "Back Door Man" with earlier, tamer and cleaner studio versions, and then shuffle the tracks out of the original album order because of the dates they were recorded. By the mid-1960s, LPs were presentations; the best albums had a pace and a narrative that boxed-set dismemberment by chronology sabotages. The procrustean bed of the timeline may be useful for the scholar and informative for the curious, but it's not entertainment, and it's not art. Me, I'd rather the reissue gathered the two key albums, *Live at the Café Au Go Go* and *Projections*, plus singles, and forget the later and earlier tracks confusing the story here. But that's not how compilation product gets made these days.

Product versus Project: for the first time in 30 years, while I strained to listen to these discs, I thought about the significance of this seminal band's name. The liner essay suggests that it's misleading; after all, they weren't just a blues band. That's true but, like other points in the essay, misleading by default. Project was precisely what these guys, and their scene, and their audiences, and their times were about. The archer and the arrow were meant, at least, to be one. It was an era when American culture had become suddenly self-conscious again, aware of its voices and powers coming of age in a world that seemed, so much more than today's, a place that could be made better. The process was the goal. In their idiosyncratic, sometimes cranky stylistic gropings and reworkings and achievements, the Blues Project encapsulated that extraordinary American moment when folk culture and mass popular culture over-lapped, a place where art was possible, however accidentally, in a broad commercial forum, possibly more than at any time before or since.

When the band finally quit, exhausted by internal tensions and ignored by the larger rock world, Kooper and Katz started Blood Sweat & Tears, an early jazz-rock fusion group with sharp-eared charts and a horn section of jazz players and a ranginess that gave it heft. Its only peer was Bloomfield's swaggering, soulful Electric Flag, whose first album opens with a recorded segment of an LBJ speech about Vietnam that dissolves into laughter, then a smooth-running, 12-cylinder version of Howlin' Wolf's "Killing Floor," pumped with stuttering horns, fired by trebly blues Telecaster snarls, focused by the understated delivery of Nick Gravenites' smooth vocals. Introduced by Bob Dylan for *Highway 61 Revisited*, Kooper and Bloomfield reunited on *Super Sessions*, largely improvised instrumental outings in soul-jazz and blue; "His Holy Modal Majesty" was a Grateful Dead–inspired jam based on the language of Miles Davis and John Coltrane. On the record's other side, Kooper and ex-Buffalo Springfield guitarist Stephen Stills joined forces, with Stills's sweet countrified wah-wah wafting across the "Season of the Witch," the Donovan folk song Kooper recast into a jolt-filled 10 minutes of crescendos and decrescendos, by rippling horns and rumbling, sinewy Hammond organ. No wonder the track was an early FM rock radio mainstay—which is why the record entered the top 20 in late 1968.

In the original *Super Session* liner notes by Michael Thomas it's clear how thoroughly the Beat-jazz mythos permeated this period in flux: "Always, the best things happen after hours, by accident, while the cat's away, when the moon goes behind a cloud and there's no one else around; certainly the best music in America is made after twelve, deep in the rock and roll dungeons, little clubs in New York and California, when whoever's in town and feeling restless . . . rock and roll strays, they get together and jam, sometimes they collide, more often than not they tempt each other to take more and more risks, always they discover something they'd perhaps had in mind but couldn't quite bring home before."

Flaws and all, the Blues Project and its radiating semihidden influence centered on that—the element of risk frozen out of American mainstream culture by its neurotic emphasis on security and predictability and banished to the margins. Was it any wonder that so many kids followed the siren call? Maybe that's why as I get older I find I'm still laughing at a lot of the same places, and startled or moved by some new ones, when I listen to the Blues Project.

17

Buffalo Springfield

Somethin's happenin' here
What it is ain't exactly clear.
                    —Buffalo Springfield

Do you have a movement?
Yes. It's called Dancing.
                    —Abbie Hoffman

In the dark times will there still be
singing? Yes, there will be singing, there
will be singing about dark times.
                    —Bertolt Brecht

UNSTABLE CHEMISTRY can cause spectacular effects—that's one way to think of Buffalo Springfield. Or frame them as an American musical smorgasbord (though three of them were Canadians). Or see them as defining much of 1960s rock.

Or you can notice that their lifespan marked the moment when West Coast folk-rock renegades joined mainstream commercial culture at its heart, in Los Angeles, when AM radio played "protest" songs amid teenybopper treacle, and record labels competed for the weirdest, most outrageous bands, trying to read marketing cues in the emerging counterculture: how to channel inchoate energies of folk art into commerce. TV shows for teens proliferated: *American Bandstand, Shindig, Hullabaloo.* Satiric comedy infiltrated the mainstream on *Laugh-In* and the *Smothers Brothers Comedy Hour,* hosted by two folksingers, where bands like the Springfield appeared. Movies sprouted rock soundtracks. The music industry's delivery systems adapted only slowly: FM radio and counterculture impresarios like Bill Graham only came along when Buffalo Springfield had ended.

The larger society was buckling, as the icy repressions of the 1950s thawed: civil rights legislation, the war in Vietnam, the prophetic scripted selling of Richard Nixon in 1968, assassinations, race riots, the Chicago

Democratic convention. The "silent majority" and the southern strategy, crime and welfare queens—the murky idioms and repressions of American politics from Ronald Reagan onward were being sketched.

BUFFALO SPRINGFIELD OWED ITS START to a traffic jam. Richie Furay and Stephen Stills pulled up behind Neil Young's 1953 Pontiac hearse with Ontario plates on the Sunset Strip. They knew each other from the folk-revival circuit of colleges and coffeehouses. Stills had come to LA to audition for the Monkees; he failed because of bad teeth. But producer Barry Friedman, looking for a youth-market hit, suggested Stills could have a deal if he formed a band. Sitting in Young's hearse was fellow Canadian Bruce Palmer. They'd come back to LA, after an abortive side-trip to Motown to cut a record, to find Stills. They agreed on the spot to form a band, and went to pick up drummer Dewey Martin. They lived and rehearsed at Friedman's house, and when they spotted the nameplate on some road equipment they had their name.

By the time they debuted at the Troubadour, they were already the subject of buzz. They toured briefly with the Byrds and the bluegrass Dillards, then got a six-week gig at the Whiskey A-Go-Go (thanks to the Byrds' Chris Hillman) and signed with Atlantic for $12,000. They cut their first single, "Nowadays Clancy Can't Even Sing," less than two months after the traffic jam.

Between 1966 and 1968, the Springfield held together, often just barely, as pot busts banished their bassist back to Canada, and ego blowups between Stills and Young escalated and sent Young packing for part of 1967. They had only one big hit. But for a while they were possibly the most important rock band in America. Then in May 1968, after yet another pot bust in Topanga Canyon and the financial collapse of a southern tour following Martin Luther King's assassination, Buffalo Springfield disintegrated.

BUFFALO SPRINGFIELD IS A PROSAICALLY TITLED four-CD set that, for better and worse, captures the band's kaleidoscopic range. They could be blandly commercial. On their first album, Beatlesy efforts like "Sit Down I Think I Love You" and "Do I Have To Come Right Out and Say It," with earache-inducing harmonies right out of the British Moppet Handbook, inadvertently highlight meatier material. For when the Sunset Strip riots hit in 1966 as the LAPD cracked down on Pandora's Box, a teen rock club, Stills penned the group's only AM hit, "For What It's Worth"; when it made the charts, it was inserted into the hastily revamped first album.

The song marked a new sound: ominous, with its identifying riff of two single reverb-dripping guitar notes over rumbling bass, its vaguely threatened and threatening lyrics, its stark yet sweet harmonies. The lyrics are deliberately shadowy, even amorphous, but embedded in that sound they captured the lurking sense of foreboding and opposition. When the song made the *Billboard* charts in February 1967, it spoke to the crystallizing counterculture—the resonant chamber of a potential mass audience.

"For What It's Worth," a deliberately throwaway and dismissive title, filed Buffalo Springfield forever under folk rock, although it's hard, listening back, to imagine why. Live, the Springfield's shows were renowned for their volume and violence, as guitarists Young and Stills dueled and thrashed for power—a stagebound parable of the group's inner workings, perhaps, but also a fabulous generator of sonic ideas. Young's experimentalism and lunges into feedback were complemented by Stills' sweeter melodic turns—though they could, and often did, switch roles at the drop of a beat. Furay's rhythm guitar nestled between the athletic, R & B-meets-McCartney bass of Bruce Palmer and the shape-shifting drumwork of Dewey Martin. They ignited awesome homemade improvisations.

The box set's second disc gives glimpses of those, via previously unreleased jams. "Kahuna Sunset" is a hippie fantasy, an updated surf-guitar lilt that left-turns into a raga-inspired jam. (Not to worry that raga is a complex form demanding discipline and knowledge: Ravi Shankar, discipled by the Beatles and John Coltrane, was the moment's international-music icon. And thousands of teen guitar players, fascinated by the altered sounds that would flower most fully in Jimi Hendrix, wanted to sound like a sitar doing modal runs.) It closes with Young's Yardbird-influenced rave-up style, though his attack is almost diametrically opposed to Yardbird guitarist Jeff Beck's: Young frets slowly with his left hand and with his right picks feverishly.

On "Buffalo Stomp," guitars wind in and out until the jam revs into squalls of feedback against a backdrop of interwoven solos—rock Dixieland. Among the players is Skip Spence on kazoo; he was Jefferson Airplane's first drummer and would soon cofound Moby Grape, a multi-vocalist guitar army from San Francisco's Flower Power era, much like Buffalo Springfield itself. And pieces like "Bluebird," a guitar-stuffed four-minute mini-suite on disc, would open onstage into mammoth jams.

In the studio, Buffalo Springfield grazed even more widely. They could unchain their pop imaginations and their record collections, and run wild across an American landscape that had recently been opened wide by Bob Dylan and the Beatles.

When British rockers invaded the United States in 1964, they peddled reworked American R & B, rockabilly, and other pop to American kids tired of saccharine hits by voiceless commercial fabrications named Bobby and Fabian—forerunners of today's teenypop idols. The Brits were especially good at recycling R & B hits by black artists, often invisible on the white-dominated pop charts of the time, into guitar-powered pop with Everly Brothers vocals. Far from the land where these forms were born, British kids heard them as a release from the boredom of homemade UK folk-revival offshoots like skiffle; they became building blocks to be played with as much as styles to be mimicked. It was the same energy that had led 1950s blue-collar southern kids to refashion R & B and country into rockabilly in their backyards.

Eclectic, populist, postmodern—choose what terms you like—this was key to the 1960s transition of rock and roll into rock. The guitar, portable and cheap, made music-making widely available; garage bands were the ubiquitous result. As electric amplifiers became smaller and cheaper, even basement-bound guitarists could experiment with sound shaping—punching holes in a speaker to get fuzztone, loosening tubes for distortion, rolling the volume pots for violin effects. Early effects boxes for plugging into the signal chain started to appear. It was like getting a do-it-yourself art kit.

It was also an extension of America's postwar cultural renaissance. Whitman's heirs—jazz artists, the Beats, the Abstract Expressionists, the folk revivalists—all shared a romantic, if sometimes romantically cynical, critique of that hangover from the Great Depression and World War II, the gray flannel 1950s. As counterweight they reemphasized the value of play, long recognized as one of art's core cultural values; influenced by jazz improvisation and the civil rights movement, they revamped play into an artistic and a moral code. The subcultures of black America were valued even when they were misunderstood.

The romantic notion of authentic popular culture—a folk culture where there is minimal mediation between artists and audience—is an elusive grail. In modern commercial pop culture, that polarity is always in flux, but the folkie notion was a potent one during the 1960s. It was ironic that Bob Dylan, in a characteristic paradox, translated that model into both artistic and commercial success; inevitably, he was accused of selling out. And yet, he personified the folk revival's longing for a popular hero who would forge a new sound and, incidentally, a new sense of community.

He had plenty to play with: postwar America was full of new musical syntheses, broad cultural and social curiosity—an openness that has been bled from our society over the last two decades by the twin scalpels of fear and complacency. Both jazz and folk musicians were interested in music from Africa and India, the Caribbean and Asia, for instance, as well as African American gospel and blues. Thanks to the likes of Dylan and the Beatles, this legacy energized garage bands, crackling across the Anglo-American world, where making a band became something countless thousands of kids did. Think of garage bands as the inheritors of the 1950s folk-revival aesthetic, and as the precursors of hip-hop: the street-level site where the reassimilation of pop culture becomes a feedback loop. In that sense, Buffalo Springfield was one of rock's ultimate garage bands.

They were also late for the party that was already cresting toward the Summer of Love and Woodstock, but they quickly made up for lost time and joined the central cast. Soul music was their touchstone; it wasn't just an accident that they recorded for Atlantic Records, a big indie label that made its fame by recording black artists from Joe Turner to Solomon Burke. And in the mid-1960s, soul music ruled the dance floors of America. The Rascals and the Righteous Brothers lifted blue-eyed soul into artistic and commercial payoff. Even whitebread folk-rockers like the Byrds were, thanks to Gram Parsons, countrifying soul hits like "You Don't Miss Your Water."

Neil Young wrote "Mr. Soul," a fierce attack on celebrity (including his own) and the record biz; his wispy vibrato quavered with metalloid and country guitars over thundering Four Tops–style bass. He also wrote "Burned": "Been burned," he yelps, "and with both feet on the ground," a characteristic verbal incongruity backed by musical incongruity. Chugging Motown bass and honkytonk piano share center soundstage: the piano takes a just-enough-out-of-tune solo, followed by Hawaiian-flavored slide guitar, which downshifts into a Beatles-knockoff rideout. This was the band's second single.

With its demos and remixed and finished tracks, Buffalo Springfield amply demonstrates how explosive and creative the band's chemistry could be. It leaves a curious fan wanting more when a more casual fan has had more than enough. In me, it inspires a list of highlights: two Young demos of early interior dreamscapes—the painfully ethereal "Out of My Mind" and vulnerable "Flying on the Ground is Wrong." The tight-wound Stills-Furay harmonies and beautiful acoustic simplicity on the demo for "Baby Don't Scold Me," ultimately released as a mix of stiff Supremes' drumbeats, reverb, and psychedelic guitar raunch that overshadowed the bittersweet lyrics. "Nowadays Clancy Can't Even Sing," an early Young art-rocker with twining guitars, opaque lyrics, and a time-signature shift that highlights Furay's unpleasantly blocky phrasing. The massed-guitar country rock and Miles Standish triangle of "Go and Say Goodbye." The R & B goodtime feel of Stills's "Hot Dusty Roads," with its heavily treated guitar solo and whimsical genre twist of a city boy who stays at home. The Zombies-ish jazz-bossa inflections of "Pretty Girl Why," and the walking bass and jazzy modal drone of "Everydays," cut in the same year as Miles Davis's *Bitches Brew*. The guitar-orchestra suite called "Bluebird." The drippy psychedelic orchestration and Moody Blueslike choir on "Expecting To Fly." The vocal handoff, straight out of two-tenor gospel groups, on "Hung Upside Down," where Furay's soulful lead yields the chorus to Stills's raunchy wails. The gently stinging ironies of "A Child's Claim to Fame," underlined by hired hand James Burton's dobro solo. (Burton played guitar with Ricky Nelson and Elvis Presley and Gram Parsons.) The galloping drive and stinging guitar lines of "Rock and Roll Woman" that leave you feeling like you've just danced with a truck. The Dylan-modeled imagery and phrasing of Young's demos like "The Rent Is Always Due." The arthouse melodrama and Sergeant Pepper orchestration of "Broken Arrow." The dark blues of Stills's husky musings and piano on the demo for "Four Days Gone." The punk flipping the bird to convention of "Special Care," where Stills plays all the instruments but drums.

That last cut is from *Last Time Around*, which was recorded over nearly a year; as time wore on, the band was disintegrating, as the Beatles did during *White Album*. Stills and Young started producing their own sessions; Stills sung and played nearly all the parts on cuts like "Questions," here a biting soul-rocker with blues-drenched vocals, later cutely rearranged as a harmony piece for Crosby Stills & Nash.

Is the box set an effective representation of the legend? Well, it's got the same middle-finger attitude the group itself had: the booklet, perhaps as a tipoff to its sensibility, opens with a Wallace Stevens–inspired page titled "Various Accounts of Their Meeting in Hollywood." And it's taken 10 years to put together because of the same old egos. It's definitely worth complaining that the 26 duplicated album cuts could have been replaced by additional rarities. The booklet's sometimes hard-to-read design, a postmodern swirl of artfully collaged documents and pictures, leaves misinterpretation rampant, though the one-page historical essay by Pete Long is fact-packed. The fan's-eye view by Ken Viola jumps disconcertingly around the booklet. The discographical annotation is thorough, but could use explication. And there's a complete tour schedule, which ends with Buffalo Springfield opening for the Beach Boys and Strawberry Alarm Clock on the last 1968 tour. As another perspective on an overly mythologized period, it's worth recalling that at just about the same time Jimi Hendrix was opening a tour for the Monkees.

YOUNG WAS OUT OF THE BAND when Monterey Pop launched Summer of Love. He was back for the Topanga Canyon bust. From then on his bandmates recombined like pop-culture DNA: bassist Jim Messina first with Richie Furay in Poco, then with pop singer Kenny Loggins. Stills joined with the Byrds' David Crosby and the Hollies' Graham Nash and played Woodstock. Young wandered between their band and solo work.

Less than a year after Woodstock came the Kent State shootings. Within days Young had a tune about tin soldiers and Nixon coming and four dead in Ohio. Its abrasive guitars and Young's incongruous yelping vocals pushed "Ohio" into the top 25, thanks to FM rock radio and adept record industry executives, who had learned again that outrage and opposition could fuel a hit.

18

Gram Parsons and Emmylou Harris

We drink our fill and still we thirst for more
Asking, "If there's no heaven, what is this hunger for?"
                    —Emmylou Harris, "The Pearl"

No doubt they all Got What Was Coming To Them. All those
pathetically eager acid freaks who thought they could buy
Peace and Understanding for three bucks a hit. But their loss
and failure is ours, too. What Leary took down with him was
the central illusion of a whole life-style that he helped create
. . . a generation of permanent cripples, failed seekers, who
never understood the essential old-mystic fallacy of the Acid
Culture: the desperate assumption that somebody—or at least
some *force*—is tending that Light at the end of the tunnel.
                    —Hunter Thompson, *Fear and Loathing in Las Vegas*

I DIDN'T EXACTLY LOSE TRACK of Emmylou Harris between the late
1970s and the mid-1990s, but she did fade from my list of preoccupa-
tions. I'd been listening to her on and off since I first heard about her
making records and touring with Gram Parsons, the man who turned
the Byrds (and subsequently, it seemed, nearly all of LA's burgeoning
rock scene) toward what became country rock, founded the Burrito
Brothers, partied (and cowrote songs like "Wild Horses") with the
Rolling Stones, elevated Harris to national attention, and in September
1973 was found dead (of coroner-ruled "natural causes" that included
morphine and tequila) in a motel in Joshua Tree. A friend stole his body
and burned it in the Joshua Tree National Monument.

How rock and roll can you get? Parsons, never widely famous,
instantly became a mythic cult figure. His life seemed appropriate: as a
kid in 1956, he went backstage at a touring Grand Ole Opry show to
meet Elvis Presley, who blew him away and made him want to play
music, which from then on totally absorbed him. In the early 1960s, he

joined folk groups modeled on hitmakers like the Kingston Trio and Peter Paul and Mary, one of which made it to Greenwich Village coffee-houses. After one semester at Harvard, he started a country-rock garage band in 1965, the International Submarine Band, which previewed tunes like "Luxury Liner," later to number among the genre's touchstones. Already Parsons's eccentric American mixture of cosmopolitan rock outlaw and Christian country boy was combining with his sense of guilty privilege (his dark childhood was shadowed by family problems and wealth) to fuel his charisma and his songwriting talent while (mostly) overcoming defects like his wispy, often off-key voice and, for a while, his hellbent chase after drug-and-booze-fueled insulation from reality and concomitant bouts of despair.

Parsons put together rhythm and blues and country in rock in ways no one had since 1950s rockabilly and updated it. Although he was only a contracted sideman, not a charter member, of the Byrds, he transformed them with tunes like soul singer William Bell's "You Don't Miss Your Water," reimagined as a sweet-harmonied, pedal-steel-lined lament. Ironically, when Roger McGuinn, the Byrds' leader, erased and redubbed most of Parsons's lead vocals on the *Sweethearts of the Rodeo* album, it underscored how much the disc owed Parsons. Left untouched was his unironic reading of "The Christian Life," a waltz adapted from the Louvin Brothers.

Hunter Thompson had his points about the mysticism at the heart of the 1960s, but Parsons exemplifies how complex and American all that confused ambivalence is. Drug-addled or drunk or screwing every available woman, Parsons maintained that he was a Christian. Is this due to his southern background, the bouts in boarding schools, the saturation of American culture by that Puritan claim to the City on the Hill? Parsons never traded in his old-fashioned Bible Belt beliefs for hip revivals of Eastern philosophy. But he still managed to incarnate the contradictions and self-destructive aspects of the 1960s so perfectly that they killed him.

Maybe like Elvis Presley, his earliest idol, whose first recording was for his mother and who sought grace between sin-soaked descents and shooting up TVs, Parsons just ignored the glaring internal contradictions. This is the man whose garish Nudie suit, pictured on *Sacred Hearts and Fallen Angels: The Gram Parsons Anthology*, had on its back a red cross emanating rays of light.

Parsons was a restless and tortured American Romantic in the fashion of the day. Cross or not, he hung out in London to party with the famously debauched Keith Richards instead of touring with the Byrds, so the band fired him. Back to LA, he hooked up with ex-Byrds Chris Etheridge and Chris Hillman, picked up the name Flying Burrito Brothers, and organized a loose aggregate of country rockers to continue where his edition of the Byrds left off. Sneaky Pete Kleinow augmented his pedal steel with fuzztone and distortion, Hillman and Parsons warbled Everly Brothers harmonies, and the band devised a sound between Nashville and Memphis soul.

The Burrito Brothers' first album was called *The Gilded Palace of Sin*. Parsons's two years with them marked a creative period when he wrote definitive tunes. "Christine's Tune (Devil in Disguise)" opened with driving rock rhythms, careening pedal steel, and a typically direct lyric that ran, "A woman like that, all she does is hate you." Then there was a surreal Beach Boys version of Aretha Franklin's "Do Right Woman." On "Sin City," Parsons and Hillman impersonated the Everly Brothers rejecting runaway American materialism. And then there was "Wheels," almost quintessentially American, the urge to jump in the car and get away, light out for the territory on the road like everyone from Huck Finn to the Beats, amid the existential questions tearing Parsons, a shrunken Elijah, apart.

By the Burritos' more subdued second album, *Burrito Deluxe*, Parsons was relegated to a supporting role; by 1970, he was out of the band for the same reasons he'd been bounced from the Byrds: unpredictability, unprofessionalism, drug-induced disappearances for benders with pals like Richards. He spent, he told one interviewer, the next two years "getting lost." But he came out of his blurry hiatus creatively rewired, if with a much more ragged, weakened voice. He went to Vegas to steal the core of the band he'd long wanted to record with from Elvis, who was now beginning his long-term residency in America's Casino-and-Divorce Central: rockabilly guitar ace James Burton, who'd backed young Ricky Nelson and then moved on to Elvis, amid myriad studio dates, punched up Parsons's newest recordings with his tastefully outrageous fills and solos, abetted by versatile pianist Glen D. Hardin, who later anchored Merle Haggard's jazz-inflected country outfit, the Strangers. (The Burritos covered Haggard's "Sing Me Back Home," a blue-collar country blues that, like most of Haggard's ruggedly individual, Bakersfield-style honky-tonk music, found no home in countrypolitan Nashville. It's impossible to say whether Haggard, notorious for his later "Okie from Muskogee" flag-waving during the Vietnam war, would have liked Parsons, but Parsons wanted Haggard to produce his first solo effort, which didn't work out.)

In the dying days of the Burritos, Parsons met Emmylou Harris. He'd been looking for a female duet partner; now he'd found one whose devotion would outlast his life and help enshrine his artistry in rock history. With the manic energy that possessed him when he wasn't crashing or smashed, Parsons put all his new friends in a studio and pulled out material from punchy country weepers like "We'll Sweep Out the Ashes in the Morning" to weaker originals like "A Song for You." The result: the 1972 album *GP* was an uneven, weirdly mixed but suggestive semi-wreck with small jewels. Parsons's voice, by now shredded, could still intimate a great deal; Harris's, almost entirely intuitive without much road seasoning, adds timbre and strength without polish or certainty. Their tour, which kept derailing thanks to Parsons, nevertheless tightly wound their voices together, which showed a year later when they released *Grievous Angel*: sharper material—the autobiographical title cut, the brutally honest "Love Hurts," the careering Sin-City Redux called "Ooh Las Vegas, the prayerful "In My Hour of Darkness," in which the Nudie-suited country boy asks with disarming directness for peace—and more sophisticated recording, better rehearsal, and all that roadwork together gave this album more consistency.

And that was that. The hickory winds called Gram Parsons home from the Mojave two months after *Grievous Angel* was finished.

THE DEATH OF GRAM PARSONS wasn't unexpected but still shocked Emmylou Harris. Her natural harmonizing had wowed Parsons and completed his vision, and her personal empathy for him was as deep as the music. Wrenched by his enthusiasm from her small niche in Washington, DC, as a folk artist, lifted into the aborning world of folk-rock, she suddenly was left to carry on his musical legacy and plot her future.

When the teenaged Harris discovered folk music on the radio, she grabbed a guitar and learned to play. (She also played alto sax in her school's marching band and was a cheerleader.) "Here I was," she told *Rolling Stone* in 1975, "a 16-year-old WASP, wanting to quit school and become Woody Guthrie." Like so many, she headed to Greenwich Village in the late 1960s, performed at coffeehouses, and lived at the YWCA.

A marriage that broke up, a kid, and a move to Nashville led her back to her parents' Virginia farm, until Chris Hillman of the Burritos heard her at a DC club in 1971. That was the Parsons connection. As she told Holly George-Warren for the notes to the uneven *Emmylou Harris Anthology: The Warner/Reprise Years*, "Gram showed me that you can bring all your influences together if you have a focal point. . . . Singing with him, I learned that one of the universal things about country music at its best is the restraint in the phrasing, the economy of the emotion. . . . I went from being a person who thought drummers were evil, the killers of music, a folksinger with an attitude, to just going, 'More more more more more—let's get out there and rock.'"

Parsons's death stopped her cold; she regrouped in LA, where she sang backup on Linda Ronstadt sessions. Parsons's ex-manager got her a label deal and a producer, she regrouped the Parsons/Presley outfit as her Hot Band, and in 1975 released *Pieces of the Sky*; one track, her own "Boulder to Birmingham," was the first of many yearning Parsons tributes, but the Louvin Brothers' "If I Could Only Win Your Love" became her first country hit. Her lilting, sweet-natured voice, with its bluesy scoops and catches, was amplified by the Dillards' Herb Peterson, whose subtly moving voicings were more jazz and bluegrass than Nashville.

I first saw Emmylou Harris in the 1970s, when she was making records like *Pieces of the Sky*, *Luxury Liner*, and *Elite Hotel*, records that weren't quite country and weren't quite rock but had more idiomatic integrity than, say, the Eagles. On 1979's *Blue Kentucky Girl* she got into bluegrass. A year later came *Roses in the Snow*, country classics from Bill Monroe and Jimmie Rodgers, the Carter Family and the Stanley Brothers, with a Paul Simon tune tossed in. After this she lost me: her focus got more diffuse, her mood too tied up with ballads and weepers. I didn't get the 1987 trios with Dolly Parton and Linda Ronstadt. On the other hand, her all-acoustic *Angel Band*, with its desolate, soulful country-gospel hymns, grabbed me; only later did I find out she'd been inspired by Bruce Springsteen's bleak album *Nebraska*.

The sound of *Wrecking Ball*, Emmylou Harris's 1995 album produced by former Brian Eno/Neville Brothers associate Daniel Lanois, drew me back toward Harris. But it was her energetic if unevenly recorded live disc, 1998's *Spyboy*, and the tour that followed with her post-psychedelic power trio that made me seriously want more for the first time in a decade. So I went back and replayed *Pieces of the Sky*, *Luxury Liner*, and *Elite Hotel*, and even 1972's *GP* and 1973's *Grievous Angel*. For me, her pretty, soulful folky voice with the surprisingly resilient country-meets-blues *cri de coeur* got under my skin less as it settled into Nashville's more predictable contours. I kept waiting for the shakeup, for the rock in country rock to reemerge and maybe even, with luck, take over.

To my ears, that's what happened on *Wrecking Ball* and *Spyboy*. Fired first by Lanois's Eno-inspired, wall-of-sound approach, then by her interracial power trio (guitar whiz Buddy Miller, bass monster Daryl Jones, agile drummer Brady Blade), Harris didn't so much tear up her country roots as reinfuse them with another set of musical ideas. Thick-toned distorted guitar, galloping bass, a cyclone of sound surrounding that angelic voice with the heartachy tremolo, even on the old spirituals that have been part of her show for decades.

Then came *Red Dirt Girl*, Harris's first studio disk since *Wrecking Ball*, this time via arty Nonesuch Records, home of the sleeper hit *Buena Vista Social Club*. There may be ironic hay to be made by somebody (not me) out of the fact that Nonesuch has made its bucks as the trendy yuppie label of the 1980s and 1990s, marketing leather-and-lace Euro-trash hits like the Gypsy Kings. The label's stock in trade is its (justly) critically ratified, near-automatic intellectual heft, and its consequent ability to target boomers who scan the Sunday *New York Times* each week for what to absorb.

They could do a lot worse than Harris's *Red Dirt Girl*, most of which—rarely, for her—she wrote herself.

It's a cliché that most people in America want someone else's life. Ever since the Gold Rush was augmented by Hollywood and John Steinbeck's Depression, California has been the golden wet dream for Americans imagining new identities, the place where you can retool your self and ditch the nasty nagging past you might someday have to answer for— or to.

Harris, like Springsteen, doesn't leave folks or home or culture or ideas behind. In fact, she has been a kind of bellwether of pop music's directions for almost three decades, partly because she's so rooted in her past she's aware of where changes of direction are likely to blow in from. When she started singing with Parsons, country and rock hated each other; over the last decade, as her boomer generation settled comfortably into middle age, country stars all sound like the Eagles, who were just reading some pages from Parsons's book. Before the current refashionability of bluegrass and that already-gone moment of alt-country, Harris was there. On *Red Dirt Girl*, she connects the dots between the 1960s, Springsteen, and the post-Hendrix production style Lanois has refined.

You could argue that *Red Dirt Girl* updates Hendrix by way of electronica, but with a (relatively) conservative ear cocked backward, for the boomer audience's sake. The entire album is a potpourri of sonic styles, somehow overstuffed and lavish and rippling with suggestive overtones even when it's spare. On the title track, for instance, wisps of overdriven guitar leak almost discreetly into the corners of the soundstage, a sympathetic echo of the lyrics' successive dislocations. Multiple basses rumble and snort through "I Don't Wanna Talk About It Now," reflecting the disoriented but overwhelming focus shaping the singer's emotions. Every cut finds sounds spurting, drifting, wafting, insinuating, poking, or sizzling into the deeply textured stereo image with unexpected and sometimes unsettling bits of shock, humor, recognition. Repeatedly jigs and reels, the staples of Appalachian-descended country, get bushwacked and overlayed and saturated with fuzz and wah-wah washes and distant jangly electric piano and guitars, of course, always guitars of every aural hue and cry.

The guitar, rock and roll's conceptual anchor, is the symbol that links Harris and Springsteen. Consider her in-concert staple, "Born To Run"; not Springsteen's song, it takes an angle on men-women relationships that puts the woman in the rock and roll driver's seat. In fact, the title track of *Red Dirt Girl* is a very Boss-like tale of doppelgangers, one of whom gets stuck in the old hometown, has five kids by age 27, starts downing whiskey and pills and ends up dead.

Like Springsteen and Tom Waits, Harris often imagines the characters in her songs as people (or aspects of herself) she's left behind. But in contrast to America's standard-issue California dreamin', she doesn't want to erase her past. She doesn't disappear beneath each new persona. Which is one of several reasons Gram Parsons never hovers far from her music.

"Michelangelo," the CD's second tune, is yet another in a long line of Harris tunes that invoke his ghost, the tragic figure of the flawed genius surrounded by his past choices, via a melody that could have come out of Leonard Cohen and a spare but textured aural background speckled with rumbling bass and acoustic guitar strums and jetstream wisps of overdriven feedback. "Tragedy" sets its tensions between industrial drumming, a clutch of guitars (including a hovering pedal steel), and Springsteen and wife Patty Scialfa on backup Everly Brothers-go-rhythm-and-blues-flavored vocals after the Bossish opening about how we all harvest our own destinies.

That sense of responsibility is why Harris never forgets or erases history, no matter how she may recast it in literary or imaginative terms. ("Bang the Drum Slowly," her eulogy for her father cowritten with Guy Clark, is unabashedly sentimental and biblical, for instance, with an e-bow winding through it like a church organ.) It's also why, along with the likes of Springsteen and Waits, she has struggled with the theme of redemption time after time, whether singing refurbished old hymns in her soaring vibrato or switching to more profane journeys taken from her own and others' searching. Understanding, guilt, salvation, and love are all bound together in songs like "The Pearl" which pictures humans neoplatonically cast form a world of light into a dark world of pain where we earn our destinies.

It's a story older than *Piers Plowman*, but may seem quaint in a day when the word character has been vastly reduced in meaning, when the world appears like a welter of wannabe victims lining up for a camera shot. The process of living leaves us scarred like it did Michelangelo, but that's the price. Cameos come relatively cheap. On the other hand, there's always the twilight solace of Prozac Nation.

Startlingly produced by Malcolm Burn (who engineered and mixed *Wrecking Ball*), featuring a dozen or so musicians (also including Dave Matthews and Jill Cunliffe), *Red Dirt Girl* is roughly two-thirds dyna-mite, one-third breathing space. Sonically, it never stops pushing into post–Hendrix wah-wah soundscapes, including telephone rings and background conversations, tunes starting with the whirr of a tape machine being turned on—all the deliberate post–electronica careless-ness of sonic references outside the soundstage that paradoxically underscore that stage's fierce integrity. Conceptually, it does what the best country music (which it only vaguely is) has always done: tells us stories about where we come from and warns us to look twice about where we're going.

For Harris never forgets for long that our only inevitable destination is death—which is one big reason you might call this music for grown-ups. Sure, it's boomer music, so there's inevitably nostalgia, but in Harris's capable, determined, ironic hands, the disc raises more questions than it settles neatly down to bed. And you can hum nearly all of it through the jabs at the job and downers from your parents and/or kids and adrenalin rushes of joy and outbreaks of road rage and those late, ominously clear and sparkling nights when everyone else is finally out cold and you're rhapsodically wishing you had a telescope.

The Grateful Dead

19

Frenesi took her hand away from Flash's and they all
got back to business, the past, a skip tracer with an
obsessional gleam in its eye, and still a step or two
behind, appeased for only a little while. Sure, she knew
folks who had no problem with the past. A lot of it they
just didn't remember. Many told her, one way and
another, that it was enough for them to get by in real
time without diverting precious energy to what, face it,
was fifteen or twenty years dead and gone. But for
Frenesi the past was on her case forever, the zombie at
her back, the enemy no one wanted to see, a mouth
wide and dark as the grave.
　　　　　　　　　　　　—Thomas Pynchon, *Vineland*

Q: How do you know when Deadheads have been
　staying with you?
A: They're still there.

We're American. What we do is as American as lynch
mobs. America has always been a complex place.
　　　　　　　　　　　　　　　　　—Jerry Garcia

THE GRATEFUL DEAD avoided social pronouncements like bad acid, but
they helped create the contemporary concept of lifestyle. Even in the
1990s, when the band's audience was mostly middle-aged, Deadheads
felt they stepped out of prefab social roles and into an alternate universe
of possibility.

For those off the bus, the Dead's culture was childishly dangerous. So
were taking drugs and dropping out to sleep on the street and scamming
money, food, and tickets to the band's infamously uneven shows, as
young Deadheads did.

So then, why did it work? The Dead and Deadheads persisted and thrived, despite being the butts of jokes and harassment and rejection. What could this tell us about the 1960s, the epicenter of the American culture wars?

"The Dead," wrote *Entrepreneur* in the 1990s, "found a way to sell without appearing to sell out." Their long strange trip there went the hard way. In 1969, after recording their first three albums, the band owed Warner Bros. $185,000. The company's frustration about cost overruns in the studio was exacerbated by the Dead's lack of hit singles. Then *Live/Dead*, a live double album, went gold in 1970, the label gave them $75,000 to re-sign, and Lenny Hart, drummer Mickey Hart's father, the band's interim manager, walked off with it. By 1971, they had been arrested repeatedly for drugs. One bust in New Orleans sparked "Truckin'," their only AM radio hit.

FM radio saved the Dead. *Live/Dead* was the first in-concert album recorded in 16-track stereo, and its long jams fit the more relaxed album-cut format that predominated on FM rock radio. Widespread play on FM coupled with a multi-city US tour: the band's concerts were simulcast on local FM stations, and listeners were encouraged to tape them—despite the entertainment industry frowning on piracy. The gambit won over thousands of listeners who had never seen the Dead and cemented their outsider reputation.

When Warner Bros. executives first met them, they were startled to realize that this unknown bunch of weirdos would take a deal only on their terms, and as a result the Dead kept rare control of their publishing and licensing rights. They also pioneered the contemporary concert industry: by 1971, tables at their shows sold T-shirts, and they unveiled The Wall of Sound, a modular behemoth of vari-sized PA speakers that filled two tractor-trailers, at a time when arena concerts barely existed. That same year the cover of their second live double-album, *Grateful Dead*, had a notice: DEAD FREAKS UNITE! Who are you? Where are you? How are you? Several hundred wrote to the San Rafael, California, P.O. box, and the first Dead newsletter went out. By 1974, the list had 80,000 names. In 1983, they opened Dead Tix to control ticket access and prices and promoters. They asked that bootleg tapes of their shows be swapped, not sold, and tried to prosecute violators. Their Rex Foundation was funded by concert earnings and gave away $7 million.

Their corporate headquarters was a small house in Marin, north of San Francisco, where they all lived for years. They evolved Dead versions of corporate structure and *Roberts Rules of Order*. "The question," Garcia said to *Rolling Stone* in the early days, "is, can we do it and stay high? Can we make it so our organization is composed of people who are, like, pretty high and not being controlled by their gig but who are actively interested in what they're doing?"

At first, people just showed up and hung out and maybe worked; sixty stuck, and got well-paid, secure jobs with profit-sharing, health and dental and retirement plans, home and car loans. Roadies were on salary year-round, six figures. Grateful Dead Productions ultimately dealt with all Dead business: mail-order tickets, catalog merchandising, concert-site merchandising, their label and publishing company, the fan club, the foundation. "It is certainly the rock industry's most fully formed company," *Inc.* wrote admiringly in 1994. The chairmanship rotated among band members as the staff ran their bailiwicks. No wonder *Inc.* was enthusiastic: 1990s business consultants had caught up with the Dead's decentralized style of team management.

During the 1970s, the Dead placed among the country's top-grossing live acts. In 1985, trapped in a deepening addiction, guitarist and resident guru Jerry Garcia was busted in Golden Gate Park for cocaine and heroin possession. The band, which had avoided the issue, finally confronted him, and he entered drug rehab. In 1986, he had a diabetic coma and nearly died. But in 1987 the Dead made *Forbes*'s list of top-paid entertainers. In the 1990s, they slowed their pace to three to four week-long bouts on the road three or four times a year, but in 1992 they pulled in $32 million; they were the highest-grossing act in show business. Garcia collapsed again. In 1993, 81 concerts earned $45.6 million.

After Garcia died in August 1995, the press had a field day. His widow and his second wife and kids fought over $10 million in cash and annual royalties of $4.6 million from his music and art, plus spinoffs like painted neckties, an action figure, and branded Birkenstock sandals. His bandmates fought over the hand-crafted guitars he'd willed to the man who made them, claiming they were communal property.

But for 30 years, while the straight world jeered or shrugged, the Dead lived in a parallel universe and made it work.

GRATEFUL DEAD MUSIC WAS AMERICAN MUSIC, polyglot, popular, spiked with jazz, folk, rock, rhythm and blues, country, blues, electronic, aleatoric, classical, and any other sound the musicians decided they could use. The band's background had a lot to do with why that worked.

Garcia's father, a Dixieland bandleader, named him after Jerome Kern, but rock and roll and bluegrass made him want to play guitar and banjo. His solos are an Armstrong-like process of melodic sugggestion and searching: plangent lyricism, bursts of triplets, crying glissandos, unexpected icy edges of irony and wit. Ron "Pigpen" McKernan grew up in black neighborhoods, where his father worked as a DJ on black radio; he was the Dead's sacred monster, its black-in-whiteface front man. Bassist Phil Lesh learned violin at age eight, trumpet at 14, studied with Luciano Berio at 22, and at 25 took up the bass, for the first time, two weeks before he first played the then-Warlocks. As a teen, Bill

Kreutzman drummed for years in R & B bands, and drummer Mickey Hart studied folk percussion around the globe: the Dead were charged by a powerful generator of polyrhythmic, odd-meter grooves. Guitarist Bob Weir was mostly self-taught, but he learned from Garcia to avoid patterns and phrase like brass sections. "He used to listen to trumpet—like Miles (Davis), for instance," Weir remembered, "and so I started listening to John Coltrane's pianist McCoy Tyner. He was good at phrasing, but he was also good at what I call a textured harmonic carpet that he'd lay down for a soloist. There'd be a given key he'd be playing in, and then there'd be an overlay of notes on top of that that were basically suspended on the back half of the bar. I learned that you're not there to make a point—you're there to serve the music. Jerry taught me to listen."

In the 1990s, jazz musicians jammed with the Dead regularly, and jazz groups put on Grateful Dead tributes. Ornette Coleman had Garcia guest on an album; asked what it was like, the guitarist told *The New Yorker*, "Like filling in the spaces in a Jackson Pollock painting."

Garcia was the Dead's psychic and symbolic hub, and embodied the cultural strands knotting the Beat and hippie periods, and thus jazz, folk, and rock. Born in San Francisco in 1942, Garcia was Chicano. Not long after the five year old lost part of a finger in a wood-chopping game of dare with his brother, he saw his father drown. After a few years living with his mother's parents, where he had piano lessons but preferred reading comics and Ray Bradbury and Edgar Rice Burroughs, he moved into his mother's sailors' bar and hotel in downtown San Francisco.

"My grandmother listened to country music," he said, "and my mother listened to opera. My father was a musician; I was in the middle of music. . . . Nobody was telling me rock and roll was out of tune. I didn't get that." But when he was 15 and stung by Chuck Berry and Buddy Holly and asked his mother for an electric guitar, she got him a Neapolitan accordion from a sailor. He swapped it at a pawn shop for a Danelectro, one of the cheapest electric guitars of the period, a postwar triumph of functionality with its pressboard body, cheap finish, and pickups made from lipstick holders. He taught himself to play: "The most important thing I learned," he told Bruce Barich, "was that it was okay to improvise."

He hung out with pot-smoking beatniks who went to poetry readings in North Beach at the Coexistence Bagel Shop, so his mother moved to the Sonoma County coast to get him out of trouble. It didn't work. Like Jimi Hendrix, he was busted for stealing a car and joined the army at 17. As with Hendrix, Garcia's army time sharpened his interest in music. The paratrooper Hendrix translated the Doppler effects he heard as he fell into his outrageous space-age blues. Garcia was drawn instead to the discipline of bluegrass: "When you're blasting along straight eighth notes at a quick tempo, it requires a lot of control and a lot of practice." Near-death in a car crash that killed a friend made him fanatical about music. He slowed down Earl Scruggs records to learn five-string banjo. By the early 1960s, he was good enough to tour bluegrass festivals and meet one of his heroes, Bill Monroe, the man who'd brought jazzy polyrhythms and harmonies into old-time string music.

By 1962, a member of the loose community of Beats around Palo Alto and Menlo Park on the peninsula south of San Francisco, he devoured records: string bands and blues, R & B and jazz, the Harry Smith *Anthology*. His bluegrass and jug bands had period-piece names: Asphalt Jungle Boys, Sleepy Hollow Log Stompers, Hart Valley Drifters, Thunder Mountain Tub Thumpers, Wildwood Boys, Black Mountain Boys, Mother McCree's Uptown Jug Champions. In 1964, he met David Grisman, who a decade later fused bluegrass with the hot jazz of Django Reinhardt and Stephane Grappelli, which he dubbed Dawg Music. During the late 1970s, Grisman and Garcia (on banjo) formed in Old and In The Way, a jazz-bluegrass string quintet with fiddler Vassar Clements.

Menlo Park was home to writers Ken Kesey and Robert Stone, who were taking LSD, initially as part of Stanford University studies. (At Harvard, Timothy Leary, with the advice of Aldous Huxley, was giving LSD to creative people like Thelonious Monk and Allen Ginsberg.) In 1965, the Warlocks debuted at Magoos Pizza Parlor, playing anything from plugged-in jug-band music to roiling rhythm and blues with spontaneous jams. Then they met Bill Graham, actor turned promoter; less than a month later, they were the Grateful Dead, house band for Kesey's Acid Tests, and Garcia morphed into Captain Trips. For most of 1966, they played constantly around the Bay Area for free. By the time they cut their first Warner Bros. recording, they'd been performing nonstop for two years.

I FIRST SAW THE GRATEFUL DEAD in New York's Tompkins Square Park on June 1, 1967. A schoolmate was hip to the new San Francisco bands and heard about them doing a free afternoon concert. For us, the Dead were a rumor, so we cut class and went.

The park looked full. The thick sweet scent of pot wafted over, but though there were plenty of cops dealing with outraged Ukrainians from the neighborhood we couldn't see any busts. The Diggers seemed to be keeping things together. The Diggers organized squat housing, food distribution, first aid, and other vital services around the hippie and runaway communities that suddenly sprang up in San Francisco and the East Village. They hustled donations, worked out barter, but always their watchword was "free." They rejected money and The System it oiled.

The Dead were playing "Dancing in the Streets," with Pigpen the anti-hippie, a greasy, ugly, beery biker, centerstage. It reminds me now, after decades of hearing how trippy and abstract and slo-mo their live shows were, that the Grateful Dead I saw so much in the late 1960s was a dance band. Rhythms were their fuel, that New Orleans-flavored lilt of their sprung beats that swung with such joy and freedom. In 1967, I felt it, like everybody else, but I didn't realize they'd absorbed jazz syncopations and modal improvising into psychedelic rock, that they grasped Miles Davis's modes and melody and Herbie Hancock's way of turning the beat around repeatedly, a cyclonic effect that suspends time. But I didn't have to realize it to move to it.

The Dead and the Diggers scared and repelled the American mainstream, but they descended from an American tradition: the ecstatic utopian community, a consistent but repressed side of American history that stretched from peyote-taking, tobacco-smoking Native Americans through the Quakers and Shakers and Baptist snake-handlers and Jim Jones. Psychedelic drugs were this sect's casual sacraments, mostly pot, hash, mescaline, peyote, psylocibin, and LSD, though speed and downers and cocaine flickered around the edges.

Forty years later, it still seems bitterly hilarious to me that after spending countless billions of dollars America's perpetual War on Drugs continues without evident effect, except for millions in prison, while more millions gobble proliferating pharmaceuticals marketed by drug conglomerates, like Viagra and Prozac, spurred by what are now called "lifestyle choices," despite the spotty knowledge about their long-term effects.

Welcome to Brave New World.

Psychedelic drugs deepened the tribalism and distrust of ideology fundamental to the Diggers' vision. They rejected the use of money, the totem of American society, because they rejected The System where everything had a dollar value or else had no value. So they begged, scammed, panhandled—the modes the straight world despised and feared in white youth. "Diggers are niggers," a slogan that was obviously less than true, was really the sound of some who had grown up absurd, slouching out the exit from the rat-race and Manifest Destiny.

But, in 1967, black and white America were separate worlds ruled by economics and racism, not ecstasy. Black Power and black separatism replaced the religious-led civil-rights crusade in the South; Martin Luther King was broadening his political platform to oppose the Vietnam War. There were few Deadheads or Diggers of color, and as few whites in black revolutionary groups. As the war escalated, Lyndon Johnson slashed Great Society programs to fund it, and the rage broke in the firestorm of riots that swept the nation's cities around the time the Dead coalesced outside San Francisco, crescendoed just about the time their New York City blitz converted thousands into Dead freaks. From then on New York was their second home: we saw them a lot at the Fillmore East, three- and four-hour phantasmagorical shows that inexorably fed the legend.

They headed back west to play the Monterey Pop Festival, rock's first, blanketed with media coverage that showed the counterculture in confusing, frightening, blissful drug-powered glory onstage and off, culminating (in the movie) with Jimi Hendrix making his debut and, after burning up the music, smashing and burning his guitar. Was this a representation of the politics of ecstasy? What about the playfulness, the way he detonated "Wild Thing" while casually chewing a huge wad of gum? Despite the noise and cavalcade of stars, the movie *Monterey Pop* lost money and slowed Hollywood's rush toward rock: I saw it in a Kips Bay theater, the seats mostly empty and the screen washed with deep blue and black for Otis Redding, who died soon after the festival, the speakers bursting with sound and fury and hippie irreverence and Marx Brothers-inspired subversion.

The Dead did the concert but not the movie. They wanted the show's profits to go to the Diggers, refused to sign releases for their performances when that didn't happen, stole amplifiers and gave a free all-night show at a local college to retaliate, and returned the equipment the next day.

A month after Monterey, *Time* magazine did its cover story on "The Hippies," and 75,000 middle-class white kids looking to drop out and party, most with no street smarts, poured into San Francisco during the Summer of Love, and the deluge buried the Diggers and their fragile experiment. On October 6, 1967, the first anniversary of the outlawing of LSD, the Diggers marched in a symbolic funeral procession for "The Death of Hippie."

The attempt to set up a viable alternative infrastructure in the physical world was over before Woodstock or Altamont ever happened.

GARCIA GREW MYTHIC, aureoled with curly black hair and thick beard, his glasses glinting with merry irony. Like Dylan, he used double-talk and put-ons to slide out from the role of leader. He did not direct or speak for the Dead, the Deadheads, the hippies, the Diggers, the antiwar movement. Each of us had a path for our steps alone that we had to find.

Enigmatic, Zenlike: Garcia's best solos led the Dead to the risk of the unforeseen to seek those moments of transport, walking on air; sometimes he seemed like a cartoon character, Pynchon's Benny Profane, fine as long as he didn't look down. Sometimes he fell. Sometimes he fought his way free of gravity and, pumped by the Dead's oscillating feedback loop, stepped back into space and searched again. If the quest for musical ecstasy imbued the Dead with homemade drama that hooked their audience, it also displayed character in their endless willingness to try.

The 12-CD set called *Golden Road (1965–1973)* gathers their 10 albums for Warner Bros. (The individual albums with outtakes have also been reissued.) With improved sound, original art, multiple sets of well-informed notes, and elaborate packaging, it can be riveting, then downshift into something so painful you wonder all over again how these guys ever made it. Then you hit *Live/Dead* and hear the onstage torque this band could put out, its kinetic ability to spot problems and trampoline them into possibilities, send Garcia back out soaring on those skipping triplets and crying glissandos, those sudden unexpected edges of irony and wry wit, those clean, crisp, cascading lines that wink like shooting stars on a clearing night.

Not for nothing was "Dark Star" the totemic Deadhead hit: it epitomized the Dead's participatory musical democracy. The volume rolls up on Lesh's bass and Garcia's guitar twining in a contrapuntal canon that clarifies gradually into John Coltrane's themes from "India" and "Your Lady," burnished by double-drummer cymbals and finessed by Weir's guitar, which scratches and claws two-note and three-note chords and hammered-on and pulled-off fills. The modal conversation hovers, then swells into full view: the voices in the band wind in and out, bob and weave through the foreground, dancing in their heads as they sway (if you'd seen them, you knew this) gently out of time onstage. The Dead's command of dynamics was exceptionally deft, and "Dark Star" pivoted on it. The improvisation was dominated by modal interaction, but, as later Miles Davis would, they also segued into patches that were less thematic development than sidebars, sudden sonic windows opening along the way because of something one of the musicians said.

Their first recording sessions, for the Autumn and Scorpio labels, included on the box set, are forgettable, except for a weird track with jazz's master of scat vocals Jon Hendricks. The first album for Warner Bros., *Grateful Dead*, sounds like the Ritalin they were swallowing: the folk songs and blues from their huge repertoire were transmogrified into amphetamine blues. Engineer Dave Hassinger was flummoxed by the snorting psychedelic behemoth he faced in the studio for four days, so he turned the volume down and edited out the jams. (The reissues restore them.) When I finally heard the album, it didn't sound much like Tompkins Square, except for the material. ("Birth of the Dead," an early live disc in the box, comes closer to what they sounded like.) There was Pigpen's dirty-old-man reading of Sonny Boy Williamson's "Good Morning Little Schoolgirl," riding that bouncy Dead beat, Lesh's bass loping with his eerily agile grace, stirring lyricism, and daredevil timing. There was "Cold Rain and Snow," whose double-guitar solo set the pattern for the Allman Brothers and their ilk.

"Sitting on Top of the World," an old Mississippi Sheiks tune redone by Howlin' Wolf, revved into a high-speed, key-shifting chase. "Morning Dew," a contemporary folk song about nuclear holocaust, was a longtime Dead setpiece, at its best a tour de force of their rock-meets-Dixieland call-and-response. "Viola Lee Blues," the album closer, put this over a march beat that accelerates into a one-chord rave-up, a rolling avalanche that climaxes with feedback billowing—a glimpse of what the Dead sounded like live. Only the explosively galloping opening of "Golden Road (to unlimited devotion)," aswirl with Hammond and combustible guitars, matched it.

The album introduces the American patchwork quilt of material that remained the Dead's trademark: tunes from Gus Cannon's Jug Stompers, the Memphis Jug Band, Otis Redding, Smokey Robinson, Howlin' Wolf, Noah Lewis, Reverend Gary Davis, Bob Dylan (their single largest source of outside material), Jesse Fuller, Merle Haggard, and the ever-popular Anonymous filled their bulging songbook. This was one reason they never made set lists; the other was to take the risk, and try to read the audience via the feedback loop that eliminated the fourth wall of the stage.

Anthem of the Sun took them into conceptual-art music, sonic collage, tape manipulations, lapping overdubs, and endless splices, parts inchoate and other parts brilliant as they learned the latest technology, the eight-track recording studio. Their Buddha's grin and jug-band history periodically surface: Pigpen's "Alligator" opens with cheerfully sneering kazoos as horn section. Next came *Aoxomoxoa*, which spent almost as much time and money while they tackled the new 16-track studio; it also marks the appearance of Robert Hunter's lyrics, and with them, a new direction. "Dupree's Diamond Blues" is the first of a line of Dead originals: twists on old folk lyrics into a comic tall tale of the surreal or deadly supernatural, with mostly acoustic instruments in a densely subtle arrangement stippled with eccentricities (an ersatz calliope, for instance), and, at the end, a cosmic shrug.

Recorded in the midst of *Aoxomoxoa*, *Live/Dead* was cut onstage at a few shows to let kids who hadn't seen them find out what the buzz was about. "Dark Star," which opened the double album, was an instant FM radio hit. But as popular on the airwaves was the earthy balls-to-the-wall rhythm and blues of Smokey Robinson's "Turn on Your Love Light," which wrecked the house whenever I saw them go for it: the band pumps and chugs and snorts in a multifaceted arrangement behind Pigpen's lewd asides, comic grunts and gestures, and soulful vocals. Garcia's scratchy thin tenor yelp alchemized the dread of Reverend Gary Davis's "Death Don't Have No Mercy": he learned to use his hiccups and even the cracks in his fragile voice skillfully, phrasing with a story-teller's timing, translating bluegrass's high lonesome sound into psychedelic blues even as his guitar navigated around the blues clichés choking nearly every other rock guitarist of the time.

And so the next two albums were a shock at first: the Dead were trying to be Crosby Stills and Nash or The Band. Then I listened to the sturdy song construction, the nuanced arrangements, the narratives that were harrowingly dark and surrealistically funny and sometimes both at once. This makes sense, I thought, from a band named from one of the annotations for *Child's Ballads* that describes "grateful dead," the unavenged who wander without rest until the wrong done them is righted—which grants them peace and makes them "grateful."

With *Workingman's Dead* and its follow-up, *American Beauty*, lyricist Hunter and Garcia (they teamed up far more than the others) explored the nature of evil, the casual damage inflicted by time, history, loved ones, society, life—an American version of the Brothers Grimm, with lots of Dylan-style storytelling etched with steel and tenderness. So there's little sentimentality but plenty of misfits and outcasts, laughs and fear, fables and tall tales and even folk realism. And always there is the genial acceptance of fate tempered with irony and spine. Even when "Uncle John's Band" calls you home, the dire wolf lurks everywhere, and the best you can do is sit down and let him deal the hand though every card in the deck is the "Queen of Spades," shrug like Humphrey Bogart, cornered but in the moment, and play out the scene, knowing that you can run but you can't hide and that sometimes you can't even run, like "Black Peter," a dying old man who wants be surrounded in peace by a couple of close friends but whose neighbors run to see him suffer and die in pain.

Live, the Dead were among rock's worst ensemble vocalists—even when they hit the right notes, their voices didn't blend texturally. That made these albums, full of elaborate harmonies demanding nuance, more of a shock. The Band studied the Staples Singers to learn to max out on their limited voices, emulating the gospel singers' staggered entry and pacing. The Dead were far less inventive. Still, *Workingman's Dead* and *American Beauty* have some lustrous singing, like the taut harmonies of "Cumberland Blues" and "Uncle John's Band." And if "Till the Morning Comes" sounded like the Beach Boys straining, well, fallibility made the Dead more approachable and reminded us that human perfectibility was an ongoing activity, a road that never ended.

These two albums went gold, thanks to FM radio, and gave the Dead a place among rock's most accomplished songwriters. So naturally their next two albums—their last for Warner Bros.—were recorded live.

Deadheads call *Grateful Dead*, their 1971 live double album, the "Skull and Roses" album, because of the four-color skeleton adorned with roses that stretched across the fold-out cover. The name was a last-minute compromise; the band, mischievously provocative, demanded it be called Skullfuck. (*Spinal Tap*, anyone?) It leaked to FM radio even before it was released.

I was at one of the Fillmore East shows where parts of the album were taped, and all I remember was that the band smoked. Pigpen was sick with a much-reduced role; Merl Saunders added occasional organ.

Mickey Hart, shamed by his father's theft, was on sabbatical. So the Dead regrouped around their quartet fundamentals and got even tighter. "Bertha" galloped on Lesh's bass, which suddenly climbed out of its soul-music patterns to loosely double and pump Garcia's solo; "Mama Tried" and "Me and My Uncle," their "cosmic cowboy" tunes, put Weir on ironically smooth lead vocals framing solo sections where Garcia and Lesh danced in fierce telepathy; "The Other One" was as smart and sophisticated a long-form improvisation as "Dark Star"; "Big Boss Man" gave the sadly diminished Pigpen (and the Dead's R & B side) a moment in the spotlight; "Wharf Rat" was a long tale of hope crumbling but unabandoned set to chiming guitars and rumbling, prowling bass rippling with the Dead's dynamic finesse; and the closeout medley, "Not Fade Away/Going Down the Road," was so open-ended, so buoyant, so good that Dylan copped the arrangement.

Europe '72 closed the Dead's time working, as Hunter put it, "for Bugs Bunny." It was also their first tour outside America, so they naturally brought The Wall of Sound (which they pictured inside the fold-out cover) and 50 or so family members, dependents, staff, and roadies. They had added a keyboard player and female backing vocalist, Keith and Donna Godcheaux. They had a clutch of great new tales, like "Jack Straw" and "He's Gone" and "Ramble on Rose," from times that never quite happened about people who never quite lived in places that looked like you might've been. And they had old ones revamped as well: "China Cat Sunflower" undulates on snarling, braided lines that could have been Sly and the Family Stone's. Godcheaux was a busy pianist; what he added in texture and support he could subtract in the breathing room essential to the Dead, but they usually managed to absorb him into their dialogues, and his wife shored up their woeful live harmonies.

And with that they were off to start Grateful Dead Records, which folded, though they did not. During the 1980s their shows lacked edge: after Pigpen's death in 1973 they banked their R & B fires. But the sold-out crowds of Deadheads, aging and newbies, filled airplane hangars like Nassau Coliseum, so far from the Acid Tests, those complicated moments of transcendence that inevitably look dangerously goofy after the fact: mysticism is never clear in words, and the utopian dreams bursting from beneath America's Puritan Taylor-ized crust aren't always easy to decipher. Or maybe, in our dwarfish and cynical age, they are: "In essence," wrote *Entrepreneur*, "the Dead weren't selling music, they were selling a unique, spontaneous experience, a version of lifestyle marketing embodied by Harley-Davidson and Nike. Each concert was a unique event, with the same songs rarely repeated for weeks or even years."

20

The Band

W HEN I FIRST SAW *The Last Waltz* in 1978, I almost walked out, although I was a fan of both director Martin Scorsese and The Band. I admit I was one of the folks whose tickets for the original 1976 show at San Francisco's Winterland were refunded by impresario Bill Graham in light of the scheduled movie shoot, when he decided to have a sitdown Thanksgiving turkey dinner precede the concert, which translated into a then-hefty $25 price tag.

Twenty-six years and a new DVD version with compelling video and redone audio have changed, or at least made subtler, some of my reactions. But I still think two of Scorsese's typical dynamics are in play: seeking out America's underbellies, and monumentalizing or sacramentalizing them. And so *The Last Waltz* teeters between grit and awe—perhaps unintentionally but tellingly, like rock itself at the time and rock history ever since.

When it premiered, Pauline Kael famously dubbed it "the most beautiful rock movie ever." As a formalist she had a point. With seven cameramen who included Vilmos Zsigmond, Scorsese professionalized the deliberately nonprofessional documentary sensibility of DL Pennebaker and the Maysles. Now that seems a fitting sign of the times. In the 1970s, mainstream rock had been professionalized, from the boring arena-ready music itself to the new national distribution systems, while pop sputtered with the industry's search for commercially viable trends, like disco. Almost in answer, new forms of folk art appeared. Bruce Springsteen prowled stages toward apotheosis with shows that exploded somewhere between Elvis, an R & B revue, and *West Side Story*. Breakdancers with turntable artists were appearing on the streets of cities like New York, as punk rockers were in the clubs. It was another return to the do-it-yourself folk aesthetic consistently underlying evolutionary developments in American popular culture.

And so now *The Last Waltz* gives me a kind of double-vision: it's an elegy to The Band that is also, perhaps unwittingly, an elegy to an era. The sense of reverence toward the motley parade of music stars trooping across its lenses is intercut with open-eyed realism during the best of the connecting interview segments—though those too are frequently tinged with Scorsese's romanticism.

The opening scene is a good example. Rick Danko, scarred face and blurred eyes and coiled street-punk energy, gets ready to shoot pool when Scorsese asks him what the game is. "Cutthroat," he replies, swaggering slightly while he explains that the object of the game is to knock everyone else's balls off the table, then smashes the cue ball into a newly racked, now caroming pack.

WHEN *MUSIC FROM BIG PINK* appeared in 1968, it sounded to me like it came from some musical Bermuda triangle sketched by the *Anthology of American Folk Music* and Booker T and the MGs. Its album cover was a painting by Bob Dylan.

Dylan heard about the quintet through blues revivalist John Hammond Jr., who used them on the recording sessions for his 1963 album *So Many Roads*. (Hammond's father was the famous John Hammond who signed Dylan, Billie Holiday, and Bruce Springsteen.) When Dylan called to hire them for shows at New York's Forest Hills tennis stadium and the Hollywood Bowl, they didn't know who he was.

This kicked off Dylan's revolutionary 1965–66 tour. He and the Hawks, as they were known then, revved up his music into garage grunge while being booed coast-to-coast by folk purists. It was enough to make one band member quit. Al Kooper remembers that at shows he played with Dylan during this time audiences sang along with "Like a Rolling Stone," and *then* booed. But the crowds weren't all hostile: in Berkeley, Allen Ginsberg brought Ken Kesey, Michael McClure, and Gary Snyder. There's a picture of the poets with Dylan that shows Robertson standing a bit apart, as if wanting to join but not sure he should—or could.

After his 1966 motorcycle accident, Dylan pretty much disappeared from view, and there were regular rumors of his death or disfigurement. But the smartest word was that he'd been hanging out at Big Pink, a nondescript house at the foot of Woodstock's Overlook Mountain, jamming and writing songs with The Band. (These would soon surface as bootlegs; selections have been remixed and officially reissued on *The Basement Tapes*, intercut with other material by The Band alone.) Dylan encouraged them to find their artistic vision. No surprise that *Music from Big Pink* opened with one Dylan track, "Tears of Rage," and closed with another, "I Shall Be Released."

Dylan's near-invisibility only augmented his cultural aura, a marketing lesson his widely disliked, thuggish, Svengaliesque manager, Albert Grossman, absorbed and soon applied to his latest clients, The Band. Hadn't there already been a major-label bidding war to sign them thanks to their time with Dylan? The word of mouth preceding their first album release was amplified by then-emerging FM rock radio, which played album tracks, not hit singles. This late 1960s development created openings for groups like The Band, who were not really top 40 AM-radio material, but could survive from FM airplay thanks to album sales and touring. (Even so, *Music from Big Pink* was certified gold—recognition of 500,000 copies sold—only in 2001.)

From the late 1960s on, power and money shifted to FM rock stations as audiences and album sales grew exponentially, displacing other genres in the music business's hierarchy. Classical, jazz, and folk stations dwindled. Through the 1970s, standardization of format and consolidation of ownership proceeded apace with the rest of American business trends. By the century's end, virtually 90 percent of all American radio stations were owned by two or three corporations. But at the time, the birth of FM rock radio seemed to bring gusts of fresh air through newly opened windows.

Inside the double sleeve of *Music from Big Pink* were pictures of The Band: five guys dressed like extras in an early Hollywood western, visual kin to the road-warrior hobos and evicted tenant farmers who peopled *Grapes of Wrath* and Woody Guthrie tunes. Their mothers and fathers and kids. Their house, Big Pink, every band's dream—a clubhouse to jam and practice and record in, surrounded by a hundred acres of mountain meadows and woods, though The Band, like millions of post-Beatles and post-Dylan American kids picking and singing in their cellars and backyards, still had to keep the volume down for fear of riling the neighbors.

Nestled in Big Pink, playing cards and getting stoned and writing and working out new stuff as well as tweaking old bar-band tunes and Anglican hymns and backwoods country and pieces of Harry Smith's *Anthology of American Folk Music*, Dylan and The Band forged a remarkable creative symbiosis. Thanks to their Dylan-paid salaries and a rent that, depending on who you believe, was somewhere between $125 and $275 a month, The Band played musical chairs with instruments as they groped for fresh ideas. As Robbie Robertson, The Band's chief songwriter and guitarist, has shrewdly observed, "Sometimes the limitation of the instrument can provide originality."

Improvising was key to their artistic process, as their shortcomings or imaginations prodded them from instrument to instrument, lineup to lineup to find what worked with the tune at hand. The result was contemporary folk music, new-minted yet old-sounding, with strains of Appalachia and the Delta, rockabilly and soul. It wobbled foggily somewhere between jug bands and Stax-Volt, surreal wet dreams and revival meetings.

DESPITE ROCK HISTORY'S STANDARD MYTHS, the instruments on *Music from Big Pink* were in many ways less unfamiliar, even in rock contexts, than idiosyncratically foregrounded and mixed and matched. Each track got a particular sound, a special treatment. The keynote was a kind of homespun versatility, at times reminiscent of Woody Guthrie's sawn fiddle tunes.

Robertson's guitar stayed mostly low-profile, rearing for occasional stabbing outbursts; he rarely sang. The three vocalists were startlingly different, but found offbeat ways to blend. As Robertson has wryly observed, "A lot of the time with The Band they were somewhere between real harmonies and, because of our lack of education in music, they would be things that just sounded interesting—or they would be only thing the person could hit."

And yet there was more art to it than that. "I wanted," Robertson has said, "to discover the sound of The Band. . . . I didn't want screaming vocals. I wanted sensitive vocals where you can hear the breathing and the voices coming in. The whole thing of discovering the voices—don't everybody come in all together. Everybody in records is working on getting all the voices together until it neutralizes itself. I like voices coming in one at a time, in a chain reaction kind of thing like the Staples Singers did."

Levon Helm's singing was gritty and soulful and at times sardonic; he doubled on drums and mandolin. Rick Danko had a clear, yearning tenor, played bass that burbled like a McCartneyesque tuba, sawed a backwoods fiddle, and strummed guitar. Richard Manuel doubled on engagingly ramshackle drums and pounded what has been described as "rhythm piano"; as for his voice, Robertson has said, "There's a certain element of pain in there that you didn't know whether it was because he was trying to reach for a note or because he was a guy with a heart that'd been hurt." Garth Hudson was classically trained, said he learned to improvise from playing at his uncle's funeral parlor, loved Scriabin and Anglican church music, and invented one after another "black box," the kinds of sound-shapers so integral to the era's musical sensibility. Hudson didn't sing, but the sounds he made became The Band's sonic glue, as they fitted parts together that breathed, leaving spaces that float, stepping into others, with the sort of interlocking discipline found in, say, the jammed-out music of Count Basie, or Muddy Waters, or Booker T and the MGs. Not surprisingly, they cut their first two albums mostly live in the studio. (See *The Band* for an informative, if talking-head-heavy, video history of the making of the group's first two records.)

"Tears of Rage," cowritten by Dylan and Manuel, kicked *Music from Big Pink* off-kilter from the start. Manuel's eccentric R & B cry and falsetto staggered dangerously, seductively, around the confessional lyrics, Robertson's treated guitar approximated organ tones, Hudson's winding churchy organ swelled and subsided, and a drunken Salvation Armyish horn section (courtesy of Hudson and producer John Simon) punctuated the flow over the spare, Booker-T-and-the-MGs-style bass and drums. Simon has observed of the distinctively moaning horn blend, "That's the only sound we could make."

The rest of the album was uneven but ear-opening, challenging, even wonderful. "To Kingdom Come" bounced airily, blearily beneath Manuel's vocals, "The Weight" mixed Curtis Mayfield guitar licks into a surreal gospel setting, "Long Black Veil" tipped its classicist hat at Lefty Frizell, and "Chest Fever" was an instant FM-radio hit, with its swelling, skirling, gnashing organ and nightmare-incoherent lyrics.

With Albert Grossman behind them, The Band—or at least Robertson, who was rapidly becoming primus inter pares—learned to use reticence and image to enhance their music. Like Wynton Marsalis a decade later in jazz, they self-consciously looked back to tradition. "We were rebelling against the rebellion," Robertson has said. "It was an instinct to separate ourselves from the pack." That instinct drew the attention of the aborning rock press, which became their champions: outlets like *Rolling Stone*, cofounded by jazz historian Ralph J. Gleason, fused the old fanzines and more critical and historical perspectives. These new media helped make The Band counterculture heroes.

As did the lyrics, which were increasingly written by Robertson. Enigmatic and vaguely religious and poetic, full of questions and retorts that never necessarily mesh, painting realistic scenes and Dadaist laments, they clearly owed a great deal to Dylan. Robertson had also been reading Steinbeck and Cocteau, thinking in terms of movies, wanting to replicate what he's called Dylan's disruption of song forms. To many, he appeared as a contemporary James Agee, determined to find the artistic secrets in the backwoods margins of America's soul.

The look and sound, the entire presentation of The Band, evoked the notion of authenticity that has underscored writing about them ever since, usually to contrast them with the countercultural rebellion they were supposedly rebelling against. As Grossman, who knew show business, surely understood, this was both an iconic extension and an ironic inversion of the folk revival's would-be purity. For the counterculture and show business were The Band's home. They were outriders on Dylan's panoramic influence, mountainside avatars of the Jeffersonian "back-to-the-land" ideal that recurred in the Woodstock generation's ideology. "The Weight" became a radio hit largely because of its appearance in the film *Easy Rider*. Their music wasn't played at the Grand Ole Opry or juke joints. They weren't Waylon Jennings or Willie Nelson or Merle Haggard.

The appearance of *Music from Big Pink* helped seal the shift to rock culture from rock and roll. Musically, this described a finely braided process of more self-conscious reassimilation of musical influences and ideas that fed a creative surge in post-Dylan/post-Beatles American popular music, washing away years of teen idols and Tin Pan Alley and crewcut collegiate folk singers dominating the radio and record industry. Everyone, following the new model, wanted to write songs.

For The Band, it was no accident that so much of their materials' imagery feels derived from southern models. The South was the part of the country they knew best; Helm was born there, the others met it first-hand from the road trips as the Hawks backing Ronnie "The Hawk" Hawkins, a second-tier rockabilly rebel, in roadhouses and clubs where tempers blew and bottles flew. But, more to the point, it was a space the Canadians already imagined clearly, since they'd grown up listening to American clear-channel radio. Seekers of native American roots music generally headed south: think of W. C. Handy or the Lomaxes. It was in the South that the raw blue-collar energy of rock and roll had first erupted, precisely because, following the Hegelian laws of inversion that seem to govern social evolution, black and blue-collar white cultures in that most overtly segregated section of the country were paradoxically closer and more alike after spending hundreds of years side-by-side than they could possibly be elsewhere.

These four Canadians and lone Arkansan were a long way from their days as the Hawks. Instead, as Greil Marcus perceptively if rather romantically noted of their early music, "It felt like a passport back to America for people who'd become so estranged from their country that they felt like foreigners even when they were in it."

Maybe. To me, a kid playing in garage bands, it felt like eccentric, fascinating sounds that reopened acres of imaginative possibilities.

"THE FIRST TWO RECORDS were almost the same project in my mind," Levon Helm has said. When *The Band* followed *Music from Big Pink* a year later, it cemented their reputation, and enhanced their Dylanesque mystique of invisibility: refusing to tour, partly because of Band members' car crashes and flip-outs, they had watched promoters' offers climb from $2000 a show to $50,000.

In the post–Woodstock Festival world, rock had accelerated its move from roadhouses and clubs, which became unable to compete financially for rock headliners, to theaters, then arenas. Bill Graham had led the way, first with San Francisco's Winterland, soon with his Fillmores West and East. The Band were in the midst of recording their second album far from the Catskills, in Hollywood at Sammy Davis Jr.'s poolhouse, which they'd converted to a studio, when they decided to resist no longer. But before they debuted onstage as themselves at Winterland in April 1969, Robertson got such a bad case of nerves (he has always claimed he had the flu) that he stayed in bed for three days of rehearsal and had to be hypnotized to go onstage.

Since they'd been musically weaned in roadhouses and spent such care on recording live, it's always been one of the odder ironies of The Band's career that they were erratic, often uncomfortable performers. Having so meticulously worked out their parts in clubhouse fashion, they seemed unable to adapt them easily to theaters and arenas. "Taking our music out and performing it, there was something very private about it," Robertson has argued. "There was some kind of yin-and-yang between our nature and what concerts were really about. It was almost more like classical music in performance." Perhaps, as with Marsalis years later, that sensibility sapped the music's vital forces. As Jim Miller wrote in *Rolling Stone*, "They displayed an awful slickness.... Even the raw edges seemed planned. These bar-band auteurs were only too ready to embalm their own work beneath a veneer of professionalism, as if to exhibit it behind a glass case in some museum."

Unconsciously extending the folk revival's ideology, many reviewers tended to explain their unevenness as an emblem of honest authenticity, which, in the ways of do-it-yourself folk-culture amateurism, it sometimes was, though this was somehow also the culture that The Band was posited to be different from. "A lot of mysticism was built up around The Band," Robertson has said. "These guys up in the mountains. . . ." At any rate, the quality of their concerts was as fully unpredictable as that of their putative opposite numbers, The Grateful Dead.

From Winterland they hit the Fillmore East, where I can testify they did at least one good show, then they finished recording at the Hit Factory in New York City. *The Band* still stands as their masterpiece. Loosely built around a harvest-is-in, carnival-is-in-town feel, it's incredibly consistent and divergent at the same time, the strength of their studies and abilities ramifying its depth and breadth. After all, their brand of self-consciousness of sources and sounds marked one key difference between rock and earlier roll and rock.

From "Across the Great Divide," with its bouncy rhythms, yearning Manuel vocal, bleary horns, and slippery guitar fills, to "King Harvest (Has Surely Come)," the surprisingly downbeat rural closer that cuts in snapshots of union struggles, the album has a rare scope and power. "Up on Cripple Creek," with its bump-grind rhythms and allusion to an old folk tune, was all over FM radio, as were the hoedowns-in-your-basement "Rag Mamma Rag," which rode its two-beat feel with one of the group's most off-kilter and inspired lineups—tuba, fiddle, acoustic guitar, drums, piano—and "Jemima Surrender." "Unfaithful Servant" gave Danko's aching tenor a Dylanesque vehicle, while "The Night They Drove Old Dixie Down" told a moving tale of one southern family's civil war hardships—though to my teen New Yorker's ears, it also echoed suspiciously like an apology, revisionist kin to the D. W. Griffith movies I'd been watching at the Museum of Modern Art. (In 1967, the ex-Hawks, still nameless, had toyed with the idea of calling themselves the Crackers or the Honkies. That, as Manuel wryly put it, "was too straight.")

With characteristic acuity, Ralph Gleason reviewed this record as a belated soundtrack for James Agee's *Let Us Now Praise Famous Men*. This fit: Agee's gothic sensibility and tortured neo-Elizabethan prose had become a classic leftist touchstone, a legacy of the New Deal's political constituencies that were, even as Gleason wrote the review, being pried apart by prosperity, civil rights backlash, the divisive war, and Richard Nixon. To shoot the evocative, Guthriesque album cover, a brown border for an outdoor group half-portrait, they stood for hours in the rain. As Danko once observed, "That's why we don't look too cheerful."

AFTER THE SECOND ALBUM, the madness and musical unevenness accelerated. In 1969, The Band played the Woodstock Festival, backed Dylan at the Isle of Wight Festival, and made the cover of *Time*—a rarity then, a harbinger now. It was already a cliché that anything *Time* covered was probably past its peak. This was sadly true of The Band.

Their substance abuse—Manuel's endless drinking and coke binges, Danko's omnivorous drug consumption, Helms' pill popping and heroin addiction—deepened, especially when they were off the road, as they were for months at a time. They took turns having serious car crashes and being incapacitated, which made touring difficult. Partly by default, partly by his devising, Robertson had become the dominant figure— reading widely and watching movies, dealing with Grossman, writing first most, then all the songs, disciplining the others into rehearsing and recording. He was standoffish, sophisticated, and managing as well as directing them musically now; he was also getting the lion's share of songwriter royalties. If, as fans insisted, the alchemical creativity of The Band depended on a relatively equal distribution of ability, the equation was now unbalanced.

Maybe they'd just hit the natural limits of their talent. Maybe Robertson's songwriter's imagination lacked some adaptability essential to longevity. Maybe their image itself, the mythic history they evoked, even the ghosts of folkie authenticity they and Grossman had conjured trapped them. Whatever the cause, most of their later albums, even *Stage Fright*, sound more airless, stale, fussy, strained. The vocalists didn't interact nearly as much in the neogospel fashion that had made the first two albums so winning. It was as if The Band was confined conceptually to an inelastic, increasingly romanticized and nostalgic space and mode. As Greil Marcus wrote, "The past no longer served them."

They didn't go straight downhill. In 1970, they headlined at the Hollywood Bowl on a bill that included Miles Davis. But for years, despite Robertson's bleary-eyed talk of "the road" in *The Last Waltz*, they performed live very little. They toured Europe in 1971, where Garth Hudson fantasized about having Ben Webster open for them. They recorded *Rock of Ages* live, mostly at New York's old Academy of Music, augmenting their tunes with horns charted by Allen Toussaint and played by jazz vets like Howard Johnson, Snooky Young, and Joe Farrell. (Johnson would later do horn charts for and perform in *The Last Waltz*.) Gleason compared the album to landmarks like *Mingus at*

Monterey, but though its energy levels were unusually high, the material felt worn, and The Band didn't tour at all the year it was released.

They played at Watkins Glen with the Grateful Dead and the Allman Brothers to 650,000 people, after Altamont was supposed to have ended the heyday of huge rock festivals. In late 1973 they rejoined Dylan to cut *Planet Waves*; it seems telling in retrospect that Robertson, at least, felt uncomfortable recording the album in the informal manner The Band and Dylan had once used so fruitfully. The Band then joined Dylan on his comeback tour, where the music they made raged as fiercely as their revolutionary howl in 1965–66, as if, critics agreed, he had once again sharpened their creative edge. This also happened to be the first major stadium tour of the new rock era, and was very well paid; according to Barney Hoskyn's book *Across The Great Divide*, "Dylan and The Band netted $2 million between them." Tickets were expensive, averaging $8; still, 658,000 were sold. Naturally, there was a live album, *Before the Flood*, which modulated between high energy and roadburn.

Their several tours with the Grateful Dead, though the pairing confused many reviewers, were studies in similarity and contrast that sometimes sparked great things. In 1970, Danko told Jerry Garcia, "We thought you were just Californian freaks, but you're just like us." They double headlined with Crosbys Still Nash & Young, whose generally ghastly live shows may have helped The Band seem sharper partly because of its relative professionalism.

On the albums, a few standout songs—"The Shape I'm In," "Stage Fright," Dylan's "When I Paint My Masterpiece"—displayed the old wit and dexterous touches. (*To Kingdom Come* offers two CDs that cull much good and some indifferent material from all their recordings.) Overall, though, everyone seemed frozen, stunted, content to coast—after all, women, booze, and money were plentiful. Robertson kept telling interviewers about some grand instrumental work they were preparing, but that was more in keeping with his growing sense of self-importance than The Band's steady disintegration and ossification. The ambitious songwriter, who'd begun producing other artists' records and thinking about movies, finally decided to pull the plug in high style. Hence *The Last Waltz*.

SCORSESE HAD BEEN ONE of the junior editors on *Woodstock*, the movie that eventually translated the myth into cash. The festival organizers had, of course, lost lots of money—millions, they said, though estimates vary dramatically starting at $2.4 million. (The festival had sold $1.1 million worth of tickets, but had also written $600,000 worth of bad checks during the event, which were later covered by one producer's trust-fund monies.) Budgets for everything (except performers, who all signed on for fractions of their usual fees) ballooned—helicopters, food, lodging, you name it. Among the steadily mounting financial woes: early in 1970 New

York State's attorney general, following an investigation, directed Wood-stock Ventures to refund ticket prices to between 12,000 and 18,000 payees who couldn't get near the site because of closed roads.

Nine months after the festival, when the movie finally leaked into theaters, Woodstock had supplanted San Francisco's Summer of Love as The Counterculture Event. But the question was, after *Monterey Pop* bombed and *Don't Look Back* didn't break the surface, would it sell tickets? Winning the 1971 Oscar for Best Documentary helped; by 1979, *Woodstock: The Movie*'s worldwide box office gross topped $50 million. This surprised Hollywood and netted Warner Bros. millions: the festival organizers had signed the movie rights over in return for $100,000 financing up front on a handwritten contract at Yasgur's farm two days before the show. (Twenty years later, they resolved their fights with each other and Warner Bros.)

Director Michael Wadleigh, just out of film school, cobbled together a crew that included young Martin Scorsese, listed as an assistant director, and Theresa Schoonmaker, who won an Oscar as supervising editor. Schoonmaker would edit several of Scorsese's films and Scorsese became identified with the split-screen technique that shapes so much of *Woodstock*. His leanings toward monumentality showed up, early but unmistakable, in the widely parodied segment with guitarist Albert Lee, singing to himself in an orgy of split screens. And there was producer Michael Lang's hogging camera time and credit as he romantically perched on his motorcycle. (Six weeks after the festival, he sold his share to two of his colleagues for $31,240.)

The Band wasn't in *Woodstock: The Movie*. Albert Grossman refused to let their footage be included. Others, including the Grateful Dead, made the same decision, though not for the same reasons. Grossman, entranced by the power of the Garboesque mystique of disappearance, decided that The Band's best marketing ploy was scarcity. The Dead, in debt to Warner Bros. for their first three albums, standing onstage in pools of water and getting electric shocks when they touched their instruments, felt they hadn't played well.

It's worth remembering, in this context, that the first day of that first Woodstock festival was devoted primarily to folk music.

THERE ARE BEAUTIFUL SEQUENCES in *The Last Waltz*, and the best are those of The Band itself. Scorsese's desire to work tight means fewer establishing shots than some (including me) might want, but the aesthetic does reflect The Band's subtle, intimate music. At its best, the film can be stunning. "Stage Fright," for example, shoots Danko from almost 360 degrees, lit only by an overhead spot, creating gorgeous interplays of shadow and light, heightening the song's lyrics. "Mystery Train," to which Paul Butterfield adds harp and vocals, has a similar self-conscious beauty, which jars with the raggedy unison singing. The Staples Singers joining on "The

Weight," in a sequence filmed after the show itself, aurally demonstrates The Band's vocal debts to them. For Emmylou Harris's turn on "Evangeline," another post-show scene, Scorsese fills the soundstage with blue-lit smoke, which feels hokey, but redeems it a bit visually with arresting camera angles that frame the stark, lovely geometries of Hudson's accordion, Danko's fiddle, and Helm's mandolin.

A concert film is ultimately about the music, however. *The Last Waltz* translates The Band's broad tastes into a narrative punctuated by interviews and special guests onstage. But the frame is only as strong as its content. Eric Clapton? Ron Wood and Ringo Starr? Dr. John? Neil Diamond? Joni Mitchell? Even Muddy Waters? Broad-based roots, far-reaching sounds, all spokes in the wheel of the 1960s rock resurgence that Scorsese's narrative contextualizes and justifies via the interviews. (Neil Diamond, for instance, is preceded by a tale of The Band in New York City and Tin Pan Alley. Probably more to the point, Robertson was producing him at the time.) But there's little about the performances of these artists that is special. No particular chemistry emerges to make this a moment—except that it's The Band's Last Waltz. I found myself wondering if part of The Band's artistry consisted of its ability to musically disappear. (The companion four-CD set, *The Last Waltz*, has state-of-the-art sound and a bunch of added music—most of it, unless you're a completist, better left unheard.)

This is part of why some critics at the time, including Marcus, Dave Marsh, and Jim Miller, raged against *The Last Waltz* as an overblown Entertainment Event, a betrayal of the do-it-yourself aesthetic—an ironic if transmuted echo of the folk-revivalist reaction to Dylan and The Band a decade-plus earlier. For Pauline Kael, however, rock wasn't a way of life or a mode of salvation. It was show business. And since she knew as much about rock as about kayaking, she judged the movie in formalist terms.

Certainly *The Last Waltz* makes clear why The Band ended. Though Scorsese tries to balance his time with the five members, Robertson's hooded eyes enthrall him. It's palpable that Robertson is surrounded by goodtimey, undisciplined mates who have trouble articulating or finishing their stories, and often steps into the breach. (Helm is incisive talking about music and cultural roots; the others work in a haze of fractured sentences, bits of cynicism and mysticism, and defer to Robertson.)

Robertson had become the group's public face, more and more the businessman, the guy who had the vast bulk of the publishing income and royalties from all that collaborative imaginative work that made the songs timeless. He was also the sole producer of *The Last Waltz*. He wanted out; if the movie is unclear what the others wanted, the fact is that the rest, minus Robertson, reformed in various configurations over the years.

Aside from The Band's own sequences, the best moments in *The Last Waltz* belong, fittingly, to Ronnie Hawkins and Bob Dylan, the two front men who helped catalyze their chemistry. Hawkins is wonderfully unselfconscious during his rave-up version of "Who Do You Love," cuing and teasing The Band as if a dozen years hadn't passed between them. Dylan, at the film's end, leads The Band through "Forever Young," making it their gentle envoi. Watching him goose them through his abrupt transition to the snarling reworking of Reverend Gary Davis's "Baby Let Me Follow You Down," one of the electric tunes they'd rattled audiences with in that now-legendary 1965–66 tour, offers us a glimpse into the chemistry of their fruitful relationship, and the perfect closing bookend to The Band's career.

The Last Waltz had an ironic afterlife. *This Is Spinal Tap* was a hilarious deconstructive remake by Rob Reiner, and more widely known than its cousin, *The Last Polka*. Written by John Candy and Eugene Levy soon after the demise of SCTV, the satirical group that did for TV what the Firesign Theatre did for radio and LPs, it traces the rise and ultimate breakup of The Shmenge Brothers, polka mavens born in Leutonia, where they began as child vaudevillians who played the gelkies, or glass jars, in imitation of their American idol, vibraphonist Lionel Hampton.

21

The Firesign Theatre

IN THE LATE 1960S AND 1970S, millions of us walked around with alternate visions of reality dancing in our heads. No, it wasn't just drugs and the stupidity of youth; even senators and Congresspeople dared to seek a newer world, to argue about social dynamics and priorities, to doubt and oppose Official Lines and corporate power.

Now that everything has changed so drastically, that the 30-year-old conservative backlash has so engulfed America that alternative visions are, as they were in the 1950s, pushed to near-invisible margins, it gets hard to remember that tens, if not hundreds, of thousands of us were getting deeply coded comic messages about the structures of official reality from our record players and a four-man, multivoiced, multitalented madcap troupe called The Firesign Theatre.

The 1960s may be dead, but they aren't—far from it. It was absolutely fitting that, on the eve of the millennium, the group reunited, as they regularly do, to release *Give Me Immortality or Give Me Death*, a brilliant send-up of America's obsessions, foibles, and unawareness that razors the chattering detritus filling a cultural void left by an absence of dreams.

"They've come to steal my dreams," whimpers a female voice. A series of male voices drift past: "Get up, lady." "It's the trade of the century." "There's monster money in every sweaty mattress when you trade in your used dreams at Unconscious Village." "But those dreams have been with me since the beginning," she asserts weakly. The very masculine ad voiceover cuts in: "Don't be stuck with leftover dreams in the terrible days to come."

That's the kickoff that brought the Firesign Theatre back from the shadows again in 1999 and onto Radio Now ("If it's not now, it's too late"). There's the digitized Princess Goddess ("She may be dead but she's obviously a very caring person"), now starring in Bottom Feeder Films' "Pull My String." ("She had to die to star in the movie of her life. Now she'll live for you.") Princess Goddess passed on while mud-boarding in the Alps—straight into a landmine. She's a spokesperson for Princess Goddess Airlines ("Let her take you for all you're worth") and sponsors "doll drops" at Homeless Stadium ("Bring a kid and maybe a doll will drop on her").

Y2K obsessions? Replacement body parts, from and for Americans ("You can live forever while your friends fall apart like rotten fruit")? Celebarazzi taking pictures of each other? Contests like triple ripoff, millennial scratch and lick, and, of course, itch-and-sniff (one winner exults tearfully, "Finally I can afford to have someone kill my husband")? Dr. Onan Winkydink, expert on self-help? Promise Breakers causing massive traffic tieups in Metroburbia? Fundamentalist preacher-politicos running eternal sales on mattresses? Slo-mo SUV chases down freeways infested by plagues of locusts and "helmet heads" checking motorists for circumcision, while "funny foam blocks the seven exits between Perdition Pass and Great Satan's Village"? Straitjacketed formats ("desensitized environmental radio") that change up on DJ Bebop Loco with every shift, thanks to endless focus groups? Low-key corporate-image ads, complete with plausible deniability, for US Plus ("We own the idea of America")?

The Firesign Theatre—Phil Proctor, Peter Bergman, David Ossman, and Phil Austin—don't own the idea of America, but we'd all be better off if they did. Back in the 1960s, they walked by night, waiting for the electrician or someone like him, trying to figure out how to be in two places at once when you're not anywhere at all. They translated classic radio into the TV and psychedelic eras, via Joycean stream of consciousness, jazzy improvisation, and rapidly evolving technology that amplified their mind-bendingly discontinuous plots and characters. In the process, they revolutionized comedy and comedy recording.

The Smothers Brothers were battling censors on network TV and George Carlin was unpacking Seven Little Words on campuses when the Firesign Theatre became a counterculture cult. They toured sporadically, appeared on virtually no national media, and survived on word of mouth. But the buzz among fans was devoted and nonstop to the point of obsession; decades later, Firesign cultists can't bump into each other without reenacting favorite sketches: Pastor Rod Flash and that rousing hymn, "Marching to Shibboleth"; The *Howl of the Wolf* movie "presenting honest stories of working people, as told by rich Hollywood stars"; Porgie and Mudhead in "High School Madness," the saga of the struggle between Communist Martyrs and Morse Science high schools that segued, via the TV channel-surfing that was one of Firesign's vital narrative devices, into World War II ("Don't eat with your hands, son, use your entrenching tool"); and, inevitably, Vietnam (from *Don't Crush That Dwarf, Hand Me the Pliers*):

LIEUTENANT TIREBITER: How was it out there?
PICO: Weird! We been shootin' reds and yellows all day.
ALVARADO: Hoo boy! Am I sleepy!
LT. TIREBITER: What about the gooks?

PICO: Bad news, Lieutenant. There're gooks all around here.

ALVARADO: They live here, Lieutenant. They got women and pigs and gardens and everything.

PICO: I was talking to this one little gook . . .

ALVARADO: I was talkin' to his daughter. She's got the biggest . . .

LT. TIREBITER: That's swell, Corporal, but we got orders to surround these little gooks.

ALVARADO: That'll be easy, lieutenant. There's millions of them on all three sides of us.

LT. TIREBITER: That means we've got these little gooks right where we want them, right?

IT WAS SILLY, STRANGE, exhilarating, scary—a roller-coaster ride of the mind. As Proctor told me years later, "Remember, the Firesign Theatre was an opportunity for a bunch of mavericks to liberate people from set ways of thinking, which came out of accepting a certain presentational form as a reality. If you heard it on the radio, it must be true. If you saw it on television, it must be true. But we all know how slippery reality can be. Truth is a relative idea. We built our comedy—our COMEDY, mind you—on that premise."

How very 1960s, eh? But as the Iraqi war spills out into TVs across America in herky-jerky green video-game images, as CNN and MSNBC fill their screens with right-wing talking heads to stanch their losses in the ratings war that Fox is sweeping with its steady assault on objectivity and truth, screaming all the while about the alleged left-wing biases of the media, as the culture and society fracture into unresolved oppositions and interest groups who, thanks to the proliferation of targeted media, never have to leave the cocoons of their beliefs, maybe it's time again to jack into Firesign's nonstop perceptual shifts, their sci-fi tumbling between superficially unrelated events and situations, and be jolted as the familiar suddenly becomes as strange as it should be. According to Proctor, "Things have become so distorted in America today that surrealism has to compete with hyperrealism."

The Firesign Theatre made hyperliterate outsider comedy for hip college insiders who wanted out. They were sharper and funnier than Mort Sahl, who struck kids like me as a brainy professor—interesting ideas but boring. They made Lenny Bruce seem old-fashioned, even quaint. They hooked you because their alternate sketches of America and its history were hilarious. The fertile wordplay echoes Abbott and Costello and the Marx Brothers and old radio comedians like Bob and Ray, with a dash of Kafka and a dollop of Joyce; the surreal perspectives evoked Ernie Kovacs and Stan Freberg, Marcel Duchamp and Marshall McLuhan; the kinetic interplay mimicked jazz and jam bands like the Grateful Dead. The Firesign Theatre records were, like good musical recordings, palimpsests that demanded and repaid study; it was as if all of American popular culture and history had been sliced and diced, tossed into a blender, and spewed back via a recording studio in high-speed dissolves, a Rorschach test for your soul. Knowing the lines and routines meant you had a glimmer, at least, of the machinery framing the pictures most people thoughtlessly accepted as reality.

If high art and popular entertainment merged in Firesign, the cultural space for them was created by recording and sonic experiments in rock and the rise of FM radio. The quartet harnessed multitrack studio effects to comedy, creating satiric soundscapes that sprawled across an entire album: not Bill Cosby bits, but extended-form satire. The staggering range of oddball voices and bad-joke names popping out of corners of the audio image, the dissolves and crossfades and collages and jumpcuts mimicking channel-surfing, the reams of winceable puns, the multiple Bizarro narratives zigzagging through time and space—as the needle rode through 20- and 30-minute-long album sides, the impact was disorienting and dizzying, could make you laugh so hard you couldn't breathe or catch the next five lines, since those four Bozos were riffing like machine guns armed with Mel Blanc's voices and Chuck Jones' panache. Once you were sucked in, reality forever became an issue, an open question. This may explain why their fanatical followers include Steve Martin and Robin Williams.

Surreal, questioning, philosophical, snotty, stoned, acute, ideologically restless, technologically prescient, and, above all, side-splittingly funny, the Firesign Theatre was more than the sum of its parts: their work represented participatory democracy as comedic process. The foursome's backgrounds dovetailed, making them, as Proctor explained, "a comics' committee. We had the advantage of a built-in audience. None of us was so aware of what was going to happen next that we couldn't be caught up in the spontaneity of creation and expression of the work."

In 1964, Peter Bergman, Firesign's catalyst, participated in a Ford Foundation gathering of playwrights in Berlin, with Tom Stoppard and Piers Paul Read, part of a larger workshop that included Shirley Clarke and Roman Polanski, the Living Theater and Gunther Grass. "I could go to my window," he recalled, "and see Allen Ginsberg and Tim Leary going into some consortium where they were going to show images on the wall and take acid." He hung around The Factory in New York with Andy Warhol's gang, then headed west, where LSD was mushrooming through hippie streets. "It seemed so passé to me by then," he said.

Moving from San Francisco to LA, Bergman did a benefit to raise money for his rent on KPFK, the Pacifica Foundation's listener-sponsored FM radio station in LA, which was on the tip of FM expansion into the aborning youth market. (A hand-to-mouth politically leftist foundation, Pacifica Radio was a counterculture staple; it could afford what were soon choice FM radio slots in New York, San Francisco, and LA because at the time FM radio meant classical music and low audience numbers, which in turn meant broadcasters weren't fighting over the FM dial yet.) Once he got on the air, Bergman revved into a nonstop tornado. Austin pointed out, "He becomes *more* candid when he performs." The station signed him up to spearhead their 1966 fundraising marathon, and then gave him a show. He called it *Radio Free Oz*; it was a wacky call-in talk show where he tried to pull back the curtains on the machinery generating Official American Reality. Soon he met Ossman, an actor-poet who'd been laid off as KPFK's program director and hired by ABC-TV, which he hated. Austin, a musician–actor–director, was Bergman's engineer, who kept joking his way into the show. Proctor knew Bergman from their studying at Yale Drama School, so he called him when he fled the stale New York theater scene for LA. The Firesign Theatre—the name evokes FDR's Depression-era fireside radio chats as well as the fact that they're all air signs—was open.

"So there we were, FOUR FRIENDS," Austin wrote in *The Firesign Theatre's Big Book of Plays*, which collects some of their early scripts. "You see, we had no ambitions. It was a pure jam and the instrument we each played was verbal glibness or radio." Hard to imagine these days, when careers and ambitions are all most people seem to dream of. Or, as Bergman told me, "There hasn't been anything like the Firesign Theatre because you can't get four extraordinarily strong egos to come together, as we did, under what I consider war and hippie conditions. It was like a platoon: nobody goes out of the foxhole until everybody agrees."

When their records filtered back to the East Coast and college towns around the land, they sounded like a sort of electronic cubism enhanced by LSD, an omnidirectional perspective-exploding gaze that panned and zoomed and tracked in and out, cutting and pasting its dizzying scrambled way across America's sense of itself, channel-changer at the ready, decoding hidden agendas by means of what looked like loopy associations. They were a lot more fun than Noam Chomsky.

Because they are artists, not academics or politicians, when they went into the recording studio they wanted to show, not tell; they etched their process of search and discovery into the vinyl grooves, forced their listeners to join, not overhear, their searches, U-turns, speed bumps, and all. Proctor explained, "When we started on the radio as a four-man group, taking the audience on a crazy ride and seeing how far out we could go with them, we learned to interact in a live moment, sustain comic characters and comic ideas, feed off each others' themes—almost like playing jazz. Then, when we started performing our stuff as radio plays at the Magic Mushroom, when *Radio Free Oz* went into a live-audience format, we began to add sound effects, to experiment a la the Goon Shows—the style of simultaneous comedy. If somebody was saying something funny and we could augment with a funny sound behind it, we would. In the early radio shows, we did an awful lot of spontaneous comedy by responding to what whoever was performing was doing. That was experimentation with the freedom that the multitracking allowed us. It was a very musical approach to comedy."

Over the last three and a half decades, the Firesign Theatre came out of their foxholes with 22 albums, seven radio series, and several videos; they've been nominated for two Grammys, celebrated by the Museum of Broadcasting, and, in 2002 were tapped to boost fundraising by local PBS channels, offering their latest album and their first four reissued albums as premiums. "We are," Proctor deadpanned, "the American Monty Python." They don't have endless PBS reruns, but they tour every couple of years, started their own website in the 1990s, and regularly broadcast new episodes of *Radio Free Oz* over satellite radio.

According to them, the most famous Firesign segment is what they call the Ralph Williams mantra from "How Can You Be in Two Places at Once When You're Not Anywhere at All?" (Its subtitle was "All Hail Marx and Lennon"; its cover pictured Groucho and John.) Ralph Spoilsport (like most Firesign Theatre characters, his name changes but he recurs across their work) began life as a parody of Williams, an LA car shyster whose ad spiels were notorious: "Hiya, friends! Ralph Spoilsport, Ralph Spoilsport Motors, the world's largest new used and used new automobile dealership, Ralph Spoilsport Motors, here in the city of Emphysema. Let's just look at the extras on this fabulous car! Wire-wheel spoke fenders, two-way sneezethrough windvent, star-studded mudguards, sponge-coated edible steering column, chrome fender dents, and factory air-conditioned air from our fully factory-equipped factory. It's a beautiful car, friends, with doors to match!"

The album's hero Babe, one of the group's Kafkaesque characters who, like Benny Profane, is a schlemiel, buys a car so he can get out, and careens across American history. Right after he metamorphoses into Woody Guthrie ("This land is made of mountains! This land is made of mud!"), he is shown how things really are: the immigrants from Smegma, Spasmodic, and the far-flung Isles of Langerhans flee here from poverty, injustice, the Law, and the Army, to help Them steal America and its natural abundance from the Indians. "We needed," Babe is told, as voices ricochet around the audio stage, "the Hope, the Faith, the Prayers, the Fears, the Sweat, the Pain, the Boils, the Tears, the Broken Bones, the Broken Homes, the Total Degradation of . . ." "Who?" he whimpers. ". . . you! The Little Guy." A train chuffs over the steel rails flung across The Little Guys, the chanted swoosh of

Rockefeller, Humphrey, Nixon, Kennedy, Wallace, Ford overlapping and entwining, the sound of hope for America pulling out of the station. In the end, Ralph Spoilsport fades, slightly out of phase, into Molly Bloom's final soliloquy from *Ulysses*—the optimistic reinstatement of natural flowing reality over the power of The Grid.

Have we outgrown the Firesign Theatre, like we have the rest of the childish decade that nourished them? Turn on your TV and decide for yourself.

22

Bruce Springsteen

HEAD UP I-95 THROUGH CONNECTICUT, pass through the I-95/I-91 linkup and on out of New Haven toward Hartford, and the clustered cityscape and small suburban sprawl slip away after a few minutes. By the exit for Wallingford, about halfway between those two ethnically divided and economically blighted urban centers, the landscape is almost pastoral: open fields dotted with lakes and rimmed with hills, darkness deepening under a rising moon. On September 18, 1996, I'm driving that way, for the second show on the second leg of Bruce Springsteen's acoustic tour—a tour that, by year's end, will land in 33 cities around the Northeast, Midwest, and South.

For this swing behind *The Ghost of Tom Joad*, his thirteenth album, Springsteen is packing a 6- and a 12-string guitar and a box full of harmonicas and neck racks. He's been at it on and off since the disc's release the preceding November, hitting 20 US cities, swinging over to Europe for 35 dates, taking a break for summer, then back on the road, where he's been hustling for 30 years now.

I turn off I-91, part of a small line of cars snaking through the hilly plain, past open fields and a sudden construction-equipment-clogged acre, looking for the Oakdale Theatre. After curves and climbing appears first a spreading parking lot, then a complex. Until recently, the Oakdale Theatre was a supper club, home to tired acts like Steve Lawrence and Eydie Gormé. Now it's a 5,000-seat venue with clean sightlines and good sound, with a 150-degree seating plan on a gentle grade with tight mezzanines that make it feel half its size. It splits its bookings between rockers avoiding hockey rinks and ballparks, and subscription deals like "Family Broadway," which includes *Grease* and *Hello, Dolly*. Like politicians and everybody else in show biz, its owners are trying to cobble together several audiences, chasing the vanishing masses in the age of fragmentation.

The venue is as welcoming and intimate as a mini-arena can get. Still, several folks, from the *New Haven Register*'s Entertainment Editor to a local cop, run variations on a theme for me: "They've sunk an awful lot of money into this, and everything else that's been here before has flopped. I sure hope this works." Their rooting for the underdog home team, tugged by anxiety, speaks to their downsized America, its bewildering decline, its confusing loss of values and hope, the ebbing of its dreams in their lives.

This is one of the places that Springsteen's audience has lived ever since he came out of the bars along the Jersey Shore. So the Oakdale Theatre is a handy metaphor for this threshold in his career. Can its refurbishment make people come out to it more than once? Is it making a comeback— or staving off the inevitable?

Thirty minutes before showtime, the parking lot roads inch lines of cars toward ever-more-distant spaces, like mice pulsing through snakes. Slowly the sprinkling of plates from New York and Massachussetts and even New Hampshire and Pennsylvania and, of course, New Jersey among the dominant Connecticut tags find slots. The cordoned-off area for limos is full. The folks leaving their cars: New Haven and Hartford yuppies and students, thirty- and fortysomethings in casual mallwear, snatches of twentysomething Bossalikes with bandannas wrapping their heads and bearded scraggle. No big hair on the women: this ain't Jersey. The small memorabilia concession in the spacious lobby is tucked discreetly next to the center-orchestra entrance and the men's bathroom, and does a steady but not crunching business.

Kinda like *The Ghost of Tom Joad Itself*. Springsteen's latest disc, a Woody Guthrie-meets-John Steinbeck look at what used to be called The New Depression, has gone gold—in sharp contrast to his twelfth album, *Bruce Springsteen Greatest Hits*, which hit double platinum. The tour is selling out: tickets for the theatre's 5,000 seats were gone in a few hours. But paralleling the Boss's roadwork is a deliberate fudging of his neofolkie direction, no doubt thanks to sales. Last week, for instance, saw the release (on laser disc) of the fine documentary, first aired in March on the Disney Channel, about his 1995 reunion with the E Street Band for songs included on *Greatest Hits*. (The videotape comes later this year, with a limited-edition EP included.) Those sessions marked the first time he'd joined his longtime sidekicks since his commercial peak, 1984's *Born in the USA*—a fact that helps explain the distance in sales between *Hits* and *Joad*. One reason I'm in Wallingford is to take another measure of that distance.

Bob Dylan's "John Wesley Harding" is the last song on the preconcert tape, and ends once the audience finds seats and the lights drop. A ragged harmonica flourish stabs the hall. The spotlight—the show is resolutely low-tech—hits Springsteen as he strides centerstage, anchored between the microphone and the bins to his left, each with a different-keyed harmonica mounted in its own neck rack. The house finds its feet, the ovation pouring out like a premonitory Brechtian catharsis, lapsing into quiet only when he starts "The Ghost of Tom Joad."

Knowing how to get intimate with huge crowds is a key trick to being a pop star, and no one's better at it than Springsteen. We root for him so hard because he came up the same way we did and can speak to and for us, and we ignore the fact that he's become The Boss living in the Hollywood Hills mansion, whose music and career outline a fin de siècle summary of rock's history, a narrative reworking of its genetic strands into one final, do-not-go-gentle scream. But with this tour, as with the album, he's straddling several fissures, any of which can open beneath him at any time—as the Wallingford show illustrates.

The audience revs up at the close of "Joad," prompting the first of Springsteen's characteristic between-songs asides. "We're gonna rerelease the album," he deadpans in his sandpapery drawl, "as 'The Ghost of Tom Macarena,' so we can sell a few more. The video's gonna have 16-year-old girls in silver hot pants and all." The fans love it. Here he is, poking fun at himself, not taking his serious folk songs *too* seriously, and in the process positioning himself somewhere in the American psyche between Will Rogers and Woody Guthrie—a nuanced, evocative site he'll try to inhabit for the rest of the show. At the same time he's spoofing the brave new post-MTV world of pop that he's never seemed comfortable with—that is, in effect, after his time.

Cut to halfway through the two-and-a-half-hour set. "Forget about *Born in the USA*; that was ten years ago," he says, with at least a trace of exasperation. The crowd isn't rock and rolling any more. We break out sometimes, like for the "Pinball Wizard"-y recasting of "Darkness on the Edge of Town," but mostly we're respectful, quiet, supportive, a bit baffled, hanging in there for The Boss but not always quite sure why, except for the intricate, unspoken allegiances that have bound us to him, and him to us, for decades now. His asides keep us connected, but remind us who's in charge. He asks for quiet, explaining it's for the show's effectiveness, and to an astonishing degree, gets it. (One preteen, sitting with her dad in the row behind me, is almost alone in yelling out between nearly every tune: "Bruce, play 'The River'." He never does.) Several times he growls, "Will you please put those Brownies and Instamatics away—or step on 'em?" And so flashes pop in relatively rare bursts.

There's no intimacy without trust, and he doesn't hesitate. When his 12-string keeps going out of tune, he interjects, "That's 30 years of experience there, folks." For a new song, "Sell It and They Will Come," which lists the horror-mall wonders of late-night cable TV, he explains, "I got the idea from watching one of those shows about the stuff that you spray on your head to make your hair look like Astroturf." He tells a story about a guy from Belgium who's followed him for six months, asking for "My Father's House," and how he's consistently refused to play it—until tonight. And, to finish up the tale of how he and his roadie had this $100 bet on the correct spelling of "friend" (Springsteen lost), he quips, "That's the kind of drama we've got on this *Tom Joad* tour, folks."

Springsteen doesn't condescend. His intro to "Straight Talk": "Sometimes the things that make you feel alive are the very things that are bringing you down." For "Spare Parts": "The tricky thing about getting older is not giving in to cynicism." About having kids: "As we get older, part of what people search for is ways to get grace into their lives. Kids are like open windows; they let it in." The audience sits hushed, hoping for rapture, wanting to share it with the small figure onstage. And yet . . .

It's hard to be a folkie in an arena. It's hard to bring your audience, hungering for the slamming backbeat that's your musical signature, into a reflective mood for two and a half hours. It's hard to reroute your image after 20 years. It's hard to be the avatar of recapitulation, the man who sums up rock and roll in time for it to trail off into history.

Bruce Springsteen wants to matter, has always been about mattering. But the culture has moved since *Born to Run*—and not just politically. The seismic shifts have fractured it. No more do subcultures meet at the mainstream. Markets, like politics, are micro. Celebrity, like power, is balkanized, making Andy Warhol seem like an optimist. Consensus is a box of jigsaw puzzle pieces that don't fit back together. Springsteen's job is reassembly, not innovation. His stardom is permanent, but possibly irrelevant. His fans want to stand with him, but can't quite always get there from here. His music has to find a new way to be. Hence *Tom Joad*. It's no accident that as Springsteen struggles to reinvent himself, he reaches back to the Depression, evoking the furnace that forged the last American consensus. What's doubtful, in 1996 America, is whether scared or nostalgic yuppies and suburbanites, twentysomething hotrodders, and blue-collar refugees are forgeable into a meaningful group, culturally or politically.

But Springsteen's gonna give it his best shot. At Wallingford, his audience strains to be on his side, even when he launches into a quiet story-song trilogy about the hardscrabble life of immigrants and the evils of the Border Patrol. We accept it, because he's Bruce. We listen as he quotes Carlos Fuentes about California being part of Mexico, and the border between the United States and Mexico as a scar that never heals. But we don't love it the way we love "Thunder Road." We can't. The whiff of possibility, of hope, the touch of bravado in the restless search for even a marginal way out that powered the music we love is gone— from him, from us, from the country. Now, we have to face the scars that crisscross America, and hope for grace from our kids.

Late in the show, he pauses to tell the story of how he first saw John Ford's classic film: "When I was 26, a friend showed me *The Grapes of Wrath*. It really hit me. I'd wanted to do something like that, my whole life. I wanted to make something that would be a thread running through people's lives. . . . Before Tom leaves, there's a scene where everybody in the camp is dancing. The looks on their faces—it's like John Ford was holding out the possibility of beauty in a brutal world."

Affirmation against the darkness made Bruce Springsteen a culture hero. The bravado may be lost to us now, but the beauty of what he does lingers—his effect on his audience, who knows him and roots for him. At Wallingford, Springsteen is hammering uptempo, trying to recreate a rock and roll stomper on a 12-string guitar, giving 'em what they want the way he wants it—a key ingredient of leadership, as well as celebrity. He busts one, then two, finally a few of his strings. He reaches into his harmonica shelves for a solo, to cover his confusion, and picks out a wrong harp several times—something he discovers only as he blows, time after time, into the microphone. At long last, somewhere between nonplussed and disgusted, he gives up trying to finish the tune he's so doggedly chasing. While his roadie resets the equipment and The Boss waits, softly at first, then quickly gathering strength, the crowd begins singing to the stage—an impromptu "Happy Birthday." Five nights from now, Bruce Springsteen will turn 47.

FAMILY VALUES WERE A HOT-BUTTON ISSUE when *Blood Brothers* came out in 1997. My kids didn't care much about Bruce Springsteen, so I loaded the video and was watching it myself when, after a few minutes of overhearing it, they edged one at a time into the den and sat down and, to my surprise, got into it. "They're a real band," exclaimed the older one into trance-dance and electronica. "I had no idea they worked like that in the studio." "They act like family," said the younger one, "the way they clown around. But he really runs things, doesn't he?"

Yes, he does. Gary Tallent, the E Street Band's longtime bassist, kicks off *Blood Brothers*: "In his striving for spontaneity Bruce often won't tell you what key or what song we're gonna play—it's 'Follow me, boys'." That could be right out of Mingus. What's fascinating is the shorthand exchanges that telegraph between him and the band, spending their first few days together in the studio after 11 years, the to-and-fro-ing while The Boss alludes to and sketches and implies what he and the songs need: sometimes he's very specific (the piano figure in "Secret Garden" should be less defined, and yo, Steve van Zandt, drop that "Never On Sunday" mandolin part) and sometimes he leaves it to them ("Atmosphere on the guitar," he grins crookedly and waves broadly at Nils Lofgren). He's a good Boss, uses street versions of nicely turned diplomacy. When drummer Max Weinberg wants to flatten the video's title track with his typical arena 4/4 snare beat, Springsteen sidesteps him, says, "I hear those cymbals"— and the next shot shows Max sitting rather glumly behind the snare, a little kid corrected, doing like he was told.

Striving for spontaneity is one way Springsteen keeps it real, the need jazz and acting (and hip-hop, the child of both) share to stay in the moment. Reenacting the tribal community of the E Street Band is a big lure for him (and us) to go back into the world of MegaMusicBusiness, after the perpetual tours of the 1980s, the burnout, the contractual lawsuits, the Reagan campaign attempts to appropriate one of the most coruscating antiwar songs since Vietnam, the disappearance (not end) of the New Depression and fracturing of his effective social coalition, the audience he built of his threatened and marginal and disaffected blue- and white-collar fans, the relative commercial failure of his folkie directions. That last, of course, is the compelling reason the E Street Band is sitting around the studio in the opening shots of *Blood Brothers*, clustered as he straddles a chair with his battered acoustic and strums the song that gives the documentary its title, their notebooks open and felt pens scraping down chord changes and rhythmic and other inflections as he picks and mumbles through this piece they've never heard, which they're about to record.

Welcome Home, Boss.

Ernie Fritz's 90-minute documentary, which covers the sessions that put together the title track and "Murder Incorporated" and a couple of other new sweeteners for a *Greatest Hits* album The Boss needed, is a reasonable insider look at how this garage band works. "All the years I've known him" mutters Miami Steve Van Zandt, *The Sopranos* tough guy, "he's never had less than five songs ready to go on a given day. I hate that about him." So we see Springsteen, the garage-band Ellington, leaning against the packing cases in the studio to scribble while the group goofs off. He stays up all night to figure out why their two earlier takes of "Blood Brothers" didn't click, worries at the rhythms, comes back in fingerpicking it a la Merle Travis on acoustic in a modified shuffle, lets the band listen and find and follow that groove so that the song breathes the way he's dreamed, and voila—the last take is the keeper, another jigsaw piece of Springsteen bittersweet that promises to transcend what "time and memory fade away," and the band dances in the control room listening to the playback.

Fritz sees, too, how encircled The Boss is by layers of handlers and managers, how only his personal integrity and charisma keep it at all real. It's amazing this Brechtian rocker can hold the multibillion dollar industry at bay at all, but he can only as long as he sells, even if he's Bruce. Hence this record. Three decades ago Jon Landau wrote for *Rolling Stone*, "I have seen the future of rock and roll and its name is Bruce Springsteen," and found himself with a job when Springsteen spent years in contractual suits. Now he's the manager, aka the "official pontificator." He choreographs the intricate pas-de-deux around a big commercial property making a big record: the press releases, the photo shoots, the number of tracks, the deadlines, the expectations of fans and marketers. It's fun to watch the machinery whirr around the Wizard of Oz. And at least these guys don't bore us by telling us how real they are; they just do what they do, craftsmen at work, making music inside the family most of them have been with for most of their lives.

The distance between what they actually do and what everyone around them does focuses at Tramps, the small New York club that specialized in blues and R & B and soul for decades. That's where director Jonathan Demme shot the music video for *Murder Incorporated*; Fritz shot his shooting. It was an intense night: we watched the band charge headlong into the song a few times for Demme's multiple cameras and hot lights, then they roared into random songs till about one in the morning. That generosity is their strength, the virtue that ties fans to them as surely as Deadheads to the Dead. What strikes me now ("They just recorded this live, Dad?") is how superior Fritz's underexposed grainy footage is to Demme's glossy finished product: Fritz understands and mimics the experience, but the maker of *Something Wild* and *Silence of the Lambs* tries to distill it—his video is too finished, airbrushed; the lighting too good, the staging too staged. Is this Demme's fault? Or is it because music video conventions, designed in the MTV era for prepackaged acts, don't breathe, can't capture live shows that run on real in-the-moment existential drama—why bands like E Street and the Dead toss set lists and fly into the wind with their audience at their backs?

"Hey mister can you tell me / what has happened to the seeds I've sown?" I watch my kids watching "This Hard Land" and its opening question, think of the dreams of the 1960s erased, buried, replaced by greed and opportunism and lies. The sense of hope that a change is gonna come is gone, along with the notion that there could be a different better world built on the wealth and power and achievements of the greatest nation on earth. Now, no one imagines alternatives. Few want them. They just want a bigger piece of the existing pie. So when my kids tell me they still hate Springsteen's videos but see how the band was really a band and how come nothing like that exists any more, I don't say a thing, just bask in the vestigial glow of hope that, for a moment, fills me like a dream of this hard land.

WHEN BRUCE SPRINGSTEEN AND THE E STREET BAND, reunited to tour behind *The Rising*, came to Madison Square Garden on August 12, 2002, they juxtaposed "41 Shots," Springsteen's powerful song about Amadou Diallo's shooting by NYPD officers, with "Into the Fire," the new album's uplifting gospel tribute to the emergency workers who climbed into the burning Twin Towers never to emerge. Stripped to incantatory simplicity, the newer song's chorus—a litany, really—invokes the healing circle of community that on 9/11 magically materialized-as hordes of volunteers and photo-covered memorial walls abruptly elevated the NYPD and NYFD and EMS to hero status. The crowd, mostly middle-aged in suburban summer attire, stood in rather stony silence for the first tune, which drew boos and threats from the NYPD when Springsteen unveiled it at the Garden in June 2000; for the second they eased into a reverential hush. Everyone around here knows, after all, that Springsteen's music, especially "Thunder Road" and "Born in the USA," resounded through countless post-9/11 memorial services for the many blue-collar victims.

Springsteen's set lists are typically narratives; a sort of rock cabaret, they build emotional tensions and releases to tell some larger story. So at the Garden, he donned his plaid shirt as High Priest of the secular religion rooted in his audience's belief that he is somehow one of them writ magically large, as were the Local Heroes who flocked toward danger that beautiful, deadly September day, transfigured by necessity, rising to the call. Here he stood, with the E Street Band, his own symbolic community, ready to transform this site not three miles from the fallen towers into a temple of expiation, release, remembrance, hope, loss, despair, acceptance, resolve, love—and, of course, a rock and roll party.

Like the strain of American populists he springs from, Springsteen has always seen this country as a dichotomy, the Promised Land that waits within the dream of This Hard Land. Originally inspired by what he has called "class-conscious pop records" like the Animals' 1960s hits "We Gotta Get Out of This Place" and "It's My Life" ("I'd listen . . . and I'd say to myself: 'That's my life, that's my life!' They said something to me about my own experience of exclusion."), during the 1970s he delved into Flannery O'Connor and John Steinbeck, William Carlos Williams and John Ford, country music ("a very class-conscious music") and Guthrie, Walker Percy, and Robert Frank.

"I've made records," Springsteen told Percy's nephew Will several years ago, "that I knew would find a smaller audience than others I've made. I suppose the larger question is, 'How do you get that type of work to be heard—despite the noise of modern society?' . . . There's a lot of different ways to reach people, to help them think about what's really important in this one-and-only life we live. There's pop culture—that's the shotgun approach, where you throw it out and it gets interpreted in different ways and some people pick up on it. And then there's the more intimate approach like I tried on *Tom Joad*."

For *The Rising* he grabbed the shotgun. For the first time ever, the E Street Band blasted through endless TV talk shows and promo spots and you-name-its to launch the record and tour. When the CD was released on July 30, 2002, it was ubiquitous, and the marketing campaign looked like an avalanche. The number of editorial pundits in places like the *New York Times* and the *Economist* who've felt they had to comment on what is, after all, a pop record struck me as remarkable. No wonder, issues of artistic quality aside, the disc debuted at number one and went gold in the first week—an unprecedented hit for The Boss.

Boss or not, Springsteen hasn't exactly been burning up the charts since the breakup of the E Street Band, except—predictably—for the *Greatest Hits* packages. But he has been looking for new entrance ramps onto the artistic freeway. In 1992, he made *Human Touch* and *Lucky Town*, essentially by himself, and got complaints that he'd lost the old power, that the songs had gotten clichéd, or repetitive, or superficial—all of which had some merit. He tried touring with a mostly black, largely female band, but the new group was loud and oddly bland. With *The Ghost of Tom Joad* he walked the footsteps of Steinbeck and Guthrie and Ford, but for whatever reasons—the prosperity of the times? The alien heroes? The lack of Max Weinberg's bedrock backbeats and Clemons' predictable sax?—despite a terrific acoustic tour, most of his fans bought in only because the themes and approach interested them. They really wanted the Friday-night adrenaline rush of his earlier hits, their imaginary glory days represented to them in rocked-out concert form, but still they came, in reduced but dedicated numbers, to see Bruce because . . . hey, he's Bruce.

One PR edge about *The Rising* pushed Springsteen's calling victims and families, piecing together reportage for the album. There's a queasiness about this among longtime fans, including me, although Springsteen's genius has always shone in his talent for telling other people's stories. Which may be the main reason fans like me believe in Springsteen: this pop megastar who describes what he does as a job and bikes around the country during his down times. Unlike Michael Jackson, Springsteen doesn't live in Neverland. He believes in his ability—his duty, the requisite for his gift of talent—to move us to more than adoration and sales. His human touch is the ghost in the pop industry's machinery.

"I'm more a product of pop culture: films and records, films and records, films and records," Springsteen told Percy. "I had some lofty ideas about using my own music to give people something to think about—to think about the world, and what's right and wrong. I'd been affected that way by records, and I wanted my own music and writing to extend themselves in that way."

My first reactions to *The Rising* album were mixed. I don't know what I wanted to hear, but the marketing onslaught about 9/11 had shoved me into an emotional corner. Listening however expectantly, I felt my enthusiasm drain: a lot of these songs sounded like retreads whose earlier incarnations told fuller-bodied stories. Some of them, despite the hype, were barely if at all about 9/11. Shifting critical gears, I postulated problems—the limits of realism, the boundaries of Springsteen's talents and vision, the impossibly tangled American weave of commerce and culture, Reagan's attempt to appropriate "Born in the USA" as a campaign tool, all kinds of intellectual reasons why I wasn't blown away. I groused about the sketchy thinness of the tales, their flatness, their itchy transcendental yearnings, their failures. It didn't, I kept repeating to friends I played it to, really work.

A month later, I still think that whole chunks of *The Rising* don't work. I just don't care. Why, I keep asking myself, does the album's title track choke me up every time I hear it, its call-and-response gospel chorus with Bruce listing the sky's contradictory attributes and the chorus answering each entry, "A dream of life." The story of a rescue worker who left his house on the fly to alarm bells everywhere, wearing his red cross and burning rubber, an apocalyptic Elijah who ends up inching through the dusty dark lit by bright-eyed spirits to his death, and the vocal erupts into the wordless jigging chorus. This mini-epic opens with drawling guitar and spare backing gradually thickened by swirling keyboards and more guitars, grinds into a blues-rock basher for the race to the disaster site and the climb, dissolves into kaleidoscopic textures as the hero dies dreaming of his children dancing in a sky filled with light—a dream, he says, of life. It closes with gusts of contrapuntal voices that fade into the band's final unresolved chord.

The opening of "Into the Fire" is the last time the narrator sees his comrade, who climbs into the flames because of love and duty. Its incantatory chorus is backed by an organ figure over a taps-derived beat. The instruments growl and skate with that understated amazing grace the E Street Band at its best can dazzle with. On "Empty Sky," Patti Scialfa's ghostly, quavering vocals frame Springsteen's tight-lipped narration in a stark rock ballad with doomed minor-major modulations and a fore-ground-shifting mix. "The Fuse" chuffs electro-tech industrial sounds while a couple grope for comfort in sex as funeral processions wind through town-carrying on, living, as time's beats tick into forever.

These are the songs I can't stop playing.

The reunion of Springsteen and E Streeters reaffirms The Boss's basic mythic community; musically the album integrates the surprisingly varied styles the World's Greatest Garage Band has tackled over 30-odd years. The album's title signals reassurance. The Boss has gathered us tonight in the Church of Rock and Roll, as he used to holler in those ferocious live gospel set pieces, to gather us, to bear witness, to go on—to live. Because that, as cliched as it is, is what we do, with a snatching of images, pangs of emotion, and a gazing at the skies.

One musician I know called *The Rising* "comfort food—classy, well-done comfort food." He was right, but it didn't really matter. Over the years Springsteen has become part of the soundtrack for our lives, as the Animals were for his. The album's failures are part of its package, its blandness a necessary function of the affirmation, reconciliation, and healing. Think of Springsteen as the plugged-in troubadour who shapes his artistry into what his audience wants and needs, not cynically but because he wants to bring them with him, and its structure comes clearer.

Structure and intention, however, can't save all the songs. They move effortlessly, though not always successfully, from one tempo and sound-scape to another as they talk of heroism and transcendence, devils in the mailbox and dreams of the garden of a thousand sighs. There are no Big Statements; there are sketchy stories. The standard imagery of romantic love and loss is tilted into the post–9/11 world. Sometimes, as in "You're

Missing," this leaves us with a catalog of unsatisfying cliches against generic synth backgrounds. On the R & B-flavored "Countin' on a Miracle," which explodes after a gentle acoustic-guitar intro, it plays off Springsteen's long-standing hope-against-hope in love trope. The familiar language tries to embrace the unimaginable; mostly, inevitably, it fails.

But when it doesn't it cuts deep. Among the album's speakers are the dead, the determined and fragile living, the suicidal and transfigured and living dead: "Nothing Man" is a breathy ballad about a working-class hero who makes his hometown paper, gets glad-handed and bought rounds, and, like Coleridge's Life-in-Death, mutters about praying to find courage others can understand in the pearl-handled revolver on his night table. The linguistic conceit gets tangled, stretched. The earnest "Worlds Apart," where star-crossed lovers meet to an Arab-music inflection and a Pakistani chorus, is camp-hilarious. "Sounds like Sting on a bad day," quipped one pal who hates Sting. Every three or four tunes is a party piece like "Skin to Skin," a throwaway emotional release.

Still, even the failures reflect Springsteen's vision of an unpredictable, hostile world in which individuals overcome, evade, understand in defeat, or are simply crushed by the loaded dice of the Powers-That-Be, whether they are the fates, the rich, the government, or the lonely crowd. He sees community as a necessary refuge: "Mary's Place," bubbling R & B, is about a survivor throwing a post-9/11 party while haunted by her dead lover's voice. These songs don't lay out a political agenda. Who needs more of that in a world where endless voices politically spin What Happened every day? Catch the Rashomon-style perspective shifts in "Lonesome Day."

This is the ineluctable lure of Springsteen's storytelling at its best—its suggestions of life's complexity. His voice, soaked in blues and gospel, sounds incredible, and its sheer allure, its phrasing and catches, its demands and pleas, carry many of the weaker songs. The singing's allusive cracks and crannies evoke empathy and redemption, separation and defeat, wrapped in religious imagery that suggests, among other things, that the ways we were on 9/11 are more complicated than anyone can capture. How long, after all, did it take for Vietnam to yield *Going After Cacciato* and *Dog Soldiers* and "Born in the USA?"

Which brings us back to the Garden, where the band pranced through nearly three hours, delivering note-perfect renditions—the blues-rock throb of "Into the Fire," the chug-a-lug suspensions and industrial-metal thrust of "The Fuse," the stark-yet-full acoustic colors of "Empty Sky," the skirling keyboards and snarling guitars that alternate sections of "The Rising"—that often flared but never quite built into the emotional peak that is their hallmark. The crowd leapt from its seats and sang the show's carefully salted oldies like "Prove It All Night," "Darkness on the Edge of Town," and "The Promised Land." They danced to "Mary's Place" and cheered the second half of the line from "Empty Sky" that runs, "I want a kiss from your lips, I want an eye for an eye." For the rest they mostly milled and sat and drank. The encores were all classics, from "Thunder Road" to "Born in the USA."

Careful, controlled, scared, wondering if the glory days are past, sifting for omens. That's how the concert felt. Maybe that's who we are now. What kind of oracle did we expect?

23

Tom Waits

Mass market nostalgia gets you hopped up for a past that never existed.... Only a reckless verisimilitude can set that line straight.

> —James Ellroy, "American Tabloid"

What price freedom? Dirt is my rug.

> —Tom Waits

TOM WAITS IS AN IMAGINARY HOBO. He cruises the oddball corners of American pop culture and collects the deft and moving and loopy short takes he sees and imagines there. Like Raymond Carver, he judges only when judgment is utterly unavoidable, a last resort on the journey through life.

Back in 1973, *Closing Time* first caught Waits's then far less grizzled voice on disc, growling about unguarded moments in real lives. Unlike that era's Me-Generation singer–songwriter crop of hit-generating navel-gazers, the solipsistic James Taylors and Carole Kings and Carly Simons, Waits made you feel other people because he did. He was ironic or direct, caustic or unabashedly torn open by loss and hope and love and fear and the pivotal emotions that daily face folks who don't live inside recording and movie and TV studios, ivy-covered towers, newspaper and magazine offices, the Beltway, or their own swollen heads.

His sense of being on the outside may have started at birth: the story goes that he was delivered in the back seat of a cab outside a hospital in Pomona, California, on December 7, 1949—Pearl Harbor's eighth anniversary. His parents, both schoolteachers, were divorced when he was 10; growing up, he and his two sisters moved around California a lot. As a teen, Waits hung back from the regional craze for surf music, hotrod music, or even psychedelic music. Instead, he listened to his parents' 78s of Perry Como and Bing Crosby, and tacked Bob Dylan lyrics up on the walls of his room. This was when he started writing down ideas that came to him during the night, taught himself piano at a neighbor's house, learned to play some guitar. At school he was a clown who'd blow harmonica and do a soft-shoe during his loosey-goosey art class. Cars consumed him. A beloved beat-up station wagon inspired the song "Ol' 55," which the Eagles covered on their first album, after it appeared on *Closing Time*.

Waits, working as a doorman at LA's Heritage Club, was exposed early to the opening up of pop culture. As he told *Rolling Stone*'s David McGee in 1976, "I listened to all kinds of music there, all kinds of stuff from rock to jazz to folk to anything else that happened to walk in. One night I saw a local guy onstage playing his own material. I don't know why, but at that moment I knew I wanted to live or die on the strength of my own music. I finally played a gig there. Then I started writing down people's conversations as they sat around the bar. When I put them together I found some music hiding in there."

He started reading—Jack Kerouac, Gregory Corso, Allen Ginsberg, Beat after Beat. He started listening more widely—Irving Berlin, Johnny Mercer, even Stephen Foster. When he got a shot at the famed stage of the Troubadour in 1969, Herb Cohen, manager of the Mothers of Invention, Captain Beefheart, and Linda Ronstadt, liked Waits enough to sign him. Then, in 1972, Waits recorded *Closing Time*, which got nice reviews and slid down the charts even faster than it rose up them.

But the album established Waits's Beat persona and noir sensibility; it's not hard to imagine Sam Fuller directing Sterling Hayden and/or Susan Hayward in video versions of some of these tunes. And there's a tenderness and understanding about America's marginal types that reflects that. Randy Newman, who emerged as a singer–songwriter at about the same time, and Warren Zevon, a friend of Jackson Browne's, shared with Waits an irascible sense of irony and the conviction that the world was surreal and tragicomic, that individuals were surrounded and molded and buffeted by the absurd. They served as a useful astringent to counteract the cloying, soppy wave of Me-Generation singer–songwriters. But while Zevon (a favorite of Hunter Thompson's) cast himself as a swashbuckler gloating over startling images like "Roland the headless Thompson gunner," Newman and Waits could look without shame or embarrassment into the odd angles of the human heart, and were far more inventive about musical attire for their storytelling.

In fact, "Martha" from *Closing Time* could be a genre tune from the Newman songbook, a vaguely parlor piano piece looking back in genuinely sweet, if eccentric, nostalgia. (Newman and Waits, The Band and the Grateful Dead were among the few pop and rock musicians in 1972 interested in Stephen Foster.) The title track portrays a subtle series of empathetic vignettes at a bar: a man and a woman (the woman is sitting with another man) exchanging crossing but not quite meeting glances, an abandoned seat next to her, tentative but never actually realized gestures toward meeting, a refrain that alternates "and I hope that I/you don't fall in love with you/me," the final nonintersection and a resigned shrug into the night.

And there are gifted musical touches: the breathily muted horn that winds like a ribbon through the album to evoke Miles Davis; the Lead Belly flavor and Dylanesque vocals of the exuberant waltz "I'll Be Gone"; the hilarious homage to lovers' betrayal called "Rosie"; the abstracted stepwise blues of "Lonely"; the subverted Tin Pan Alley of "And It's You," with Davis-style trumpet and Satchmo-style scat. Like the best musicians of the time, Waits was a kind of amateur archaeologist.

It was natural that he gravitated toward films and acting, consistent with his Charles Bukowski outlook, even. For an adept musical character actor like Waits, it was only a short step from creating and realizing imaginary scenes to movie stardom in roles about outsiders and eccentrics.

WHEN WAITS'S DEATH-AND-SOUND-OBSESSED 1992 disc *Bone Machine* won him his first Grammy, *Rolling Stone*, by way of yuppified praise, summarized his output to date this way: "For more than twenty years, Tom Waits has chronicled the grotesque losers of the seedy underworld." More revealing and to the point, Bruce Springsteen covered Waits' "Jersey Girl"—one master chronicler's homage to another.

Waits's long career falls into two congruent pieces. For his first 10 years and eight recordings, the So Cal boho (remember Rickie Lee Jones? She was his girlfriend, shared his Beat existentialism and love of jazz, which she inflected into her music) collected noirish pictures for his outsider's album of Americana. He started acting in 1978, with a small part in *Paradise Alley*. He's notched four Coppola flicks (he did Robert Altman's *Short Cuts* and half-a-dozen others since), but his most telling performance was in Jim Jarmusch's offbeat 1986 *Down by Law*, which teamed him with a then-little-known Italian comic named Roberto Benigni.

What led Waits to outsider auteurs like Jarmusch and Robert Wilson (Waits's 1993 album, *The Black Rider*, is music for the folk-tale-based opera Wilson directed) was his eccentric muse's 1983 pivot. With *Swordfishtrombones*, Waits hopped a creative freight train into the downtown New York arts scene, where postmodern genre-scramblers like John Zorn and John Lurie and Laurie Anderson searched in parallel (and sometimes in combination) with hip-hoppers like Run-DMC for ways to recombine and recycle musical ideas. *Swordfishtrombones* ditched hifi recording and noir songwriting for Impressionistic soundscapes dreamed in rude facilities—bathroom echo chambers, a hotel room in Mexico, a concrete-and-wood bunker studio on a chicken farm. Waits began amassing an 18-wheeler's worth of weird instruments—calliopes, Balinese metal aungigongs, glass harmonicas, bowed saw, pump organ, accordion, mellotron, bass boo-bams, brake drums, parade drums, even one he built called a condundrum. Hanging out with these grotesques has helped Waits grow into an American original, a wonderfully gifted miniaturist with a Romantic's seeing touch and bruised ironies, like Sherwood Anderson.

Mule Variations was Waits's first album since 1993, but it's unmistakably the sound of him opening up his outsider scrapbook again. A sharp pal who's a fan heard the advance CD and said to me, "Good, huh?" He paused, a shade defensive. "A lot like the last two." Another beat. "But that's who he is." Exactly.

It's hard not to be yourself when you're as much who you are as Waits is. With cowriter/producer and wife Kathleen Brennan, he covers so much stylistic and dramatic ground, you could call him a musical avant-archivist. *Mule Variations* naturally catalogs a lot of American music. There's gospel ("Come On Up to the House," parlor songs and civil war ballads ("Take It with Me," "Pony," "Georgia Lee"), jazz noir ("Black Market Baby"), Stax-Volt soul ("House Where Nobody Lives"), jungle funk ("Big in Japan"). There's electro-blues-surrealism out of Captain Beefheart ("Eyeball Kid," "Filipino Box Spring Hog"). There's the gently insistent, buoyant clave of "Hold On." There's more than a hint of Weill and Brecht in "Chocolate Jesus," with a coruscating chorus about the cellophane-wrapped Messiah melting.

An old-blues hound, Waits now makes his own. "Lowside of the Road" rides a lo-fi sonic rumble made by Harry Partchesque instruments with names like Optigon and Chumbus and Dousengoni. The booze-soaked raunch called "Cold Water" stumbles along like an imaginary hobo who's hooked down some LSD with his hooch; Marc Ribot's bitingly thick-tongued guitar is hilarious. "Get Behind the Mule" marshals Delta-blues doggedness, a saying attributed to Robert Johnson's father, and Chicago 1960s blues revivalist Charlie Musselwhite's lurking harmonica to back-jabbing vignettes of murder and fear that finish with a simple moral: "Never let the weeds get higher than the garden/Always keep a sapphire in your mind."

Our imaginary hobo ain't churchgoing, but he believes how you live matters. His lyrics put old queries in moving ways, and don't mind exploring "standard" answers. Between simple maxims and irony, comedy and satire and suspense, tragedy and surrealism, Waits is never afraid or embarrassed. Take the heartbreaking (and real) story of "Georgia Lee," where he comes back over and over to the basic, unadorned, chilling question, "Why wasn't God watching?" You can sense he's probably a lapsed Catholic boy before you confirm it—that sense of impatience and baffled anger in the face of the world's repeated failures, its daily litany of banal evil. This is a different side of the coin from Randy Newman's "And The Lord Said," with its Joblike irony: "Oh Lord if you won't take care of us, Won't you please please let us be?"

Waits has a smashed foghorn of a voice, somewhere between Beefheart's and Howlin' Wolf's, and he uses it to ruminate and yelp and scream and croon and plead and threaten. It can be a blunt, heavy instrument, but he wields it with incongruous dexterity—even, at times, lightness. The ways he can ask "Why wasn't God watching?" makes your pulse bump. His clashing vocal overtones sometimes surround a note like a clot forming around a gash.

You can't make a hobo, even an imaginary one, flinch easily, and Waits's scrapbook is full of things we'd mostly rather sidle past or turn our backs on.

Like "What's He Building?" Musique-concrete clanging and hissing and the like sets spoken lyrics that start by wondering about the neighbor who has subscriptions to vague magazines, who never waves when he passes, who makes building noises in his workshop, who must be hiding something while he keeps to himself. Sound familiar? Don't you recognize the face of American paranoia?

With all these snapshots rolled into his knapsack, Waits is an American bricoleur. Before you grab a brick to heave at me, let's say that just means he's one of our very own cranks from a very long line, the yowling and yawping sort of Romantic barbarian seer who gets tossed into the tank by bored cops and takes in the turned backs and locked doors as he passes through town, sympathizes with the pregnant women and Vietnam vets begging on the freeways, steps into the cool and still graveyard for a nap, and then hunkers down with an old stray dog in front of the furniture store window to catch a little TV. In fact, you probably don't want a guy like him hanging out in your neighborhood, even if he's named Walt Whitman or Harry Partch or Kenneth Burke, Woody Guthrie or Charlie Mingus or Allen Ginsberg. You're thinking 911 if he's named Howlin' Wolf or Captain Beefheart. Why put up with Tom Waits?

Here's one reason. He can show you what you already know and make you believe it again.

part V **Possible Futures**

Ken Burns, the Academy, and Jazz

LET'S CUT TO THE CHASE on Ken Burns's *Jazz* by invoking Wallace Stevens.

1. Is it entertaining TV? *Mostly, in PBS fashion.*
2. Does it leave out people and places and whole periods and genres normally considered vital parts of jazz history? *Yes.*
3. Does it need more editing? *Yes.*
4. Does Louis Armstrong claim 40 percent of its 19 hours? *Yes.*
5. Does post-1960s jazz claim 10 percent? *Yes.*
6. Does it tell an informed and informative story? *Usually.*
7. Does it identify the 500-odd pieces of jazz that serve as its soundtrack? *Rarely.*
8. Does it have rare and evocative pictures and film footage? *Absolutely.*
9. Is it good history? *It's made-for-PBS history.*
10. Will it satisfy jazz fans and musicians and critics? *Even before it aired, and before most of them saw a fraction of it, it didn't. Once it came out, there was plenty of noisy debate about it, sometimes with good reason, more often not.*
11. Will it save the jazz industry? *That depends: CDs labeled Ken Burns's* Jazz *are bullish.*
12. Will it make jazz a part of mainstream American culture again? *Not likely, but it may help make it an official part of popular American history.*
13. Is it part of the transition jazz has been making for three decades into the academic world? *You bet.*

Now let's dolly back and try to tell the story.

THE NUMBERS HAVE TO COME FIRST. The 10-episode, 19-hours'-long series was six years in the making, and it sprawls: 75 talking heads, tens of thousands of still photos, 500 pieces of music, and so on. Costing some $13 million, about a third of it from General Motors, it's the biggest documentary that's ever been done about jazz.

And yet a lot of jazz musicians and critics and fans, in print and on the Web, started complaining even before it was aired that it's too constrictive. It's easy to see why. It's certainly not comprehensive. For Burns and collaborator Geoffrey C. Ward, history unfolds in the textures of individual lives. (Ward won the Francis Parkman prize for *A First-Class Temperament*, one volume of his biography of FDR.) Jazz for them is the story of a few great men (and the odd woman) who changed the way Americans, then the world, hear and think and act. Chief among them: Louis Armstrong and Duke Ellington. There are places of honor for the likes of James Reese Europe and Jelly Roll Morton, Sidney Bechet and Bix Beiderbecke, Benny Goodman and Count Basie, Artie Shaw and Charlie Parker, Miles Davis and Dave Brubeck. This sort of survey is easier to sustain until about 1929, because jazz musicians were few (though not as few and or as limited to New Orleans and Chicago and New York as the movie implies). But Burns & Co. can tell a credible if reductive story of jazz's first decades using a handful of pioneers.

One reason for the noise from the jazz community is that this overlaps the story of jazz according to Jazz at Lincoln Center, a flashpoint in the jazz world. J@LC teaches that jazz is a clear-cut genealogy of a few outstanding figures, and it excludes many important artists, especially after 1960, often for ideological reasons. The basic plot for both: taking its building blocks from slave music and marching bands and blues and the church and European dance and classical music, jazz began life as a mongrel in New Orleans, came up the river to Chicago, met up (via Armstrong) with New York proto-swing bands and Harlem stride pianists, and exploded, drawing young white players into a black-developed music. It's a true enough, though it ultimately means ignoring uncomfortable parallel developments (Red Allen and Armstrong) or scenes (between-the-wars LA jazz) or entire genres (Latin jazz, European jazz). But schematic history can be good TV, and Burns, like earlier PBS filmmaker Frederick Wiseman, makes long, long movies that depend on strong, heavily delineated characters and themes to keep them from dissipating.

His story's heart is Armstrong. Its head is Ellington. And its soul is the Jazz Age and the Swing Era.

In Episode 5, "Swing: Pure Pleasure (1935–1937)," writer Albert Murray declares, "Jazz is primarily dance music." Though that hasn't been true for nearly half the music's history, it's clear he's speaking for Burns: three episodes, nearly six hours, discuss the big band era, when jazz underpinned America's popular music and lifted Depression-era spirits, saved the record industry, and dominated that then-new omnipresent technology, radio. Nevertheless, as the often intrusive talking heads tell us, from Ellington on down the musicians knew the difference between the business and the music: stage shtick and chart slots were as important then as now. This is a bittersweet Golden Age of speakeasies, hoods, the Great Depression, squealing bobby-soxers, lynchings, jitter-bugging, novelty tunes, and early moves toward racial integration. It is described without apparent irony as a time of "adult sensibility," and is the series' gravitational center.

The great-man schematic creates escalating difficulty for the plotting starting with Episode 7, which begins with Charlie Parker and spends nearly as much time on Armstrong as it does on bebop. By the mid-1940s, the musicians had multiplied and moved on—out of Harlem and swing time. And so jazz dissolves into hundreds of musicians searching for different sounds, styles, approaches, languages, multimedia formats. The last 40 years of Ken Burns's *Jazz* are a choppy and unreliable ride; a lot disappears, and what's left can be telegraphic or confusing and look exactly like J@LC speaking.

Burns says post-1960s jazz is too controversial even in the jazz world to be history. Maybe he should have ended, then, with John Coltrane; his series *Baseball*, after all, stopped at 1970. For in less than two hours, faces from Charles Mingus's to Sonny Rollins' flash across the screen between inevitable reprises of Duke and Satchmo. Miles Davis's push into fusion shrinks to his alleged desperation for teen fans. Ornette Coleman is dismissed. Keith Jarrett and Chick Corea don't appear. The 1970s and 1980s are a quick-blur artistic wilderness until the arrival of Wynton Marsalis, Artistic Director of Jazz at Lincoln Center and the film's Senior Creative Consultant and prime talking head. And there, after a brief survey of new stars (Cassandra Wilson, Joshua Redman) and a recapitulation of key figures and themes, it ends.

The signal irony: if Burns had cut the final episode and billed this as *Jazz: The First 50 Years*, more of the discussion might be where it belongs—the movie.

UNTIL PRETTY RECENTLY nobody thought enough of jazz to point a movie camera in its general direction for very long. There are snatches of footage of Armstrong and Ellington and Fats Waller and Bessie Smith and the like from the early days. By the mid-1930s the popular swing bands cropped up in films and then in "soundies." But the video record of what fans like to call America's greatest art form is sporadic and discouraging.

This problem plays to Burns's strengths: he loves having his staff dig up old photos (for this, they turned up millions), and he loves working stills to make them kinetic. He pans across and slowly zooms in and out of a single shot to give it a movielike temporal depth. In one vignette about Harlem's Savoy Ballroom, where drummer Chick Webb held court and introduced Ella Fitzgerald in the 1930s, he intercuts shots of separate white and black dancers to hammer home the voiceover's point about its integrated patrons—a first in America. He assembles a deft mix of photos and film to recreate the stage-fright-to-triumph of Benny Goodman's 1938 "Sing Sing Sing" concert at Carnegie Hall.

The series boasts tours de force. The evocative segment called "The Road" strings out a head-turning daisy chain of wondrous footage: bands on trains and buses and touring cars, chugging 500 miles a day six days a week, making whoopee and changing tires, riding high onstage and coping with breakdowns and prejudice offstage. The recently deceased bass and photography great Milt Hinton recalls how at band stops his wife would head into town looking for black homes where the musicians could eat and stay, how musicians were people of prestige in the community. Readings from journals and newspapers and diaries sample big band life's dizzying ups and downs, while the film rolls from impromptu baseball games to a couple of female jazz fans puffing fake reefers while hugging the sign of a town named Gage.

And in the background rolls out more jazz by far than 99 percent of America has heard. Much of the time, it's as snippets in the background when one after another talking head pops up. The heads are duly identified time after time. The tunes aren't, unless they're key to a biographical or sociological set piece. Why not flash a subtitle to tell the audience what's playing?

Because jazz is the soundtrack for this series as much as or more than its subject. To put it another way, this isn't really a movie about jazz history. Think of Burns as PBS's Oliver Stone. Like the civil war and baseball, jazz for Burns and Ward is a lens to focus on basic questions: who are Americans, and how do they manage to get along—or not? And their central query concerns race.

So they film jazz as the tale of black redemption in and of America, a narrative of conversion and triumph whose shape recalls St. Augustine and Dante. From the days of slavery through the humiliations of Jim Crow and minstrelsy to the assertive freedom of the blues and jazz, Burns's movie resounds with the apocalyptic ring of apotheosis, as it examines a few crucial candidates for cultural sainthood. For it wants both to carve jazz greats into the American pantheon and to underline jazz's pivotal centrality to 20th-century America as an affirmation of African American creativity and endurance.

This, coupled with Marsalis's camera-savvy polish as a spokesman as well as his insistent championing of jazz education over the years, explains why a filmmaker like Burns would feel drawn to J@LC's version of jazz history. (Actually Dan Morgenstern, the respected head of the Rutgers Institute for Jazz Studies, was the film's senior historical consultant and vetted the script, and there were 17 consultants in all, so until the final episode there are inevitable contiguous plot and character points, but not necessarily identity, with Lincoln Center's tale.) But dramatic necessity also helps explain why some characters, like Armstrong and Ellington, are the story's recurrent focus.

Swing, you might guess, is a buzzword in this series, and you'd be right, even though the film itself doesn't swing much. The earnestness that suffuses PBS cultural products won't let it float for long. At times, the music's lilting ease and fire contrast vividly with its deliberate, self-conscious pace. That's exacerbated by Burns's 75 talking heads: watching can be like sitting through a course team-taught by the UN.

Besides Marsalis, Burns's other main soloist is writer Gary Giddins, and Giddins swings: his wide-ranging learning rides his love for jazz easily. Other commentators—Stanley Crouch, Murray, Artie Shaw, Gerald Early, James Lincoln Collier, Dave Brubeck—give good camera and consistent historical edutainment. But too many proffer vague impressions, cliched memories, breathless interpretations, and warmed-over anecdotes. They could easily have been edited or edited out. Then there are periodic pileups. In Episode 7, Joya Sherrill, and Ellington's granddaughter, and a few others repeat that Duke and Billy Strayhorn were a rare and wonderful match. In Episode 5, the same two dancers appear twice with virtually the same observations about Harlem's Savoy Ballroom.

Sometimes the anecdotes are fun or fabulous, and sometimes they're bad history. Take Jon Hendricks, who in Episode 4 retails the disproven mythic origins of Armstrong's scatting (sheet music fell off his stand at a recording session). Or director Bernard Tavernier, who gushes about Django Reinhardt and Stephane Grappelli introducing the guitar-violin combo to jazz, though they themselves would have fingered Eddie Lang and Joe Venuti. Ballplayer Buck O'Neil rambles good-naturedly about Billie Holiday giving listeners "the greatest moments" and "the saddest moments," amply demonstrating how a tighter edit could have sliced the series' lapses into vacuity.

Marsalis's starring role has several sides. He delivers very effective musical glosses and explanations, polished by years of shows and clinics with adults and teens and kids. His knowledge of and passion for the jazz he loves, and his conviction that it represents American life in full, is infectious, if sometimes hyperbolic. But when he holds forth about Ellington and Armstrong and the semilegendary Buddy Bolden as if he knew them intimately, it's TV, not history.

History can be light-fingered instead of heavy-handed, and *Jazz* could use more humor, more of "the light" Marsalis ascribes to the best jazz musicians. It has some fabulous vignettes from Crouch, the series' third-ranked talking head. Except for the last two hours, Crouch swings. In one priceless bit, he mimics pre-Armstrong pop vocalists and then Armstrong himself, and asks why anyone would want to revert. "That would be a bad choice," he deadpans. Anybody who makes that choice, he adds, should be deported—count a beat—"to somewhere." Another beat. "Maybe Pluto." It's impossible to disagree, especially when you're laughing.

To SOME EXTENT, Burns has himself to blame for the unjoyful noise that greeted his film in the jazz world. In conversation, he tends, rightly, to underplay his work's ambitions. It's not the history of jazz, he says.

Viewers will get to know a handful of musicians, meet another dozen or two, and brush past a few dozen more. He can't possibly compete with books like Giddins's *Visions of Jazz* or jazz histories like Ted Gioia's or Marshall Stearns's; he's made a movie that tells an educational story for a mass audience. This is reasonable and accurate and no small feat. And, in fact, the movie is steeped with rich human detail of the sort most music historians rarely touch on. But the PR bombast trumpets him as jazz's Joan of Arc, and once he's on-message he can't stop selling. Jazz, like academia, is small and marginal with plenty of defensive, combative types; "the music" is a secular religion. Burns's perceived power inevitably lights territorial fuses.

As it happens, the jazz industry, now down to under 1 percent of US music sales, once you exclude Kenny G and his clones, looks incongruously like a Victorian maiden lashed to the tracks awaiting her hero. Burns's movie is a mantra, as labels crunch despairing numbers and weed out personnel and artists after the latest wave of megamergers and Internet terrors. For his well-designed five-CD companion set (subtitled *The Story of America's Music*), the filmmaker brokered a deal between Sony and PolyGram, bitter corporate rivals, then brought in other labels; all are hoping for sales like the companion book's, which had a 300,000 first printing. This is mind-blowing if you're a jazz label head used to dealing in niche sales (Marsalis himself rarely moves more than 10,000 CDs, Cassandra Wilson and Joshua Redman several times that many) and waiting for the next guillotine.

Potential audience numbers were tossed around fervently in advance of the show's screening: 40 million viewers for *Baseball* and *The Civil War*, and probably *Jazz* will draw less, but. . . . (Ultimately it reached about 12 million.) It fascinates me that few of the film's critics ever addressed that. Why not consider an America where 20 million more people—or 3 million, or however many watch this in repeats or on DVD—know something, anything, about Louis Armstrong, Duke Ellington, Charlie Parker, Miles Davis, and a few others? Where, if they survive the overstatments, talking heads, and pacing, they learn some hidden history?

Am I Pollyanna? Maybe. Reality check: this is a made-for-TV movie. But I too think race is America's central issue, even more multifaceted in the 21st century. What holds this joint's pasted seams together, beyond the Founding Documents, is the frequently intangible glue called culture. TV is a major place American culture gets made. Can anyone measure what it meant to have Bill Cosby playing an upper-class Dad next door for a generation? What it means now that there are black and Hispanic and Asian and gay and you-name-'em channels filling cable and satellite TV? Can anyone guess what it might mean in five years to have *Jazz*, whatever its warts, playing over and over to a country as terminally divided and in search of itself as this one?

These are not delusions of grandeur about the power of jazz or Ken Burns. They are possibilities written in the history of jazz in America. Take Burns's vignette about Charlie Black, a white Texas teen who saw Armstrong perform in the 1930s. It changed his life. He joined the NAACP'S legal team working on what became *Brown v. Board of Education*. The sociology of jazz is full of such stories. And they are very real.

For instance, no one with a brain disputes that jazz was initially an African American creation. But as Marsalis, Giddins, Crouch, Murray, and Early point out over and over, jazz was welcoming, inclusive, open. It replaced minstrelsy with a cultural site where all Americans could participate, speak to each other, override or ignore or challenge or slide by the society's fixations on racial and ethnic stereotypes. Black Americans (and other ethnic outsiders) could use it to enter mainstream society, white Americans could flee to it from mainstream society, and the transactions created a flux and flow that powered American cultural syntheses.

Jazz, the theme goes, represents America at its best—the dream of America. In the Depression, as Early reminds us, it rivaled MGM musicals in lifting the country's spirits. Of course, since jazz is a human activity, it also reflects the deepest divisions as well as the ideals at America's core. Race, sex, money, power, capitalism, creative freedom, the interaction of the individual and the group—these are all questions embedded in jazz history. They're the questions Burns and Ward are truly interested in. At its best, *Jazz* gets us interested in them too.

Burns admits he never listened to jazz until he started considering it as a subject. Ward became an Armstrong fan at age 10, when he was hospitalized with polio. Jazz is lucky they're interested in it.

RIGHT NOW, JAZZ'S COMMERCIAL FUTURE is murky. The major labels are wreckage. Marsalis, who used to get $1 million a year to make niche-market records in hopes that they would turn into catalog gold, for years didn't have a label. High-profile jazz promoters are hemorrhaging. The Knitting Factory is reported in the hole for $2 million, after luring a big entertainment firm to take a stake, opening a club in LA, and losing its annual jazz-festival sponsor. The Blue Note chain is said to be spurting red ink from expansions into Las Vegas and midtown Manhattan. Nor are jazz's nonprofit arms thriving. The Thelonious Monk Institute, so closely aligned with the Clinton–Gore administration its head was reportedly hoping for an ambassadorship if Al won, has resituated its rump organization in LA. And the long-dormant board of Jazz at Lincoln Center fired executive director Rob Gibson in a swirl of intrigue: changed door-locks and computer codes, fired and rehired personnel, and persistent rumors of financial malfeasance, bullying, and drug abuse.

Jazz has been on a commercial slide since the 1970s, when it racked up 10 percent of US retail music sales. At the same time, it began entering the groves of academe. Today, most jazz musicians are trained at schools; jazz history is laced through American Studies and music curricula.

This process has already fundamentally changed jazz itself and its relation to American culture, though how isn't always clear at first. As a colleague reminded me recently, in the jazz heydays celebrated by Burns's *Jazz*, musicians fashioned their own idiosyncratic solutions to musical problems, drawing on oral tradition (which varied considerably) and their own ingenuity and needs. This meant individual creative solutions to problems—how to finger this note or sequence, how to get that timbre, how to connect those chord changes. Now, a professor distributes computer analyses of famous solos, templates for solutions that are shared by hundreds and thousands of students. This has a paradoxical effect: it raises the general level of and standardizes jazz training, but it also tends to vitiate the individualism traditionally at the music's heart. This is why older musicians routinely complain that younger schooled players all sound alike. On the other hand, they're well suited for jazz repertory programs like J@LC.

That is part of jazz's changing contemporary dynamics. So is Ken Burns's *Jazz*.

OVER THE LAST DECADE, "What is jazz?" became a hotly contested issue in cultural circles. But while the debate about the jazz canon and other such issues swirled around neotraditionalists and avant-gardists and their advocates and critics, jazz was opening new paths into contemporary pop music and revisiting others, like the jazz-rock fusions of the 1960s and 1970s, that had been discredited, debased, or dead-ended. Out of this came some of the most interesting trends of the 1990s.

Meanwhile, to a greater extent than ever before, the question "What is Jazz?" has become academic, because jazz programs are being taught at more and more US campuses, even though there's less and less steady work for the graduates, fewer big bands like Maynard Ferguson's that they can get road educations with. Nevertheless, the programs grow. These are the first generations of jazz musicians trained more in the academy than on the bandstand.

What do these newcomers want from jazz? What is jazz getting from them? How does an academic jazz program deliver—and fail to deliver—on its implicit promise to create a better musician? Does it help students in dealing with day-to-day scuffling?

Many middle-aged and older musicians grouse that the youngsters they hear sound more and more alike. "They're processed, like Velveeta," says 51-year-old bassist Ray Drummond, one of the most in-demand sidemen in jazz, veteran of more than 200 records and countless club and concert dates.

"Technically they can be very good, but they sound like they come out of a generic white box. Developing a personal sound, a personal vision of who you are as an artist, is not an issue they address. It's not important to them. Neither their peers nor their elders are making them address it. And it's a serious issue that cuts to the heart of the credibility of the artistic process. And it's why so many younger players on all instruments sound the same.

"When I was coming up, younger guys hung out on the scene, looking for any way to break in we could find. We'd already sat down and listened to hundreds of tunes, learned and practiced them, developed our ears. And you've got to know who you're playing with, so you can figure out how they'll approach whatever you're doing. That's the kind of discipline you're supposed to bring to this job."

Bill Pierce is head of the woodwind department at Berklee School of Music, which has one of the oldest and most respected jazz training programs. A performing veteran as well as an academic, the baby boomer has played tenor with Stevie Wonder, Marvin Gaye, and his own former student Antonio Hart. In these ways and others, he straddles the cusp between the old and new worlds of jazz performance.

Though he has a college degree in music himself, Pierce broke into the major leagues via Art Blakey's Jazz Messengers. So he knows how jazz education used to be. "In the past," he begins, "you studied with masters, you worked with some older guys who showed you the ropes. I was fortunate; I had that and college training. I got to hang out with Blakey and Freddie Hubbard and Tony Williams, and listen to what they did and how. I took lessons and hung out with older guys like George Coleman. But that's not the case so much these days. A lot of the older masters are gone now. So it's less learning by doing than by being incubated in academia.

"At Berklee, the students are getting their training the same way most people have been doing it for a while. It's secondhand information, in a sense. Instead of going in and listening to Coltrane, or all the masters who have already passed on, they listen to recordings and do analysis, applying the tried-and-true procedures of music study to jazz. But everything we use is somewhat tempered by the fact that jazz is a different animal, with a different aesthetic and history. The idea that jazz is at its root a black American music that's based on the blues and improvisation—that permeates what we teach."

Pierce notes that not all good musicians make good teachers, which could make jazz's traditional on-the-road education a spotty curriculum. "In academia, people know how to teach," he insists, although anyone who has nodded through classes taught by professors who can't lecture might disagree. "Some of the older guys didn't always know how to share information, or didn't always have the time. 'Oh, learn that for yourself,' they'd say. Now that was good for some people—it forced you to use your own ingenuity, to develop your own methods for learning. But for other people it was less helpful than someone with a background in education who knows how to teach."

Still, Pierce admits that jazz-in-academe has a central problem: "It's always better to have someone who's actually done something explain it, but there are more younger guys coming up through jazz programs who are now just teachers. They haven't played seriously. So I guess the music's life's blood is thinning a little bit."

That's one key point older working musicians criticize. Another is the clubhouse atmosphere of the dorms, where friends cheer each other while cutting enemies down—judgments that can be more social than musical. Of course, you could argue that the old cutting sessions did the same. But a dorm is more a womb than any scene or club, and the variety and levels of experience and understanding among musicians there vary far less than in the real world.

As Pierce sees it: "On a certain level, the students can learn to interact improvisationally, but it's really an introductory level. The interaction between musicians, in this music, comes before the interaction between musician and audience. So students can learn the techniques, though it's one or two steps removed from the actuality, and it's definitely not the oral tradition.

"But you still have to learn how to create soul, emotion, feeling, a spiritual connection—whatever you want to call it. You have to connect with people that way. All the technique in the world doesn't make you a real jazz musician if you can't do that. It's not just about technique. People study Trane like they study Mozart, and sometimes they glean the technical aspects but they miss all the spirituality that's the core of his music. And look at Monk: people used to think he couldn't play the piano at all, and yet he expresses so much.

"That's one of the drawbacks of studying jazz in the conservatory setting: the spiritual and emotional contexts of the music don't get emphasized. And that's important. Jazz started as black American music. For the early musicians, it was about the aspirations and the feelings of being excluded. There are still white kids from the suburbs taking that life out of context and trying to live it. You don't have to go that far. But you do have to address those issues—and it's hard to do in the conservatory context.

"More and more, though, teachers are realizing that's lacking in the musicians we're putting out. They're very competent, but they're not necessarily touching the soul. Music has to make you feel something. It always has to come back to that—and whether that can be taught in school, I'm not sure. But we have to try to get it across."

One of Pierce's better-known ex-students is Javon Jackson, who was drawn to the tenor by his father's love for Gene Ammons' burly Texas tenor lines. In his early 30s, Jackson sits on the cusp of pre- and post-academic jazz. In the early 1980s, Branford Marsalis, then with Blakey's Jazz Messengers, heard Jackson play, and suggested he study at Berklee with ex-Messenger Pierce. Jackson went, but didn't finish the four-year course. Instead, boosted by Marsalis and Pierce, he left after two years to join the Messengers himself—one of the last of the great drummer's informal "graduates." In the decade since, he's become a leader himself, with a rare major-label contract: he's recorded a couple albums for prestigious Blue Note.

"At Berklee, a lot of the teachers are musicians who are actually working, so they can give you good information about the real world," Jackson begins. "And Berklee puts all these kids who might be big fish locally into a very competitive situation, which puts things in perspective. It humbles you, and puts you around other musicians you can share ideas with. The networking is maybe the most important aspect. There are so many musicians and so few slots out here, anything helps.

"Of course, university training doesn't prepare you for most of life on the road. My first two weeks with Art Blakey almost cancelled a lot of my schooling. What happens when Sarah Vaughan walks into the club where you're playing in mid-set?

"Then there are the practical things. You have to grow up. You're getting this amount of money. You have to make sure you have your passport before you get on the plane. You've got to find your own places to eat, deal with credit cards and bills, figure out what to do before and after the gig. You're on your own. It's like going from high school basketball to the NBA."

"And you can't develop yourself as a musician in the university settings the same way. Playing for a few friends is not the same as playing for an audience that's got a 60-year-old man or a 30-year-old woman. You have to learn to articulate varied emotions for audiences. You learn to play ballads, medium-tempo things. You learn to balance a set. You have to learn these things on the job, not in school."

Still, Jackson understands that the old world is gone: "There aren't a lot of clubs any more, so musicians have to develop within the universities, even if it would be better for them to develop in the clubs. I was part of the last generation of musicians who worked with bands. So Blakey would tell me to go hang out with Clifford Jordan, or Junior Cook, or whoever—these are the cats who will show you how to do what you need to know how to do. It got me thinking about hanging around older people who had the information. Now musicians come to New York looking for a record contract, because it's not really possible to do what I did anymore."

Jackson believes younger musicians are responsible for gathering the oral information that school doesn't provide. "It's like a library: it's not the library's fault if the books don't fall off the shelves and hit you on the head," he insists. "If I walk past a 50-year-old musician and don't ask him about his experiences, that's my own fault."

Pierce agrees. "Innovation is something that just happens," he says. "I don't think Trane or Bird started by saying, 'I want to be an innovator.' It happened because of their talent and their work ethic, how they went about what they were doing. Some of the attitudes I see in some of the younger musicians amaze me: they see themselves on the same level as these guys, and they haven't done anything that legitimizes that."

Even if they're still wannabes, many jazz students have big plans—and according to Pierce, who agrees with Drummond, the distortion starts on the business side: "Jazz is driven from the top down these days, by the music industry. Who's making it big is kind of odd: people who get a shot because of the way they look and dress, their potential marketability. That's not the musicians' fault. Do you tell them to give the big bucks to the other guy?"

"But it's changing people's aspirations in jazz. A lot of kids see Wynton Marsalis and Josh Redman and want to be instant leaders, stars. They start worrying about getting an agent, marketing themselves. It's a different perspective from the one people my age went into the music with. And it's not really what the music is about. If you don't take care of the music, the rest of it won't do you any good. There only about five people on the industry's top shelf, and everybody else is scuffling."

Jackson concurs: "There are older musicians who are bitter about some of the younger stars. There are probably older basketball players bitter about Michael Jordan. But it's not his fault. He exploited the situation, and the situation exploited him. Still, just because people have more and live better than earlier generations doesn't mean that they know more. The way I see it, it's my responsibility to seek a rapport with a Cedar Walton and a Ron Carter. But it's very hard; not all those musicians are accessible. How many young sax players can get to Sonny Rollins? There isn't the access there was 30 years ago."

Sam Thomas recently graduated Berklee, and is confronting the move from the sheltered world of school life to the very naked world of jazz—and the music business that surrounds it.

Like most Berklee students, Thomas got his musical start in elementary school. He chose the sax because, he says, "when the teacher came around with the instruments, it looked flashy." In junior high school, he switched from alto because the newly started jazz band had an opening for tenor sax. Soon he was listening to Coltrane and Joe Henderson records, and was hooked on the tenor for life. "Once you find heroes like that, you want to emulate them," he says almost shyly.

An older high school pal dazzled Thomas one day when he came off the field from marching-band rehearsal reeling off signature licks from Charlie Parker. The pal was going on to study at Berklee—the first Thomas heard of the school, which gave him a degree in jazz composition.

Like Jackson, Thomas perceived that being a jazz student in academia would have advantages and disadvantages. So he exploited it for both its insider and outsider aspects. He says: "The good thing about Berklee is I got systematically exposed to many different areas of music. I graduated with a degree in jazz composition. I could have had a dual major in performance. But who needs a performance degree to work in jazz? And besides, I could study with more teachers with more varied ideas and approaches outside Berklee, thanks to the school's reputation and connections."

"The drawback," he continues, "is that it's not real life; it's not like being on the road with a band. So when you do hit the real world, you have to learn to put your ego in place. Or else you sink. So I now have a realistic perspective on myself. See, your first inclination is to be really competitive. Some of that comes from dorm life and the academic environment, some of it's just natural, because we're young. It's a lack of maturity. But music isn't a competition. So I had to rethink what I was doing."

Or, as Jackson puts it from his veteran's perspective, "You have to be humble enough to take criticism—because it's sure going to come back at you."

One survival strategy Pierce tries to implant in his students is to branch out in their skills: "Be diversified, I tell them, so they can do other musically related things to sustain themselves. If I don't think they're ready to go to New York, I'll suggest they go back home, if they come from a reasonably large city, and see what they can develop there. And if I think they're ready, I'll send 'em to New York, which is still the center of jazz, the ultimate testing ground for jazz musicians. But no matter what, I stress versatility. If you've got the inner strength to stick with it, you might, at the end of the process, be able to consider yourself a player. It doesn't mean you'll be wearing Italian suits with money in the bank."

Thomas has been following his teacher's advice on both counts. "I worked my way through Berklee on computer graphics," he explains. "So I can apply that to my music for notation. And I can use it to develop my own package for record labels, public relations people, and marketing, and make it professional and attractive." And, of course, to supplement his musician's earnings.

He plans on heading back to his California roots. "Breaking in to the jazz world," he says wryly, "still relies a lot on the old method: jump in and get your ass kicked and learn. But I know some people in San Francisco, so I'll start doing self-promotion there and see what develops. I feel the move-right-to-New-York thing that a lot of young guys do is actually disrespectful to the music. They don't have the experience. I know I need more practical experience. If you don't have it, you're setting yourself up for some real hardship.

"Besides," he continues, "that's the kind of thing that makes me understand why older guys see us as primarily technicians. It's true in a lot of cases. Music is about deeper things, and I know I need to develop that. I don't have it yet. Then, too, the whole premise of jazz is to push the music further. Lots of my peers are just regurgitating. I feel I'm just on the cusp between regurgitating and a deeper understanding. It's why I'm doing it the way I'm doing it. Music has to be real."

Or, as his teacher puts it, "Out of all these hundreds of real competent students, maybe five or six will be the real item. That's all anyone can hope for."

25

The Politics of Music
Don Byron and Dave Douglas

EVERYONE KNOWS HOW Plato mistrusted the politics of music. And some may remember that Theodor Adorno saw pop music, in particular, as an insidious form of brainwashing. That current runs through philosophy and theology worldwide, reminding us to be grateful we don't live in Plato's Republic or fundamentalist theocracies. In 2002, the return of music to Radio Afghanistan became an instant symbol of castoff oppression. In this context, Nietzsche was rare in his praise of music's historical and social functions, an embrace that let him appropriate its textures and effects into his sensibility and prose.

It's clear that music, even popular music, which includes jazz, has some power that frightens philosophers and politicians, enough so that they try to harness it when they're not censoring or disparaging it. The figure of the bard, the Orphic seer whose power can penetrate the world's veils and change its bent, still exerts a powerful, if largely subliminal, pull on the imaginations of artists and audiences alike.

And why shouldn't it? *Homo ludens*, whom the artist represents at his best, is fundamental to our nature, and a wondrous and compelling thing to behold, whether it's Michelangelo brooding on his scaffolding in the Sistine Chapel or Derek Jeter dancing at shortstop at Yankee Stadium. As Nietzsche wrote in *The Gay Science*: "Every great human being has a retroactive force: all history is again placed in the scales for his sake, and a thousand secrets of the past crawl out of their hideouts—into HIS sun. There is no way of telling what may yet become history some day. Perhaps the past is still essentially undiscovered! So many retroactive forces are still required!"

But unlike the forces in Newtonian physics, these never operate in a social vacuum. Both left and right nurture a disdain for and suspicion of popular culture, unless it's nostalgic or carefully defined and hence safe. Today in America, art swims in a near-all-encompassing commercialism that functions, at times, as gatekeeper and censor. Under Stalin, Lenin, and the tsars, the governing powers made sure art was molded and censored and suppressed. As a Russian expatriate professor-friend once remarked to me, "At least we valued art enough to censor it. Here you just let anyone shout whatever they want." I cited Lenny Bruce, whom he'd never heard of and, when I tried to explain, didn't want to understand. "Dirty words?" he asked, shaking his head. My attempted point: gatekeepers exist always and everywhere, and even in freewheeling consumer America, entertainment capital of the world, art is understood, at least by some, to possess gravity.

So there are always some artists who aspire to be Shelleyan bards, no matter what their medium. They take the time to study and learn, some-times in tidy or systematic ways, like ants converting a fallen leaf to portable pieces, and sometimes in meandering, maddening fashion, like bees seeking nectar. In our postindustrial culture, their status and power, like old magic, ain't what it used to be. That loss is one motivation behind the multiplication of New Age phenomena in recent years.

Still, most people, like most philosophers, tend to think of musicians as talented beasts. Rafi Zabor's fairy-tale novel, *The Bear Comes Home*, inverts that notion with whimsical charm and some nice satiric turns. Zabor's bear plays cutting-edge jazz saxophone, and develops a whole quasi-human life, including human lovers, inside the jazz world, where he's mostly accepted, even considered a star. Now jazz musicians, thanks no doubt partly to race, have long been treated as, well, semi-trained bears—especially insulting given the body of work and extended disci-pline jazz artists developed in half a century. Some, like Charles Mingus and Anthony Braxton, to name two men who are very dissimilar in most other ways, raged against it in extensive writings and speaking. Louis Armstrong and Duke Ellington, in their very different ways, sidestepped it or ignored it, at least in public. Beboppers subverted it, as Amiri Baraka pointed out in *Blues People*, adapting and tweaking the costumes and mannerisms of European bohemians in their claim to be artists.

Political or social commentary has always been part of jazz, implicitly or explicitly. How could an art form originally formulated by outsiders be otherwise? There are famous examples: "Black and Blue" by Armstrong. *Freedom Now* by Max Roach and Abbey Lincoln. "Fables of Faubus" by Charles Mingus. *Jack Johnson* by Miles Davis. "Alabama" by John Coltrane. But now, post-9/11, new resonances have been added, unlooked-for surplus value, to art that has something to tell us about who we are now, much as it has to so much else—normal bits of life in our times, like airplanes falling out of the sky, suddenly acquire newly active potential meanings, a spreading shadow of possible contexts.

Enter clarinetist Don Byron, 42, and trumpeter Dave Douglas, 37. Both have garnered lots of press coverage, gathered awards, attracted musi-cians and followers, produced varied and important bodies of work that are stylistically and conceptually diverse as bandleaders and composers. Both are those fortunate jazz rarities, possessors of major-label deals. Both are widely read and intellectually cultivated, and infuse that sensibility into their art, which includes how they use liner notes, album illustrations, the whole package surrounding the disc that effectively embeds it in a perspective. Both recorded their latest albums before the World Trade Center came down. Each had particular social as well as musical concerns, creative speculations, the process of rebraiding reality's DNA into something that, in that magical way of art, steps out of time while simultaneously reflecting a vision, a personality, a series of moments rooted like Yggdrasil in our world. Both albums have acquired new echoes, courtesy of history, as inevitable as they were unforeseen.

BYRON FIRST. Articulate and funny with a sarcastic wit, he says: "I don't think everything I do has to be explained. That's one of the weak parts of this era: everything has to be literal, you have to get it right now. I often end up having to justify what I'm doing in interviews: something about me rubs up against their belief-systems."

Twenty years ago, studying clarinet at the New England Conservatory of Music, he discovered Mickey Katz, whose klezmer music, which featured intricate possibilities for clarinet, was pretty much forgotten. He revived it, and became a novelty act that was extremely smart and musical. The elderly Jewish couples who came to Manhattan's old Knitting Factory years ago for his shows loved it, maybe even more because Byron is dreadlocked and black.

Byron is generally credited with bringing the clarinet back into jazz as more than an instrument sax players double on. Stiffer, less able to flow and bend notes and sounds than the saxophone, the clarinet stopped being crucial to jazz's mainstream around the time of Benny Goodman and Artie Shaw, despite subsequent technical extensions like Buddy DeFranco's bebop clarinet. During the 1960s and 1970s, it was mostly avant-gardists or nostalgic traditionalists who picked it up.

Byron's clarinet, which carries this history within its sound, is at once ancient and modern. His licorice stick moves from dry woody piping to edgy squeals to hiccups and vocalizing growls, and his penchant for chromaticism, polytonality, and hanging odd passing tones in unexpected places evades nostalgia. His circuitous, unexpectedly jumping lines are stamped with his harmonic knowledge and melodic invention, informed by Bach and Schoenberg, Armstrong and Coltrane. And his rhythmic sense is sharp: he can make any two notes dance. A tireless experimenter, he's played silent movie accompaniments, hip-hop rhythms, spoken-word performance pieces. That range was one reason Byron was jazz artistic director at the Brooklyn Academy of Music's Next Wave festival for four seasons.

As a composer, Byron is eclectic, thoughtful, and provocative, usually with a political or social agenda. Attitude bursts from his personal and artistic DNA. His album debut as a leader was *The Tuskegee Experiments*, inspired by the federal government's horrific wartime syphilis experiments on unsuspecting African Americans. His first *Music for Six Musicians* album followed.

"Most of that record," he explains, "was inspired by political events around the time I was writing it. So there are pieces about Ross Perot and Clarence Thomas and Shelby Steele. My music refers all the time to intellectual concerns. Why do that? Why not just play? My answer is, I think a lot about Max Roach and Abbey Lincoln and Mingus, and you can't strip the politics away from that music. The music holds up without it— if it didn't, it wouldn't be worth discussing—but it's the motivation. If you read what they were saying and thinking then, it makes even more sense. People can learn the notes Coltrane played, but unless they're willing to embrace some of the politics that produced them, there's a whole piece of him they're skirting.

"The flip side is, listeners expect political music to sound a certain way: if it's about race, it's either got a McCoy Tyner sound or it's free. But every tune on that first *Six Musicians* record has techniques that dealt with the subject matter differently. Take 'Shelby Steele.' It states the melody, then states it upside down in the clave, then states it two beats off in the clave; so it talks about how if you state something out of context it changes meaning. My point is that you can talk politically in any context, even repertory. Any lump of clay you pick up, you can use to say anything you need."

And Byron has become an accomplished bricoleur. *Bug Music*, like *The Music of Mickey Katz* demonstates what he means about the cultural politics of repertory music. In his historical revisionism, Duke Ellington, Raymond Scott, and John Kirby are presented side by side, as implicit equals. Everyone knows Ellington. Scott wrote wacky music often used as cartoon soundtracks. Kirby pursued chamber jazz. Byron's sly goal: to recontextualize Ellington and the others, changing the angle of vision and hence the potential meanings of the music. His album *Romancing the Unseen*, did something similar with ghosts from Benny Goodman to Walt Disney.

Byron's second, recent album for *Music for Six Musicians* is entitled *You Are #6*. It alludes to *The Prisoner*, the late 1960s TV show starring Patrick McGoohan as a British spy who tries to resign and is kidnapped to The Village, a pleasantly surreal totalitarian holding pen for such as he, where he is expected to be broken. Instead, he mounts one escape attempt after another and plots to undermine the nameless powers, which seem to include his own government, who run the place. Failing to get cover art from the show, Byron substituted A. G. Rizzoli's equally surreal "The Bluesea House," an intricate system of buildings and symbolology that, as it sprawls across the opened CD booklet's innards, resembles a board game for a Platonic life system. It had, Byron felt, the right resonances to enhance his music.

Why *The Prisoner?* "What's interesting about that show," says Byron, a self-described connoisseur of pop culture, "is the scenario. Essentially, The Village is a comfortable place, a nice place to live, had all the amenities, but no one was really free. They kept wanting The Prisoner to get relaxed in that. In some ways they were right: once you're clean and comfortable and everything is taken care of, it really doesn't matter what's happening, in a certain kind of way."

Byron is of West Indian descent; his father played bass in calypso bands in the Bronx when the clarinetist was growing up. Hence another embedded context for his music: the Anglo-Caribbean tradition, whose cultural roles in the West African diaspora he feels may be forgotten in the current Latino renaissance. "Calypso," he says, "Haitian music, they're part of it; the English-speaking part of Nicaragua and the Caribbean is part of it. When people see me they often think, you're an avant-garde guy. Actually, no, I'm very West Indian. My politics, the way I approach the humor in my music. West Indians are pretty ironic, nastily judgmental, frugal, angrily political and yet joyfully political—West Indian politics is usually a band. When I was growing up there were lots of Sparrow songs about Martin Luther King. The lyrics unfold into pretty long stories, always with a twist and irony. Take my approach to Brazilian music—funny twists and turns, Schoenberg type of harmonies, stuff in places that if you look hard they shouldn't necessarily be together and yet they go together, because they're in my imagination."

That, and the fact that clave resides partly in the ambiguity between duple and triple meter—which multiplies out to six—helped shape an album that is wide-ranging, effective, and shot through with knowing, releasing humor.

It opens with Henry Mancini's "Theme from Hatari (Baby Elephant Walk)," which Byron has remade in clave with percussionist Milton Cardona overlaying a santeria chant—a wicked irony for a comic film starring John Wayne as a big-game hunter in Africa. "You Are #6" Latinizes the show's theme, tagging the end with a taped quote from a sardonic panhandler, who classifies people's habits about giving on the street. "Klang" mixes Brazilian and funk beats with deft sonic touches, like plinking guitar as mbira. "B-Setting," with its musical and extramusical puns, draws on classic soul—the bridge is pure acoustic-jazz-style James Brown—and sports a witty vocal mixed nearly into the background. "A Whisper in My Ear" nods to Afro-Cuban jazz architect Mario Bauza; the band here best demonstrates its rhythmic suppleness and torque. "Shake 'Em Up" was a local calypso hit for the band his father played in, and it grooves like Eastern Parkway's annual West Indian Day parade, which it invokes. "No Whine" is pointedly blues-free but poignant, resigned, moving. "Dark Room" blends Miles Davis, film noir, and Machito. "Dub Ya"—taken, Byron says, from a suite he is writing "about animals that look and sound dumb"—is a tape-loop foray with Mingusy overtones that's hilarious. And one of Byron's growing number of film pieces, "Belmondo's Lip," gets two treatments, the second a stuttering, psyche-delicized remix by DJ Spooky that reassembles its deconstructed pieces over its irresistably chugging beats. That closes the disc.

FROM ONE PERSPECTIVE, Dave Douglas's *Witness* got a horrible boost when the Twin Towers fell. Inspired by Edward Said's *Representations of the Intellectual*, the suite-like album draws extensively on Arabic music sources for its celebration of cultural activists: the Ruckus Society, Nawal El Saadawi, Eqbal Ahmad, Naguib Mafouz, Taslima Hasrin, Pramaoedya Ananta Toer, and Ken Saro-Wiwa. Though it sidesteps the complicated, tangled role of music within Islamic and Arabic societies, it does, with good reason, stake a claim for Douglas.

Like Byron, Douglas has become a jazz-based bricoleur. In fact, one of his first prominent recording gigs was with Byron's Mickey Katz lineup. He attended both Berklee and the New England Conservatory, came to New York in 1984, and studied and worked with Joe Lovano. In the late 1980s he got interested in Central and Eastern European folk musics, which later led to his forming the Tiny Bell Trio. He worked with pianist Myra Melford and joined John Zorn's Masada, which uses eastern and central European Jewish idioms as thematic materials for free-ish impro-visation.

His chosen horn was already the subject of a renaissance, thanks to Wynton Marsalis. Whatever you think about Marsalis's abilities or depth as either player or composer, you'd be hard pressed to argue he isn't the best-known jazz musician alive, that he's pursued Armstrong's position in American cultural mythology, the iconic man with the trumpet, with single-minded intensity and success. Besides, unlike the clarinet, the trumpet had never been benched with jazz's backup squads. In fact, in his early days, Douglas sometimes seemed like a downtown white alternative to Marsalis: in his serious and self-conscious intellectualism (he wowed jazz critics with references to Benjamin and Foucault and Said, much as Marsalis had by talking about Thomas Mann and Ralph Ellison), in the cerebral virtuosity and golden tones of his horn, in his carefully controlled approach to music and the world, in the image he cultivated of straddling the classical and jazz genres.

Sometimes I tend to think of Byron as more Dionysian and Douglas as more Apollonian, sometimes I think of them as the fox and the hedgehog, sometimes I think of them in McLuhanesque terms as warm and cool. For me, as Douglas unfolded a variety of projects with different personnel and goals, his solos, especially in Zorn's group Masada, exhibited more of that unselfconscious grace that I look for in matured artists, what Castiglione called sprezzatura. I admired Douglas's work with his Tiny Bell Trio and Sextet and *Charms of the Night Sky*, but from a distance, where I felt the music's sensibility in some ways kept me. But his tribute to Mary Lou Williams struck me more deeply; Douglas seemed more emotionally attached to this project, and it coincided with Linda Dahl's *Morning Glory*, a solid biography.

Now he's assembled a first-rate cast of players for *Witness*, which grew from his several-year-old "Thoughts Around Mahfouz." He says: "The music, just like the culture and the society, has retreated from experimentation quite a bit, retreated into entertainment. And yet I think—and I don't want to generalize—that in the American improvised idiom there's a lot of awareness of other art forms—dance, poetry, and so on—but also of politics—social justice movements and the like. But it's been muted in the ways it's been able to speak. Over a period of time it became much harder to make any kind of statement in the art itself. While we're seeing things like Ani DiFranco and Steve Earle and even Springsteen making statements in song, for those of us who are instrumentalists and dancers and even novelists in the United States it's been harder to make any kind of impact. The resurgence of community spirit and activism in the wake of 9/11 has made that easier to do, in some ways."

He's also looking to move beyond what he sees as the end of postmodernism. "I don't relate at all to postmodern ideas. If anything, what's going on in the music now is post-postmodern, if there can be such a thing. I think artists are believing in something again. This music is passionate. There are melodies and harmonies and sequence and flow. The juxtaposition of genre language is not happening gratuitously or in a forced way. If you look across the spectrum of the music, that's a fairly universal new area, that there's not this edgy self-awareness and self-consciousness, that artists are looking for meaning."

This is somewhat disingenuous; like Byron, Douglas will talk on, given the chance, of how he's mixed and matched previously unmixed-and-matched genres and style in unique ways. But more than Byron, who prefers to be subject to interpretation, Douglas has embedded his music as deeply in extramusical signposts as he can to fix the inherent instability of the relationship between sounds and meaning, especially when translated into another idiom. And so his CD booklet cites and briefly glosses the people and materials that inspired each piece, proffers lists of suggested readings (Arundhati Roy, Howard Zinn, and so on) and websites, describes the epiphanic moment behind his need to speak out more directly in his music, which produced this project (reading a newspaper on the Yugoslav border "on the rising stock of American weapons makers during the NATO assault on Yugoslavia"). He released a formal interview as part of the accompanying press materials for the disc, which he refers to regularly during other interviews as a vetted source. Some of this, of course, is simply information-sharing; some is simply control, artistic or otherwise, of a process—translating music into emotion, thought, action—that is necessarily messy and virtually unduplicatable.

For like Byron, Douglas is well aware that the history of engaged music in whatever form is littered with detritus that was neither good propaganda nor good art. He says: "One of my big fears was that the message not cut into the artistic strength of the project. That was one of my reasons for not using dogmatic statements, even on the tune where I chose to use voice. I don't think anyone is gonna want to listen to it if the art doesn't come first. Said being such a big influence on how I think about the world, the quote on the liner notes steered me along: maintaining a constant state of alertness. The message of the record is, if anything, for people to think. I think that's what the arts are capable of doing—getting people to think. The music in itself confronts a lot of categories, people's assumptions about what jazz should be or could be, what world music should be. Where do I put this in my cultural file?"

Listening to the album's enveloping, often dazzling sense of textures and depth, which adheres and coheres as the well-paced CD runs, should also be enjoyable and entertaining, and it is. "Ruckus" kicks off lustily by doffing Douglas's cap to the Seattle riots against the WTO; it also rather neatly fits Byron's observation about genre-expectations for "protest" music, with Arabic sounds replacing Coltrane's Indian sounds. The title track, emotionally centered on a brilliant, achingly beautiful violin solo by Mark Feldman, juxtaposes plaints with bursts of rage over a droning backdrop. "One More News" is a short and lively dance piece about "tragedy fatigue." "Woman at Point Zero" takes its title from Saadawi's novel and boasts a scintillating use of moods and tension-and-release tactics. "Kidnapping Kissinger," dedicated to Ahmad, lacks Ahmad's "sharp sense of humor" but is an effective genre piece, right down to the electronic music portions. As for "Mahfouz," the nearly 24-minute-long work is the album's deserved centerpiece, and allows Douglas and several sidemen (there are 11 in total on the album) extensive improvisational freedom within well-developed arrangements, and they all shine. Tom Waits reads excerpts from Mahfouz and Gilles Deleuze, his voice mixed as far back as Mick Jagger's on the early Stones recordings, occasionally dissolving into smoker's laughter. Here, in the music, Douglas finds meaning by layering, interweaving, creating possibilities for interpretations, and, in fact, loosening his control.

"How do you protest a system," Douglas writes in the liner notes, "that coopts and marginalizes almost every unique and original thought that confronts it? And how do you stay silent?" When I read that, I thought of my old Russian professor. One critic, reviewing the album, raised and dismissed this issue by noting that Douglas has a rare major-label deal. I'd just note that such Chomskyite rhetoric, the self-defeating vision of totalitarian control of culture that arises from Adorno, can't adequately account for the shape of Douglas's own career.

Consider that idea another external puzzle piece of meaning to ponder while you spin this disc.

26

Cassandra Wilson

AFTER MORE THAN TWO DECADES of hustling and a series of overlapping personas—the Joni Mitchell-wannabe days of her youth, the time with avant-jazz alchemist Henry Threadgill, the experimental jazz-funk fusions with the 1980s M-BASE Collective, the commitment to the Black Rock Coalition's antiracism-in-the-music-biz drive, the major-label recasting as a mainstream diva, the follow-up sidelong plunge into hip-hop/jazz crossover—after all that and more, Cassandra Wilson became, at 40, an overnight success.

Born in Jackson, Mississippi ("As long as I've been in New York I still retain some southern values—some southern black woman values," she drawls), Wilson grew up in a musical household. Her mother was a pop, especially Motown, fanatic; her father, a semipro musician who played trumpet, then electric bass, then guitar, was a swing-band lover with a taste for Monk and vocalists like Ella Fitzgerald and Sarah Vaughan, Dinah Washington and Nancy Wilson. At six, Wilson took piano lessons, then moved on to guitar—an instrument her dad started her on, that would return decades later as the epicenter of her breakthrough to jazz stardom. The instrument focused her evolving artistry in much the way that Jerry Wexler's sitting Aretha Franklin down at the piano while she sang and recorded unleashed the fullest thrusts of that singer's jazzy gospel fervor and creativity. So, too, her early tastes, typical of the times she grew up in, would reenter her field of focus in the 1990s as potential material ripe for radical redesign: the Monkees, female folksingers like Joan Baez, Judy Collins, and especially Joni Mitchell.

After touring coffeehouses in the South, a stint in New Orleans, and a first marriage, Wilson found herself in New York in the early 1980s. Heavily into her bebopper phase, studying and singing Charlie Parker solos and absorbing Betty Carter's nervy model and hard-won lessons about vocal rhythmic elasticity, she landed gigs with Woody Shaw, Abbey Lincoln, Dave Holland, and Olu Dara. (In a small parallel movement, Dara, an avant-garde cornet player in the 1980s, subsequently remade himself, first as an entertainment-oriented dance-bandleader, then more successfully as a guitar-toting bluesman.) When Wilson met Steve Coleman at a jam session celebrating Bird's birthday, the duo began a partnership that was one core of M-BASE. She refined her undivalike musicality with Threadgill, who cast her sensual, warmly timbred voice as just another instrument that had to find its appropriate place within the ensemble—a role she insists still shapes her approach.

Wilson has been one of the lucky artists in jazz or any other medium: for her, success and the chance for artistic reintegration of her various past selves have coincided. *Blue Light 'Til Dawn*, her groundbreaking, critically acclaimed 1993 album with then-neophyte producer Craig Street, racked up six-digit sales figures, and set her on tour steadily as her star climbed rapidly. TV and radio loved her too. So by the time *New Moon Daughter*, also produced by Street, was released, she was working larger venues and selling more albums. Within a couple of months of its release, *Daughter* clocked nearly 300,000 copies worldwide, phenomenal numbers for jazz, even jazz with accessible pop strains.

Much of this was due to Street's acute instincts about music and his ability to tune into Wilson's often intuitive insights. I first met Street in the 1980s; he was a member of the Black Rock Coalition, and devoted to the legacy of the blues, rural and electric, and James Marshall Hendrix. He was widely cultivated and intense—an avid film buff, a curious reader of philosophical texts, an oddly low-key yet insistent guy who seemed to home in on both the weaknesses and central points of arguments, a man who was amassing a catalog of sounds. He admired famed producers like Jerry Wexler and Leonard Chess; one of his favorites was Tom Wilson. In 1988, when the first Black Rock Coalition event took place at the Kitchen, a night of Hendrix and other stuff from an orchestra that included Wilson, pianist Geri Allen, and guitarist Vernon Reid, Street steered it. Now he's producing A-list vocalists like k.d. lang.

With Wilson, Street was a natural fit, and it showed in the affinity that brought Wilson's cultural politics closer to the surface. "Strange Fruit," the horrific, powerful protest song Billie Holiday first gave voice to at Café Society, is one of *New Moon Daughter's* most powerful cuts. The haunting lyrics, the unusual cantilevered structure of a brilliantly disguised blues, were written by Abel Meeropol in reaction to the widespread lynchings across the South spurred, in part, by D.W. Griffith's *Birth of a Nation*; Meeropol was a Bronx schoolteacher who flirted with the Communist Party during the Depression, and, with his wife, adopted the sons of Ethel and Julius Rosenberg. Wilson revels in the tune's dark brilliance, its suffocating atmosphere. A native of a city where churches were burned and children shot, Wilson is the dispassionate teller of a passionate tale, yet lures the listener to see through her eyes, the eyes of innocence and terrible understanding, the unavoidable, towering Tree of Knowledge of Good and Evil that is racism in this county.

Wilson is the right diva for the fractionating cultural landscapes of the post-1990s: syncretic yet unique, a voice for a generation that grew up listening to more rock and soul and pop than it did to Ella and Sarah and Billie and the rest.

For this interview, I met Wilson at her spacious Harlem apartment. Looking from her seventh-floor living-room windows across the Harlem River, winding its way from the George Washington Bridge to the Triboro, I watched the Met Life blimp hover over Yankee Stadium on the other side, celebrating with the rest of us the Bronx Bombers' first Series shot in 15 years. "I can hear the crowds," says Wilson in her honeyed drawl, "and I'm glad."

GENE SANTORO: Just this fall, you opened for Ray Charles—a man who's made musical crossovers in any number of directions—at Radio City Music Hall. What was it like?

CASSANDRA WILSON: It went by so fast, the whole evening, I didn't have time: didn't have time to get nervous, didn't have time to really react to the event. All I could do was live through it. I'm still digesting that—and all the things that have happened over the last few months. Radio City's just part of that. God, it's the biggest place—just cavernous. It was the first time I experienced not being able to touch or see or feel or sense an audience, them being so distant I was feeling like I was in a fishbowl.

GS: That's a different kind of output demanded from you onstage. How did you deal with it?

CW: I think you have to create your own universe on the stage. That's what you have to rely on, in the end, to give to the audience: the feeling that you have about being in that circle of musicians, and the relationship that you have with them. You invite the audience in. At times it got pretty vocal, actually—reminded me that there were a few thousand folks out there. But I could not see them. And when they talked they sounded as if they were miles away.

GS: Like early Brother Ray, you've been through a number of different personas. What you're doing now seems to summarize or recap most of them in some ways. Talk a little bit about your chrysalis stages.

CW: Oh, trying to get me to talk. But you're right: now is a pivotal point, the end and the beginning. It's like a summation of everything—well, not everything, but ... well, unexpected things came out of the box. Like the guitar playing. It was the first instrument that I really started improvising with, but I was never really able to connect the dots, to bring together the knowledge and foundation that I have in jazz with that part of my musical personality. Bringing that and the stint with M-BASE, Henry—all of that really came together in these records, in these last couple of years.

GS: It's gotta be a little dizzying when that first happens: my life's caught up with me.

CW: You know it. When you start doing Monkees stuff—yeah, my life has really caught up with me now, the sixth grade. Shewwww! It's an elevating experience, clarifying, gives you continuity. And it lets you build a firmer foundation to get to the next place.

GS: This foundation started with Craig Street and his broken foot.

CW: You know the story. Craig and I have known each other for 10 years. We did a gig together for the Black Rock Coalition at Citibank, downtown on Wall Street. So we've been running into each other for a long time. I had just signed with Blue Note, and Bruce (Lundvall, Blue Note's president) was pushing me to find a producer. He had made some suggestions: George Duke, coupla other people. But I told him I wanted somebody who was completely fresh, somebody who was familiar with my work, who knew that I need to stretch out, who'd understand that that is a really important part of my musical personality. So I kept running into Craig in the lobby here, because his foot was broken from a construction accident, and he was just hanging out at home a lot. We started talking about this album I was supposed to do, and I told him I needed to find a producer. He suggested himself and . . . I laughed. I mean, he was doing construction. But he talked, and we just kept talking. It occurred to me that he had a thorough knowledge of my background, my history, and he had these incredible ideas, these wild, bizarre ideas about stringed instruments, and the songs from the folk period of my life. So I said, Let's do a demo. The first tune we did was "You Don't Know What Love Is." He knew that I'd played guitar—I'd mentioned it to him in passing years before—and so he forced me to sketch the song out on guitar, which really opened me up. That clinched it: when he made me do that, I knew he was the producer I wanted.

GS: He was thinking about Jerry Wexler and Aretha. She'd done stuff for John Hammond that didn't quite gel, but Wexler sat her down at the piano when she was singing, and it changed everything.

CW: It was amazing. I felt new. I felt as if I'd just stumbled onto a whole other space—the tunings, the song. I just thought, Wow, here's a space I can go! I think I'd backed myself against the wall in a lot of ways by that point. The idea I'd pitched to Bruce was going in (to the studio) to do a bunch of R & B tunes with a jazz interpretation. I had my piano trio, and I was trying to do that: I gave him "Can't Stand the Rain" and "Loveland" and a couple of other tunes. Bruce was checking it out, but he said, Why don't you go back to the drawing board? That's when Craig and I started really talking. I played Craig the demo, and he said, Well, this is cool, but it's mostly pedestrian. He's a Taurus to the bitter end. But he's very comfortable with it, very Zen about it, so you don't feel this massive opposition. He's got a subtle approach. So we argue a lot.

On the first album, there was a lot of give and take. We had arguments about all kinds of things. We had arguments about the drums, problems with what part would the drums play. That was the biggest thing that we faced off on. Specifically, we disagreed about "Blue Light 'Til Dawn." Craig is into the minimal kick, and I tried to explain to him that "Blue Light" is a slow drag, and there's a certain thing that the kick has to do, the kick and the snare, actually, and they were the only things I really wanted to make sure made sense with the song because the song is supposed to evoke a particular kind of body movement. Well, Craig's from Oakland, California, and . . . well, if they do slow drag they don't call it slow drag, so it wasn't a pattern he was familiar with. I even danced with him to try to show him what I meant. I won that one. There were two mixes, and the other one is cool, but it's just . . . airy. It flows just a little too much.

See, the thing about Craig is he had so many terrific ideas. And actually, with a few exceptions like the ones I've told you, we agreed about all of them—in the end.

GS: What happened when you went in to do *Daughter?* You already had *Blue Light* as a model.

CW: I was scared to death for *New Moon Daughter*, because I wasn't at all prepared for it. I had three or four tunes done, and I wrote "Solomon" while I was up at Woodstock. "Find Him" I didn't write until we went back in the studio two months later. We had sketches of things. I'd sketch things out on the guitar and then pass it on to Craig, who'd listen and then pass it on to Brandon [Ross, guitarist and music director], who'd do the arrangements.

The thing about it I learned was, it's okay to go into a project with maybe six or seven tunes you have a sketch of. We had that leisure this time, the time and the money. So we could actually go up to Woodstock, I could hang out for three days before the rest of the gang came up. Craig had them make the barn at Bearsville Studio into a studio, and it was open, so we could interact. We started with "Memphis," something I pieced together with Brandon's help. Then we did what we did the whole time we were there: hang around at night and talk about what the next day would be like. Bearsville is really special; if I could make music like that all the time I'd be happy.

Oh, the Monkees—yeah, I had fun with that one. It's nice going back to the sixth grade. I really got excited when I could hear that piece out front, the intro, stretched out in 9. When I stumbled onto that, I thought, Okay, now I can bring this piece of knowledge into this other thing and see how we can get it to swing. Onstage now, it's evolved into this interesting kind of swing piece, a combination of swing and what it was before. I really love it now. It's okay on the album, but it's really fun to watch the songs grow onstage, evolve.

GS: Staging this band has to be real tough, given the instrumentation.

CW: It is, because it's very delicate, and Brandon's very precise about what he wants. So it's been difficult. But Brandon's pretty much on top of it: he's the maestro. He's very meticulous and very patient. It takes him two hours for soundcheck, but when he finishes you know he's got the perfect guitar sound. That's the hardest part. Lonnie [Plaxico, bassist] can pretty much just dial his sound quickly almost anywhere. As we play bigger places, it obviously gets more difficult. It's not like bringing a saxophone or a piano out. The guitar is a delicate, nontempered instrument, and we have to deal with all that. There were many nights—many nights—at the beginning of this where I didn't know where I was. Charlie [Burnham, violinist] would be in one place, Lonnie would be in another place, and Brandon would be in yet another place. And I'd hear this A somewhere, this one somewhere else, and this one somewhere else again. But after a while, it was liberating. I could just kinda swim around, because I knew how to tune my ears, rather than relying on that A440 from the piano.

GS: A little harmolodics, there.

CW: Oh yeah, it was harmolodic many a night! We got into some serious harmolodics. But eventually we moved toward each other. Now I really enjoy the timbre of the strings and the nontempered aspects of it.

GS: What do you like about it?

CW: It's thick. Thick and spare at the same time. Everything isn't spelled out, but the sound is dense, rich. I don't know any other way to describe it.

GS: Like with Ray Charles 40 years ago, your musical setup and success is one of the signs, I think, that some aspects of jazz are doing their once-a-generation crossover into the broader culture.

CW: Hi, we're over here! Yeah, and it's all exciting. The music has to reinvent itself to keep going, to get where it's going. I think that's the nature of jazz. As hard as some people fight against it, that just propels it forward even more. It just gets to the point where you find you're desperate. I am desperate to get excited. I'm so desperate . . . I think I'll go and play guitar! It's that kind of immediacy.

GS: You're playing with people who are trying to extend that bridge too.

CW: You mean Vinx and Courtney Pine? Well, I had to get involved; I always have to challenge myself. I get bored with myself. If I'm inside my thing for too long I have to get out and do something else. It stimulates me. I just love Courtney's playing, and he's got an incredible imagination. His music is . . . happenin', a nice kind of mix: jungle and jazz. Anyone who's doing that I want to support. If it's not the formula that I would use, well, that's why I'd support it. And if I can go inside it maybe I can see something else, and learn something. Like Wynton.

GS: Let's talk about that: *Blood on the Fields*.

CW: It's a work in progress, and Wynton wrote all of that music in some ridiculous amount of time, so it's a really impressive body of work. And he's a terrific bandleader; he's got this tremendous wisdom for somebody his age. Yet there's another side that's still kind of young. I have to study him more.

There's a big difference, in terms of the music and what we can do for each other, from 10 years ago. I guess I now feel like an equal. Maybe I didn't feel that way then. I feel like I can actually have a conversation with him about music, share my ideas. We certainly didn't have that 10 years ago. Ideas that would've gotten a sneer and a dismissal are now possible for him. And I'm glad to see that he's open to that. There's a lot more middle ground now we can meet on, because of the way the music's moving.

Walking into Lincoln Center is still like walking into the biggest boys' club in the world. But what I like about it is that Wynton appreciates what I bring to it, which is what makes it really rewarding for me as well—this kind of . . . skewed approach that I have to the music. Maybe it's just skewed in his eyes; it might seem a little off. But I'm happy that he appreciates it enough to invite it into his context. He knows who I am, and he's not afraid of it.

GS: What did he want that you can do?

CW: I don't know if there's a word for it. I heard him say my voice was thick with the South.

GS: It's where you come from.

CW: Yes, and he as well. Different part, but we have more in common than not. I think he's beginning to see that. I've even heard him call himself country. A couple of years ago, it'd be unimaginable that he'd admit to being country, which is something that I do every day. Yes, I'm country. That's why my records sound like that now: it's all in there. It's not as if I stepped outside myself to find something that might sound good for me to sing.

GS: One jazz singer said to me a while ago, "Jazz singers really don't find themselves until they're older."

CW: It's really true. There's a whole lot of experience that you have to absorb to do justice to the tradition of jazz singing. It's a storytelling tradition, and unless you have the experience to give it an emotional depth you're not really doing anything. You're just benchpressing some changes. Age equals experience. The older you get, the more you have to place inside of the music. You have more to call on. I don't really know very many singers who don't age into something better. Even Sarah: listen to early Sarah and it's a beautiful voice, but it doesn't have nearly the weight that it has when she gets older. Certainly people like Billie Holiday had a fullness of life early on, a massive amount of experience. I led a pretty sheltered life compared to Billie Holiday.

GS: Compared to Billie Holiday that wouldn't be hard.

CW: True. But compared to a lot of that generation of singers as well. For the next generation the way has been paved a little bit more, so you don't have to run into as many obstacles. Still, the obstacles are there; there's still a course that you have to run.

GS: Let's talk about the obstacles.

CW: The chick singer thing is still the biggest obstacle to overcome, from the audience and the musicians. Being the object instead of the subject determining the context. Being able to communicate with the band and really mold them so that they are able to get past all of the preconceived notions about the way singers communicate music. See, singers have a very different way of communicating music. Even if they're really well-schooled and really understand the language and theory, there's still a really different way of communicating ideas, because you're dealing with words, the emotive quality of a song. You're painting with words as well as music, and it's really difficult to relate that to an instrumentalist. Traditionally, the language of the singer has come, for the most part, from women; and traditionally, the language of the musician has come, for the most part, from men. So bridging that gap is a big task, still. It's just a matter of everybody coming closer.

GS: Does it make it easier that you're a schooled musician?

CW: Oh, yeah, definitely. A lot of singers who aren't musicians can't really communicate well at all, and they confirm the musicians' prejudices. And I understand how they feel: you go through years of training to be a musician, master the language, and someone comes up and stands in front of you and then begins to dictate to you what to do musically— and they reap most of the benefits, the applause, the money. I really understand it. Singers have a tendency to be a little bit lazy in terms of learning theory, in terms of learning what they can do when they sing. A lot of my scatting technique comes from having dealt on the front line with the horn players with Henry Threadgill and Steve Coleman. I've had to develop a style of improvising that's not imitating them— didn't make any sense to me to go brrp-brrp-de-frrp-fop. I think there's a way to do what the horns do, though. They're dealing with very difficult intervals that singers don't sing because they don't listen to them and don't work on that. If you listen to a singer improvise, most of the time they're just dealing with some very simple intervals and using some syllables—and that's it. But you listen to horn players and you hear them dealing all over, moving up and down. Which is why I really encourage singers to become musicians. That's a large part of breaking down that wall.

THE GENEALOGY OF FEMALE JAZZ SINGERS reaches back to Bessie Smith and Ethel Waters, who took blues out of the juke joints and put it into vaudeville theaters, and snakes its way through the distinctly unbluesy

Ella Fitzgerald, who otherwise followed Louis Armstrong's formidable lead and sang and improvised like a horn, through Dinah Washington and Sarah Vaughan, who bridged jazz and R & B. Of course, there's a host of others: Carmen McRae, Betty Carter, contemporaries from Diana Krall to Dianne Reeves. But historically speaking, they all have shared a mission: to personalize and make audible jazz's often esoteric art for folks who short out on sax and piano solos unless they're trapped in supermarkets or elevators.

For the historical facts speak plainly: divas have always been the primary way jazz has leaked its musical and cultural advances and attitudes into the mainstream society. (There are, of course, major exceptions, notably Louis Armstrong and Miles Davis.) The fact is, most Americans don't like instrumental music. Just ask any radio station program director, any record label head, Nissan (which threw in the piano after dropping a couple of million dollars in sponsoring two years of the Thelonious Monk Institute awards on network TV), or any of the guys and dolls slouching down today's mean streets with Walkmen and MP3s clipped onto their bobbing heads.

Historically, this American lack of interest in instrumental music has created some significant sales problems for jazz, whose early 21st-century market share of recording sales is hovering below 2 percent. Jazz can hardly avoid being labeled a mostly instrumental music; worse, it doesn't necessarily adhere to simple melodic and harmonic forms. Still making its listeners think isn't a complete turnoff works as long as they can dance to it—witness the Jazz Age, when Americans apparently liked the idea of jazz best—or make out to it—when cool stars like Miles Davis helped young people seduce each other.

And while the last two decades have marched to a steady beat of reappraisals for the likes of Louis Armstrong, it's still essential to note that yeah, he revolutionized music by outplaying Gabriel on cornet and reinventing the virtuoso improvising soloist European classical music had lost inside a new homegrown American musical format. He wowed flapper-age hipsters and thrilled and inspired musicians of all sorts in the process, but he only became every American's Satchmo when he opened his mouth to sing standards like "Wonderful World," "Hello Dolly," and "Mack the Knife."

Even other apparent exceptions to the rule of divas in pop-jazz culture, like Duke Ellington, aren't. Amid the more ambitious works he started during the 1930s, Ellington continued to pen hit songs that were sung so endlessly as pop fare by others they became mainstream standards. Even so, it was his carefully forged combination of elegant charm and iron will—touring 300-plus days a year for decades, including stops at roller rinks and aquacades—and nonstop composing on trains and in hotels that kept his name out there. Meanwhile, his steady stream of composer's royalties subsidized the beloved instrument that otherwise he, like virtually every other bandleader by the late 1940s, would have had to give up—his orchestra, the reason and mode of his composing to begin with.

Let's play What If. If John Coltrane hadn't hit with his exotic version of "My Favorite Things," an inane but lilting Broadway waltz-time hit that every right-thinking American could hum by the time Trane reimagined it, many folks who today know his name but not his searching, revolutionary music wouldn't know either. As it happens, when he operated on "My Favorite Things," Trane was working very much within a traditional jazz mode for dealing with pop music: take the latest hits, however banal, and tweak them, move their parts around, add jazz's inevitable irony as it undercuts or toys with pop's contrived innocence or sleek commercial sophistication. Why is the irony inevitable? Because jazz, thanks to its cultural roots and its time and place of development, has played an unmistakable historical role in our culture: it functions as the return of the repressed, whether race, sex, drugs, or other less targeted American problems. Even before Armstrong broke across the color bar, jazz gave voice to the dark sides of the American psyche. At its best, its Socratic irony questions its materials, its methodologies.

I've been thinking about this for the last decade, as I've watched the industry try to sell jazz as lifestyle, the perfect accompaniment for coffee or fashion or sophistication. And I've listened to musicians and critics and industry executives explain how contemporary pop and rock tunes are too "simple" for jazz musicians to deal with.

My notion is different: that jazz must regularly sharpen its creative teeth on its far more successful sibling rivals in pop—the process I've described earlier—or risk becoming purely historical art music out of touch with the popular mind. That may be what's occurring: the upsurge in jazz-school registrations and the success of Ken Burns's *Jazz* may indicate that jazz has no future as contemporary pop art. And that would be too bad. Fortunately, lots of younger jazz musicians are following Cassandra Wilson's lead and their own souls to disagree.

Is Wilson the Miles Davis of this time? She discusses him in circuitous, mystical terms: a light that recedes as you near, a Chesire Cat smile that mocks anyone, including himself, who gets too comfortable.

And yet Wilson seems quite at home on *Blue Light 'Til Dawn,* a studio backporch of acoustic guitars and bass and gently persistent percussion and odd daubs of color, like floating steel guitar or a skirling fiddle. The dense arrangements swayed to allow improvised solos and ideas into radically revamped material ranging from Son House to The Monkees. As it has been throughout jazz history, rhythm was the engine of change, here embodied by the nuanced athletics and emotional charge of Wilson's brooding, introspective vocals.

And so next she confronted Davis directly, with a provocative disc called *Traveling Miles.*

With guests like violinist Regina Carter, altoist Steve Coleman, and vibist Stefon Harris augmenting her crew, Wilson takes on tunes from all over Miles's long and checkered history, including the evil post-fusion days. The disc's first single (for EZ-listening jazz radio) is her deep-blue revision of Miles' version of Cyndi Lauper's hit, "Time After Time."

Crossover, anyone?   Even Miles would have smiled.

OVER THE LAST DECADE, Cassandra Wilson has become jazz's prima diva. And she did it her way: by making her sultry voice the gravitational center of an expansive musical cosmos encompassing soulful improvisation, back-porch acoustic blues, and contemporary pop.

Belly of the Sun, which she produced herself, continues filling in the map Wilson (and then-producer Craig Street) started to chart on 1993's *Blue Light 'Til Dawn*. On *Belly*, new and familiar galaxies enter Wilson's orbit and are altered: The Band's "The Weight," which launches the album's civil rights subtext; a dreamy "Wichita Lineman" ("I'm a big Jimmy Webb fan," she says, "and watched Glen Campbell's TV show growing up"); bossa novas by Antonio Carlos Jobim and Caetano Veloso laced with country; James Taylor's "Only a Dream in Rio"; Bob Dylan's "Shelter from the Storm"; Robert Johnson's careening "Hot Tamales"; and a worksong, "You Gotta Move," that the Rolling Stones covered in the 1970s. Rounding it out are originals, like Wilson's "Justice," a funky call for racial reparations.

This is the new vision of jazz Wilson has been exploring since *Blue Light*—a sophisticated yet rootsy feel that is creative, catchy, and spontaneously elastic.

Delicate yet taut arrangements and instruments that don't sound or look like standard-issue jazz—resonator guitar, bazouki, mandolin, steel pan drums—weave an engaging sonic web around Wilson's voice, whose earthy force ensnares listeners. Meanwhile, the band and vocalist bend and flutter notes, redraw melody lines, warp time and shift accents in ways that can sometimes seem subliminal.

To record *Belly*, Wilson took the 26-hour train trip ("I don't fly," she says) to Clarksdale, Mississippi, the Delta center of blues lore and home of the Blues Museum, to reconnect with jazz's blues roots.

Partly she was inspired by her ongoing model, Miles Davis. "Miles never left the blues, no matter how far into experimentation in forms and electronic stuff he took his music," she says. "So that was the impetus. Which meant I had to go home, really get an education about myself."

And so she retraced her steps to nearby Jackson, Mississippi, where in 1955 she was born to a teacher-mother and a jazz-musician father; where she grew up hearing Billie Holiday, the Stones, Aretha Franklin, and Joni Mitchell; where she performed folk music at political rallies before heading off to New York's jazz scene.

"We went down to Clarksdale," she explains, "and the train station became our studio." She had a few sketches and ideas—a couple of blues, Jobim's "Waters of March," "Wichita Lineman," pieces she and the band had been messing with.

But only after she started jamming with Boogaloo Ames, an 81-year-old local jazz-blues pianist of a dying breed who'd also worked at Motown, did the album's shape fully emerge.

"Listen," Wilson explains, "to the Latin rhythmic feel on 'The Weight,' and the Caribbean thing happening on 'Wichita Lineman.' That's because we were in Clarksdale. Or the bluesy quality of the Jobim: bossa nova, a friend of mine says, is Brazilian blues, a joy born of sadness. So bossa nova is superimposed over Clarksdale. 'Waters of March' has chord changes that are not busy, so they allow me to do a lot more with the melody, take space to improvise, create more colors."

For Wilson, jazz is less form than process, an improvising approach applicable anywhere. Here she joins a long tradition. Billie Holiday, Dinah Washington, Sarah Vaughan, and Nina Simone infused whatever they sang with jazz's ad-libbing craft, its rhythmic play and melodic freedom. After all, Ella Fitzgerald's first hit was "A-Tisket, A-Tasket." "It's about the rhythms," Wilson says.

Her rhythmic finesse underpins her virtuosity. On "Wichita Lineman," her molasses voice pours artfully out of what seem pent-up pressures; it's an introspective struggle become improvised siren song, a la Miles Davis's trumpet, where the spaces between notes hover with a suggestiveness that articulation would only diminish.

She says, "For me, Miles is the embodiment of Legba, the god of the crossroads, the trickster. You have no idea what's gonna happen with him; he will play with you just to play with you. I study that. There's a lot to study about it. It's mercurial. It recedes as you come closer. It's something that you can never fully know or understand or analyze."

ON DECEMBER 5, 2001, a concert titled "Made In America," featuring hours of jazz musicians, was staged at New York's Town Hall—a benefit for some of the many funds dealing with the aftermath of 9/11. Despite the long list of jazz artists—Kenny Barron, Ruben Blades, Michael Brecker, Paquito D'Rivera, Bela Fleck, Kenny Garrett, k.d. lang, Joe Lovano, Brad Mehldau, Greg Osby, Danilo Perez, Dianne Reeves, John Scofield, and Cassandra Wilson—the nearly full house was mostly nonpayers.

Jazz, a marginal form, is disappearing from the major labels—which, to me, is a good thing. Besieged by their own poor planning and arrogance, the entertainment conglomerates that grew from the endless mergers of the 1990s are too big and dumb to deal in the small sales numbers jazz generates. The exception is Wilson's label, Blue Note, which still uses the old corporate model of subsidizing new or "prestige" artists via profitable acts. The small labels that have been popping up like mushrooms have no choice but to operate within economies of scale. Radio, owned by two conglomerates, is hopeless, but the Web beckons, once jazz musicians get the hang of how to use it. Maybe they should study folkies and garage bands and hip-hoppers.

At the fundraiser that night at Town Hall, Wilson joined bluegrass-jazz banjoist Bela Fleck, who picked behind her while she sang "This Land Is Your Land," drawling into the mike, "I'm gonna sing the verse that's always left out."

27

Marty Ehrlich

THE LONG VIEW IS APTLY NAMED. With this album, multireedman and composer Marty Ehrlich shoulders a series of challenges that go to the heart of what jazz composition is, or might be. His musical dialogues with the paintings of a St. Louis compatriot, Oliver Jackson, yield a strikingly original and thoughtful musical work that doubles as a recapitulation of the manifold ways earlier key jazz composers from Duke Ellington to Charles Mingus to Andrew Hill have responded to similar offbeat but stimulating situations.

Ehrlich is a rarity: he crisscrosses the often self-segregating scenes that proliferate within the jazz milieu as they do across America. Partly this is because Ehrlich, once an aspiring poet and married to an established poet, has a rather philosophical and historical bent. And his music, from his "outside" excursions to his through-composed pieces, reflects his sense of continuity with the past (as he, like any artist, defines the past, which is to say in his image) alongside discontinuity. To put it another way, his art is subtle enough to speak to Darwin and Foucault.

An adept student of jazz history, Ehrlich grabs fewer fanzine headlines than more outrageous or outspoken or controversial sorts. He is not a post-modernist seeking to *epater les bourgeoisie*, replicate the shock of the new that animated the avant-gardes of 20th century European modernism. To underline the contrast, witness the two-decade long and provocative history of John Zorn. Zorn has built several groups and musical formats, an independent record label and a "family" of contributors (including Ehrlich) who both perform with his bands and record for his company, and several versions of the "downtown" New York scene in various venues. Zorn's musical and career trajectory has been fascinating, as he's moved from using game theory to create diverse improvisational and compositional structures to recomposing spaghetti-western soundtracks to Naked City, his blistering punk-jazz pomo amalgam.

Then there's Masada, his brilliant reconception of Eastern European Jewish music and Ornette Colemanish free jazz. Here Zorn made an emotional commitment that enhanced his playing: he practiced so fiercely for years that his technique has grown fluid and daring, thanks to the depths of feeling freshening his music. Unlike Ehrlich, though, Zorn has a large cult partly because of his music but also because of his punk persona (snarling, Minguslike, at ringing cash registers and noisemakers during his shows, scuffling verbally with "the press"). But with Masada Zorn has creatively exited from postmodernism and the aging and mislabeled avant-garde.

Will postmodernism and the worldwide web and omnipresent cell phones help accelerate the Death of Interiority, the space where artists have historically resided? Does the virtually constant feedback loop reassure the plugged-in that their lives exist because they are always monitored even if it hollows experience into a kind of eavesdropping? This is not the sort of world Marty Ehrlich has created *The Long View* for.

At his age, and with his background, training, focus, and introspective cast of mind, perhaps it's not surprising Ehrlich steers toward *The Long View*. Born in 1955, he started clarinet at seven in St. Paul, and when his family moved to St. Louis the young teen moved to sax as well. He studied classical music until his high school orchestra director asked him to leave because he'd improvise during pieces. In his teens he hooked up with BAG; he also wrote poetry and performed at jazz-poetry readings.

His credits as a sideman, starting from his days at the New England Conservatory (where he began on classical clarinet and finished as a jazz major) read like a *Who's Who* of jazz innovators, from avantists to Third Streamers: George Russell, Jaki Byard, Gunther Schuller, Ran Blake, Julius Hemphill, Chico Hamilton, Anthony Braxton, Roscoe Mitchell, Leroy Jenkins, Muhal Richard Abrams, Anthony Davis, John Carter, and Andrew Hill. Along the way, Ehrlich built a reputation as composer and instrumentalist.

The Long View, Ehrlich told me, is "a kind of retrospective musical autobiography that recapitulates back to my life in St. Louis. All the ensembles I've written for, like the brass quintet and sax sextet, find places here. I combine those two, which are among this piece's building blocks, into a big band of a sort too. This was a very flexible strategy. I didn't want to cut and paste. I did not censor my impulses to use any kind of material but I wanted to avoid pastiche, keep the music moving without fetishizing its components, which collage is always in danger of doing."

The first of six "movements" nods to Mingus like a poetic invocation: the long postbop melody that dominates the movement's midsection, accelerandos, springy hard-bop 4/4 walking bass, call-and-response sections, Eddie Allen's a cappella trumpet solo. Mingus, frustrated by the limits of bebop and popular tune structures, probing for new ways to structure jazz composition and improvisation, was fascinated with mixed-media works. Outside of Louis Armstrong, he was jazz's most literary voice, writing his own powerful (if distorted) autobiography, and he always befriended painters; a painter was his closest mentor. In the early 1950s Mingus's friend Franz Kline listened to Mingus's music while he worked, using a house painter's brushes to wield thick, bold lines, often stark black, that were his gestural language, his equivalent of Jackson Pollock's drips and Willem de Kooning's sign painter's strokes. One of Kline's paintings, *Blue Center*, artistically mirrored Mingus pieces like "Haitian Fight Song": it was structured around a handful of varied visual riffs that recalled the bridges and elevated trains of Kline's earlier work as an Ashcan School urban landscapist. Like Mingus's music, Kline's art could seem abstract but unearthed its roots in realism with his predominant dirty blacks and whites, which evoked the manufacturing lofts and coldwater flats where postwar artists huddled cheaply in nameless neighborhoods now called Soho and Chelsea, long since remodeled and upscaled and housing corporate officers and lawyers.

It is this world Ehrlich wants Mingus to evoke for us, in order to shed variant light on his—and our—own.

In spring 2000, Ehrlich had a residency at Harvard; his stay overlapped with Oliver Jackson's. They'd known each other for decades; Ehrlich's musical mentor and founder of the radical Black Artists Group, saxophonist Julius Hemphill, noted for his tenure with the World Saxophone Quartet, introduced them. From the 1970s, BAG, like other local groups across the United States, seized culture as its platform for commentary on the ongoing social wars, sometimes directly, sometimes by suggesting expanded conceptual possibilities. And so part of its agenda encouraged multimedia collaborations by jazz musicians, an echo from the 1950s and 1960s.

"There were several reasons, besides liking them, that working with Oliver's paintings appealed to me," Ehrlich told me. "They can be abstract and figurative at the same time, which parallels how I think of my sense of musical expression, mixing tradition and innovation but not quite either, in a pure sense. His work ranges from very minimal to very dense and layered, and that represented some visceral thing that translated to my musicmaking." Or, as he writes in his album notes, "Jackson's paintings ... have long acted as a visual counterpoint to what I have imagined in sound."

And so the duo decided while at Harvard to collaborate. Jackson created six paintings that Ehrlich used as inspiration. Though, Ehrlich continues, "there is no direct correlation between specific movements and specific paintings. My compulsion was to give expression to the place where beauties that should not be forgotten and beauties that have yet to be imagined collide, coexist, and transform. It is in this place that my artistic heart resides."

The fruits of this collaboration, dedicated to Hemphill's memory, were installed at Harvard's Sert Gallery from August 2002 to January 2003. The exhibit created a zone of potential interactions to be defined and improvised by each attendee. Jackson's paintings limn many moods but share a sense of passion and energy distilled into form; the inchoate chaos suggested by his more abstract tactics is transmuted into visual rhythms and shaped by structural organization and the suggestion of realism emerging from his segments of black lines. (The cover and fold-out liner booklet for *The Long View* reproduce two of the paintings, inviting the listener to recreate, if more narrowly, the experience.)

Ehrlich's music is his response to Jackson's creative modalities. After their dual residency, he writes, "I began working backwards and forwards in composing the musical images, much as I had observed Oliver paint, his large canvases stretched on the floor, moving in a circle around the emerging visual images." The resulting opus for saxophone sextet, brass quintet, string ensemble, and combinations thereof, he explains, "has a dual life: as music interacting in exhibition with paintings by Oliver, and as a through-composed, autonomous work."

In fact, four of the movements were through-composed, except for improvised solos. Two were recorded with different combos; the results were then edited into a fully realized form, a la Mingus or Miles Davis with producer Teo Macero. "We had two days in the studio," Ehrlich told me—typical for jazz albums.

This one doesn't sound it. Each diversely structured movement suggests both an individual mood and an overarching cohesion to Ehrlich's reaching, shape-shifting piece. The second movement evokes a somber contemplative air: spare cymbals alternate with a simple string trio figure, then a burst of short themes is topped by pirouetting solo clarinet. About halfway through the movement's 12 minutes, cellist Erik Friedlander, violinists Mark Feldman, violist Ralph Farris, and bassist Helias swell into simultaneous motion somewhere between Dixieland and a late Beethoven quartet. The final section insinuates Afro-Cuban rhythms beneath the strings, which can skid across dissonant glisses, float almost serenely, or stab angular harmonies above; the coda is pizzicato, suggesting the circular pentatonic riffs of an African kora. And yet there is an integrity rather than disjunction of elements.

All the movements delve into complexities of tone and texture, tension and release, form and plasticity. Movement three features the full ensemble with modernist classical dissonances and discontinuities, so influential on bebop; its flute solo heralds a suspenseful thematic recapitulation flecked with the blues while skirting final closure. The fourth movement evokes Ornette Coleman, its nursery-rhyme themes devolving into simultaneous spontaneous composition. In movement five, the blues dilate into a noise fest of sonic effects. The sixth movement refracts hip-hop through an acoustic ensemble, laying the foundations with the resonant power of Marcus Rojas's tuba, Pheeroan AkLaff's precise, powerful 4/4 snare, and building to a rousing and fierce finale.

One of the by-products of certain wings of jazz having become art music is that they demand listeners willing to shed their passivity. Ehrlich's music offers a portal into the rich interior dialogues that have always powered human imagination in a world threatening to shrink into virtual narcissism.

28

New Jazz Fusions

JAZZ FANS LIKE TO SAY that jazz history compressed into a century developments that took European classical music 400 years. The last 25 years held to that breakneck pace—although it often didn't seem that way, especially to detractors and warring factions.

After the economic collapse of the popular big bands 50 years ago, jazz lost most of its mass commercial appeal. But until the mid-1960s rock explosion, it managed to draw audiences of collegians and beatniks and debutantes, the disaffected for whom jazz opened an exit from the gray conformities of American mass culture to a largely African American devised art form that began as folk art from a marginal subculture.

Bebop insisted that jazz was art, not entertainment; in its wake, jazz idioms diverged, annexed, multiplied: hard bop, Third Stream, modal jazz, soul jazz, free jazz. Soul jazz found broad audiences in the 1960s, but first the era's folk revival, then the British Invasion siphoned off younger listeners. No surprise, then, that by 1970 jazz-rock fusion dominated jazz.

The story of fusion was more interesting and complex—and raised more serious creative issues—than it seemed to at the time. In hindsight, jazz and rock were as inevitable a pairing as jazz and Tin Pan Alley; Bill Graham's putting Miles Davis and the Grateful Dead on the same bills only acknowledged what the musicians were doing. After 30 years of dodging the issue or leaving it in the flaccid hands of radio noodlers like Kenny G, more serious jazz artists are revisiting how to meld jazz and rock. Some, like John Lurie and Steven Bernstein, are old enough to have lived through rock's heyday two and more decades ago. Some are young enough, like Vijay Iyer or Ethan Iverson or Brad Mehldau, that 1960s rock is their Tin Pan Alley, the standards of an older generation.

Evolution, according to the late Stephen Jay Gould, can be described best as punctuated equilibrium: it proceeds in fits and starts almost behind the scenes. That applies equally well to cultural history.

Though jazz record sales and venues shrank after the 1960s, jazz festivals mushroomed around the globe. Their draws were older stars: Duke Ellington, Lionel Hampton, Miles Davis, Ella Fitzgerald, Sarah Vaughan. Only a few younger figures like Keith Jarrett, with his ecstatic gospel solos-cum-Glenn-Gould vocalizing, or Herbie Hancock and Chick Corea, who simultaneously played fusion and jazz and classical music, could successfully headline halls.

Today the jazz industry's economic backbone is radio, which means instrumental treacle like Kenny G and nostalgic romance like Diana Krall. Jazz fans and critics generally disdain the stuff, with good reason: its risk quotient is close to zero. (Krall is a much better musician, cunningly packaged, than the wheezy soprano saxophonist, but her recordings and concerts are scripted for only a frisson of uncertainty, not its reality.) The existential drama that fires jazz's soul has nowhere to dance, although in a culture as averse to risk on every front as America's this would probably be the sort of mild distraction most people wanted to hear even if radio wasn't owned, operated, and programmed by two corporations with nothing but demographics, ad dollars, and focus groups on their minds.

Off the mainstream, away from classical jazz, other voices have been evolving. For instance, although jazz fans mostly scorned hip-hop, musicians from M-BASE to Max Roach got interested in the beats, the lyrics, and the culture. DJs began to appear as parts of avant-jazz bands; in the 1990s Disposable Heroes of Hiphopracy, Cypress Hill, 3rd Bass, Jungle Brothers, and Us3 stirred jazz into hip-hop. Then came TJ Kirk, Charlie Hunter, Medeski Martin & Wood, Phish, Dave Matthews, Govt Mule, String Cheese Incident, Iverson wailing on Blondie's "Rapture" without being hobbled by the "simple" structure (what could be more direct than modal soloing? What could be simpler than "rhythm changes?"), Iyer reshaping Hendrix's "Hey Joe" into an acoustic jazz quartet without losing the raw emotional power of the blues.

The unfinished business of 1960s fusion has been reopened. And yes, some of the impetus for this comes from cynical and desperate commerce looking for a profit line, the undignified scramble of an industry drowning in its own waste and trying to woo boomer buyers back into stores after alienating Gen Xers and Yers, who download their music. But trying to prosecute instead of accommodate, refusing to drop retail prices to the $8.95 that surveys show would drastically curtail, if not quash, what the RIAA insists on mislabeling "piracy," well, that's the business of American music.

JASON MORAN IS AN OUTSTANDING exemplar of how, in cultural as in biological evolution, nobody can realistically expect what directions or form a new artistic breakthrough will take until it presents itself. The cultural historian, like the biologist, then works backward from effects to causes. So think of Moran as simultaneously an effect of recent jazz history and a probable cause of possible futures, as sketched on *Modernistic*. It suggestively sets new spins on sounds from James P. Johnson to Afrika Bambaata.

In his late twenties, Moran is young enough to have absorbed hip-hop as a native, not an acquired, language, and he's schooled enough to have absorbed lessons from a century of jazz and classical music. Born and raised in Houston, he and his brothers started music lessons young, were in the school orchestra, and then quit. But Moran's father had an extensive record collection, which the boy enjoyed overhearing, especially Thelonious Monk's "'Round Midnight." By the time he was in high school, he said, "That gave me the kicking in the butt I needed to go back to the piano." For college he headed to New York, where he studied for four years with Jaki Byard at the Manhattan School of Music.

The late Byard, a unique pianist with a wide-angle conceptual lens, is unknown to the general public, but he shouldn't be; his music is a cornucopia of Americana. Born in 1922, he doubled on many instruments, and in his long career worked everywhere from strip joints to the New England Conservatory, playing ragtime, greasy R & B, adventurous Third Stream, free jazz, and whatever else struck him or was needed; like Charles Mingus, with whom he worked over several years, he ignored convention, which is why his big band, the Apollo Stompers, dished such an eclectic potpourri laced with dollops of humor on songs like "Aluminum Baby."

"Jaki," Moran said, "used the entire piano. Certain piano players and instrumentalists stay in a certain range because it is comfortable, and that is what you are used to listening to." Moran recalls seeing Randy Weston, for instance, at a solo concert of Duke Ellington material: "He made that piano sound like an entire band, made the bass register of the piano really sing, the rhythm and time wasn't all straight. He really surprises you; the same with Muhal (Richard Abrams) and Andrew (Hill)."

What's most interesting about Moran's piano heroes, including Byard, is their distinctive combinations of broad scope and individual attack—and their repeated attempts to reexamine jazz composition and its recombinant relationship with improvisation.

Weston, the eldest living member of Moran's pantheon, studied informally with Monk—a rare claim—and is admired for his African jazz pieces and rough-grained, sweeping piano; his tunes "Hi Fly" and "Little Niles" are now jazz standards. Abrams, who founded the Association for the Advancement of Creative Musicians, reaches to stride piano and Schoenberg on *Blues Forever*. Hill, 65, studied with Hindemith, played bop as a teen, was music coordinator for (then) Leroi Jones's Black Arts

Repertory Theatre, and has been a Smithsonian Fellow; *Point of Departure* illustrates his Monkish piano and elliptical compositional sense.

Hooking up with alto saxophonist Greg Osby (who has worked with Hill for years) not long after graduation marked Moran's first step into a major-league career. Osby, his senior by two decades, has mentored Moran both within his own band and outside it. Their rapport is evident in their seamlessly nonstop live sets and their recordings.

Osby's album *The Invisible Hand* projects the new logic of his music against the backdrop of established material. Over the last decade, Osby has come a long way from the M-BASE collective. He has always had a richly mature tone, and on ballads he plumbed uncanny depths of soul.

His poised maturity on this disc is supported by his choice of material and collaborators. There's his longtime employer Andrew Hill, whose deeply introspective music twists and tugs at basic elements like time and harmony. Guitarist Jim Hall, whose band Osby also joined, is one of jazz's subtlest harmonic colorists. Bassist Scott Colley (of Hall's band), drummer Teri Lyne Carrington, and flute/woodwind player Gary Thomas mingle in several configurations from piano-sax duo on up.

The record is serious fun. Osby takes Fats Waller's "Jitterbug Waltz" and stretches its rhythms and harmonies: the postbop abstract alto lyricism, wispy intrusion of cymbals, skittering piano teetering around the beat, times lagging way behind chord changes. Yet it seems natural, thanks to the discipline of the players. The foreboding version of "Nature Boy" makes sense once you remember it wasn't just a Nat King Cole hit but also the signature tune for the 1948 antiracist/anti-Communist witchhunt sci-fi thriller, *The Boy with Green Hair*; it braids Hall's slurring guitar, Thomas's sinuous flute, and Colley's stuttering bass around Osby's edgy, fluttering alto. There's "Indiana" (a flagwaver for Swing Era soloists frequently rewritten by boppers and here reformulated into postbop cell-like structures), and Quincy Jones's "Who Needs Forever" (from 1967's *A Deadly Affair*, about a British spy and a turncoat Communist official). There's superb original material: Hill's "Ashes," a brooding, cantilevered ballad; Osby's "The Watcher," an impressionistically yearning, Wayne Shorteresque piano-sax duo; and Hall's "Sanctus," an intricately textured piece with a sinewy structure and snaking melody that like most of Osby's work, avoids the bop head-string-of-solos-head approach.

That brings us back to Moran's *Modernistic*, where six Moran originals nestle alongside compositions by Johnson ("Modernistic"), Abrams ("Time into Space into Time"), Schumann ("Auf Einer Burg"), and Bambaata ("Planet Rock"). The title cut skips and dances through rhythmic breakdowns and shifts into impressionistic abstraction. "Body and Soul" tethers its romantic deconstruction to a recurrent figure. "Planet Rock" is rendered via prepared piano, tape reversals, and several

overdubs. And Moran's continuing series of "Gangsterism" compositions (all based on a theme from Hill's "Erato") are like short takes from
a jazz movie in process.

Call what Moran is doing not deconstruction, from that lingering but
passed postmodernist moment, but reconstruction. Did I mention how
much fun it is to listen to?

THE LAST TWO DECADES WATCHED American pop culture reliving the
postwar era, so it shouldn't be a surprise that *The Grand Unification
Theory*, from vibist Stefon Harris, surfaces a re-emerging Third Stream.
A tone poem of 11 movements for 12 instruments, it skillfully avoids
pastiche while weaving a rich musical tapestry that tells a story of birth,
life, death, and rebirth against the backdrop of a multifaceted universe.
Moving from grander themes ("The Birth of Time") to more focused
ones ("The Velvet Couch") and, via death, back to Big Ideas (the title
track), this piece's ambitious program includes translating Harris's fasci-
nation with physics and philosophy into musical form.

Harris seems born to do this sort of thing. Still shy of 30, he has
rapidly risen to an enviable tier among jazz artists: he has a major-label
deal with three albums as a bandleader, plays name-brand clubs and
festivals, and collects rave reviews from national publications. But what
shaped his talents was an education in two too-often divorced modes:
academic and on-the-bandstand training.

Born in 1973 in Albany, New York, hardly a hotbed of jazz, the boy
taught himself piano from age six, and could read music by the time he
hit first grade. By eighth grade he was taking classical marimba instruction and could play all the band instruments. "One of my teachers used
to say, 'If we needed a trombone, we gave it to Stefon,'" he jokes. He
saw the Empire State Youth Orchestra on TV, auditioned on clarinet and
percussion, and eventually became principal percussionist.

While he was studying on a full scholarship at the Eastman School of
Music, his roommate played him some Charlie Parker records and
changed the direction of his musical life. "Two things," he says of
hearing Bird. "The first was spiritual liberation. He sounded extremely
free, like he could go wherever his imagination took him. Second, I realized how much harmony you had to understand to do what he was
doing—how you had to hear the chord the pianist was playing and be
able to use it right then—and I found that extremely challenging intellectually." He instantly dropped his plans for a career in classical
music—plans that weren't possible for earlier generations of black musicians who became jazz players, like Charles Mingus, an early stalwart of
the original Third Stream—switched from percussion to vibraphone,
transferred to the Manhattan School of Music (though still as a classical
performance major), and began learning to play jazz and improvise with
other students.

The vibraphone and jazz have an almost coextensive history. As with all instruments, jazz musicians have tested its capabilities, probed its multiplicity, adapted it to their self-expression. In 1930, Lionel Hampton, who died in 2002, improvised an introduction on vibes to Louis Armstrong's "Confessin'"; he was a drummer, but Armstrong encouraged him to take up the decade-old mallet instrument. Hampton's highly extroverted performance style on drums and vibes and his appearances in movies with Les Hite's band brought him wide recognition; his shimmeringly fast vibrato and quick, articulated touch became lifelong trademarks.

In 1936, Benny Goodman, who had reached the first peak of his popularity, decided to add Hamp to his big band's "chamber jazz" trio, already (unusually, for the times) integrated with pianist Teddy Wilson and drummer Gene Krupa. (Goodman's radical and wealthy brother-in-law, John Hammond, pushed him hard to do this, just as he'd later push Goodman to sign up guitarist Charlie Christian.) Hampton crossed the racial divide to mainstream stardom, and soon led his swaggering powerhouse of a band; in 1942, a young tenor saxophonist named Illinois Jacquet ignited a burly, raunchy solo that launched rhythm and blues for the Hampton band's hit version of an old Goodman small-group piece, "Flyin' Home."

This being jazz, different hands brought the vibes different sounds. For Red Norvo, moving from xylophone in 1944, it was a vibratoless attack, the opposite of Hampton's. Milt Jackson, an early bebopper who played with Parker and Dizzy Gillespie and cofounded the Modern Jazz Quartet, favored a long, almost drawling vibrato to yield sonic pools, enhanced by soft mallets and blues-based lyricism. Within the Third Stream MJQ, Jackson's vibes counterpointed the precise, Basie-esque understatement of John Lewis's piano.

Since he's been in New York, Harris has joined a variety of musical situations to stretch and season himself. He worked with Max Roach, Charlie Hunter, Wynton Marsalis's Lincoln Center Jazz Orchestra and the Lincoln Center Chamber Music Society. He toured with Blue Note New Directions, a feisty postbop group that included Osby and Moran. And he recorded two tunes with Cassandra Wilson for *Travelling Miles*.

Harris's touch on vibes reflects his devotion to melody, but it's also functional: he's an ensemble player who tweaks his tone and attack to suit the environment. And so he's adept at his complex instrument's technical aspects, varying motor speed and vibrato for effects, for instance. It's Harris the Composer and Leader, not Harris the Soloist, who informs *The Grand Unification Theory*.

Doubling on vibes and marimba, Harris takes only a handful of solos on this extended composition, but his sonic sensibilities and compositional map shape its soul. Avoiding players who might be more brilliant soloists, he's chosen a team that can harness ego to structure while creating contrasts and tensions. The result is a tone poem that's a worthy successor the works of Duke Ellington, Gil Evans with Miles Davis, and Mingus.

Utilizing elements from jazz and musique concrete, Impressionism and funk, each section of the programmatic piece moves differently. Following the percussion rumbles (the Big Bang) and tick-tick funk of "The Birth of Time," the soul-jazz of "Velvet Couch," with its winking stereo horns and easy grooving, represents a kind of garden of earthly delights. The circular African beat of "Transition," with its last breaths, the sonic atmospherics of "Corridor of Elusive Dreams," and the cool-jazz-horns-plus-salsa of "Escape to Quiet Desperation" ease us into Death. "Song of the Whispering Banshee," a funeral dirge, features part of the Koran keened by bassist Tarus Mateen Kinch. The odd-metered "March of Angels" and dark, quavering ostinato opening the multipart "Mystic Messenger" begin the transition to "Rebirth," with its Ravelish interludes, lush Gil Evansy harmonies, and cloudy vibes finish. The title track resumes three of the pieces key melodies within a rotating backdrop drawn from all the sections—a summa.

Though it's acoustic, the piece is redolent of Harris's intimacy with hip-hop and electronica, whose sonics are gracefully translated into acoustic-instrument textures, while stereo imaging effects remind us this is the 21st century, not 1930. In fact, Harris says his next project is an electric band. "My generation," he points out, "expects sound to be big. I was able to do that acoustically with this project. But we all grew up listening to all kinds of music. Our job as a generation isn't to produce great soloists—how many have there really been in jazz?—but to learn to compose more than rhythm changes and blues forms using all these sounds and idioms."

THE YEAR 2002 MARKED the tenth anniversary of the Jazz Composers Collective, a noteworthy New York-based entry in the long history of jazz-musician cooperatives. Gen X composers like bassist Ben Allison, pianist Frank Kimbrough, and drummer Matt Wilson form the JCC's core. Each has a distinctive approach: Kimbrough's *Chant* tends toward cool; Allison's latest, *Peace Pipe*, integrates kora and cello into a brand of world jazz; Wilson's postmodern playfulness infuses *As Wave Follows Wave* and *Arts and Crafts*. And yet they and others central to the JCC maintain a group cohesion—playing on each other's albums and tours, exchanging business info and cross-pollinating creative ideas about how to reopen jazz's past.

Since 1992, The Herbie Nichols Project has been one of the JCC's central undertakings, yielding three signature discs: *Love Is Proximity* and *Dr. Cyclops' Dream* and *Strange City*. Meanwhile, its members stepped out as individual leaders while seeking alternative venues and methods for producing and showcasing their work. The JCC is building a homemade creative and distribution system outside the mainstream music industry. In the Internet era, that's clearly the way to deal with a marginal art form—especially since the corporate megaliths resulting from a decade of mergers are staggering under debt, firing staff and dropping artists, and muddling around looking for The Next Thing while fighting rear-guard actions against "piracy" that alienate the very consumers they need.

The JCC musicians have signed with small independent labels that give them creative control, and have developed presenting partnerships with not-for-profits nationwide; in 1996, they forged an alliance with the New School, where they mount an annual concert series (so far, 90 shows debuting 300 pieces by 45 composers) and sell CDs at the door. Their website and newletters (sent to 3500 people) attempt to foster dialogue and word of mouth. (Wilson, who regularly tours heartland America in non-jazz venues, notes, "This generation of high school and college students are the most receptive people to hit with improvised music, whether it's because of grunge or acid jazz or whatever.") Like alterna-poppers such as Ani DiFranco, the JCC has revived and expanded the old vital model that, until the entertainment megamergers, was fundamental to interaction between performing artists and audiences since prehistory: tour, tour, tour. That means also stepping outside "usual" clubs and spots and using the Web to shape audience and support systems.

For the JCC, Herbie Nichols was an astute choice as calling card. A contemporary of Thelonious Monk, formally trained from age nine, Nichols is a quintessential overlooked jazz artist—a near-pleonastic usage that unfortunately suits him well. He apparently didn't fit in around Minton's, the postwar bopper academy, though he participated in seminal swing-to-bop sessions there. His working bands rarely lasted, he performed more smooth swing and raw stripper accompaniments than arty bop, and only a small percentage of his often gnarly work reached records. His funny and/or pungent song titles—"Love, Gloom, Cash, Love"; "Argumentative"; "Infatuation Eyes"; "Step Tempest"; "Cro-Magnon Nights"; "Blue Chopsticks"; "Hangover Triangle"; "Riff Primitif"; "Shuffle Montgomery"—reflect his frequently whimsical, provocatively offbeat art. But in the bop pantheon of characters—smack addicts and musical giants, deliberately cartoonish goatees and hornrim glasses, and jive talk unintelligible except to initiates—the retiring Nichols was elbowed out of what little limelight there was.

From the late 1940s to the Korean War, the live-music scene catastrophically collapsed; jazz musicians scrambled for work in then-aborning television, or played "toilets" behind strippers and "dirty" comics like Lenny Bruce, or backed blues and soul singers for indie labels like Atlantic. Mingus, who was incessantly organizing new venues and cooperatives, and Max Roach convened a 1950s meeting in a

Brooklyn warehouse for a one-night hole-in-the-wall concert that drew the scrambling likes of Miles Davis and MJQ pianist John Lewis. Independent labels, some artist-operated like Roach and Mingus's Debut or Dizzy Gillespie's DeeGee, tried to fill the void as major labels withdrew from jazz, but many artists like Nichols got little studio time, though he counted Mingus and Alfred Lion, founder of Blue Note Records, among his champions.

In fact, the couple of dozen cuts Nichols recorded for Blue Note (*The Art of Herbie Nichols*) and on *Love, Gloom, Cash, Love* pretty much sums up his output as a leader. These trio tracks present bracingly nuanced sketches of potentially far richer compositions. Take "Shuffle Montgomery," Ellingtonian in its onomatopoeic echoes of street life, the cultural parade in flux. "Hangover Triangle" flashes glints of Monkish discordance for a chromatic melody that typically seems to meander without obvious resolution, like a drunk the morning after. Or "Love, Gloom, Cash, Love," a ambitious waltz with interpolated tempo shifts and turnarounds of jagged scalar riffs, a skeletal X ray of a deeper psychological picture.

Listening to pieces like "Hangover Triangle" clarifies why critics compared Nichols to Monk. Both were preoccupied with revamping the Tin Pan Alley format, though Monk's pithy deconstructions gyred and stung, while Nichols' liked to linger, and Nichols' piano technique is refined and polished, where Monk's is percussive and disjointed. Still, their common focus was on strong short pieces that instill respect for form while soloing—a discipline Monk drilled into Sonny Rollins and John Coltrane.

Kimbrough began researching Nichols' legacy in 1985, and from the JCC's birth it became a central issue, leading to discoveries that included nearly 30 unrecorded pieces at the Library of Congress. Why Nichols? His music has an intellectual aspect that I suspect appeals to the JCC sensibility: like Nichols' their music has fire but more often burns like ice. Then there's his sly humor: along with skill and taste, what enlivens the best JCC material is evident intelligence, supple irony, and satiric wit. Unlike 1980s jazz neocons, these urbane neoclassicists have fun while paying homage to a past they want to extrapolate and extend in their own work.

Strange City, the most recent Nichols Project CD featuring Kimbrough, Allison, and Wilson, is a coolly unpredictable yet genre-smart treat of tunes Nichols himself never got to record. It can also function as a kind of primer about fill-in-the-dots jazz composition and arranging, the organic mesh linking written and improvised music woven by jazz performance. Onto these pieces' bare bones the band has layered some alluring skin. "Moments" leads off with four horns improvising on the intro and outro in now twining, now dissolving harmonic lines to the typically lengthy Nichols melody—a nicely doubled irony, since Nichols never recorded with horns, and this piece survives only as a solo-piano acetate. The music's tensile delicacy is underscored by Wilson's seemingly hand-played drums—thumping his fingers on the snare or cymbals, for instance—in gently wry commentary. "Delights" is translated from 4/4 to 6/4 and 3/2, allowing the head to sway even more asymmetrically over half-time drums. "Happenings" boasts another four-horn improvised head, then opens into noir dappled with sunsplashes, a movement vaguely reminiscent of Mingus pieces like "Far Wells, Mill Valley." It's apt that Nichols is said to have used the March Theme from Prokofiev's *Love of Three Oranges* as its intro.

WITH *NU BOP*, pianist-composer Matthew Shipp leads what is now, in some circles, becoming a normal jazz quintet—it includes D. J. Flam on synths and programming. Flam's insidious synth work helps make the disc a thought-provoking, at times circuitous journey; in part, it aims to reincarnate the ever-present ghosts of a century of jazz-pop fusion via drum-'n-bass and contemporary sounds, which it does with real success.

"Space Shipp" evokes Herbie Hancock's "Rockit"; the title cut finds alto saxophonist Daniel Carter scrawling Ornette Colemanesque lines across a funky backdrop. "ZX-1" features angular, post-Webern solo piano. "D's Choice" opens with Asian piano pentatonics integrated with Flam's quickwitted sonics. "X-Ray" is a cool flute-bass duo by Carter and Shipp's mentor/sideman William Parker that sports Hendrixy delay on the flute. "Rocket Shipp" nods again to Hancock, crossing him and Cecil Taylor in Shipp's now-scrunched, now-skittering piano. "Nu Abstract" offers 1970s-style burbly sonics against stark Satie piano and grumbling arco bass. "Select Mode 1" and "Select Mode 2," which finish the album, ride (and often turn around) rock rhythms and are engineered for pop radio.

Nu Bop is not merely survey or menu: its diversity has integrity, and means to challenge and provoke as well as titillate and seduce. Shipp is usually called an avant-gardist, and if that outmoded term indicates anything, it's attitude. But let's put him in context rather than label him. Over the last few years, more musicians have been revisiting the intersections open to present-day jazz and pop. Shipp was one of the first on the block.

He came at music directly and indirectly, in the same multitiered, nonlinear fashion his compositions and improvisations still favor. Born in Wilmington, Delaware, 40-odd years ago, at 12 Shipp decided he wanted to be a jazz musician after seeing Ahmad Jamal, whose sense of space so influenced Miles Davis, and Nina Simone, whose crossover hits rendered her jazz credentials suspect to some, on TV. His father, a now-retired police captain, encouraged the boy, who at 14 read a biography of John Coltrane and found a lifelong hero, whom he venerates for creating probing, visionary music from mysticism—one of his own aspirations. A religious youth who read Carl Jung and links his way of thinking to Emerson and the American Transcendentalists, Shipp got early lessons from his church organist, then studied jazz with Boysie Lowery, who also taught trumpet great Clifford Brown, and classical music. In high school he learned bass clarinet and listened to Coltrane, Jimi Hendrix, and Led Zeppelin. A quick stop at the University of Delaware, where he spent his time practicing, listening to jazz classics, and working in a record store, led to the New England Conservatory of Music, where Ran Blake, a lonely practitioner of Third Stream jazz, was his mentor. But the most overt influence on his emerging, very un-Blakean piano, dense and furious with note clusters and pronged dissonance, was Cecil Taylor, a dean of the postwar jazz avant-garde. A 1991 MacArthur Fellow, Taylor also attended the New England Conservatory, in 1952, but left because he felt it was culturally racist.

In 1984, when Shipp hit New York, the downtown scene was in its heyday: 1950s- and 1960s-vintage pioneers of its idioms were alive and working, and young and old neotraditionalists, spearheaded by Wynton Marsalis, were patrolling jazz orthodoxy. Shipp, then shy of 30, found his musical choices very limited, and felt he had to pick a side. For a while, he was the Anti-Wynton. His dense piano work, the aural equivalent of layers of impasto, was often compared to Cecil Taylor's: both used classical training and ideas in their aggressive, even when tender, and non-linear approaches. With albums like *Circular Temple*, Shipp threw down impressive credentials in the now-traditional avant-garde idioms: dense tone clusters, serrated solo lines, multiple time signatures—cubism in motion. And he built a longterm working relationship with Taylor's ex-bassist William Parker.

But over the last few years, Shipp has been at the tip of expanding the conception of and the audience for alternative jazz. He makes regular appearances at College Music Association conventions, and his recordings make the CMA charts; there's something about the headlong flight of Shipp's music, maybe its mystical roots and yearnings, maybe its sometimes baffling flow, maybe the personality that shows through— Shipp speaks in a soft but insistent flurry, with an intellectual focus that shows in his marshaling of arguments toward key points and conclusions. The cliché is that jazz musicians often speak as they play—but once you think about it, why wouldn't they, since a traditional goal for a jazz soloist was to find his own voice? At any rate, Shipp is a cult star on college campuses.

That hasn't stopped his questing. He renounced the studio, à la Glenn Gould, then released several drummerless "chamber jazz" albums like *Gravitational Systems*, where he duetted with violinist Mat Maneri, and *Strata*, with his Horn Quartet. Most strikingly, he stripped his playing into a lean and hungry style.

Nu Bop is the impressive yang to those yins. It reached the number one jazz album slot in 2002.

WITH *BLUES DREAM*, an album that interprets the blues as the foundation for jazz, bluegrass, Thelonious Monk, soul, Western Swing, heavy metal, and other styles, guitar hero Bill Frisell closes several circles in his life and music. Or, more accurately, he opens a spiral of possibilities that, viewed two-dimensionally, looks like circles being closed.

For the truer perspective, let's fade out and then iris back into postwar Colorado. There, in the shadow of the Rocky Mountains, Frisell played clarinet in his school band but picked up a guitar because of B. B. King and Paul Butterfield's Blues Band, and worked with local bar bands doing James Brown covers. That musical bifurcation—the trained artist versus the populist player—took years to resolve.

King, a postwar blues idol, pioneered soul-blues hybrids with *The Thrill Is Gone*. Butterfield, a white harmonica virtuoso who mastered the moves of black pioneers like Little Walter, fronted Chicago's foremost white blues band; featuring guitarist Mike Bloomfield, Butterfield band is given credit by some (including me) for an early jazz-rock fusion record, *East West*, which tackled Nat Adderley's "Work Song" and the title track's raga-blues-rock. Everybody knows that James Brown invented whatever Ray Charles didn't. And don't forget Jimi Hendrix, whose pyrotechnics and sonics influenced even Miles Davis.

But Jim Hall's lambent harmonies and complex melodic sense lured Frisell's guitar into jazz. He went from the University of Northern Colorado to Berklee and became a jazz snob. Which means he dumped his soundshaping boxes and 1960s roots—no more fuzztones, overdrives, blues, soul, whatever. Time to master theory and make his music deep, difficult—art.

By the mid-1980s, though, he was making his name in New York as a sonic pioneer, an avid extender of Hendrix's psychedelic soundscapes into abstract music. After squeezing into the "vintage" 1950s jazz guitar sound, Frisell fell back in love with soundshaping devices like delays and choruses. Like guitarists Adrian Belew and Vernon Reid, he was looking for new jazz-rock fusions that weren't about blizzards of notes, that reimagined sound with wry and resonant effects.

Then as now, Frisell's sense of history anchored him. Even on the radical *Smash and Scatteration*, where he and Reid deconstruct guitar-duo music from the 1920s on, the insightful, often hilarious results are grounded in knowledge and understanding. Hooking up with John Zorn in the iconoclastic late-1980s combo called Naked City accelerated his development. Naked City drew on Ennio Morricone and the Meters, Japanese anime soundtracks and blistering hardcore punk, surf music and Henry Mancini. Zorn's jumpcut compactness prompted Frisell to pare back his own music; blues forms, then country and blues forms, merged into modal jazz to become his building blocks. He avoided flashy solos, absorbing from Miles and Monk and Muddy Waters invaluable lessons about space and the value of a single note—and the spice of wry humor.

Like Miles or Monk, he made his sound his signature. It expanded from bleary delay rippling with looped phrases to embrace molten metalloid raunch and blues grit, acoustic guitars and pedal steels. He was reaching into the history of several sorts of American chamber music.

Jimmie Rodgers, the Father of Country Music, learned to pick guitar from a black railroad hand. (Virtually all modern American vernacular musics share this creation story—originated with blacks, adapted by others.) In the 1920s, Gid Tanner and his Skillet Lickers wed hillbilly string-band music to jazzy fiddle and guitar improvisations. By the late 1930s, Bob Wills and his Texas Playboys forged Western Swing from big band jazz and country. (This paralleled the rise of electric-guitar pioneers in jazz like Charlie Christian, whose hornlike solos made him a star with Benny Goodman—and gave him a role in the birth of bebop when he jammed with Monk and Dizzy Gillespie at Minton's in Harlem.) By the 1940s, Bill Monroe formulated bluegrass's "high lonesome sound" from old-timey string bands, jazz, blues, complex time signatures and harmonies, tight ensemble work, and solo improvisations.

The process never stops. As post-1960s experiments and hybrids washed across American culture, a Grateful Dead pal named David Grisman, a mandolin virtuoso, created Dawg Music—an amalgam of Django Reinhardt and Monroe. The Dead themselves flew on Django-inspired guitar and modal improvisations: one of them, "Dark Star," reworks John Coltrane themes from "Your Lady" and "India."

So, can country music be jazz? (Hint: ask Merle Haggard.)

On *Blues Dreams*, these echoes merge and collide and mix, where the sound of the prairie and the mountains and the hollers is laced with the hard-earned tang of the blues and the surprise of jazz and the textures of rock, where it's all transformed into a wonderfully evocative, surprisingly and even sneakily off-kilter and thought-provoking musical world. *Blues Dream* paints a rootsy, atmospheric place rife with complexity, with so many diverse elements that only art, rooted in dreams, could make them this coherent. Like Cassandra Wilson, Frisell envisions a musical world that is charming, simple-seeming—very American, and very subtly rich, in its range and contradictions.

The album charts many paths across the American landscape. The tremolo-shimmery title track is a brief minor-mode intro, an evocation of post "Kind of Blue" Mile Davis. Track two, "Ron Carter," named for the great Miles 1960s bassist, opens with metallic horn squiggles that wind over a brief bass ostinato and off-kilter guitar licks, then builds with horns and overdriven guitar solos and electronic and bottleneck-guitar squiggles at the soundstage edges. It evokes 1960s experimentalism while organizing and updating it—no mean feat, which the rest of the disc continues.

Music has one big advantage over the real world: resolution is always possible, if you want it. Take "The Tractor." It kicks off as backporch bluegrass, drummer Kenny Wolleson and bassist David Piltch laying down a shuffle behind Frisell's arpeggiated rhythms and sometime doubling of Greg Leisz's mandolin strumming doubletime and picking hot licks. Suddenly a snaky, slightly dissonant horn section slices across it. A chorus goes by before it cuts in again: this time, two asymetrical riffs. More furious bluegrass. And horns. With each chorus, the fine section—trombonist Curtis Fowlkes, saxist Billy Drewes, and trumpeter Ron Miles—connects the riff-dots, filling in until they're almost continuous, a Monkish counterpoint to hillbilly jazz heaven.

It's a brilliant piece of work, a wondrous musical portrait of a melting pot or tossed salad or whatever metaphor you prefer for the multiracial, multicultural place America has never, in sad reality, managed to become.

29

Ani DiFranco

As the 2002 election results came in, I surfed through 100 cable channels with nothing on and hit an infomercial hosted by John Sebastian for a Time-Life eight-CD set of 1950s and '60s folk and folk rock. For the nth time I thought, What hath the Coen Brothers wrought with *O Brother Where Art Thou?* Who would've guessed a hillbilly cross between Homer and Preston Sturges would make America friendly again to the idea of folk music, catalyze the latest generational revival that follows two earlier upsurges: the New Deal, which sent researchers and artists to delve into and chronicle and represent America's myriad pasts, and the postwar McCarthy era, when the crust of American political and cultural monism hardened while, seething below, countercultural currents were flowing toward the mass reaction of the 1960s and '70s?

Santayana's adage about how those who don't know history are doomed to repeat it crossed my mind. Here in the lengthening shadow of the Reagan era, we seem to move outside history in a kind of projected nostalgia, like Plato's fools in a cave of their own device. History textbooks have been dumbed down and decontextualized along the lines Frances FitzGerald drew at the dawn of Reaganism in *America Revised*; our mass media have no memory. The timeless imaginary space they help create allows opportunistic replays of the 1950s, Reaganism's favorite era, when the need for a united front against our Great Satans (communism, sex, drugs, Big Government, taxes, Al Qaeda, Iraq) stifles dissent, opposition, and even discussion by branding them anti-American—ploys recurrent in American history, right out of Richard Hofstadter's *Paranoid Style in American Politics*. Remember how, in 1984, a torrent of pundits mused how Orwell imagined the future wrong? Guess they never imagined a contemporary day spent being ahistorically glared at by CNN and Fox and talk radio.

The bedrock of Reagan's legacy was the invention and spread of a language, from "tax and spend" to "partial-birth abortion," that successfully banishes opposition to the margins in near-total silence. Which is why one lesson from 1950s America seems pertinent: when opposition can find no voice within the government and public arenas, it runs underground to surface elsewhere, as it did in McCarthy's heyday. So the question is: since the governing classes can no longer manage their own opposition and the governed are fractured by slogans of ever-narrowing self-interest or bloody banners, or bored into passivity, or simply hiding out, who will open the possibility of debate?

That brings us to Ani DiFranco, who says that for her politics and art are inseparable.

As the 32-year-old tours the country in a return to her roots as a solo singer with an acoustic guitar, her recent live double CD, *So Much Shouting So Much Laughter*, instead features the kinetic, musically polymorphous sounds of her now-defunct band of the past two years and the growing sophistication of her vocal delivery. The two merge into generally enticing mixtures of jazz, R & B, funk, hip-hop, bossa nova, and salsa that recall Gil Scott-Heron's similar 1970s melanges, like "The Revolution Will Not Be Televised."

The album opens with the sound of DiFranco screwing up a guitar lick—an overt nod to her overall project's resolutely homemade nature. Reviving the antique model that served musicians for centuries and the record industry for decades until the 1990s entertainment megamergers, DiFranco developed her audience via constant touring; she then graduated to packaging and selling her own product via her own Righteous Babe label. (It's worth noting that the last peaks for indie labels were the postwar era, during the rise of blues, rockabilly, R & B, rock and roll, country and soul, and the 1980s, when Reaganites began to dream America back to those glory days.) Like other early-adapting musicians, DiFranco started using her website as a combination marketing springboard/fan chatroom, thus updating the pre-web feedback loop: performers building fan lists so they could mail info about performances and recordings. And she's set up a foundation funneling money to what she describes as "grassroots cultural and political organizations around the country."

Americans still love Horatio Alger, which offers DiFranco her marketing opening into the mainstream—and like Dylan a generation ago, she's savvy enough to use it. Then there are her attitudes and language: she gives her slacker fans an indisputably recognizable voice in her hip sarcasm, cutting put-downs and political alienation, as well as in her nuanced focus on relationships and power. Her audience, mainly college and postcollege women, has grown so large that she routinely nets mainstream-media headlines and big-hall dates despite, and often because of, her outspoken political beliefs and sexual preferences. For Big Media, controversy is raw meat. How far controversial ideas are neutered or proliferated in this process is a conundrum that recalls the arguments about mass culture rampant among postwar public intellectuals like Dwight Macdonald—a conundrum made even more complicated by the now ubiquitous presence on mass media of familiar songs, even "protest" songs, as decontextualized advertising soundtracks.

What is certain is that DiFranco has come a long way from her early neofolkie outsider days, when she was scuffling around Buffalo and clubs of other Rust Belt cities with an acoustic guitar, passing the hat and looking for crash pads. And thanks to the way she's built her career, her fans adore her not just for what she says but what she represents to them—which is down-the-line opposition to official America, outsidership in political and personal terms.

Recorded on the band's last tour, *So Much Shouting So Much Laughter* showcases DiFranco in the round as an artist, with often stunning singing backed by abstractly conceptual as well as hard-driving music. "Swan Dive," the opener with her flubs, catches her at her nihilistic damn-the-torpedoes, Romantic-with-a-capital-R best. The bridge's odd-meter horn licks wind and curl around her increasingly elastic phrasing, her palpably maturing confidence, to head back into the verse's rhythmically layered, edgily staccato funk. As she told one interviewer, "I'm slowly learning, as my life whizzes by me, how to sing them [her songs]—maybe in a slightly calmer voice, maybe with a little bit more self-possession."

Most of the songs revamped by this jazzy sextet will be familiar to fans. Take "Letter to a John": a lapdancer's dismissively sarcastic refrain, "I just wanna take the money I make," unfolds into a hurt and angry admission that she was a molested child, and offhanded observations about how social mores have set back women (and simultaneously imprisoned men) now more than at any time since the 1950s. The pumping rhythm section and sinuously suggestive horns, the well-paced and spiky dynamics, DiFranco's free and easy rhythmic phrasing that rides across as well as on the beats, all underline her artistic growth. She's learned a lot from Dylan; still, even in her most "poetic" forays, she generally forgoes his surrealistic leaps for realism.

As with Dylan, the rawness that dominates DiFranco's more personal tunes about love and yearning, like "Grey," packs the immediacy that's one of her strengths. Or, as she sings in "Dilate," "You always disappoint me . . . / I just want you to live up to the image of you I create." Her slacker sarcasm delivers plenty of good zingers, like "I live in New York, New York, the city that never shuts up" on "Cradle," whose high-energy funk is laced with stop-time breaks and atonal curlicues. She shares that ironic-punk sensibility with a galaxy of her generation's alternative stars, from the late Kurt Cobain to David Rees. (In fact, Rees's online cartoons, popular after 9/11, have been published as *Get Your War On* by Soft Skull Press.)

On "Self Evident," her long exploration of 9/11, DiFranco, to her credit, once again wants to bite the hand that feeds her with a sometimes moving, sometimes naïve mix of the personal and the political. "Us people are just poems," she recites in the opening to background keyboard squiggles, "We're 90 percent metaphor ... rushing down a long hall in a building so tall that it will always be there." She shifts from setting "that beatific day" to "the day America fell to its knees, after strutting around for a century without saying 'thank you' or 'please.'" She scoffs equally at "hypocritical chants of 'freedom forever'" and newscasters struck dumb watching the Twin Towers fall, as if the two were somehow equivalent or implicated; she throws down a countertribute to El Salvador, Mount Rushmore, inmates on death row, and "all those nurses and doctors who daily provide women with a choice, who stand down a threat the size of Oklahoma City just to listen to a young woman's voice." These days in America, the cultural agendas linking Muslim and Christian and Jewish fundamentalism are usually blurred or submerged; when DiFranco makes the connection in concert with this song, fans scream in approval. She finishes by lamenting "3000-some poems disguised as people should be more than pawns in some asshole's passion play" and suggesting Borschtian action.

In an interview, she described performing "Self Evident" at Carnegie Hall several months after the World Trade Center fell: "There was something very ritualized for me about going back to New York, where I was on September 11, and bearing witness before ... all of the other witnesses.... About three seconds in, panic just hit me, like how dare I? Who knows who these people in this audience are, what happened to them that day, or whom they lost?" She found the experience cathartic and empowering. And yet her sense of trepidation, her momentary uncertainty in the face of a complex horror, wasn't unfounded. Listening to lines like "Keep each and every TV that's been trying to convince me to participate in some prep-school punk's plan to perpetuate retribution," I wondered what impact a pamphleteer can have on the language of opposition when official policy in America is routinely disguised as airless slogans.

You can, for instance, revel in her Bush-bashing and still have trouble imagining how turning off CNN could transform Al Qaeda into reciprocal pacifists. Contrast her approach with Rees's: Arabs, Muslims, radical Islamists, whoever, the spectrum of millions actually involved in American policy don't much appear in DiFranco's political sallies, in sharp contrast to the shaded insights that enliven her depictions of gender and personal politics. Although she rejects what she sees as the media-framed "big picture," it can frequently feel as if she's replacing one America-centered mode of seeing the world with another. Is this partly a consequence of her own brand of personal/political ahistoricism? Does it bare the limits of the truism underlying so many of the positive changes as well as the ferocious culture wars of the last three decades, the axiom that the personal is the political?

These are not questions that spring to mind with Guthrie or Seeger, Baez or Dylan. (Much as Dylan was accused in the 1960s of deserting social protest for personal examination and pop stardom, his acute sense of The Other, apparent in his overtly political songs, never fully deserted him; and in his surreal world, where the figures, like Goya's or Dante's, are distorted by the artist's penetrating vision of their inner light, multiple frames of reference, including politics and sociology, are almost always in play.) On the other hand, DiFranco's intractable opposition to All War All The Time has already had potentially significant ripple effects. Hearing "Self Evident" in concert fired Chuck D of Public Enemy to record and release the song before DiFranco's own version came out. This illustrates one of the more promising cultural undercurrents of the last decade-plus—the linking of alternative rock and nongangsta hip-hop. (Prince, who's also tried this, is one of her biggest boosters.) Continuing to nurture those connections musically and politically may ultimately go down as one of DiFranco's most durable contributions to the emerging countercultures of the 21st century.

Meantime, there's her winning black humor and well-honed personal sensitivity and obvious talent to help spur her continuing artistic development. Just as in a Guthrie/Dylan talking blues, DiFranco's asides often shoot her best barbed lines: "Take away our PlayStations, and we are a Third World nation under the thumb of some blueblood royal son." And she wants to move her audience to action: "To the Teeth" begins "Schoolkids keep trying to teach us what guns are about" and ends with exhortations to besiege media and politicians with antigun messages. Will she be a torchbearer out of Reaganism's long twilight? Who knows what America these days will follow as it wanders its deepening chasms of alienation? But that's not really the point. Right now, it's enough that she's out there.

Index